新编21世纪经济学系列教材

Stata/EViews 计量经济分析

第二版

Introduction to Modern Econometrics Using Stata/EViews

胡志宁 编著

中国人民大学出版社
·北京·

作 者 简 介

胡志宁（Zhining Hu），现任 Gettysburg College 副教授。2003 年从 Boston College 获得经济学博士学位；2003—2004 年，在 University of Mississippi 任访问教授；从 2004 年至今，在 Gettysburg College 从事教学科研工作。曾教过初级经济学、中高级宏观经济学、货币财政学、东亚经济发展和初高级计量经济学。目前研究东亚经济、货币财政、金融和房产，以及宏观经济。

About the Author

Zhining Hu，Associate Professor of Gettysburg College. In 2003，she received a Ph. D. in Economics from Boston College; From 2003—2004，she worked with the University of Mississippi as a visiting professor; Since 2004 up to date，she has been teaching and researching at Gettysburg College. She has taught introductory economics，intermediate and advanced macroeconomics，money and banking，East Asian economic history and development，and introductory and advanced econometrics. Currently her research areas include East Asian economy，monetary economics，housing economics，as well as macroeconomy.

前言

笔者在教学和科研工作中，深知学习并掌握计量经济学理论和应用方法的重要性。本书的出版目的就是试图引导国内外高等院校学生如何系统地、循序渐进地学习各种计量经济模型并将理论应用到实践中。本书也可作为学术界同仁的参考用书。

本书较为全面地介绍了计量经济学的基础理论和各种常用回归模型的分析及检验。强调实用性是本书的第一个特点。在美国的很多高等院校、科研机构甚至是公司的 R&D 部门，Stata 这种统计计量软件经常使用。同样，EViews 常常用于时间序列分析。本书特意为计量分析的学习和计量软件的学习架起一座桥梁。通过对本书的阅读和理解，国内外高等院校的学生们能由此了解到如何使用 Stata 和 EViews 软件进行计量分析，并从本书中获知如何建立并分析自己的计量模型。相信本书也会对学术界同仁和计量研究爱好者有所帮助。

本书还介绍了现代计量的分析方法并提供了很多有趣而实用的例题和上机操作的习题。每一个习题都尽量配有 Stata 或者 EViews 的使用说明。读者完全可以根据例题在 Stata 或 EViews 软件上操作模拟，从而很快地掌握这两种软件的使用，并根据本书对软件运行中得到的图表数据的分析和讨论加深对现代计量分析方法的理解和运用。这是本书的第二个特点。

第三个特点是本书使用两种语言（英文和中文）同步讲解现代计量理论和应用，读者可以比较清楚地了解现代计量的专业术语在英语国家的教学科研里是如何被解释和阐述的。另外，本书每一章里的上机操作习题都是英文书写的，并附有中文对照。这样的方法是希望能提高读者的自信心，更好地集中注意力，并提高他们的学习记忆。而且，笔者也希望读者通过这样的练习机会加强和巩固对计量的英文学习，从而可以更为轻松地阅读其他有关计量经济的英文书籍，以便更好地和国际接轨并保持同步。

Preface

The author, involved in research and teaching work, is well aware of the study and mastery of econometric theory, and understands the importance of the application of econometrics. Hence, the aim of this book is to guide university students, both in China and abroad, in a systematic and step-by-step manner to learn a variety of econometric models and how econometric theory is applied in practice. The book can be also used as a reference book for academic colleagues.

This book provides a pretty comprehensive description of the basis of econometric theory and a variety of commonly used regression analysis and testing. Practicality is the first and most stressed characteristic of this book. In many colleges and universities in the United States, research institutions, and even R & D departments of company, Stata is a very often used software package for statistical and econometric analysis. In a similar fashion, EViews is often used to deal with time series models. This book specifically strives to bridge a gap between the study of quantitative analysis and econometric/statistical software. Using this book, students of domestic and international economic research institutions of higher learning can learn how to use econometric analysis software, especially Stata and EViews, and discover how to establish their own econometric model analysis. I believe this book will be of use to academic research associates and other econometric enthusiasts as well.

Furthermore, the book provides modern applications of econometric analysis, and lots of interesting, practical examples and computer exercises. Exercise and practice are essential to the mastery of Stata or EViews, and helpful instructions are presented in furtherance of this quest. Readers can follow examples on either Stata or EViews to learn to operate and quickly master the use of both software packages. The book also provides charts and data to be analyzed and discussed in order to deepen understanding of econometric analysis. This is the second feature of the book.

The book's third feature is its use of two languages (English and Chinese) to explain modern econometric theory and methods on the synchronization, enabling readers to more clearly understand the terms of modern econometrics in English-speaking countries. In addition, in each chapter of this book, computer exercises are written in both English and Chinese, which give readers a confidence boost, make them focus better, and enhance their working memory. Also, I hope that through these exercises the readers will be granted the opportunity to strengthen and consolidate the learning of econometrics, allowing them to more easily read other econometric books in English and the world at large, in order to keep pace.

鸣 谢

感谢我的家人和所有帮助过我的人们!

本书得益于许许多多在中美工作的非常杰出的研究人员和学者甚至学生的帮助。他们在百忙之中阅读了本书的早期文稿，并提出了很多修改建议。特别感谢的是郑江淮教授。

我的 Gettysburg College 的同事们也给予了我大力的支持。他们对于计量经济学教学的想法以及建议使我能更好地理解如何教授这门棘手的学科。另外，本书之所以能顺利完成还得益于 Gettysburg College 提供给我的科研发展基金。

感谢我的 Gettysburg College 的学生助理们！ Yujie Zheng 和 Humenghe Zhao 负责核对本书的中英文术语的对照工作，Christopher Carrier 核对并校正了本书的英文部分。他们在本书的每个细节上努力地确保语言的准确性，为此作出了很大的贡献。

我衷心地将这本书献给我的先生和我的儿子，感谢他们的支持和配合，以确保我写书所需要的大量时间。还要特别感谢我在中国的家人，在这个漫长的写书过程中，他们给予我无数鼓励和支持。最后，我深切地感谢中国人民大学出版社的编辑们。在他们的耐心和不懈的帮助下，我才能够有此机会完成这样一本有意义的书的写作。

Acknowledgements

This book benefited greatly from the keen eyes and minds of many researchers, scholars, and students, both in the United States and China, who read the early drafts and made many suggestions for improvements. Especially helpful was Prof. Jianghuai Zheng.

I have been blessed with the unflagging support from my colleagues at Gettysburg College. Their ideas and suggestions about teaching econometrics have enhanced my understanding of how to teach this difficult subject best. I am also grateful for the Research and Professional Development Grant from Gettysburg College which makes this book project run smoothly.

Many thanks to my Gettysburg College student assistants, Yujie Zheng and Humenghe Zhao who were helpful in translating econometric terms into Chinese, and Christopher Carrier who worked very hard to proof-read and edit the English parts of this book. Their efforts contributed remarkably to the accuracy of the text in its myriad details.

With all my love, I dedicate this book to my husband and my son, who had to put up with the many hours that I spent working on this book. A special note of gratitude also goes to my family in China for their encouragement and support throughout this long process. Finally, my deepest thanks go to my editors at China Renmin University Press, who were unfailingly patient and so helpful to transform my manuscript into such an exciting and accessible book.

目 录

第 1 章

Stata 和 EViews 软件的简介

Ⅰ. Stata 软件的简介

1. 关于 Stata

Stata 是一种在命令驱动下进行操作运算的现代软件。它可以进行统计分析、数据管理以及绘图。在经济学领域，它可以用于分析各种经济数据，比如横截面数据、时间序列数据、面板数据，等等。Stata 使用方便，配有大量的参考用书，并且可以通过 Internet 在线更新该软件的旧功能以及增添新功能。

2. 基本操作命令

2.1　输入数据

insheet：从电子表格里读取 ASCII（文本）数据（该命令仅限于 . cvs 文件）
infile：读取非格式化的 ASCII（文本）数据（该命令仅限于空间分隔的文件）
infix：读取格式化的 ASCII（文本）数据（该命令仅限于 . fix 文件）
input：由键盘输入数据
use：读取 Stata 格式的文件，也可以读取网上在线的 Stata 文件
describe：描述存在内存里或磁盘上的数据内容
compress：压缩存在内存里的数据
save：以 Stata 数据格式存储在内存里或磁盘上
count：显示变量的长度
list：列出变量的数值
clear：清除整个数据集和所有的显示

memory：显示内存使用情况
set memory：设置内存的大小

2.2 分析数据

codebook：列出数据集里的详细内容
log：创建一个日志文件
summarize：描述数据的基本统计特性
table：创建统计表格
graph：画高分辨率图
sort：按变量的观察数值由大到小排序
histogram：画连续变量和分类变量的直方图
tabulate：画单向和双向的频率表
correlate：描述变量之间的相关性
type：显示 ASCII 文件

2.3 修改数据

label data：给数据集加上标签
order：把数据集里的变量排序
label variable：给变量加标签
label define：定义分类变量的数值意义
label value：赋予一个变量标签值
rename：重新命名变量名
recode：重新给予变量新编码
note：给数据文件加附注
generate：创建一个新的变量
replace：替换新值
egen：是 generate 命令的扩展——具有特殊的功能，可以用来创建一个新的变量

2.4 管理数据

pwd：显示当前目录（pwd＝打印工作目录）
dir 或 ls：显示当前目录中的文件
cd：改换目录
keep if：保持观察值，如果 if 条件得到满足
keep：保持变量（去掉其他变量）
drop：去掉变量（保持其他变量）
append using：附加新的数据文件到当前文件

merge：把新的数据文件与当前文件合并

3. 上机操作练习[①]

请注意，括号里的字句是备注。首先，在应用程序里找到并双击 Stata 图标。启动 Stata 后，根据出版社提供的数据链接找到 **stata. cvs**，然后你可以逐一输入以下命令。请记住，Stata 是区分大小写的。

如何输入数据

insheet using "H：\ stata. cvs"　（输入你存储数据文件的路径名）

save stata

count

describe

compress

clear

use stata，clear　（仅适用于 Stata 数据文件，也可以读取网上的数据）

memory

set memory 5m　（最大取值：256MB）

如何研究数据

use "H：\ stata"，clear

describe

list

codebook

log using unit1，text replace　（打开一个命名为 unit1 的已存日志文件，所有将要输入的命令和对应的处理结果会被保存，但原有的日志内容会被删除）

summarize

display 10^2

log close　（关闭日志文件）

type unit1. log　（查看日志文件）

如何修改数据

use "H：\ stata"，clear

order id gender

label variable schtyp "The type of school the student attended."

label define scl 1 public 2 private

label values schtyp scl

codebook schtyp

---

① 关于本书所涉及的数据，读者可登录 www. crup. com. cn 在检索框输入本书书名进行下载。资料来源：http：//www. ats. ucla. edu/stat/stata/notes/hs0. csv.

```
list schtyp in 1/10
list schtyp in 1/10, nolabel
encode prgtype, gen (prog)                    （创建字符串变量 prgtype 的数字版本）
rename gender female
gen total=read+write+math
replace total=read+write+socst
list race if race==5
recode race 5=.
list race if race==.
generate total=read+write+math
sum total
codebook total
notes race: values of race coded as 5 were recoded to be missing
egen zread=std (read)                                    （使用特殊公式 std (.)）
save stata1
```

如何管理数据

```
use "H: \ stata1", clear
pwd
dir
cd H: \ stata1
keep if read >=60
describe
summarize read
save hsgoodread, replace
use hsgoodread, clear
drop ses
save hsdropped, replace
list in 1/20
```

Ⅱ. EViews 软件的简介

EViews 是一个在 Windows 操作系统下运行的统计软件。它主要用于处理以时间序列为主的各种经济模型。它使用方便，操作者可以通过菜单界面较轻松地分析复杂的时间序列及其各类模型。

启动 EViews 时，要在应用程序文件里找到并双击 EViews 图标。退出 EViews 时，选择“文件/退出”。打开 EViews 后，通常你需要采取以下步骤。

第一步，创建工作文件。

EViews 要求数据、图形和回归结果存在工作文件里。要创建一个新的工作文件，你可以选择“文件/新建/工作文件”。在工作文件范围的窗口，选择适当的观测频率和样本大小，例如：季刊，1952：1 至 1996：4，然后点击“确定”。如果你想打开已有的工作文件，可以选择“文件/打开/工作文件”。

第二步，输入数据。

EViews 提供了多种方便的输入方法。其中，最主要的方法是：

(1) 手动输入数据：在主菜单栏里选择“快速/空白组”，一个电子表格窗口随之将会跳出来。您可以逐一输入数据并击回车键。EViews 将默认这一变量为 SER01。为了改变变量名，返回你的工作文件，选中 SER01，右击它，然后选择“重新命名”。

(2) 上传数据：EViews 允许三种数据格式：ASCII，Lotus 和 Excel 电子表格。为了读取这些数据，可在你的工作文件的菜单栏选择“步骤/引进/读写 ASCII-Lotus-Excel”。然后，在标准的文件对话框里，你可浏览到适当的目录并指定文件类型。

第三步，选出需要的一组变量，画时间序列图。

移动鼠标，同时按住 Shift 键，你便可以选出需要的一组变量（例如，GDP 和 M1），然后单击“显示”按钮。一个含有这两个变量的电子表格将会出现。点击“命名”按钮（例如，填入 GRP1 ）。这个新创建的文件可在工作文件窗口找到。

如要查看时间序列图，选择“查看/多图/线”。也可以尝试其他的选择，例如条形图、描述性统计，等等。

Chapter 1

Brief Introduction to Stata and EViews

Ⅰ. Brief Introduction to Stata

1. About Stata

Stata is a modern and general command driven package for statistical analyses, data managements and graphics. In the field of economics, it is capable of analyzing different types of economic data, such as cross-sectional data, time-series data, and panel data, etc. Stata is user friendly. It has an extraordinary set of reference books and has internet capabilities (such as installing new features and updating) .

2. Basic Operations

2.1 Entering Data

insheet: Read ASCII (text) data created by a spreadsheet (. cvs only)
infile: Read unformatted ASCII (text) data (space delimited files)
infix: Read formatted ASCII (text) data (. fix files)
input: Enter data from keyboard
use: Read Stata files, can be used to read Stata files over internet
describe: Describe contents of data in memory or on disk
compress: Compress data in memory
save: Store the dataset currently in memory on disk in Stata data format
count: Show the number of observations

list: List values of variables
clear: Clear the entire dataset and everything else
memory: Display a report on memory usage
set memory: Set the size of memory

2.2 Exploring data

codebook: Detailed contents of a dataset
log: Create a log file
summarize: Descriptive statistics
table: Create a table of statistics
graph: High resolution graphs
sort: Sort observations in a dataset
histogram: Histogram for continuous and categorical variables
tabulate: One-and two-way frequency tables
correlate: Correlations
type: Display an ASCII file

2.3 Modifying Data

label data: Apply a label to a data set
order: Order the variables in a data set
label variable: Apply a label to a variable
label define: Define a set of a labels for the levels of a categorical variable
label value: Apply value labels to a variable
rename: Rename a variable
recode: Recode the values of a variable
note: Apply notes to the data file
generate: Create a new variable
replace: Replace one value with another value
egen: Extended generate—has special functions that can be used when creating a new variable

2.4 Managing Data

pwd: Show current directory (pwd=print working directory)
dir or ls: Show files in current directory
cd: Change directory
keep if: Keep observations if condition is met

keep：Keep variables（dropping others）
drop：Drop variables（keeping others）
append using：Append a data file to current file
Merge：Merge a data file with current file

3. Computer Exercise[①]

First，please start Stata by double-clicking on the Stata icon in the Applications folder. Please find **stata. cvs** from the data link provided by the book publisher. Then，you can type the following commands one by one. Remember that Stata is case sensitive.

How to Enter Data

insheet using "H：\ stata. cvs" （*Enter the directory where you store your data file*）
save stata
count
describe
compress
clear
use stata，clear （*only for Stata files，can read the online data over internet*）
memory
set memory 5m （*maximum*：256MB）

How to Explore Data

use "H：\ stata"，clear
describe
list
codebook
log using unit1，text replace （*open an existing log file called unit1 which will save all of the commands and the output in a text file and delete the contents and places the current log into the file*）
summarize
display 10^2
log close （*close the log file*）
type unit1. log （*see what is in the log file*）

How to Modify Data

use "H：\ stata"，clear
order id gender

① This exercise is modified based on the Stata class notes provided by UCLA Academic Technology Services. Data source is http：//www. ats. ucla. edu/stat/stata/notes/hs0. csv.

```
label variable schtyp "The type of school the student attended."
label define scl 1 public 2 private
label values schtyp scl
codebook schtyp
list schtyp in 1/10
list schtyp in 1/10, nolabel
encode prgtype, gen (prog)
```

(create a new numeric version of the string variable prgtype)

```
rename gender female
gen total=read+write+math
replace total=read+write+socst
list race if race==5
recode race 5=.
list race if race==.
generate total=read+write+math
sum total
codebook total
notes race: values of race coded as 5 were recoded to be missing
egen zread=std (read)
```

(using special function std (.))

```
save stata1
```

How to Manage Data

```
use "H: \ stata1", clear
pwd
dir
cd H: \ stata1
keep if read>=60
describe
summarize read
save hsgoodread, replace
use hsgoodread, clear
drop ses
save hsdropped, replace
list in 1/20
```

Ⅱ. Brief Introduction to EViews

EViews is an easy to use statistical software package for Windows catering mainly to time series econometrics. The menu interface makes complicated time series look effortless.

To start EViews：double click on the EViews icon in the Applications folder. To exit EViews：select "File/Exit". After opening EViews，usually you have to take the following steps.

First，create a workfile.（EViews requires that data series，graphs，and estimation output be contained in object containers called workfiles）.

To create a new workfile，select "File/New/Workfile".

In the Workfile Range window，select the appropriate frequency and range of the data you intend to work with，e. g. Quarterly，1952：1 to 1996：4，followed by OK.

If you want to open an existing workfile：select "File/Open/Workfile".

Second，enter the data.

EViews offers a number of convenient options，among which the following two are commonly used.

（1）To enter data manually：Select "Quick/Empty Group" on the main menu bar of the EViews window. A spreadsheet window with the specified range will appear. You can begin entering your data hitting the return key after the entry for each cell. EViews will set the default name of this series to be SER01. To change this，go back to your workfile，highlight SER01 and right click it，and select Rename.

（2）To import data：EViews allows importation in 3 formats：ASCII，Lotus and Excel Spreadsheet. To read these data，select "Procs/Import/Read Text-Lotus-Excel..." from the workfile menu. A standard File dialog allows you to navigate to the appropriate directory and specify the file type.

Highlight the desired series objects using the mouse while holding down the shift key（example *GDP* and *M*1）click the Show button. A spreadsheet of these 2 series will appear. Click on Name to name this object（example *GRP*1）. This will appear as a group object in your workfile window.

To view a time series plot select "View/Multiple Graphs/Line". One can also try a number of other options，for example Bar Graph，Descriptive Statistics，etc. for the selected series.

第 2 章

计量经济学简介

Ⅰ. 计量经济学定义及其学习意义

计量经济学是一门建立在统计方法基础上用来估计和检验各种经济理论及其经济模型的学科。

学习计量经济学的理由以及意义何在？主要理由如下。第一，它可以帮助我们分析估计各种经济关系。很多经济理论是建立在分析两个或多个变量之间相互关系的基础上的。例如，我们感兴趣的关于教育和收入的关系、需求和供应关系，或者通货膨胀和失业预期关系，等等。为了分析估计这些关系，计量经济学提供了一系列的研究方法。第二，计量经济学可以用实际数据和检验假设帮助我们评价经济理论的正确与否。要检验经济理论，我们把总结出来的经济关系转换为一些重要的未知参数。然后进行抽样，估计未知参数，以及进行假设检验。第三，最常见的计量经济学的应用就是预测经济变量的未来走势。例如，我们可以使用一系列的计量经济方法来预测主要经济指标的未来趋势，比如生产、通货膨胀、利率、失业率，等等。

Ⅱ. 学习计量经济前需思考的问题

在我们为了进行计量研究而通过收集数据来验证某个经济理论或关系之前，我们有必要探讨回答以下几个问题。

问题 1：如何在经济理论或模型的基础上建立一个计量经济模型？

在大多数情况下，计量经济分析开始于如何建立一个计量经济模型。通常情况下，一个计量经济模型的建立取决于一个正式的经济模型、经济理论，甚至是直觉的存在。例如，我们想调查在职培训对工人生产力的影响，进而对他/她的工资的影响。经济学家们早已采用一些基本的经济分析工具来解释工人的工资与他们的生产力之间的关系（例如，Wooldridge，2006）。这种推理有助于建立以下的计量模型：

$$wage=f(education,experience,training) \tag{2.1}$$

很明显，除了以上三个决定要素，还有很多其他要素可能会影响工资率，但上述经济模型涉及以下两个问题的实质：是否在职培训和工人的工资之间存在着正相关的关系？在职培训对工人工资的影响有多大？在我们确定上述经济模型之后，我们需要把它转换成一个相关的计量经济模型。假设经济模型里各种关系是线性的，我们可以建立起这样一个完整的计量经济模型：

$$wage=\beta_0+\beta_1 educ+\beta_2 exper+\beta_3 training+\mu \tag{2.2}$$

在该计量经济模型中，常数β_0，β_1，β_2 和β_3 是参数，用于测量工资和其决定要素之间的正负相关性以及各种工资决定要素对工资水平影响的强度。此外，μ 包含影响工人工资的其他要素。一旦我们建立起所需的计量经济模型，我们就可以把重点放在对 β_3 的分析上以便回答上述提到的那两个问题。

问题 2：如何识别不同类型的数据？

经济数据有多种类型。因此，我们必须学会识别计量分析中那些经常使用到的重要数据结构。

第一种类型：横截面数据。这种数据是通过随机抽样的方法，在同一个时间点上收集到的有关一群人或是一组公司等的信息。比如，2008 年，100 个家庭的收入和消费支出情况。如果数据不是随机抽样得到的，我们会面临样本选择偏差的问题。

第二种类型：时间序列数据。不同于横截面数据，时间序列数据没有随机抽样的特性。它是在一个指定的时间段里收集到的有关某人、某物或某事件的信息变化——例如，股票的价格。时间序列数据强调时间顺序的重要性，因此，我们如果要处理时间序列模型则需要考虑如何解决趋势和季节性的问题。例如，2000—2008 年，同一个家庭的收入和消费支出的变化。

第三种类型：混合横截面数据。我们可以把几组横截面数据合并在一起，并仅视之为一组普通横截面数据。然而，我们需要考虑到时间差异问题。例如，我们将两组不同时间段里收集的样本合并起来，一个样本是 2007 年 10 个家庭的收入和消费支出情况，另一个样本是 2008 年另外 10 个不同家庭的收入和消费支出情况。

第四种类型：面板或纵向数据。它观测的是每一个横截面单元在时间序列上的变化情况。该数据既可以用于分析个体之间的差异情况，又可以描述个体的动态变化特征。例如，2000—2008 年间，我们观察 30 个家庭的收入和消费支出情况。

注意：第三种类型和第四种类型都包含了横截面数据和时间序列数据的成分。但是，两者最大的区别是，当我们收集第四种类型的数据时，我们观察的是同一组人或物其自身的情况随时间的推移发生的变化。

问题 3：如何区分因果关系问题？

有关因果关系的提问是不可避免的。许多经济学重要的总结都存在因果的论述。例如，需求法则指出，假定其他因素不变，产品价格的上涨将会减少对此产品的需求量。计量学家也甚为关切从统计结果里确定因果关系的可能性，以及因果关系和参数估计值一致性之间的相互关联。

以教育收益问题为例。

人力资本投资模型意味着，一个人获得的教育程度越高，其收入水平随之也越高。在最简单的情况下，收入方程写为：

$$Earnings=\beta_0+\beta_1 education+\mu \tag{2.3}$$

β_1 的估计值代表了教育程度的收益值，但它能不能被用来衡量教育程度和收入的因果关系呢?

虽然误差项 μ 包括除教育程度以外其他影响收入的因素，但是有些东西仍然无法观测到，因而有可能会造成一些问题。例如，一个人的内在能力可能会影响收入的高低而被包含在误差项 μ 中，同时个人的内在能力很有可能和他/她的教育程度有关。如果我们不能排除内在能力对教育程度的影响，我们就不能清楚地知道教育程度如何影响收入。这是因为个人的内在能力会通过对教育程度的影响而影响收入水平的变化，故而，教育系数 β_1 并不能真正衡量教育和收入之间的因果关系。

Chapter 2

Introduction to Econometrics

Ⅰ. What is Econometrics? Why study Econometrics?

Econometrics is a combination of statistical methods which are used to estimate and test economic theories and models.

How useful is econometrics? Why should we learn econometrics? The major reasons are as follows. First, it helps us to estimate economic relationships. Most economic theory is directed toward establishing a relationship between two or more variables. For instance, we might be interested in a relationship between education and earning, a relationship between demand and supply, or a relationship between inflation and unemployment, etc. To estimate these relations, econometrics provides a set of tools. Second, it helps us to confront economic theory with facts and hypothesis tests. To test economic theory, we will summarize an economic relationship into some key unknown parameters. Then we will draw a sample from the population, estimate the unknown parameters, and conduct hypothesis tests. Third, the most common application of econometrics is the forecasting of the behavior of economic variables. For example, we can use a series of econometric methods to forecast the future performance of major economic indicators, such as output, inflation, interest rates, and unemployment, etc.

Ⅱ. The Must-be-discussed Questions Prior to Learning Econometrics

Before we focus on an empirical analysis which uses data to test an economic theory or estimate a relationship, it is worth considering the following relevant questions.

Q1: How to specify an econometric model from economic theory or models?

For the most part, econometric analysis begins by developing an econometric model. Typically, the formation of an econometric model begins from a formal economic model, economic theory, or even intuition. For example, we would like to examine the effect of job training on a person's productivity and consequently his/her wage. Economists have used basic economic tools to explain that workers are paid in line with their productivity (e. g. Wooldridge, 2006) . This reasoning leads to a model such as:

$$wage = f(education, experience, training) \tag{2.1}$$

Certainly, there are other factors that may affect the wage rate, but the above economic model captures the essence of the following two questions: Is there a positive relationship between training and wage rate? What is the magnitude of the effect? After we specify an economic model, we need to turn it into a related econometric model. Assuming that the relationships in the economic model are linear, we can develop such a complete econometric model as:

$$wage = \beta_0 + \beta_1 educ + \beta_2 exper + \beta_3 training + \mu \tag{2.2}$$

where the constants β_0, β_1, β_2, and β_3 are the parameters of the econometric model, measuring the directions and strengths of the determinants for wage. In addition, the term μ contains the other factors that can affect a person's wage. Once the econometric model has been specified, we can move forwards by focusing on β_3 in order to answer the above two questions.

Q2: How to identify different types of data?

Economic data sets come in a variety of types. Thus, we need to identify the most important data structures that often appear in applied work.

First type: Cross-Sectional Data. It is a random sample where each observation is a new individual, firm, etc. with information at a point in time. If the data is not a random sample, we have a sample-selection problem.

Second type: Time Series Data. Unlike cross-sectional data, time series data is not a random sample. It has a separate observation for each time period—e. g. stock prices. Since the order of observations in time series data is important, we need to deal with the problems of trending and seasonality when estimating a time series model.

Third type: Pooled Cross Section Data. We can pool random cross sections and treat them similar to a normal cross section. However, we need to account for time differences.

Fourth type: Panel or Longitudinal Data. It consists of a time series for each cross-sectional member in the data set.

Note: Type three and Type four have both cross-sectional and time series features. The big difference between these two types is that we follow the same random individual observations over time in the panel data set.

Q3: How to answer the question of causality?

Causal inquiry is unavoidable. Many important generalizations in economics are causal claims. For example, the law of demand asserts that a price increase will (ceteris paribus) diminish the quantity demanded. Econometricians have also been deeply concerned with the possibilities of determining causal relations from statistical evidence and with the relevance of causal relations to the possibility of consistent estimation of parameter values.

Example：Returns to Education.

A model of human capital investment implies getting more education should lead to higher earnings. In the simplest case，this implies an equation like

$$Earnings=\beta_0+\beta_1 education+\mu \tag{2.3}$$

The estimate of β_1 is the return to education，but can it be considered causal?

While the error term，μ，includes other factors affecting earnings rather than education，some things are still unobserved，which can be problematic. For instance，a person's inner ability which could affect earnings and is included in the error term might be highly correlated with his/her education level. If we can't block the impact of inner ability on education，we can't clearly tell how education causally affects earnings because the inner ability can affect earnings through its effect on education. Thus，the coefficient on education β_1 does not truly measure the causal relationship between education and earnings.

第 3 章

线性回归模型

Ⅰ. 简单线性回归模型

1.1 简单线性回归模型的基本建立

简单线性回归模型是 $y=\beta_0+\beta_1 x+\mu$。通常，我们定义：

y——因变量，左侧变量，被解释变量，或从属变量；

x——自变量，右侧变量，解释变量，回归变量，协变量，或控制变量；

μ——随机误差项，包含除解释变量 x 外所有影响被解释变量 y 的其他因素；

β_0——截距参数；

β_1——斜率参数。在假定 μ 不变的情况下，它用来衡量解释变量 x 对被解释变量 y 的影响。

此外，我们需要两个假设，以使回归分析简单化并符合因果关系的法则。

假设 1： 随机误差项的均值（数学期望）为 0。也就是说，$E(\mu)=0$。注意，这不是一个严格的假设，因为我们可以随时使用 β_0 将 $E(\mu)$ 化简为 0。

假设 2： 零条件均值。

我们需要一个有关随机误差项 μ 和解释变量 x 是否相关的重要假设。我们希望的是，随机误差项 μ 和解释变量 x 相互独立，互不相关。也就是说：$E(\mu \mid x)=E(\mu)=0$。这意味着随机误差项 μ 和解释变量 x 各自对被解释变量 y 的影响是完全独立的，因此，$E(y \mid x)=\beta_0+\beta_1 x$（简单的线性函数）。

1.2 普通最小二乘法 （OLS）

我们并不能获知总体参数 β_0 和 β_1 的取值，但希望通过观测到的样本数据进行估计并使这些估计值 $\hat{\beta}_0$ 和 $\hat{\beta}_0$ “接近”真实/未知的总体参数值 β_0 和 β_1。事实上，我们有许多种方法来估计 β_0 和 β_1。这里，我们采用的方法是剩余平方和最小化的法则。其基本思想是，用来自总体的随机抽样样本估计总体回归参数。假设 $\{(x_i, y_i): i=1, \cdots, n\}$ 为随机抽样的样本，样本中有 n 个观测值，对于每一个观测值，下面的情况总是成立：

$$SSR = \sum_{i=1}^{n} \hat{\mu}_i^2 = \sum_{i=1}^{n} (y_i - \hat{\beta}_0 - \hat{\beta}_1 x_i)^2 \tag{3.1}$$

下一步，通过求 SSR 关于 $\hat{\beta}_0$ 和 $\hat{\beta}_1$ 的偏导数并令其等于 0，我们可以得到：

$$\hat{\beta}_1 = \frac{\sum_{i=1}^{n} (y_i - \bar{y})(x_i - \bar{x})}{\sum_{i=1}^{n} (x_i - \bar{x})^2} \tag{3.2}$$

$$\hat{\beta}_0 = \bar{y} - \hat{\beta}_1 \bar{x} \tag{3.3}$$

其中，x_i = 解释变量的第 i 个观测值，

y_i = 被解释变量的第 i 个观测值，

$\bar{x}$ = 解释变量的平均值，

$\bar{y}$ = 被解释变量的平均值，

n = 样本中观测值的总数。

1.3 上机操作练习①

在这个练习中，我们将尝试通过看电视或电影的时间来预测 GPA。请找到并把数据文件 **gpa. dta** 上传到 Stata。在该数据集里，你会看到名为 *id*，*GPA* 和 *mediahours* 的三个变量。

（1）画出 *GPA* 和 *mediahours* 之间的关系。我们可以用多种方法找出 *GPA* 和 *mediahours* 之间的关系。因为只有两个变量，*GPA* 和 *mediahours*，所以我们首先可以采用绘制图表的方法。

在 Stata 中输入“graph twoway (scatter GPA mediahours) (lfit GPA mediahours)”。结果如图 3.1 所示。

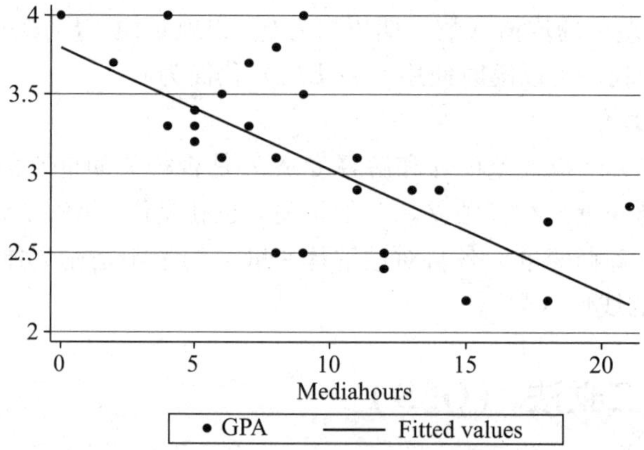

图 3.1

① 该练习受凯斯西储大学魏德海管理学院的 Eric Bettinger 的启发。数据是通过作者计量经济课堂上的学生调查收集的。

（2）图 3.1 显示：变量 *GPA* 和 *mediahours* 之间的关系趋向于线性关系。采用最小二乘法是一种方法，通常也是最好的一种方法。该方法可以根据图中的数据点拟合出一条估计线。现在，我们用最小二乘法来估计数据。

根据最小二乘法法则，最合适的估计线是：

$$GPA=\alpha+\beta mediahours,$$

其中，GPA_i＝估计线预测值，

β＝估计线的斜率，

mediahours＝在横轴上的小时值，

α＝回归线与 y 轴相交的点。

（3）测试 *gpa* 和 *mediahours* 之间的相关性。

```
. correlate gpa mediahours
(obs=30)

             |    gpa mediah~s
-------------+------------------
         gpa |   1.0000
  mediahours |  -0.6844   1.0000
```

相关系数等于－0.684 4，表明这两个变量高度相关。

（4）复制并粘贴回归结果：

```
. regress gpa mediahours

      Source |       SS       df       MS              Number of obs =      30
-------------+------------------------------           F(  1,    28) =   24.67
       Model |  4.04107489     1  4.04107489           Prob > F      =  0.0000
    Residual |  4.58592459    28  .163783021           R-squared     =  0.4684
-------------+------------------------------           Adj R-squared =  0.4494
       Total |  8.62699948    29  .297482741           Root MSE      =   .4047

------------------------------------------------------------------------------
         gpa |      Coef.   Std. Err.      t    P>|t|     [95% Conf. Interval]
-------------+----------------------------------------------------------------
  mediahours |  -.0771934   .0155405    -4.97   0.000    -.1090268     -.04536
       _cons |   3.797606    .160477    23.66   0.000     3.468884    4.126328
------------------------------------------------------------------------------
```

（5）如何解释 *mediahours* 的系数？

Mediahours 的系数是－0.077 193 4。这意味着：当你多花一小时看电视时，你的 GPA 会降低 0.077 绩点。

（6）线性回归有预测功能。

例如，如果某人看了 0 小时电视或电影，我们可以预测他的 GPA＝3.797 606。

（7）如果你的 id 是 7 号，你看了 15 小时电视或电影，预测你的 GPA 是多少？

用线性回归的方法，我们可以预测你的 GPA＝2.639 705，和你的实际 GPA 相差了 0.439 705。

Ⅱ. 多元线性回归模型

2.1　多元线性回归模型与简单回归模型的相似处

多元线性回归模型的方程式是：$y=\beta_0+\beta_1x_1+\beta_2x_2+\cdots+\beta_kx_k+\mu$。其中，$y$ 仍是被解释

变量，x_i（$i=1$，…，k）是解释变量，μ 仍是随机误差项，β_0 仍是截距参数。β_i（$i=1$，…，k）都是斜率参数。在假定 μ 不变的情况下，β_i（$i=1$，…，k）各自用来衡量每个相应的解释变量对被解释变量 y 的影响。

为了构建多元线性回归模型，我们仍然需要以下两个假设：

$E(\mu)=0$，而且 $E(\mu \mid x_1, x_2, \cdots, x_k)=0$。

我们仍然采用剩余平方和最小化的法则来估计 β_0，β_1，…，β_k。通过对 $\hat{\beta}_0$，$\hat{\beta}_1$，…，$\hat{\beta}_k$ 求偏导数并令其等于 0，我们可以得到 $k+1$ 个方程式，从而用于计算 $\hat{\beta}_0$，$\hat{\beta}_1$，…，$\hat{\beta}_k$。

2.2 对多元回归中的斜率参数的解释

以下的推导告诉了我们，每一个斜率参数可解释为：假定其他变量不变的情况下，与之相对应的解释变量对被解释变量的影响。

$$\hat{y}=\hat{\beta}_0+\hat{\beta}_1x_1+\hat{\beta}_2x_2+\cdots+\hat{\beta}_ky_k$$

于是 $\Delta\hat{y}=\hat{\beta}_1\Delta x_1+\hat{\beta}_2\Delta x_2+\cdots+\hat{\beta}_k\Delta x_k$。

所以，当 x_2，…，x_k 固定不变时，这意味着：

$$\Delta\hat{y}=\hat{\beta}_1\Delta x_1$$

注意：当我们比较简单回归 $\tilde{y}=\tilde{\beta}_0+\tilde{\beta}_1x_1$ 和二元回归 $\hat{y}=\hat{\beta}_0+\hat{\beta}_1x_1+\hat{\beta}_2x_2$ 时，一般而言，$\tilde{\beta}_1\neq\hat{\beta}_1$，除非 $\hat{\beta}_2=0$（也就是说，x_2 对 y 没有影响，或者 x_2 和 x_1 在样本里不相关）。

2.3 简单回归和多元回归的拟合优度

我们如何得知样本回归模型拟合样本数据的程度？我们可以计算样本决定系数——R^2。其定义为解释平方和（ESS）占总平方和（SST）的比重。也就是：

$$R^2=\frac{SSE}{SST}=1-\frac{SSR}{SST}\text{，其中 } 0\leqslant R^2\leqslant 1$$

而且，$SST=\sum(y_i-\bar{y})^2$ 是总平方和，

$SSE=\sum(\hat{y}-\bar{y})^2$ 是解释平方和，

$SSR=\sum\hat{\mu}_i^2$ 是残差平方和，

$SST=SSE+SRR$。

样本决定系数不会因为回归模型里添加了新的变量而相应减少。通常，样本决定系数会随着解释变量数量的增加而增加。因而，它不适合用来比较模型之间的好坏。当模型里有多个解释变量时，我们可以考虑另一个样本决定系数——调整后的 R^2。它是根据解释变量的数量调整样本决定系数：R^2，从而更切合实际地衡量变量之间的相关关系。

$$\text{调整后的 } R^2=1-(1-R^2)\frac{n-1}{n-k-1}$$

其中，n=样本数据中观测值的总数，k=模型中解释变量的数量。

2.4　上机操作练习[①]

2001 年 4 月，OPEC 开始限制原油产量到每周两千万桶。总统想知道这是否会影响美国油价，如果影响，会影响多少？请在 Stata 中打开 **gas. dta**。

这个问题中有三个变量：

Gasprice＝国内每加仑的油价（美分）

Domesticproduction＝国内原油产量（百万桶/每天）

Foreignproduction＝外国原油产量（百万桶/每天）

我们可以估测多重线性回归方程式：

$$Gasprice=\beta_0+\beta_1\times Foreignproduction+\beta_2\times Domesticproduction+\mu$$

（1）写出 Stata 中的回归结果：

```
. reg gasprices foreignproduction domesticproduction

      Source |       SS       df       MS              Number of obs =     549
-------------+------------------------------           F(  2,   546) =  102.49
       Model |  34837.1516     2  17418.5758           Prob > F      =  0.0000
    Residual |  92795.1223   546  169.954436           R-squared     =  0.2729
-------------+------------------------------           Adj R-squared =  0.2703
       Total |  127632.274   548  232.905609           Root MSE      =  13.037

------------------------------------------------------------------------------
   gasprices |      Coef.   Std. Err.      t    P>|t|     [95% Conf. Interval]
-------------+----------------------------------------------------------------
foreignpro~n |   .0191746   .0038483     4.98   0.000     .0116153    .0267339
domesticpr~n |   .0111094   .0012366     8.98   0.000     .0086803    .0135385
       _cons |   22.90343   8.743543     2.62   0.009      5.72833    40.07853
------------------------------------------------------------------------------
```

（2）现在，请注意各系数，或者“coef”列。我们可以把结果重写为：

$$\widehat{Gasprice}=22.903\ 43+0.019\ 174\ 6\times Foreignproduction$$
$$+0.011\ 109\ 4\times Domesticproduction$$

（3）解释外国原油产量和国内原油产量的影响。

$\hat{\beta}_1$ 代表在国内原油产量不变的情况下，外国原油产量每增加一百万桶，汽油价格上涨 0.02 美分。

$\hat{\beta}_2$ 代表在外国原油产量不变的情况下，国内原油产量每增加一百万桶，汽油价格上涨 0.01 美分。

（4）*SSR*，*SSE* 和 *SST* 之间的关系是什么？

$SSR=92\ 795.122\ 3$

$SSE=34\ 837.151\ 6$

$SST=127\ 632.274$

$SST=SSR+SSE$

（5）我们的样本回归模型是否拟合了样本数据？为什么？

$R^2=0.272\ 9$

---

① 该练习受凯斯西储大学魏德海管理学院的 Eric Bettinger 的启发。数据从如下网址收集：http：//connection.cwru.edu/econ326/mod1/C/gas.xls。

调整后的 $R^2=0.2703$

我们现有的模型没有很好的拟合度，因为样本决定系数和调整后的样本决定系数只能解释大概 27%的汽油价格变动。

（6）标准误差：

$\hat{\sigma}_{\beta_1}=0.0038483$

$\hat{\sigma}_{\beta_2}=0.0012366$

$\hat{\sigma}=13.037$

（7）在多元线性回归模型中，外国原油产量的下跌依然会导致汽油价格下跌。这还是与我们在新闻中了解到的相悖。这个回归结果暗示了什么？

这个结果暗示：我们省略了其他一些重要的影响汽油价格的变量，例如收入、货币政策、财政政策，等等。

Ⅲ. 附加上机操作练习[①]

打开有两个变量的数据文件 **homers. dta**。变量 *salary* 是职业联盟的棒球球员的薪金，以千美元为单位。变量 *homers* 是这些球员击中本垒的数量。两个变量都含有 2000 赛季的数据。该文件中含有 254 个位置球员的数据（不含投手的数据）。

（1）用 Stata 估计下面的回归方程：

$$salary_i=\beta_0+\beta_1 homers_i+\varepsilon_i$$

你对 β_1 的估计是什么？它的符号是你所期望的吗？

```
. regress salary homers

      Source |       SS       df       MS              Number of obs =     254
-------------+------------------------------           F(  1,   252) =   48.00
       Model |   355521440     1   355521440           Prob > F      =  0.0000
    Residual |  1.8665e+09   252  7406677.65           R-squared     =  0.1600
-------------+------------------------------           Adj R-squared =  0.1567
       Total |  2.2220e+09   253  8782625.32           Root MSE      =  2721.5

------------------------------------------------------------------------------
      salary |      Coef.   Std. Err.      t    P>|t|     [95% Conf. Interval]
-------------+----------------------------------------------------------------
      homers |   103.9471   15.00346     6.93   0.000     74.39899    133.4953
       _cons |   1253.224   312.9587     4.00   0.000     636.8762    1869.572
------------------------------------------------------------------------------
```

β_1 的估计值是 103.947 1。它的符号为正，因为如果一名球员击中的本垒越多，他的薪金越高。

（2）如果一名球员多击中一个本垒，他的薪金会上涨多少？如果他多击中五个本垒，他的薪金会上涨多少？

如果一名球员多击中一个本垒，他的薪金会上涨 103 947.1 美元。如果他多击中五个本垒，他的薪金会上涨 5×103 947.1 美元=519 735.5 美元。

（3）对于一名没有击出任何本垒的球员，你预测他的薪金是多少？

---

① 该练习经过修改，数据集从下书获取：Stephen J. Schmidt，*Econometrics*（McGraw-Hill，2005）。

他的薪金是 1 253 224 美元。

（4）用 Stata 估计下面的回归方程：

$$homers_i = \beta_0 + \beta_1 salary_i + \varepsilon_i$$

如果一名球员的薪金上涨了 100 万美元，他多击中了多少本垒？

```
. regress homers salary

      Source |       SS       df       MS              Number of obs =     254
-------------+------------------------------           F(  1,   252) =   48.00
       Model |  5264.5556     1  5264.5556             Prob > F      =  0.0000
    Residual |  27638.846   252  109.67796             R-squared     =  0.1600
-------------+------------------------------           Adj R-squared =  0.1567
       Total | 32903.4016   253  130.052971            Root MSE      =  10.473
                0
------------------------------------------------------------------------------
      homers |      Coef.   Std. Err.      t    P>|t|     [95% Conf. Interval]
-------------+----------------------------------------------------------------
      salary |   .0015392   .0002222     6.93   0.000     .0011017    .0019768
       _cons |   12.75444   .9471494    13.47   0.000      10.8891    14.61977
------------------------------------------------------------------------------
```

如果一名球员的薪金上涨了 100 万美元，他多击中 0.001 539 2×1 000＝1.539 2 个本垒。

（5）两个变量中哪个是内生变量，哪个是外生变量？你认为哪个回归模型更适合薪金市场？你能提出一种新的方法来估计这个模型吗？

homers 更像是外生变量，*salary* 更像是内生变量。因为薪金由球员的表现决定，但是一名球员的薪金不会影响球员击中的本垒数量。所以第一个模型更好。我们也可以用前一年的本垒数量来预测今年的薪金。

Chapter 3

Linear Regression Models

I. Simple Linear Regression Models

1.1 Basic Set-up of Simple Linear Regression Model

In the simple linear regression model, where $y=\beta_0+\beta_1 x+\mu$, we typically refer to:

y—Dependent Variable, or Left-Hand Side Variable, or Explained Variable, or Regressand;

x—Independent Variable, or Right-Hand Side Variable, or Explanatory Variable, or Regressor, or Covariate, or Control Variables;

μ—Error Term, it captures all factors other than x that affect y;

β_0—Intercept parameter;

β_1–Slope parameter, it measures the effect on y of a change on x, for μ held fixed.

In addition, we need two assumptions in order to simplify our regression analysis and satisfy the rule of causality:

Assumption 1: The average value of μ, the error term, in the population is 0. That is, $E(\mu)=0$. Please note that this is not a restrictive assumption since we can always use β_0 to normalize $E(\mu)$ to 0.

Assumption 2: Zero Conditional Mean. We need to make a crucial assumption about how μ and x are related. We want it to be the case that knowing something about x does not give us any information about μ so that they are completely unrelated. That is, $E(\mu \mid x)=E(\mu)=0$, which implies $E(y \mid x)=\beta_0+\beta_1 x$ (simple linear function).

1.2 Ordinary Least Squares Estimators

We don't know population parameters β_0 and β_1, but would like to use observed data to create estimates, which will (we hope) be close to the real/unknown population parameter values. There are many ways to estimate β_0 and β_1. Our method will MINIMIZE THE SUM OF SQUARED RESIDUALS. The basic idea of regression is to estimate the population parameters from a sample. Let $\{(x_i, y_i): i=1, \cdots, n\}$ denote a random sample of size n from the population. For each observation in this sample, it will be the case that:

$$SSR = \sum_{i=1}^{n} \hat{\mu}_i^2 = \sum_{i=1}^{n} (y_i - \hat{\beta}_0 - \hat{\beta}_1 x_i)^2 \tag{3.1}$$

Next, taking partial derivatives of SSR with respect to $\hat{\beta}_0$ and $\hat{\beta}_1$ and setting them to be zero, we can get:

$$\hat{\beta}_1 = \frac{\sum_{i=1}^{n} (y_i - \bar{y})(x_i - \bar{x})}{\sum_{i=1}^{n} (x_i - \bar{x})^2} \tag{3.2}$$

$$\hat{\beta}_0 = \bar{y} - \hat{\beta}_1 \bar{x} \tag{3.3}$$

where x_i=value of independent variable for ith observation,

y_i=value of dependent variable for ith observation,

$\bar{x}$=mean value for independent variable,

$\bar{y}$=mean value for dependent variable,

n=total number of observations.

1.3 Computer Exercise[①]

In this exercise, we will be attempting to predict GPA by the time spent watching TV or movies. Please find and upload the data file **gpa.dta** onto Stata. You will find three variables named *id*, *GPA*, and *mediahours* in the data set.

(1) Graph the relationship between *GPA* and *mediahours*. There are many ways to figure out the relationship between *GPA* and hours of media watched. A good place to start, since there are only two variables, *GPA* and *mediahours*, is to plot the data on a graph.

In Stata, type "graph twoway (scatter GPA mediahours) (lfit GPA mediahours)". The output is as follows, see figure 3.1.

(2) The figure 3.1 indicates that the relationship between *GPA* and *mediahours* tends to be linear. Least Squares is one rule—and often the best rule—for fitting a line to data on a graph. For now, let's look at the Least Squares method to evaluate data.

① This exercise is inspired by Eric Bettinger at Weatherhead School of Management, Case Western Reserve University. Data is collected from the student survey in my Econometrics class.

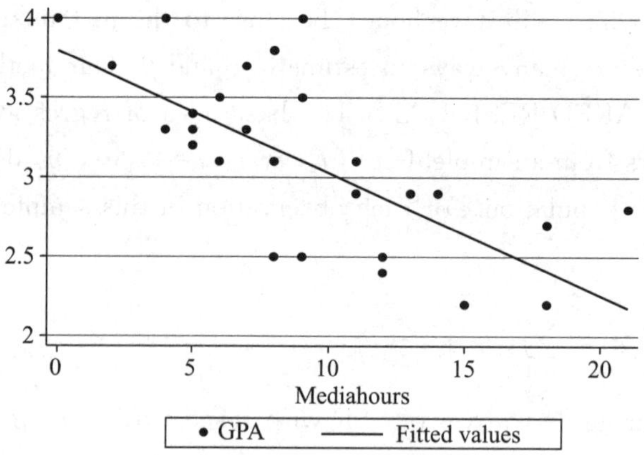

figure 3.1

According to the Least Squares rule, the best line is:

$$GPA=\alpha+\beta mediahours$$

where GPA =the value predicted by the line,

β=the slope of the line,

mediahours=the value of hours on the horizontal axis,

α=the point where the regression line intercepts the y axis.

(3) Examine the correlation between *gpa* and *mediahours*.

```
. correlate gpa mediahours
(obs=30)

             |      gpa mediah~s
-------------+------------------
         gpa |   1.0000
  mediahours |  -0.6844   1.0000
```

The correlation coefficient equals −0.684 4, showing that these two variables are highly correlated.

(4) Copy and paste your regression results:

```
. regress gpa mediahours

      Source |       SS       df       MS              Number of obs =      30
-------------+------------------------------           F(  1,    28) =   24.67
       Model |  4.04107489     1  4.04107489           Prob > F      =  0.0000
    Residual |  4.58592459    28  .163783021           R-squared     =  0.4684
-------------+------------------------------           Adj R-squared =  0.4494
       Total |  8.62699948    29  .297482741           Root MSE      =   .4047

------------------------------------------------------------------------------
         gpa |      Coef.   Std. Err.      t    P>|t|     [95% Conf. Interval]
-------------+----------------------------------------------------------------
  mediahours |  -.0771934   .0155405    -4.97   0.000    -.1090268     -.04536
       _cons |   3.797606    .160477    23.66   0.000     3.468884    4.126328
------------------------------------------------------------------------------
```

(5) How to interpret the coefficient on mediahours?

The coefficient on *mediahours* is −0.077 193 4. This means, when you spend one more hour watching TV, your GPA will be lowered by 0.077 points.

(6) Linear Regression helps to predict behavior.

For example, if someone watches 0 hours of TV or movies, we could predict that his

GPA=3.797 606.

(7) If your id is No. 7, you watched 15 hours of media. What is your predicted GPA?

Using Linear Regression techniques, we can predict that your GPA=2.639 705. We were off by 0.439 705.

Ⅱ. Multiple Linear Regression Models

2.1 Parallels with Simple Linear Regression

A multiple linear regression model takes the following form:

$$y=\beta_0+\beta_1 x_1+\beta_2 x_2+\cdots+\beta_k x_k+\mu$$

where y is still explained variable, x is still explanatory variable, μ is still the error term (or disturbance). β_0 is still the intercept, β_1 to β_k are all called slope parameters.

Two assumptions are still needed: $E(\mu)=0$, and $E(\mu \mid x_1, x_2, \cdots, x_k)=0$。

To estimate β_0, β_1, $\cdots$, β_k, we still minimize the sum of squared residuals, so we have $k+1$ first order conditions.

2.2 Interpreting Slope Parameters

The following derivatives indicate that every slope parameter measures the impact of the corresponding explanatory variable on the explained variable, holding other explanatory variables constant.

$$\hat{y}=\hat{\beta}_0+\hat{\beta}_1 x_1+\hat{\beta}_2 x_2+\cdots+\hat{\beta}_k y_k, \text{ so}$$

$$\Delta\hat{y}=\hat{\beta}_1\Delta x_1+\hat{\beta}_2\Delta x_2+\cdots+\hat{\beta}_k\Delta x_k,$$

holding x_2, $\cdots$, x_k fixed, this implies that $\Delta\hat{y}=\hat{\beta}_1\Delta x_1$, that is each β has a *ceteris paribus* interpretation.

Note: If you compare the simple regression $\tilde{y}=\tilde{\beta}_0+\tilde{\beta}_1 x_1$ with the multiple regression $\hat{y}=\hat{\beta}_0+\hat{\beta}_1 x_1+\hat{\beta}_2 x_2$, generally, $\tilde{\beta}_1\neq\hat{\beta}_1$ unless $\hat{\beta}_2=0$ (i.e. no partial effect of x_2 or x_1 and x_2 are uncorrelated in sample).

2.3 The Goodness of Fit

How do we think about how well our sample regression line fits our sample data? We can compute the fraction of the total sum of squares (SST) that is explained by the model and call this the R-squared of regression, defined as:

$$R^2=\frac{SSE}{SST}=1-\frac{SSR}{SST}, \quad 0\leqslant R^2\leqslant 1,$$

where, $SST = \sum (y_i - \bar{y})^2$ is the total sum of squares,

$SSE = \sum (\hat{y} - \bar{y})^2$ is the explained sum of squares,

$SSR = \sum \hat{\mu}_i^2$ is the residual sum of squares,

$SST = SSE + SRR$.

R^2 can never decrease when another independent variable is added to a regression, and will usually increase with the number of independent variables. Hence, it is not a good way to compara models. As a solution, adjusted *R-squared* is introduced when there are multiple x's. It adjusts the *R-squared* based on the number of x's in the model and gives a more realistic measure of relationship:

$$Adjusted\ R^2 = 1 - (1 - R^2)\frac{n-1}{n-k-1}$$

where, n = the total number of observations in the sample data, k = the number of independent variables in the model.

2.4 Computer Exercise[①]

In April 2001, OPEC began limiting oil production by 20 million barrels weekly. The President wants to understand whether this will affect the price of gasoline for Americans and, if so, by how much? Please find and upload **gas. dta** onto Stata.

There are three variables to this problem:

Gasprice = Domestic Price-Per-Gallon (in cents)

Domesticproduction = Domestic Oil Production (in million barrels/day)

Foreignproduction = Foreign Oil Production (in million barrels/day)

We can estimate our multiple linear regression equation:

$$Gasprice = \beta_0 + \beta_1 \times Foreignproduction + \beta_2 \times Domesticproduction + \mu$$

(1) Write what the regression output looks like in Stata:

```
. reg gasprices foreignproduction domesticproduction

      Source |       SS       df       MS              Number of obs =     549
-------------+------------------------------           F(  2,   546) =  102.49
       Model |  34837.1516     2  17418.5758           Prob > F      =  0.0000
    Residual |  92795.1223   546  169.954436           R-squared     =  0.2729
-------------+------------------------------           Adj R-squared =  0.2703
       Total |  127632.274   548  232.905609           Root MSE      =  13.037

------------------------------------------------------------------------------
   gasprices |      Coef.   Std. Err.      t    P>|t|     [95% Conf. Interval]
-------------+----------------------------------------------------------------
foreignpro~n |   .0191746   .0038483     4.98   0.000     .0116153    .0267339
domesticpr~n |   .0111094   .0012366     8.98   0.000     .0086803    .0135385
       _cons |   22.90343   8.743543     2.62   0.009      5.72833    40.07853
------------------------------------------------------------------------------
```

① This exercise is inspired by Eric Bettinger at Weatherhead School of Management, Case Western Reserve University. Data is collected from http: //connection. cwru. edu/econ326/modl/C/gas. xls.

(2) Now, focus on the coefficient, or the "coef" column. We can rewrite the results as:

$$\widehat{Gasprice}=22.90343+0.0191746\ Foreignproduction$$
$$+0.0111094\ Domesticproduction$$

(3) Interpret the effects of foreign production and domestic production on gas prices.

$\hat{\beta}_1$ indicates that when foreign production increases by 1 million barrels, gas price increases by 0.02 cents, holding domestic production constant.

$\hat{\beta}_2$ indicates that when domestic production increases by 1 million barrels, gas price increases by about 0.01 cents, holding foreign production constant.

(4) What is the relationship between *SSR*, *SSE* and *SST*?

$SSR=92\,795.1223$

$SSE=34\,837.1516$

$SST=127\,632.274$

$SST=SSR+SSE$

(5) Does our model have a good fit? Why?

R-squared $=0.2729$

Adjusted R-squared $=0.2703$

Our current model does not have a good fit, since each *R-squared* and *adjusted R-squared* only explain about 27% of the variation in gas price.

(6) Standard errors:

$\hat{\sigma}_{\hat{\beta}_1}=0.0038483$

$\hat{\sigma}_{\hat{\beta}_2}=0.0012366$

$\hat{\sigma}=13.037$

(7) In the multiple linear regression model, decreases in foreign production still lead to decreases in the price. This is still contrary to what we hear on the news. What does this regression result imply?

This implies that we have omitted some variables that also play important roles in affecting gas price, such as income, monetary policy, fiscal policy, etc.

Ⅲ. Additional Computer Exercise[①]

Load the data file **homers. dta**, Invalid _ string, which has two variables. The variable salary is the salary of major league baseball players, measured in thousands of dollars. The variable homers is the number of home runs they hit. Both variables are for the 2000 season. There are data on 254 position players (no pitchers) .

① This exercise is modified and the data set is collected from the book *Econometrics* written by Stephen J. Schmidt, (McGraw-Hill, 2005).

(1) Use Stata to estimate the regression equation:

$$salary_i = \beta_0 + \beta_1 homers_i + \varepsilon_i$$

What is your estimate for β_1? Does it take the sign you would expect?

```
. regress salary homers

      Source |       SS       df       MS              Number of obs =     254
-------------+------------------------------           F(  1,   252) =   48.00
       Model |   355521440     1   355521440           Prob > F      =  0.0000
    Residual |  1.8665e+09   252  7406677.65           R-squared     =  0.1600
-------------+------------------------------           Adj R-squared =  0.1567
       Total |  2.2220e+09   253  8782625.32           Root MSE      =  2721.5

------------------------------------------------------------------------------
      salary |      Coef.   Std. Err.      t    P>|t|     [95% Conf. Interval]
-------------+----------------------------------------------------------------
      homers |   103.9471   15.00346     6.93   0.000     74.39899    133.4953
       _cons |   1253.224   312.9587     4.00   0.000     636.8762    1869.572
------------------------------------------------------------------------------
```

The estimate of β_1 equals 103. 947 1. It takes a positive sign, which makes sense that, when the players hit more home runs, their salary will be higher.

(2) If a player hits one more home run, how much does his salary rise? If he hits five more home runs, how much does his salary rise?

If a player hits one more home run, his salary will rise by \$103 947. 1 thousand. If he hits five more home runs, his salary will rise by 5× \$103 947. 1= \$519 735. 5.

(3) What would you predict for the salary of a player who hits no home runs?

The salary of a player who hits no home runs would be \$1 253 224 thousand.

(4) Use Stata to estimate the regression:

$$homers_i = \beta_0 + \beta_1 salary_i + \varepsilon_i$$

If a player's salary rises by \$1 million, how many additional home runs does he hit?

```
. regress homers salary

      Source |       SS       df       MS              Number of obs =     254
-------------+------------------------------           F(  1,   252) =   48.00
       Model |   5264.5556     1   5264.5556           Prob > F      =  0.0000
    Residual |   27638.846   252   109.67796           R-squared     =  0.1600
-------------+------------------------------           Adj R-squared =  0.1567
       Total |  32903.4016   253  130.052971           Root MSE      =  10.473

------------------------------------------------------------------------------
      homers |      Coef.   Std. Err.      t    P>|t|     [95% Conf. Interval]
-------------+----------------------------------------------------------------
      salary |   .0015392   .0002222     6.93   0.000     .0011017    .0019768
       _cons |   12.75444   .9471494    13.47   0.000      10.8891    14.61977
------------------------------------------------------------------------------
```

If the player's salary rises by \$1 million, the number of additional home runs he hits would be 0. 001 539 2×1 000=1. 539 2.

(5) Which of the two variables is more likely to be endogenous, and which of the two variables is more likely to be exogenous? Which of the two regressions do you think is a better model of the salary market? Can you suggest a different way of estimating this equation?

homers is more likely to be exogenous, and *salary* is more likely to be endogenous. Salary depends on performance, whereas the number of home runs a player hits is probably not affected by his salary. The first model is better. We can use previous year's *homers* to predict this year's *salary*.

第 4 章

线性模型检验

Ⅰ. 最小二乘估计量的统计属性

在上一章，我们学习了如何使用最小二乘法来估计分析简单的线性回归模型和多元线性回归模型。为什么在数量统计学里最小二乘法能够提供最好的具有线性和无偏性的估计量？我们有必要在此章的开始部分一起讨论并理解高斯-马尔可夫定理的重要性。

高斯-马尔可夫定理指出：如果以下一系列的假设条件成立（最后一个不要求），最小二乘估计量跟其他任何线性无偏估计量相比具有最佳线性、无偏性和有效性的特点。

假设 1：$y_i=\beta_0+\beta_1 x_i+\mu_i$

假设 2：$E(\mu_i)=E(\mu_i \mid x_i)=0$

假设 3：$\mathrm{Cov}(\mu_i, \mu_j)=0$

假设 4：无完全共线性

假设 5：$\mathrm{Var}(\mu_i \mid x_i)=\sigma^2$

假设 6：$\mu_i \sim N(0, \sigma)$

换言之，假设 1 指出总体回归模型参数是线性的；假设 2 是零均值假设，即在解释变量值被给定的条件下，随机误差项的均值为零；假设 3 为无自相关假设，即误差项的各观测值之间不相关；假设 4 显示解释变量的观测值不为常数而且各解释变量之间无完全线性关系；假设 5 强调同方差，即随机误差项的方差是一个常数。根据高斯-马尔可夫定理，前五个假设被命名为高斯-马尔可夫假设。在这些假设条件下，最小二乘估计量是最佳线性无偏估计（因而称为 BLUE）。也就是说，最小二乘估计量的均值等于总体参数值，例如，$E(\hat{\beta}_0)=\beta_0$，$E(\hat{\beta}_1)=\beta_1$，…，$E(\hat{\beta}_j)=\beta_j$。同时，在所有的线性无偏估计量中最小二乘估计量的方差最小。

最后，为了知道抽样分布的情况，我们假定误差项服从正态分布。因此，我们称假设 6 为正态性假设。当所有的高斯-马尔可夫假设与正态分布假设结合起来时，我们不难证明 $\hat{\beta}_j \sim N(\beta_j, \sigma_{\hat{\beta}_j})$，也就是说 $(\hat{\beta}_j-\beta_j)/\sigma_{\hat{\beta}_j} \sim N(0, 1)$。

Ⅱ. 单一回归参数的显著性检验：t 检验

“t”随机变量（不大写）可以由一个标准正态分布和一个 χ^2 分布得到。更精确地说，如果随机变量 Z 服从标准正态分布（$Z \sim N(0, 1)$），随机变量 V 服从自由度为 m 的 χ^2 分布，并且两者相互独立，那么随机变量 t 定义为：

$$t=\frac{Z}{\sqrt{V/m}} \sim t_{(m)} \tag{4.1}$$

称之服从自由度为 m 的 t 分布。

根据 t 分布的定义，为了进行单一回归参数的显著性假设检验，我们需要下述定理：

$$\frac{\hat{\beta}_j-\beta_j}{\hat{\sigma}_{\hat{\beta}_j}} \sim t(n-2) \tag{4.2}$$

上述定理的重要性在于，它使我们能够对单个总体参数进行假设检验。我们以如下的汽车销售方程式为例：

$$CarSales=\beta_0+\beta_1 TVads+\mu$$

```
. reg  carsales tvads

      Source |       SS       df       MS              Number of obs =       5
-------------+------------------------------           F(  1,     3) =   21.43
       Model |        100     1         100           Prob > F      =  0.0190
    Residual |         14     3  4.66666667           R-squared     =  0.8772
-------------+------------------------------           Adj R-squared =  0.8363
       Total |        114     4        28.5           Root MSE      =  2.1602

------------------------------------------------------------------------------
    carsales |      Coef.   Std. Err.      t    P>|t|     [95% Conf. Interval]
-------------+----------------------------------------------------------------
       tvads |          5   1.080123     4.63   0.019     1.562565    8.437435
       _cons |         10   2.366432     4.23   0.024     2.468958    17.53104
------------------------------------------------------------------------------
```

零假设是 H_0：$\beta_1=0$，这意味着解释变量（即电视广告）不会影响被解释变量（即汽车销售）。备择假设是 H_1：$\beta_1 \neq 0$，完全和零假设相反。当零假设成立时，用于检验的统计量是服从自由度为 $n-2$ 的 t 分布。如果显著性系数是 $\alpha=0.05$，由 t 分布表，我们可以查出自由度为（5—2）的临界值是 3.182。然后，我们使用样本数据，通过最小二乘法得出 β_1 的估计值是 5，样本标准差是 1.080 123，相应的 t 值是 4.63。由于 t 值$=4.63$ 大于临界值 3.182，因此我们拒绝零假设，并得出电视广告对汽车销售有重大影响的结论。

由于 Stata 自身已配有现成的各种假设检验的执行命令，在输入 OLS 回归的命令之后，我们可以直接输入下面的代码：

```
. test  tvads

 ( 1)  tvads = 0

       F(  1,     3) =   21.43
            Prob > F =    0.0190
```

在汽车销售例子里，p 值为 0.019，这意味着对应的 t 值 4.63 是位于拥有 3 个自由度的 t 分布的尾端。由于 p 值小于显著性水平 5%，因此我们拒绝零假设，并得出相同的结论，即电视广告对汽车销售有重大影响。

更普遍的 t 检验是：我们想要检验类似 H_0：$\beta_j = a_j$ 的假设。在这种情况下，适当的 t 统计量是：

$$t=(\hat{\beta}_j - a_j)/\hat{\sigma}_{\hat{\beta}_j}$$

在 Stata 中，执行完线性回归命令后，我们可以输入“test xj＝aj”，并通过得到的 p 值来判断是否拒绝零假设。在汽车销售例子里，假如我们想知道独立变量的系数，即电视广告等于一个具体的数值，例如，$\beta_1 = 1$，我们可以输入：

```
test  tvads =1

( 1)  tvads = 1

       F(  1,     3) =   13.71
            Prob > F =    0.0342
```

由于 p 值为 0.034 2，低于显著性水平 5%，我们得出的结论是：电视广告系数不等于 1。

另外，假如我们想要检验两个解释变量对被解释变量的影响是否一样，即两个回归参数是否相等：H_0：$\beta_1 = \beta_2$。在 Stata 中，执行完线性回归命令后，我们可以输入“test x1＝x2，common”，并通过 p 值的大小来判断是否拒绝零假设。在汽车销售例子里，假如我们加入另一个解释变量——销售人员的人数，并且想知道这两个独立变量对汽车销售的影响是否一样，也就是说，电视广告的回归参数是否等同于销售人员的回归参数。在 Stata 中，我们输入“test tvads＝salesman”，然后通过 p 值来得出结论。

Ⅲ. 联合显著性检验及总体显著性检验：*F* 检验

3.1　如何进行 *F* 检验

目前我们所学的一切仅涉及单一的线性检验（例如，$\beta_1 = 0$ 或 $\beta_1 = \beta_2$）。然而，我们可能要检验有关多个回归参数的联合假设。

典型的例子是：“排除性限制条件”检验，即我们想知道是否一组参数都等于零。在此，零假设为：H_0：$\beta_{k-q+1} = 0$，…，$\beta_k = 0$；备择假设为：零假设是不正确的。我们不能逐一检查每个 t 统计量，因为我们想知道若干个回归参数在某一显著性水平下是否具有联合显著性（在该显著性水平下任何一个回归参数都有可能不具有显著性）。在检验中，我们需要回归两种模型：“限制模型”是在假设零假设是正确的情况下把相应的 x_{k-q+1}，…，x_k 排除；“非限制模型”是在假设零假设不正确的情况下仍然包括 x_{k-q+1}，…，x_k。回归之后，我们可以用以下的公式计算 F 统计量：

$$F\equiv\frac{(SSR_r-SSR_{ur})/q}{SSR_{ur}/(n-k-1)}$$

其中，下标 r 代表限制模型，下标 ur 代表非限制模型，q 代表零假设中的限制等式数目。

由于 SSR 的取值有可能会很大，导致 F 统计值计算的不便，我们可以采用另一个替代公式。其理由是因为对于任何一个回归模型，$SSR=SST(1-R^2)$ 的关系总是存在的。因此，SSR_r 和 SSR_{ur} 可以被 R_r^2 和 R_{ur}^2 替代，F 统计量可计算为：

$$F\equiv\frac{(R_{ur}^2-R_r^2)/q}{(1-R_{ur}^2)/(n-k-1)}$$

其中，下标 r 代表限制模型，下标 ur 代表非限制模型，q 代表零假设中的限制等式数目。

在各种“排除性限制条件”的检验中，有一种特殊的检验，即检验 H_0：$\beta_1=\beta_2=\cdots=\beta_k=0$，也就是，所有的回归参数都为零。在零假设成立时，限制模型所得的 R^2 为零。因此，F 统计量可简化为：

$$F=\frac{R^2/k}{(1-R^2)/(n-k-1)}$$

3.2 上机操作练习

为了强化我们刚才所学，我们一起来使用 Stata 练习下面的有关习题。

（1）我们首先回顾一下如何人工输入我们所需要的数据。

```
input y x1 x2 x3

             y          x1          x2          x3
1. 30 4 10 5
2. 20 3 8 2
3. 36 6 11 8
4. 24 4 9 3
5. 40 8 12 4
6. 38 7 10 6
7. end

regress y x1 x2 x3

      Source |       SS       df       MS              Number of obs =       6
-------------+------------------------------           F(  3,     2) =   27.29
       Model |  317.576457     3  105.858819           Prob > F      =  0.0356
    Residual |  7.75687666     2  3.87843833           R-squared     =  0.9762
-------------+------------------------------           Adj R-squared =  0.9404
       Total |  325.333333     5  65.0666667           Root MSE      =  1.9694

------------------------------------------------------------------------------
           y |      Coef.   Std. Err.      t    P>|t|     [95% Conf. Interval]
-------------+----------------------------------------------------------------
          x1 |    2.64685   .8867671     2.98   0.096    -1.168601    6.462301
          x2 |   1.183673   1.319598     0.90   0.464      -4.4941    6.861447
          x3 |   .9334516   .5046408     1.85   0.206    -1.237842    3.104746
       _cons |   1.023957   8.919619     0.11   0.919    -37.35407    39.40198
------------------------------------------------------------------------------
```

（2）如果我们要检验 x_1 和 x_2 是否有联合显著性，即 x_1 和 x_2 是否共同影响 y，在 Stata 中，我们可以选择下列三种方法的任何一种：

```
test (x1=0) (x2=0)

( 1)  x1 = 0
( 2)  x2 = 0

      F(  2,      2) =   20.61
           Prob > F =    0.0463

test x1=x2=0

( 1)  x1 - x2 = 0
( 2)  x1 = 0

      F(  2,      2) =   20.61
           Prob > F =    0.0463

test x1 x2

( 1)  x1 = 0
( 2)  x2 = 0

      F(  2,      2) =   20.61
           Prob > F =    0.0463
```

在上述方法中，Stata 提供给我们的 p 值是相同的，即都是 0.046 3。因为它小于显著性水平 5%，我们可以得出结论：x_1 和 x_2 具有联合显著性。

(3) 如果我们要检验是否所有的独立变量具有联合显著性，在这个例子中，即是否 x_1，x_2 和 x_3 一起联合影响 y，在 Stata 中，我们可以输入：

```
test x1=x2=x3=0

( 1)  x1 - x2 = 0
( 2)  x1 - x3 = 0
( 3)  x1 = 0

      F(  3,      2) =   27.29
           Prob > F =    0.0356
```

由于 p 值为 0.035 6，低于显著性水平 5%，我们可以得出结论：x_1，x_2 和 x_3 共同影响 y，具有联合显著性。换句话说，该模型具有总体显著性。

Ⅳ. 附加上机操作练习

(1) 打开数据文件 **wages1. dta**。[①] 这个文件包含了两个变量和来自于现行人口调研的 826 名工人的工资数据。变量 *wages* 是工资收入，单位为美元/年。变量 *education* 是所接受的最高教育水平。

a. 根据人力资本理论，教育可以增加工人的效率，从而增加工人的工资。考虑以下的经济模型：

$$wages=\beta_0+\beta_1 education$$

你认为 β_1 的符号是什么？简单解释原因。用图表画出数据，*wages* 在纵轴上，*education* 在横轴上。图表看起来像与人力资本理论一致吗？

在 Stata 中输入：twoway (scatter wages education)。

① 该练习经过了修改，数据集从下书获取：Stephen J. Schmidt，*Econometrics* (McGraw-Hill，2005)。

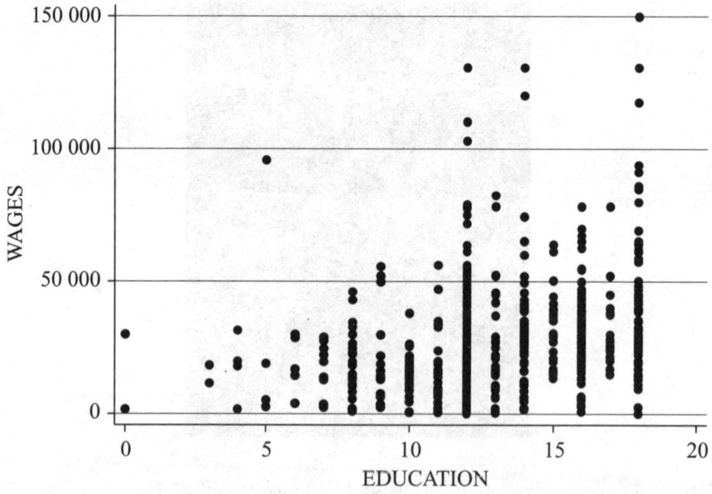

β_1 的期望符号为正，因为当一个人的受教育水平上升时，他的效率也会增加，所以他的工资会升高。图表支持了人力资本理论，因为它显示出工资和受教育水平之间是正相关的。

b. 用 Stata 估计方程：

$$wages_i=\beta_0+\beta_1 education_i+\varepsilon_i$$

预测当受教育水平增加一级时，工资会改变多少？

```
. regress wages education

      Source |       SS       df       MS              Number of obs =     658
-------------+------------------------------           F(  1,   656) =   74.29
       Model |  3.0327e+10     1  3.0327e+10           Prob > F      =  0.0000
    Residual |  2.6780e+11   656   408239273           R-squared     =  0.1017
-------------+------------------------------           Adj R-squared =  0.1004
       Total |  2.9813e+11   657   453777984           Root MSE      =   20205

------------------------------------------------------------------------------
       wages |      Coef.   Std. Err.      t    P>|t|     [95% Conf. Interval]
-------------+----------------------------------------------------------------
   education |   2182.007   253.1614     8.62   0.000     1684.903    2679.111
       _cons |   33.71045   3406.125     0.01   0.992    -6654.511    6721.932
------------------------------------------------------------------------------
```

如果受教育水平增加一级，工资上涨 2 182.007 美元。

c. 检测 β_1，即 *education* 的系数，是否显著？你得到预期的结果吗？通过 Stata 来确认你的检验结果。

H_0：$\beta_1=0$

H_a：$\beta_1\neq 0$

$$t=\frac{\hat{\beta}_1-0}{\sigma_{\hat{\beta}_1}}=\frac{2\ 182.007}{253.161\ 4}=8.62$$

p 值$=2\times P(t>8.62)=0.000<\alpha=5\%$

结论：因为 p 值$=0.000<$显著性水平 5%，我们拒绝零假设，所以 *education* 的系数是显著的。

Stata 的检验：

```
. test  education=0

 ( 1)  education = 0

       F(  1,   656) =   74.29
            Prob > F =    0.0000
```

d. 检测 β_0 是否显著。你得到预期的结果了吗？通过 Stata 来确认你的检验结果。

H_0：$\beta_0=0$

H_a：$\beta_0\neq0$

$$t=\frac{\hat{\beta}_0-0}{\sigma_{\hat{\beta}_0}}=\frac{33.710\,45}{3\,406.125}=0.01$$

p 值$=2\times P(t>0.01)=0.992>\alpha=5\%$

结论：因为 p 值$=0.992>$显著性水平 5%，我们不拒绝零假设，所以回归方程中的常数项不是统计显著的。

Stata 的检验：

```
. test _cons

 ( 1)  _cons = 0

       F(  1,   656) =    0.00
            Prob > F =    0.9921
```

(2) 打开数据文件 **tests. dta**[①]，其中有 10 个变量：*math* 和 *english* 是在一个特定的学校区域通过标准化数学和英语测试（65 分及以上）的学生的百分比；*highmath* 和 *higheng* 是在数学和英语测试中取得高分（90 分及以上）的学生的百分比；*expperpup* 是学区在教育上的花费除以该学区的学生总数；*stateexp* 和 *localexp* 是州和当地政府提供的每人教育赞助费；*stateshare* 是州政府提供的教育开销的百分比；*poverty* 是该区域的贫困率；*dropout* 是该区域的辍学率。

a. 经济学家将教育看作投入品；在投入品上花费的越多可以生产出越多商品，也就是受过良好教育的学生越多。考虑以下教育生产模型：

$$math_i=\beta_0+\beta_1 localexp_i+\beta_2 stateexp_i+\varepsilon_i$$

如果这个模型是正确的，你预期的 β_1 和 β_2 的符号是什么？

因为在投入品上花费越多可以生产出越多商品，即受过良好教育的学生越多，所以 β_1 和 β_2 的预期符号都是正的。

b. 用 Stata 回归以下方程：

$$math_i=\beta_0+\beta_1 localexp_i+\beta_2 stateexp_i+\varepsilon_i$$

哪些参数是统计显著不为 0 的，哪些不是？

```
. reg  math localexp stateexp

      Source |       SS       df       MS              Number of obs =     684
-------------+------------------------------           F(  2,   681) =    2.26
       Model |  2058.29083     2  1029.14542           Prob > F      =  0.1050
    Residual |  309890.064   681   455.05149           R-squared     =  0.0066
-------------+------------------------------           Adj R-squared =  0.0037
       Total |  311948.355   683  456.732585           Root MSE      =  21.332

------------------------------------------------------------------------------
        math |      Coef.   Std. Err.      t    P>|t|     [95% Conf. Interval]
-------------+----------------------------------------------------------------
    localexp |   .0000198   .0002121     0.09   0.926    -.0003967    .0004363
    stateexp |  -.0008982   .0005308    -1.69   0.091    -.0019404    .0001441
       _cons |   73.00355   3.495023    20.89   0.000     66.14123    79.86586
------------------------------------------------------------------------------
```

① 该练习经过了修改，数据集从下书获取：Stephen J. Schmidt，*Econometrics*（McGraw-Hill，2005）。

localexp 的系数不是统计显著的，因为它的 p 值为 0.926，比显著性水平 5%大。

stateexp 的系数不是统计显著的，因为它的 p 值为 0.091，比显著性水平 5%大。但是，当显著性系数为 10%时，*stateexp* 的系数是统计显著的。

c. 考虑如下的经济假设：来自州政府或是当地政府的教育投入没有区别，也就是说，州政府的投入和当地政府的投入对考试成绩的作用相同。与这个经济假设相对的零假设是什么？测试该假设，确定写出备择假设。你发现了什么？

H_0：$\beta_1=\beta_2$

H_a：$\beta_1\neq\beta_2$

定义：$\theta_1=\beta_1-\beta_2$，因此，$\beta_1=\theta_1+\beta_2$，将其带入原模型且修改为：

$math_i=\beta_0+(\theta_1+\beta_2)\ localexp_i+\beta_2 stateexp_i+\varepsilon_i$

$math_i=\beta_0+\theta_1 localexp_i+\beta_2(localexp_i+stateexp_i)+\varepsilon_i$

$math_i=\beta_0+\theta_1 localexp_i+\beta_2 m+\varepsilon_i$

```
. regress math localexp m

      Source |       SS       df       MS              Number of obs =     684
-------------+------------------------------           F(  2,   681) =    2.26
       Model |    2058.291     2   1029.1455           Prob > F      =  0.1050
    Residual |  309890.064   681  455.051489           R-squared     =  0.0066
-------------+------------------------------           Adj R-squared =  0.0037
       Total |  311948.355   683  456.732585           Root MSE      =  21.332

------------------------------------------------------------------------------
        math |      Coef.   Std. Err.      t    P>|t|     [95% Conf. Interval]
-------------+----------------------------------------------------------------
    localexp |    .000918   .0004453     2.06   0.040     .0000435    .0017924
           m |  -.0008982   .0005308    -1.69   0.091    -.0019404    .0001441
       _cons |   73.00355   3.495023    20.89   0.000     66.14123    79.86586
------------------------------------------------------------------------------
```

因为 $t=0.000\,918/0.000\,445\,3=2.061\,5$，而 $t_{\alpha/2}=1.963\,5$.

因为 $t>t_{\alpha/2}$是正确的，所以我们拒绝零假设。

Stata 的检验：

```
. quietly: reg  math localexp stateexp

. test  localexp= stateexp

 ( 1)  localexp - stateexp = 0

       F(  1,   681) =    4.25
            Prob > F =    0.0397
```

因为 p 值$=0.039\,7<$显著性水平$=5\%$，所以我们拒绝零假设。

结论：州政府和当地政府的教育投资对数学考试成绩的作用不同。

d. 检验 $\beta_1=\beta_2=0$ 的零假设。你发现了什么？你对这个教育模型的结论是什么？

H_0：$\beta_1=\beta_2=0$

H_a：$\beta_1\neq0$，$\beta_2\neq0$

这是联合显著性检验，所以我们运用 F 检验方法：

$$F\equiv\frac{(SSR_r-SSR_{ur})/q}{SSR_{ur}/(n-k-1)}$$

其中，下标 r 代表限制模型，下标 ur 代表非限制模型，q 代表零假设中的限制等式的数目。

非限制模型是：$math_i = \beta_0 + \beta_1 localexp_i + \beta_2 stateexp_i + \varepsilon_i$。

```
. reg  math localexp stateexp

      Source |       SS       df       MS              Number of obs =     684
-------------+------------------------------           F(  2,   681) =    2.26
       Model |  2058.29083     2  1029.14542           Prob > F      =  0.1050
    Residual |  309890.064   681   455.05149           R-squared     =  0.0066
-------------+------------------------------           Adj R-squared =  0.0037
       Total |  311948.355   683  456.732585           Root MSE      =  21.332

------------------------------------------------------------------------------
        math |      Coef.   Std. Err.      t    P>|t|     [95% Conf. Interval]
-------------+----------------------------------------------------------------
    localexp |   .0000198   .0002121     0.09   0.926    -.0003967    .0004363
    stateexp |  -.0008982   .0005308    -1.69   0.091    -.0019404    .0001441
       _cons |   73.00355   3.495023    20.89   0.000     66.14123    79.86586
------------------------------------------------------------------------------
```

限制模型是建立于零假设 H_0：$math_i = \beta_0 + \varepsilon_i$。

```
. reg  math

      Source |       SS       df       MS              Number of obs =     684
-------------+------------------------------           F(  0,   683) =    0.00
       Model |           0     0           .           Prob > F      =       .
    Residual |  311948.355   683  456.732585           R-squared     =  0.0000
-------------+------------------------------           Adj R-squared =  0.0000
       Total |  311948.355   683  456.732585           Root MSE      =  21.371

------------------------------------------------------------------------------
        math |      Coef.   Std. Err.      t    P>|t|     [95% Conf. Interval]
-------------+----------------------------------------------------------------
       _cons |    68.9693   .8171522    84.40   0.000     67.36487    70.57373
------------------------------------------------------------------------------
```

$$F = \frac{(311\ 948.355 - 309\ 890.064)/2}{309\ 890.064/(684-2-1)} = 2.26$$

p 值$=P(F>2.26)=0.105\ 132\ 6$（在 Stata 输入：display fprob（2，681，2.26））。

因为 p 值$>\alpha=5\%$，我们没能拒绝零假设。

Stata 的检验：

```
. quietly: reg  math localexp stateexp

. test  localexp= stateexp=0

 ( 1)  localexp - stateexp = 0
 ( 2)  localexp = 0

       F(  2,   681) =    2.26
            Prob > F =    0.1050
```

p 值$=0.105\ 0>\alpha=0.05$。

因此，我们没能拒绝零假设，即：$\beta_1=\beta_2=0$。

结论：当地政府投资和州政府投资对学生的数学考试成绩没有联合显著的作用。

Chapter 4

Inference in Linear Regression Models

Ⅰ. Statistical Properties of the OLS Estimators

In the last chapter, we learned how to use the OLS method to estimate either simple linear regression models or multiple linear regression models. To justify why the use of the OLS method rather than a variety of competing estimators provides us the best linear unbiased estimators, in this section, it is best for us to discuss and understand the following important Gauss-Markov Theorem.

The Gauss-Markov Theorem states that Least Squares Estimators are Unbiased, Consistent, and More Efficient than any other Linear, Unbiased Estimators if the following standard set of assumptions hold (the last one is not required):

A1: $y_i=\beta_0+\beta_1 x_i+\mu_i$

A2: $E(\mu_i)=E(\mu_i \mid x_i)=0$

A3: $\mathrm{Cov}(\mu_i, \mu_j)=0$

A4: No Perfect Collinearity

A5: $\mathrm{Var}(\mu_i \mid x_i)=\sigma^2$

A6: $\mu_i \sim N(0, \sigma)$

In other words, the first assumption defines the population model to be linear in parameters; the second one ensures that the error has an expected value of zero, given any value of the explanatory variable; the third one indicates that the errors must be serially uncorrelated; the fourth one shows that none of the explanatory variables is constant and there are no exact linear relationships among them; the fifth one emphasizes that the error is homoscedastic, given any value of the explanatory variable. Because of this theorem, these first five assumptions are known as the Gauss-Markov assumptions, under which the OLS estimator is the best linear unbiased estimator (BLUE). That is to say, the expected value of the OLS estimator is the corresponding population parameter, for instance, $E(\hat{\beta}_0)=\beta_0$, $E(\hat{\beta}_1)=\beta_1,\ldots,E(\hat{\beta}_j)=\beta_j$. Meanwhile, the OLS estimator is the most efficient with the smallest sampling variance among linear unbiased estimators.

To make the sampling distributions of the $\hat{\beta}_j$ tractable, we also assume that the unobserved error is normally distributed. Hence, we call the sixth assumption the normality assumption. When combining all of the Gauss-Markov assumptions with the assumption of a normally distributed error term, it is not difficult for us to prove that $\hat{\beta}_j \sim N(\beta_j, \sigma_{\hat{\beta}_j})$. That is, $(\hat{\beta}_j - \beta_j)/\sigma_{\hat{\beta}_j} \sim N(0, 1)$.

Ⅱ. Significance Test for a Single Population Parameter: The *t* Test

"*t*" random variable (no upper case) is formed by using a standard normal, $Z \sim N(0, 1)$, random variable and an independent chi-square random variable. More precisely, if $Z \sim N(0, 1)$ and V is chi-squared with m degrees of freedom, and if Z and V are independent, then:

$$t = \frac{Z}{\sqrt{V/m}} \sim t_{(m)} \tag{4.1}$$

Given the definition of t distribution, in order to construct a hypothesis test for significance, we need the following theorem:

$$\frac{\hat{\beta}_j - \beta_j}{\hat{\sigma}_{\hat{\beta}_j}} \sim t(n-2) \tag{4.2}$$

The above theorem is important in that it allows us to test hypotheses about a single population parameter β_j. As an example, consider the *CarSales* equation:

$$CarSales = \beta_0 + \beta_1 TVads + \mu$$

```
reg carsales tvads

      Source |       SS       df       MS              Number of obs =       5
-------------+------------------------------           F(  1,     3) =   21.43
       Model |        100      1         100           Prob > F      =  0.0190
    Residual |         14      3  4.66666667           R-squared     =  0.8772
-------------+------------------------------           Adj R-squared =  0.8363
       Total |        114      4        28.5           Root MSE      =  2.1602

------------------------------------------------------------------------------
    carsales |      Coef.   Std. Err.      t    P>|t|     [95% Conf. Interval]
-------------+----------------------------------------------------------------
       tvads |          5   1.080123     4.63   0.019     1.562565    8.437435
       _cons |         10   2.366432     4.23   0.024     2.468958    17.53104
------------------------------------------------------------------------------
```

The null hypothesis is H_0: $\beta_1 = 0$, which means the explanatory variable (*TVads*) has no effect on the explained variable (*CarSales*). The alternative hypothesis is H_1: $\beta_1 \neq 0$, totally opposite to the null hypothesis. The test statistic is t distributed with $n-2$ degrees of freedom if the null hypothesis is true. Let us select the significance level $\alpha = 0.05$. Then, from the t table, we can read the critical value $t_c = t_{\alpha/2}$ with $(5-2)$ degrees of freedom $= 3.182$. Using the sample data, the least squares estimate of β_1 is 5, with standard error=1.080 123. The value of the test statistic is 4.63. Since $t=4.63>t_c=3.182$, we reject the null hypothesis and conclude that TV ads have a significant effect on car sales.

Since Stata already has build-in commands which enable you to conduct a variety of significance tests, we may directly type the following code after running OLS regression in Stata "test tvads".

```
. test  tvads

 ( 1)  tvads = 0

       F(  1,     3) =   21.43
            Prob > F =    0.0190
```

In the car sales example, the p-value for the test of H_0: $\beta_1=0$ against H_1: $\beta_1\neq 0$ is $p=0.019$, which is the area in the tails of the $t(3)$ distribution where $|t|\geqslant 4.63$. Since the p value is less than $\alpha=5\%$, we also reject the null hypothesis and arrive at the same conclusion that TV ads have a significant effect on the car sales.

A more general form of the t statistic recognizes that we may want to test something like H_0: $\beta_j=a_j$. In this case, the appropriate t statistic is

$$t=(\hat{\beta}_j-a_j)/\hat{\sigma}_{\beta_j}$$

In Stata, after regressing y on x_1, x_2, …, x_k, we would type "test xj=aj" and read the p-value for the test to decide whether we reject the null hypothesis. In the car sales example, if we want to test whether the coefficient on the independent variable—*TVads*—equals a specific value, for instance, $\beta_1=1$, we can type "test tvads=1"

```
. test  tvads =1

 ( 1)  tvads = 1

       F(  1,     3) =   13.71
            Prob > F =    0.0342
```

In Stata, since the p-value is 0.034 2, less than 5%, we conclude that the coefficient of TV ads is not equal to 1.

Suppose, instead of testing whether a parameter is equal to a constant, we want to test if it is equal to another parameter, that is H_0: $\beta_1=\beta_2$. In this case, the appropriate t statistic is:

$$t=(\hat{\beta}_i-\hat{\beta}_j)/\hat{\sigma}_{(\hat{\beta}_i-\hat{\beta}_j)}$$

where $\hat{\sigma}_{(\hat{\beta}_i-\hat{\beta}_j)}$ is the standard error for the difference between $(\hat{\beta}_i-\hat{\beta}_j)$.

In Stata, after regressing y on x_1, x_2, …, x_k, we would type "test x1=x2, common" and read the p-value for the test to decide whether we reject the null hypothesis. In the car sales example, if we add another explanatory variable—the number of salesmen and want to test whether TV ads and salesmen have an equal effect on car sales, i. e. whether the coefficient on the independent variable—*TVads*—equals coefficient on the other independent variable—*Salesmen*. In Stata, we can type "test tvads=salesman" and read the corresponding p-value to draw a conclusion.

Ⅲ. Joint Significance Test and Overall Significance Test: The *F* Test

3.1 How to Run the *F* test

Everything we've done so far has involved testing a single linear restriction (e.g. $\beta_1 = 0$, or $\beta_1 = \beta_2$). However, we may want to jointly test multiple hypotheses about our parameters.

A typical example is testing "exclusion restrictions" —we want to know if a group of parameters are all equal to zero. Now the null hypothesis might be something like H_0: $\beta_{k-q+1} = 0$, …, $\beta_k = 0$; The alternative is just H_1: H_0 is not true. We can't just check each t statistic separately, because we want to know if the q parameters are jointly significant at a given level—it is possible for none to be individually significant at that level. To do the test we need to estimate the "restricted model" without x_{k-q+1}, …, x_k included, as well as the "unrestricted model" with all x's included. After running two regressions, we can compute F statistics using the following formula:

$$F \equiv \frac{(SSR_r - SSR_{ur})/q}{SSR_{ur}/(n-k-1)}$$

where r is restricted, ur is unrestricted, q is the number of restrictions in H_0.

The basic form of the F statistic will work for any set of linear restrictions. Because the SSR's may be large and unwieldy, an alternative form of the formula is useful. Here, we use the fact that $SSR = SST(1-R^2)$ for any regression, so we can substitute it for SSR_r and SSR_{ur}.

$$F \equiv \frac{(R_{ur}^2 - R_r^2)/q}{(1-R_{ur}^2)/(n-k-1)}$$

where r is restricted, ur is unrestricted, and q is the number of restrictions in H_0.

A special case of exclusion restrictions is to test H_0: $\beta_1 = \beta_2 = \cdots = \beta_k = 0$. Since the R^2 from a model with only an intercept will be zero, the F statistic is simply:

$$F = \frac{R^2/k}{(1-R^2)/(n-k-1)}$$

3.2 Computer Exercise

To strengthen what we just learned, let us work on the following computer exercise.

(1) Let us start by reviewing how to enter our needed data manually.

```
input y x1 x2 x3

          y         x1         x2         x3
1. 30 4 10 5
2. 20 3 8 2
3. 36 6 11 8
4. 24 4 9 3
5. 40 8 12 4
6. 38 7 10 6
7. end

regress y x1 x2 x3

      Source |       SS       df       MS              Number of obs =       6
-------------+------------------------------           F(  3,     2) =   27.29
       Model |  317.576457     3  105.858819           Prob > F      =  0.0356
    Residual |  7.75687666     2  3.87843833           R-squared     =  0.9762
-------------+------------------------------           Adj R-squared =  0.9404
       Total |  325.333333     5  65.0666667           Root MSE      =  1.9694

------------------------------------------------------------------------------
           y |      Coef.   Std. Err.      t    P>|t|     [95% Conf. Interval]
-------------+----------------------------------------------------------------
          x1 |    2.64685   .8867671     2.98   0.096    -1.168601    6.462301
          x2 |   1.183673   1.319598     0.90   0.464      -4.4941    6.861447
          x3 |   .9334516   .5046408     1.85   0.206    -1.237842    3.104746
       _cons |   1.023957   8.919619     0.11   0.919    -37.35407    39.40198
------------------------------------------------------------------------------
```

(2) If we want to test whether x_1 and x_2 are jointly significant, i. e. whether x_1 and x_2 jointly affect y, in Stata, we can choose one of the following three options " test (x1=0) (x2=0)", "test x1=x2=0" or test " test x1 x2".

```
test (x1=0) (x2=0)

 ( 1)  x1 = 0
 ( 2)  x2 = 0

       F(  2,     2) =   20.61
            Prob > F =    0.0463

test x1=x2=0

 ( 1)  x1 - x2 = 0
 ( 2)  x1 = 0

       F(  2,     2) =   20.61
            Prob > F =    0.0463

test x1 x2

 ( 1)  x1 = 0
 ( 2)  x2 = 0

       F(  2,     2) =   20.61
            Prob > F =    0.0463
```

The above alternatives provide us the same p-value, which is 0. 046 3. Since it is less than 5%, we can conclude that x_1 and x_2 are jointly significant.

(3) If we want to test whether all of the independent variables are jointly significant, in this example, i. e. whether x_1, x_2, and x_3 are jointly affect y, in Stata, we can type "test x1=x2=x3=0".

```
test x1=x2=x3=0

 ( 1)  x1 - x2 = 0
 ( 2)  x1 - x3 = 0
 ( 3)  x1 = 0

       F(  3,     2) =   27.29
            Prob > F =    0.0356
```

Since the p-value is 0. 035 6, less than 5%, we can draw the conclusion that x_1, x_2, and x_3 are jointly significant. In other words, the model has overall significance.

Ⅳ. Additional Computer Exercises

(1) Load the data file **wages1. dta.** [①]The data file contains observations on two variables, wages and salaries for 826 workers, taken from the Current Population Survey. The variable wages is wage and salary income, measured in dollars per year; the variable education is measured as the highest grade level completed.

a. According to the economic theory known as human capital theory, education increase a worker's productivity and thus leads to higher wages. Consider the economic model:

$$wages = \beta_0 + \beta_1 education$$

What sign would you expect β_1 to take? Briefly explain why. Graph the data with wages on the vertical axis and education on the horizontal axis. Does it look like the data support human capital theory, or not?

In Stata: twoway (scatter wages education).

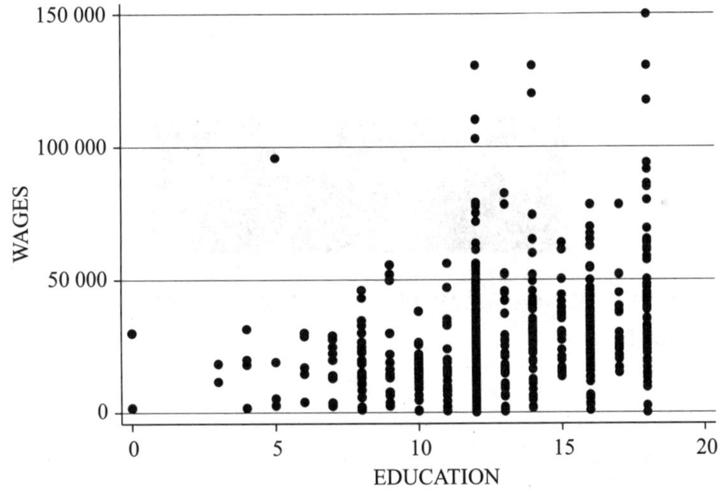

The expected sign of β_1 would be positive, because as a person increases his education level, his productivity will also increase, and thus lead to higher wages. The graph supports human capital theory, because it shows a positive relationship between wages and education level.

b. Use Stata to estimate the equation:

$$wages_i = \beta_0 + \beta_1 education_i + \varepsilon_i$$

① This exercise is modified and the data set is collected from the book—*Econometrics* written by Stephen J. Schmidt (McGraw-Hill, 2005).

Predict how much wages will change when education increases by one more level.

```
. regress wages education

      Source |       SS       df       MS              Number of obs =     658
-------------+------------------------------           F(  1,   656) =   74.29
       Model |  3.0327e+10     1  3.0327e+10           Prob > F      =  0.0000
    Residual |  2.6780e+11   656   408239273           R-squared     =  0.1017
-------------+------------------------------           Adj R-squared =  0.1004
       Total |  2.9813e+11   657   453777984           Root MSE      =   20205

------------------------------------------------------------------------------
       wages |      Coef.   Std. Err.      t    P>|t|     [95% Conf. Interval]
-------------+----------------------------------------------------------------
   education |   2182.007   253.1614     8.62   0.000     1684.903    2679.111
       _cons |   33.71045   3406.125     0.01   0.992    -6654.511    6721.932
------------------------------------------------------------------------------
```

According to the above regression results, as education increases by 1 level, a worker's wages would increase by \$2 182.007.

c. Test whether β_1 is statistically significant from 0. Do you get the expected result? Use Stata to verify your test results.

H_0: $\beta_1=0$

H_a: $\beta_1\neq 0$

$$t=\frac{\hat{\beta}_1-0}{\sigma_{\hat{\beta}_1}}=\frac{2\ 182.007}{253.161\ 4}=8.62$$

p-value$=2\times P(t>8.62)=0.000<\alpha=5\%$

Conclusion: we reject H_0, so β_1 is statistically significant from 0.

Stata Check-up:

```
. test education=0

 ( 1)  education = 0

       F(  1,   656) =   74.29
            Prob > F =    0.0000
```

d. Test whether β_0 is equal to 0 or not. Do you get the expected result? Use Stata to verify your test results.

H_0: $\beta_0=0$

H_a: $\beta_0\neq 0$

$$t=\frac{\hat{\beta}_0-0}{\sigma_{\hat{\beta}_0}}=\frac{33.710\ 45}{3\ 406.125}=0.01$$

p-value$=2\times P(t>0.01)=0.992>\alpha=5\%$

Conclusion: we do not reject H_0, so β_0 is not statistically significant from 0.

Stata Check-up:

```
. test _cons

 ( 1)  _cons = 0

       F(  1,   656) =    0.00
            Prob > F =    0.9921
```

(2) Open the data file **tests. dta**[①], which contains data on 10 variables: *math* and *english* are the percentages of students that achieved passing grades (65 percent or better) on standardized math and English tests within a given school district; *highmath* and *higheng* are the percentages of students that achieved high passing grades (90 percent or better) on the same exams; *expperpup* is the total amount of money spent by the school district on education divided by the total number of pupils in the district; *stateexp* and *localexp* are the per-pupil expenditures by state and local governments, respectively; *stateshare* is the percentage of expenditure provided by the state; poverty is the poverty rate in the district; and dropout is the dropout rate in the district.

a. Economists often think of education as a good that is produced with inputs; spending more money on inputs should produce more "output", that is, better-educated students. Consider an economic model of educational production,

$$math_i = \beta_0 + \beta_1 localexp_i + \beta_2 stateexp_i + \varepsilon_i$$

What signs would you predict for β_1, β_2 if this model is correct?

Since spending more money on inputs should produce more "output", i. e. better-educated students, I would predict that the signs for β_1 and β_2 are all positive.

b. Use Stata to estimate the equation:

$$math_i = \beta_0 + \beta_1 localexp_i + \beta_2 stateexp_i + \varepsilon_i$$

Which parameters are statistically significantly different from 0, and which are not?

```
. reg math localexp stateexp

      Source |       SS           df       MS      Number of obs   =       684
-------------+----------------------------------   F(  2,    681)  =      2.26
       Model |  2058.29083         2  1029.14542   Prob > F        =    0.1050
    Residual |  309890.064       681   455.05149   R-squared       =    0.0066
-------------+----------------------------------   Adj R-squared   =    0.0037
       Total |  311948.355       683  456.732585   Root MSE        =    21.332

------------------------------------------------------------------------------
        math |      Coef.   Std. Err.      t    P>|t|     [95% Conf. Interval]
-------------+----------------------------------------------------------------
    localexp |   .0000198   .0002121     0.09   0.926    -.0003967    .0004363
    stateexp |  -.0008982   .0005308    -1.69   0.091    -.0019404    .0001441
       _cons |   73.00355   3.495023    20.89   0.000     66.14123    79.86586
------------------------------------------------------------------------------
```

The coefficient on *localexp* is not statistically significantly different from 0, because its p-value=0. 926 is greater than $\alpha=5\%$.

The coefficient on *stateexp* is not statistically significantly different from 0, because its p-value=0. 091 is greater than $\alpha=5\%$. However, the coefficient is statistically significant at the 10% significance level.

c. Consider the economic hypothesis that it does not matter whether educational inputs are bought with state or local money; that is, suppose that state and local spending have

① This exercise is modified and the data set is collected from the book—*Econometrics* written by Stephen J. Schmidt (McGraw-Hill, 2005).

the same effect on test scores. What null hypothesis about the parameters corresponds to this economic hypothesis? Test it, being sure to specify an alternative hypothesis as well in the test. What do you find?

$H_0: \beta_1=\beta_2$

$H_a: \beta_1\neq\beta_2$

Define: $\theta_1=\beta_1-\beta_2$, thus, $\beta_1=\theta_1+\beta_2$ and then is substituted into the original model:

$$math_i=\beta_0+(\theta_1+\beta_2)localexp_i+\beta_2 stateexp_i+\varepsilon_i$$

$$math_i=\beta_0+\theta_1 localexp_i+\beta_2(localexp_i+stateexp_i)+\varepsilon_i$$

$$math_i=\beta_0+\theta_1 localexp_i+\beta_2 m+\varepsilon_i$$

```
. regress math localexp m

      Source |       SS       df       MS              Number of obs =     684
-------------+------------------------------           F(  2,   681) =    2.26
       Model |    2058.291     2   1029.1455           Prob > F      =  0.1050
    Residual |  309890.064   681  455.051489           R-squared     =  0.0066
-------------+------------------------------           Adj R-squared =  0.0037
       Total |  311948.355   683  456.732585           Root MSE      =  21.332

------------------------------------------------------------------------------
        math |      Coef.   Std. Err.      t    P>|t|     [95% Conf. Interval]
-------------+----------------------------------------------------------------
    localexp |    .000918   .0004453     2.06   0.040     .0000435    .0017924
           m |  -.0008982   .0005308    -1.69   0.091    -.0019404    .0001441
       _cons |   73.00355   3.495023    20.89   0.000     66.14123    79.86586
------------------------------------------------------------------------------
```

Since $t=0.000\,918/0.000\,445\,3=2.061\,5$, while $t_{\alpha/2}=1.963\,5$.

It is true that $t>t_{\alpha/2}$, So we reject the null hypothesis.

Stata Check-up:

```
. quietly: reg  math localexp stateexp

. test  localexp= stateexp

 ( 1)  localexp - stateexp = 0

       F(  1,   681) =    4.25
            Prob > F =    0.0397
```

Since p-value$=0.039\,7<\alpha=0.05$, so we reject H_0.

Conclusion: state and local spending don't have the same effect on math test scores.

d. Test the null hypothesis that $\beta_1=\beta_2=0$ against the null hypothesis that at least one of them is not equal to 0. What do you find? What do you conclude about the model of education as a production process?

$H_0: \beta_1=\beta_2=0$

$H_a: \beta_1\neq 0,\ \beta_2\neq 0$

This is the joint significance test, so we apply the F-test:

$$F=\frac{(SSR_r-SSR_{ur})/q}{SSR_{ur}/(n-k-1)}$$

where r is restricted, ur is unrestricted, q is the number of restrictions in H_0.

The unrestricted model: $math_i=\beta_0+\beta_1 localexp_i+\beta_2 stateexp_i+\varepsilon_i$.

```
. reg  math localexp stateexp

      Source |       SS       df       MS              Number of obs =     684
-------------+------------------------------           F(  2,   681) =    2.26
       Model |  2058.29083     2  1029.14542           Prob > F      =  0.1050
    Residual |  309890.064   681   455.05149           R-squared     =  0.0066
-------------+------------------------------           Adj R-squared =  0.0037
       Total |  311948.355   683  456.732585           Root MSE      =  21.332

------------------------------------------------------------------------------
        math |      Coef.   Std. Err.      t    P>|t|     [95% Conf. Interval]
-------------+----------------------------------------------------------------
    localexp |   .0000198   .0002121     0.09   0.926    -.0003967    .0004363
    stateexp |  -.0008982   .0005308    -1.69   0.091    -.0019404    .0001441
       _cons |   73.00355   3.495023    20.89   0.000     66.14123    79.86586
------------------------------------------------------------------------------
```

The restricted model is built under the H_0: $math_i = \beta_0 + \varepsilon_i$.

```
. reg  math

      Source |       SS       df       MS              Number of obs =     684
-------------+------------------------------           F(  0,   683) =    0.00
       Model |           0     0           .           Prob > F      =       .
    Residual |  311948.355   683  456.732585           R-squared     =  0.0000
-------------+------------------------------           Adj R-squared =  0.0000
       Total |  311948.355   683  456.732585           Root MSE      =  21.371

------------------------------------------------------------------------------
        math |      Coef.   Std. Err.      t    P>|t|     [95% Conf. Interval]
-------------+----------------------------------------------------------------
       _cons |    68.9693   .8171522    84.40   0.000     67.36487    70.57373
------------------------------------------------------------------------------
```

$$F = \frac{(311\,948.355 - 309\,890.064)/2}{309\,890.064/(684-2-1)} = 2.26$$

p-value $= P(F > 2.26) = 0.105\,132\,6$ (on Stata, type: display fprob (2, 681, 2.26)).

Since p-value $> \alpha$, we fail to reject H_0.

Stata Check-up:

```
. quietly: reg  math localexp stateexp

. test  localexp= stateexp=0

 ( 1)  localexp - stateexp = 0
 ( 2)  localexp = 0

       F(  2,   681) =    2.26
            Prob > F =    0.1050
```

p-value $= 0.105\,0 > \alpha = 0.05$.

Thus, we do not reject H_0, that is: $\beta_1 = \beta_2 = 0$.

Conclusion: local expenditure and state expenditure don't jointly have significant effects on students' Math tests.

第 5 章

建模分析和应用

Ⅰ. 如何选择合适的线性方程式

线性回归模型并不意味着解释变量和被解释变量之间必须存在线性关系，而是指该模型的回归参数和被解释变量之间具有线性关系。也就是说，该模型是“参数线性”，但并不一定是“变量线性”。基于这种理解，我们可以把变量转变成各种便捷的形式，只要所创建的模型符合线性回归模型的基本假设。

这意味着，只要回归参数和 y 之间具有线性关系。OLS 可以用于处理非线性方程中 x 和 y 之间的非线性关系，因此，只要建立的模型满足 OLS 的基本假设条件，我们就可以采用对数模型、二次模型、包含交互项的模型或采取其他方式的线性转换，等等。在本章中，我们将逐一讨论三种常见的线性模型。

1.1　对数模型

使用对数模型具有很多优点。第一，对数模型测量的是百分比的变化，因此不会随变量的测量尺度的不同而变化。第二，它们可以直接估计弹性值。第三，对于被解释变量的观测值皆取正值的模型，条件分布往往有异方差问题或者是非对称分布，而采用取 y 的对数的方法会缓解这种负面问题。第四，对数 y 的分布比较窄，抑制了非正常值/溢出值的影响。

如何解释对数模型？一般来说，我们考虑以下三种类型。

如果模型是 $\log(y)=\beta_0+\beta_1\log(x)+u$，$\beta_1$ 衡量 y 随 x 的变化而变化的量，即 y 对 x 的弹性。

如果模型是 $\log(y)=\beta_0+\beta_1 x+u$，$\beta_1$ 衡量在 x 变动一个单位的情况下 y 的百分比变化。

如果模型是 $y=\beta_0+\beta_1\log(x)+u$，$\beta_1$ 衡量在 x 变动 100%的情况下 y 的变化量。

以住房价格和空气污染为例。①

总体房价模型是：

$$\log(price)=\beta_0+\beta_1\log(nox)+\beta_2 rooms+u$$

如何解释该对数模型中的回归系数，尤其是 β_1 和 β_2？

β_1 衡量因空气中氮氧化物的变化所导致的价格变化。

β_2 衡量多出一个房间所导致的价格的百分比变化。

在收集完所需的数据并进行 OLS 回归后，我们得到：

$$\log(\widehat{price})=\underset{(0.09)}{7.23}-\underset{(0.016)}{0.75}\log(nox)+\underset{(0.009)}{0.36}rooms$$

$$n=510,\ R^2=0.714$$

这意味着，如果房间数不变，当氮氧化物含量增加 1%时，平均房价会下跌 0.75%。如果氮氧化物含量不变，每当增加一个房间，平均房价会上涨大约 100%×0.36=36%。

1.2　二次模型

如果模型是 $y=\beta_0+\beta_1 x+\beta_2 x^2+u$，我们不能仅用 β_1 来单独解释 x 的变化对于 y 的变化的影响，我们需要同时考虑 β_2 的存在。原因在于：

$$\Delta\hat{y}\approx(\hat{\beta}_1+2\hat{\beta}_2 x)\Delta x$$

所以，$\frac{\Delta\hat{y}}{\Delta x}\approx\hat{\beta}_1+2\hat{\beta}_2 x$。

如何解释二次模型里的回归系数呢？一般，我们考虑以下两种情况。

（1）假设 x 的系数是正的，而 x^2 的系数是负的，那么 y 会先随 x 的增加而增加，但最终将反过来随 x 的增加而减少。数学表达式为：

$$对于\ \hat{\beta}_1>0,\ \hat{\beta}_2<0,转折点位于\ x^*=|\hat{\beta}_1(2\hat{\beta}_2)|$$

（2）假设 x 的系数是负的，而 x^2 的系数是正的，那么 y 会先随 x 的增加而减少，但最终将反过来随 x 的增加而增加。数学表达式为：

$$对于\ \hat{\beta}_1<0,\ \hat{\beta}_2>0,转折点位于\ x^*=|\hat{\beta}_1(2\hat{\beta}_2)|$$

以住房价格和空气污染为例。②

$$\log(price)=\beta_0+\beta_1\log(nox)+\beta_2 rooms+\beta_3 rooms^2+u$$

根据收集后的数据和 OLS 回归，我们得到：

$$\log(\widehat{price})=\underset{(0.47)}{10.59}-\underset{(0.115)}{0.8}\log(nox)-\underset{(0.165)}{0.545}rooms+\underset{(0.013)}{0.062}rooms^2$$

$$n=510,\ R^2=0.63$$

---

① 参考 Example 4.5，*Introductory Econometrics*：*A Modern Approach*，by Jeffrey Wooldridge，2006。

② 参考 Example 6.2，*Introductory Econometrics*：*A Modern Approach*，by Jeffrey Wooldridge，2006。

如何解释房间数量对 log(*price*) 的影响呢？

由于房间系数是负的，房间平方项的系数是正的，这实际上意味着，在房间数量很少时，多一间房间，房价反而降低。经过某一转折点，这种影响将改变成为正面影响，而且从二次方程的图形中，我们可以看出，房价随着房间数量的增加而增加。这个转折点的取值为＝0.545/(2×0.062)＝4.4。它说明了，当房间数量超过 4.4 后，每增加一个房间将导致房价以百分比的变化量而增加。例如，房间数量从 5 增加到 6，房价上涨了 100×(－0.545＋2×0.062×5)％＝7.5％。

1.3 含有交互项的模型

对于模型 $y=\beta_0+\beta_1x_1+\beta_2x_2+\beta_3x_1x_2+u$，我们不能仅用 β_1 单独测量解释变量 x_1 对 y 的影响，我们也需要考虑到 β_3 的存在，因为：

$$\frac{\Delta y}{\Delta x_1}=\beta_1+\beta_3x_2$$

为了概括 x_1 对 y 的影响，我们通常采用 x_2 的均值。

以上课出勤率对期末考试成绩的影响为例。[①]

$$stndfnl=\beta_0+\beta_1 atndrte+\beta_2 priGPA+\beta_3 priGPA\times atndrte+u$$

其中，*stndfnl*＝期末考试的结果，

atndrte＝上课出勤率，

priGPA＝上大学前的平均成绩。

该模型包括一个交互项，即出勤率和上大学前的平均成绩的乘积。这个变量的加入是由于出勤率对期末考试成绩的影响可能会因为学生之间的学习表现不同而有所不同，这里，学生的学习表现是用上大学前的平均成绩来衡量的。

回归之后，我们得到：

$$\widehat{stndfnl}=\underset{(1.36)}{2.05}-\underset{(0.0102)}{0.0067}atndrte-\underset{(0.48)}{1.63}priGPA+\underset{(0.0043)}{0.0056}priGPA\times atndrte$$

$$n=680,\ R^2=0.33$$

我们必须十分小心地解释这个方程。如果我们仅仅查看 *atndrte* 的系数，会得出这样的结论：出勤率对期末考试成绩的影响是负的。但是，我们必须注意，不要把 β_1 和 β_3 分开考虑，根据 t 分布，这两个系数各自并不显著。如果我们检验它们的联合显著性，通过 F 检验得到的 p 值为 0.014。这意味着，在显著性水平为 5％的情况下，我们不能拒绝零假设。故而，β_1 和 β_3 具有联合显著性。

在解释 *atndrte* 对 *stndfnl* 的偏效应时，我们必须插入 *priGPA* 的均值。例如，*priGPA* 的均值是 2.59，在此基础上，*atndrte* 对 *stndfnl* 的影响是（－0.006 7＋0.005 6×2.59)＝0.007 8。这意味着出勤率增加 1％，期末考试成绩将比平均考试成绩高出 0.007 8。

① 参考 Example 6.3，*Introductory Econometrics：A Modern Approach*，by Jeffrey Wooldridge，2006。

Ⅱ．如何判定所建模型的合适性

2.1　回归误差设定检验（RESET）

我们如何知道得到的方程式是否就是我们需要的模型？当我们试图解释所建立的模型时，可以运用经济理论来加以判断。例如，x 对于 y 的影响是用百分比变化量来衡量（使用对数模型）还是用绝对值来衡量，两者哪一个更有意义？x_1 的偏导数是随 x_1^2 变化（二次模型）还是随 x_2 变化（含交互项的模型），或者本身就是固定不变的？

我们也可以通过假设检验来判断方程式的合适性。我们已经学过“排除性限制条件”检验的方法，采用此方法我们可以检验是否需要加入变量的多次方或是交互项。但是，这种检验很烦琐，需要添加新项再检验是否需要加入它（们）。另外，通过这一方法有可能发现我们需要添加平方项，但实际上使用对数模型会更好。为解决这种问题，一般采用拉姆齐（Ramsey）的“回归误差设定检验”（RESET）。

它的基本思路就是，在最初的方程式里，我们添加并检验含有 $\hat{y}$ 项的方程：$y=\beta_0+\beta_1x_1+\cdots+\beta_kx_k+d_1\hat{y}^2+d_2\hat{y}^3+u$。我们设零假设为，$H_0$：$d_1=0$，$d_2=0$，通过计算服从自由度为 2 和 $n-k-3$ 的 F 分布的统计值，即 $F\sim F_{2,n-k-3}$，我们可以得出 p 值并由此判断是否接受零假设。

2.2　上机操作练习

请在 Stata 中打开 **house.dta**。[①] 首先，我们考虑第一个模型：*price*＝*f*(*lotsize*，*sqrft*，*bdrms*)。

```
reg price lotsize sqrft bdrms

      Source |       SS       df       MS              Number of obs =      88
-------------+------------------------------           F(  3,    84) =   57.46
       Model |  617130.701     3  205710.234           Prob > F      =  0.0000
    Residual |  300723.805    84  3580.04530           R-squared     =  0.6724
-------------+------------------------------           Adj R-squared =  0.6607
       Total |  917854.506    87  10550.0518           Root MSE      =  59.833

------------------------------------------------------------------------------
       price |      Coef.   Std. Err.      t    P>|t|     [95% Conf. Interval]
-------------+----------------------------------------------------------------
     lotsize |   .0020677   .0006421     3.22   0.002     .0007908    .0033446
       sqrft |   .1227782   .0132374     9.28   0.000     .0964541    .1491022
       bdrms |   13.85252   9.010145     1.54   0.128    -4.065141    31.77018
       _cons |  -21.77031   29.47504    -0.74   0.462    -80.38466    36.84405
------------------------------------------------------------------------------

predict r1, xb
gen r2 = r1*r1
gen r3 = r2*r1
reg price lotsize sqrft bdrms r2 r3

      Source |       SS       df       MS              Number of obs =      88
-------------+------------------------------           F(  5,    82) =   39.35
       Model |  647870.676     5  129574.135           Prob > F      =  0.0000
    Residual |  269983.83     82  3292.48573           R-squared     =  0.7059
-------------+------------------------------           Adj R-squared =  0.6879
       Total |  917854.506    87  10550.0518           Root MSE      =   57.38

------------------------------------------------------------------------------
       price |      Coef.   Std. Err.      t    P>|t|     [95% Conf. Interval]
-------------+----------------------------------------------------------------
     lotsize |   .0001538    .005203     0.03   0.976    -.0101967    .0105043
       sqrft |   .0176015   .2992508     0.06   0.953    -.5777036    .6129066
       bdrms |   2.175195    33.8881     0.06   0.949    -65.23904    69.58943
          r2 |   .0003534   .0070989     0.05   0.960    -.0137687    .0144754
          r3 |   1.55e-06   6.55e-06     0.24   0.814    -.0000115    .0000146
       _cons |   166.0945   317.4325     0.52   0.602    -465.3798    797.5688
------------------------------------------------------------------------------
```

① 资料来源：http：//fmwww.bc.edu/ec—p/data/wooldridge/HPRICE1。

```
test r2 r3

( 1)  r2 = 0
( 2)  r3 = 0

       F(  2,    82) =    4.67
            Prob > F =    0.0120
```

问题 1：在进行 RESET 测试之后，你得出了什么结论？

因为 p 值=0.012，小于 5%，我们拒绝 $r_2=r_3=0$ 的零假设。这意味着最初的方程式没有包括 r_2 和 r_3。在做过 RESET 检验之后，我们得出结论：第一个模型没有采用适当的方程式。

然后，我们考虑第二个对数形式：

$logprice = f(loglotsize, logsqrft, bdrms)$。

```
reg lprice llotsize lsqrft bdrms

      Source |       SS       df       MS              Number of obs =      88
-------------+------------------------------           F(  3,    84) =   50.42
       Model |  5.15504028     3  1.71834676           Prob > F      =  0.0000
    Residual |  2.86256324    84  .034078134           R-squared     =  0.6430
-------------+------------------------------           Adj R-squared =  0.6302
       Total |  8.01760352    87  .092156362           Root MSE      =   .1846

------------------------------------------------------------------------------
      lprice |      Coef.   Std. Err.      t    P>|t|     [95% Conf. Interval]
-------------+----------------------------------------------------------------
    llotsize |   .1679667   .0382812     4.39   0.000     .0918404     .244093
      lsqrft |   .7002324   .0928652     7.54   0.000     .5155597    .8849051
       bdrms |   .0369584   .0275313     1.34   0.183    -.0177906    .0917074
       _cons |  -1.297042   .6512836    -1.99   0.050    -2.592191    -.001893
------------------------------------------------------------------------------
```

```
predict lphat
(option xb assumed; fitted values)

gen lph2 = lphat * lphat

gen lph3 = lphat * lph2

reg lprice llotsize lsqrft bdrms lph2 lph3

      Source |       SS       df       MS              Number of obs =      88
-------------+------------------------------           F(  5,    82) =   32.41
       Model |  5.32360126     5  1.06472025           Prob > F      =  0.0000
    Residual |  2.69400226    82  .032853686           R-squared     =  0.6640
-------------+------------------------------           Adj R-squared =  0.6435
       Total |  8.01760352    87  .092156362           Root MSE      =  .18126

------------------------------------------------------------------------------
      lprice |      Coef.   Std. Err.      t    P>|t|     [95% Conf. Interval]
-------------+----------------------------------------------------------------
    llotsize |  -4.191584   12.59578    -0.33   0.740    -29.2486     20.86543
      lsqrft |  -17.39336   52.49227    -0.33   0.741    -121.8172     87.0305
       bdrms |  -.9276645    2.76988    -0.33   0.739    -6.437838    4.582509
        lph2 |   3.921189   13.01484     0.30   0.764    -21.96948    29.81186
        lph3 |  -.1933951   .7521095    -0.26   0.798    -1.68958     1.30279
       _cons |   88.08799   240.9851     0.37   0.716    -391.3081    567.4841
------------------------------------------------------------------------------
```

```
test lph2 lph3

( 1)  lph2 = 0
( 2)  lph3 = 0

       F(  2,    82) =    2.57
            Prob > F =    0.0831
```

问题 2：在进行 RESET 检验之后，你得出了什么结论？

因为 p 值=0.083 1，大于 5%，我们不拒绝 $r_2=r_3=0$ 的零假设。这意味着最初的方程式不需要包括 r_2 和 r_3。在做过 RESET 检验之后，我们得出结论：第二个模型采用了适当的方程式。

问题 3：在第一个模型和第二个模型中，哪一个更合适？

相比较来说，第二个模型更好，因为它通过了拉姆齐测试。

Ⅲ. 附加上机操作练习

（1）打开数据文件 **buscost.dta**。[1] 创建变量 *logTcost* 和 *logRVM*，它们分别是 *Totalcost* 和 *RVM* 的对数形式，然后创建一个二次项 *log2rvm*，它等于 $(logRVM)^2$。估计对数一二次成本函数：

$$logTcost_i=\beta_0+\beta_1\,logRVM_i+\beta_2(logRVM_i)^2+\varepsilon_i$$

a. 写出关于产量的总成本弹性。该弹性随着产量增加而升高还是降低？

$$elasticity=d(logTcost_i)/d(logRVM_i)=\beta_1+2\times\beta_2 logRVM_i$$

弹性会随着产量的增加而升高。

b. 当 *RVM* 等于 5 000 时，估计的弹性为多少？

```
. reg  logTcost logRVM log2rvm

      Source |       SS           df       MS          Number of obs =      246
-------------+----------------------------------      F(  2,    243) =  2899.07
       Model |  460.317879         2  230.158939      Prob > F       =   0.0000
    Residual |  19.2919139       243  .079390592      R-squared      =   0.9598
-------------+----------------------------------      Adj R-squared  =   0.9594
       Total |  479.609793       245  1.95759099      Root MSE       =   .28176

------------------------------------------------------------------------------
    logTcost |      Coef.   Std. Err.      t    P>|t|     [95% Conf. Interval]
-------------+----------------------------------------------------------------
      logRVM |   .8660641   .1248086     6.94   0.000     .6202194    1.111909
     log2rvm |   .0175937   .0086463     2.03   0.043     .0005625    .0346249
       _cons |    1.30154   .4443496     2.93   0.004     .4262717    2.176809
------------------------------------------------------------------------------
```

估计的弹性=0.866 064 1+2×0.017 593 7×(ln(5 000))=1.165 762。

c. 检验随着产量增加弹性是否不变。你的结论是什么？

H_0：$\beta_2=0$

H_a：$\beta_2\neq0$

```
. test  log2rvm=0

 ( 1)  log2rvm = 0

       F(  1,   243) =    4.14
            Prob > F =    0.0430
```

因为 p 值=0.043<α=5%，所以我们拒绝零假设。

---

[1] 该练习经过了修改，数据集从下书获取：Stephen J. Schmidt，*Econometrics*（McGraw-Hill，2005）。

结论：随着产量的增加弹性是变化的。

d. 找到一个弹性为 1 时所对应的产量值；找到成本函数是规模报酬递增的产量值；找到成本函数是规模报酬递减的产量值。

当估计的弹性为 1，即 $0.866\ 064\ 1+2\times0.017\ 593\ 7\times(\ln RVM)=1$，$RVM=44.986\ 5$。

当产量小于 44.986 5 时，成本函数是规模报酬递增的。

当产量大于 44.986 5 时，成本函数是规模报酬递减的。

(2) 打开文件 **wages1. dta**。创建一个 *education* 的二次项，并估计以下方程：

$$log\ Wages_i=\beta_0+\beta_1\ education_i+\beta_2 education_i{}^2+\varepsilon_i$$

a. 写出受教育时间增加一年，年收入增加的百分比的表达式。如果一个人的受教育时间从 4 年增加为 5 年，他的工资会增加多少百分比？如果一个人的受教育时间从 13 年增加为 14 年，他的工资会增加多少百分比？这个人第 5 年的教育更有价值还是第 14 年的教育更有价值？

```
. reg  logwage education education2

      Source |       SS       df       MS              Number of obs =     658
-------------+------------------------------           F(  2,   655) =   31.08
       Model |  65.6185343     2  32.8092672           Prob > F      =  0.0000
    Residual |  691.514955   655  1.05574802           R-squared     =  0.0867
-------------+------------------------------           Adj R-squared =  0.0839
       Total |  757.133489   657  1.15241018           Root MSE      =  1.0275

------------------------------------------------------------------------------
     logwage |      Coef.   Std. Err.      t    P>|t|     [95% Conf. Interval]
-------------+----------------------------------------------------------------
   education |  -.0004559   .0657499    -0.01   0.994     -.129562    .1286501
  education2 |   .0040407   .0026061     1.55   0.122    -.0010766    .0091579
       _cons |   9.174522   .4105623    22.35   0.000     8.368345    9.980699
```

这个表达式是：

$$\%\Delta\ \widehat{wages}/\Delta education=100\ \hat{\beta}_1+200\hat{\beta}_2 education$$
$$=-0.045\ 59+0.808\ 14education$$

如果一个人的受教育时间从 4 年增加为 5 年，他的工资会增加

$-0.045\ 59+0.808\ 14\times4=3.186\ 97$ (%)

如果一个人的受教育时间从 13 年增加为 14 年，他的工资会增加

$-0.045\ 59+0.808\ 14\times13=10.460\ 23$ (%)

因此，这个人第 14 年的教育比第 5 年的教育更有价值。

b. 检验这个表达式是否随着受教育时间的变化而变化。如果不是，教育回报随着受教育时间升高还是降低？

H_0：$\beta_2=0$

H_a：$\beta_2\neq0$

```
. test  education2=0

 ( 1)  education2 = 0

       F(  1,   655) =    2.40
            Prob > F =    0.1215
```

因为 p 值$=0.1215>\alpha=5\%$，所以我们不拒绝零假设。

结论：这个表达式随着受教育时间的变化是不变的。

c. 检验 $\beta_1=0$。给出对结果的经济分析。

H_0：$\beta_1=0$

H_a：$\beta_1\neq 0$

```
. test  education=0

 ( 1)  education = 0

       F(  1,   655) =    0.00
            Prob > F =    0.9945
```

因为 p 值$=0.9945>\alpha=5\%$，所以我们不拒绝零假设。

结论：β_1 是测量一个人在没有受过任何教育的情况下（$education=0$）的工资影响状况。我们发现 *education* 的系数并不具有统计显著性。

d. 检验联合假设：$\beta_1=0$ 和 $\beta_2=0$。教育会影响工资吗？

H_0：$\beta_1=0$，$\beta_2=0$

H_a：$\beta_1\neq 0$，$\beta_2\neq 0$

```
. test  education= education2=0

 ( 1)  education - education2 = 0
 ( 2)  education = 0

       F(  2,   655) =   31.08
            Prob > F =    0.0000
```

检验结果显示 p 值$=0.000<0.05$，所以我们拒绝零假设，这意味着 β_1 和 β_2 是联合显著的。

结论：受教育水平会影响一个人的工资，但我们无法判断这个影响是线性的还是二次的。

Chapter 5

Specifying the Econometric Model

Ⅰ. How to Choose an Appropriate Functional Form

A linear regression model does not mean a linear relationship between the variables, but a model in which the parameters enter in a linear way. That is, the model is "linear in parameters", but it is not necessarily "linear in variables". Based on this understanding, we can transform the variables in any convenient way, as long as the resulting model satisfies the assumptions of the linear regression model.

OLS can be used for relationships that are not strictly linear in x and y, but linear in the parameters, in a nonlinear function of x and y. Hence, we can take the natural log of x, y or both, use quadratic forms of x, use interactions of the x variables, or take many other transformations as long as the functional form satisfies the basic requirements of OLS regression. In this section, we will mainly discuss three commonly used functional forms, one by one.

1.1 Log Models

Using Log models has many advantages. First, Log models are invariant to the scale of variables. Second, they give a direct estimate of elasticity. Third, for models with $y>0$, their conditional distribution is often heteroskedastic or skewed, while $\log(y)$ is much less so. Fourth, the distribution of $\log(y)$ is narrower, limiting the effect of outliers.

How to interpret log models? Generally, we consider the following three types.

If the model is $\log(y)=\beta_0+\beta_1\log(x)+u$, β_1 is the elasticity of y with respect to x.

If the model is $\log(y)=\beta_0+\beta_1 x+u$, β_1 is approximately the percentage change in y given a 1 unit change in x.

If the model is $y=\beta_0+\beta_1\log(x)+u$, β_1 is approximately the change in y for a 100 percent change in x.

Example: Housing Prices and Air Pollution. ①

The population model is:

$$\log(price)=\beta_0+\beta_1\log(nox)+\beta_2 rooms+u.$$

How to interpret the coefficients of the parameters in the log-form model, especially β_1 and β_2?

β_1 is the elasticity of price with respect to the amount of nitrogen oxide in the air (nox).

β_2 is approximately the percentage change in price given a 1 unit change in the average number of rooms in house ($rooms$).

After collecting the needed data and running OLS regression, we obtain:

$$\widehat{\log(price)}=\underset{(0.09)}{7.23}-\underset{(0.016)}{0.75}\log(nox)+\underset{(0.009)}{0.36}rooms$$

$$n=510, R^2=0.714$$

Thus, when nox increases by 1%, price falls by 0.75%, holding rooms fixed. When rooms increases by one, price increases by approximately $100\times0.36=36\%$.

1.2 Quadratic Models

For a model of the form $y=\beta_0+\beta_1 x+\beta_2 x^2+u$, we can't interpret β_1 alone when measuring the change in y with respect to x, we need to take into account β_2 as well, since:

$$\Delta\hat{y}\approx(\hat{\beta}_1+2\hat{\beta}_2 x)\Delta x$$

so $$\frac{\Delta\hat{y}}{\Delta x}\approx\hat{\beta}_1+2\hat{\beta}_2 x$$

(1) Suppose that the coefficient on x is positive and the coefficient on x^2 is negative, then y is increasing in x at first, but will eventually turn around and be decreasing in x.

For $\hat{\beta}_1>0$ and $\hat{\beta}_2<0$, the turing point will be at $x^*=|\hat{\beta}_1(2\hat{\beta}_2)|$

(2) Suppose that the coefficient on x is negative and the coefficient on x^2 is positive, then y is decreasing in x at first, but will eventually turn around and be increasing in x.

For $\hat{\beta}_1<0$ and $\hat{\beta}_2>0$, the turing point will be at $x^*=|\hat{\beta}_1(2\hat{\beta}_2)|$

Example: Housing Prices and Air Pollution. ②

$$\log(price)=\beta_0+\beta_1\log(nox)+\beta_2 rooms+\beta_3 rooms^2+u$$

After collecting the needed data and running OLS regression, we obtain:

$$\widehat{\log(price)}=\underset{(0.47)}{10.59}-\underset{(0.115)}{0.8}\log(nox)-\underset{(0.165)}{0.545}rooms+\underset{(0.013)}{0.062}rooms^2$$

① See Example 4.5, *Introductory Econometrics: A Modern Approach*, by Jeffrey Wooldridge, 2006.

② See Example 6.2, *Introductory Econometrics: A Modern Approach*, by Jeffrey Wooldridge, 2006.

$n=510, R^2=0.63$

How to interpret the effect of rooms on log(*price*)?

Because the coefficient on *rooms* is negative and the coefficient on $rooms^2$ is positive, this equation literally implies that at low values of *rooms*, an additional room has a negative effect on log(*price*). At some point, the effect becomes positive, and the quadratic shape means that the semi-elasticity of price with respect to *rooms* is increasing as *rooms* increases. Then we obtain the turnaround value of $rooms=0.545/(2\times0.062)=4.4$. To the right of 4.4, adding another room has an increasing effect on the percentage change in price. For example, for an increase in *rooms* from five to six, price increases by $100\times(-0.545+2\times0.062\times5)\%=7.5\%$.

1.3 Interaction Terms

For a model of the form $y=\beta_0+\beta_1x_1+\beta_2x_2+\beta_3x_1x_2+u$, we can't interpret β_1 alone as measuring the change in y with respect to x_1, we need to take into account β_3 as well, since:

$$\frac{\Delta y}{\Delta x_1}=\beta_1+\beta_3x_2$$

So to summarize the effect of x_1 on y, we typically evaluate the above at $\bar{x}_2$.

Example: Effect of Attendance on Final Exam Performance. [①]

$$stndfnl=\beta_0+\beta_1 atndrte+\beta_2 priGPA+\beta_3 priGPA\times atndrte+u$$

where $stndfnl$=standardized outcome on a final exam,

$atndrte$=percentage of classes attended,

$priGPA$=prior college grade point average.

This model includes an interaction between *priGPA* and *atndrte*. The idea is the class attendance might have a different effect for students who have performed differently in the past, as measured by *priGPA*.

$$\widehat{stndfnl}=\underset{(1.36)}{2.05}-\underset{(0.0102)}{0.0067}atndrte-\underset{(0.48)}{1.63}priGPA+\underset{(0.0043)}{0.0056}priGPA\times atndrte,$$

$n=680,\ R^2=0.33$

We must interpret this equation with extreme care. If we simply look at the coefficient on *atndrte*, we will incorrectly conclude that attendance has a negative effect on final exam scores. We must also take care not to look separately at the β_1 and β_2, each of which is not significant when we look at their t-statistics. If we test $\beta_1=0$ and $\beta_2=0$, the p-value for the F test of this joint hypothesis is 0.014. We can't reject null hypothesis at the 5% level.

To interpret the partial effect of *atndrte* on *stndfnl*, we must plug in some interesting

① See Example 6.3, *Introductory Econometrics: A Modern Approach*, by Jeffrey Wooldridge, 2006.

values of *priGPA*, for example, the mean value of *priGPA* is 2.59, so at the mean *priGPA*, the effect of *atndrte* on *stndfnl* is $-0.0067+0.0056\times2.59=0.0078$. This means a 1% point increase in *atndrte* increases *stndfnl* by 0.0078 standard deviations from the mean final exam score.

Ⅱ. How to Test the Appropriateness of a Functional Form

2.1 RAMSEY's RESET

How do we know if we've got the right functional form for our model? We can use economic theory to guide us when thinking about the interpretation. For instance, we may ask and try to answer such following questions: Does it make more sense for x to affect y in percentage (use logs) or absolute terms? Does it make more sense for the derivative of x_1 to vary with x_1^2 (quadratic) or with x_2 (interactions) or to be fixed?

To tell if we've got the right functional form, we can also turn to a hypothesis test. We have already learned how to test joint exclusion restrictions to see if higher order terms or interactions belong in the model. However, it can be tedious to add and test extra terms, plus we may find a square term matters when really using logs would be even better. A solution for this is to use the Ramsey's regression specification error test (RESET), which is designed to test if the functional form is appropriate.

The basic idea of doing the RESET is, in the initial functional form, we add and test the function of $\hat{y}$ through estimating $y=\beta_0+\beta_1x_1+\cdots+\beta_kx_k+d_1\hat{y}^2+d_2\hat{y}^3+error$ and set up the null hypothesis as: H_0: $d_1=0$, $d_2=0$. Using $F\sim F_{2,n-k-3}$ leads us to obtain the corresponding p-value and draw a final conclusion.

2.2 Computer Exercise

Please upload **house.dta** onto Stata. [1] Let us firstly consider the first model: $price=f(lotsize, sqrft, bdrms)$.

Question 1: what is your conclusion, after conducting RESET test?

Since the p-value$=0.012$, less than 5%, we reject the null hypothesis that $r_2=r_3=0$. This means that the initial functional form fails to include r_2 and r_3. After conducing RESET test, we conclude that the first model does not have an appropriate functional form.

---

① Data is collected from http: //fmwww. bc. edu/ec—p/data/wooldridge/HPRICE1.

```
reg price lotsize sqrft bdrms

      Source |       SS       df       MS              Number of obs =      88
-------------+------------------------------           F(  3,    84) =   57.46
       Model |  617130.701     3  205710.234           Prob > F      =  0.0000
    Residual |  300723.805    84   3580.0453           R-squared     =  0.6724
-------------+------------------------------           Adj R-squared =  0.6607
       Total |  917854.506    87  10550.0518           Root MSE      =  59.833

------------------------------------------------------------------------------
       price |      Coef.   Std. Err.      t    P>|t|     [95% Conf. Interval]
-------------+----------------------------------------------------------------
     lotsize |   .0020677   .0006421     3.22   0.002     .0007908    .0033446
       sqrft |   .1227782   .0132374     9.28   0.000     .0964541    .1491022
       bdrms |   13.85252   9.010145     1.54   0.128    -4.065141    31.77018
       _cons |  -21.77031   29.47504    -0.74   0.462    -80.38466    36.84405
------------------------------------------------------------------------------

predict r1, xb

gen r2 = r1*r1

gen r3 = r2*r1

reg price lotsize sqrft bdrms r2 r3

      Source |       SS       df       MS              Number of obs =      88
-------------+------------------------------           F(  5,    82) =   39.35
       Model |  647870.676     5  129574.135           Prob > F      =  0.0000
    Residual |   269983.83    82  3292.48573           R-squared     =  0.7059
-------------+------------------------------           Adj R-squared =  0.6879
       Total |  917854.506    87  10550.0518           Root MSE      =   57.38

------------------------------------------------------------------------------
       price |      Coef.   Std. Err.      t    P>|t|     [95% Conf. Interval]
-------------+----------------------------------------------------------------
     lotsize |   .0001538    .005203     0.03   0.976    -.0101967    .0105043
       sqrft |   .0176015   .2992508     0.06   0.953    -.5777036    .6129066
       bdrms |   2.175195    33.8881     0.06   0.949    -65.23904    69.58943
          r2 |   .0003534   .0070989     0.05   0.960    -.0137687    .0144754
          r3 |   1.55e-06   6.55e-06     0.24   0.814    -.0000115    .0000146
       _cons |   166.0945   317.4325     0.52   0.602    -465.3798    797.5688
```

```
test r2 r3

 ( 1)  r2 = 0
 ( 2)  r3 = 0

       F(  2,    82) =    4.67
            Prob > F =    0.0120
```

Next, let us consider the second in log-form where:

logprice=*f*(*loglotsize*, *logsqrft*, *bdrms*) .

```
reg lprice llotsize lsqrft bdrms

      Source |       SS       df       MS              Number of obs =      88
-------------+------------------------------           F(  3,    84) =   50.42
       Model |  5.15504028     3  1.71834676           Prob > F      =  0.0000
    Residual |  2.86256324    84  .034078134           R-squared     =  0.6430
-------------+------------------------------           Adj R-squared =  0.6302
       Total |  8.01760352    87  .092156362           Root MSE      =   .1846

------------------------------------------------------------------------------
      lprice |      Coef.   Std. Err.      t    P>|t|     [95% Conf. Interval]
-------------+----------------------------------------------------------------
    llotsize |   .1679667   .0382812     4.39   0.000     .0918404     .244093
      lsqrft |   .7002324   .0928652     7.54   0.000     .5155597    .8849051
       bdrms |   .0369584   .0275313     1.34   0.183    -.0177906    .0917074
       _cons |  -1.297042   .6512836    -1.99   0.050    -2.592191    -.001893
------------------------------------------------------------------------------
```

```
predict lphat
option xb assumed; fitted values)

gen lph2 = lphat * lphat

gen lph3 = lphat * lph2

reg lprice llotsize lsqrft bdrms lph2 lph3

      Source |       SS       df       MS              Number of obs =      88
-------------+------------------------------           F(  5,    82) =   32.41
       Model |  5.32360126     5  1.06472025           Prob > F      =  0.0000
    Residual |  2.69400226    82  .032853686           R-squared     =  0.6640
-------------+------------------------------           Adj R-squared =  0.6435
       Total |  8.01760352    87  .092156362           Root MSE      =  .18126

------------------------------------------------------------------------------
      lprice |      Coef.   Std. Err.      t    P>|t|     [95% Conf. Interval]
-------------+----------------------------------------------------------------
    llotsize |  -4.191584   12.59578    -0.33   0.740    -29.2486    20.86543
      lsqrft |  -17.39336   52.49227    -0.33   0.741   -121.8172     87.0305
       bdrms |  -.9276645    2.76988    -0.33   0.739   -6.437838    4.582509
        lph2 |   3.921189   13.01484     0.30   0.764   -21.96948    29.81186
        lph3 |  -.1933951   .7521095    -0.26   0.798    -1.68958     1.30279
       _cons |   88.08799   240.9851     0.37   0.716   -391.3081    567.4841
```

```
test lph2 lph3

( 1)  lph2 = 0
( 2)  lph3 = 0

      F(  2,    82) =    2.57
           Prob > F =    0.0831
```

Question 2: What is your conclusion, after conducting RESET test?

Since the p-value $= 0.0831$, greater than 5%, we don't reject the null hypothesis that $r_2 = r_3 = 0$. This means that the initial functional form does not need to include r_2 and r_3. After conducing RESET test, we conclude that the second model have an appropriate functional form.

Question 3: Between the first model and the second model, which one is more appropriate?

Comparatively, the second model is better because it passes the RAMSEY test.

Ⅲ. Additional Computer Exercises

(1) Open the data file **buscost. dta.**[1] Generate the variables *logTcost* and *logRVM*, which are the logs of *Totalcost* and *RVM*, respectively, and then generate a quadratic term *log2rvm*, which is equal to $(logRVM)^2$. Estimate the log-quadratic cost function:

$$logTcost_i = \beta_0 + \beta_1\, logRVM_i + \beta_2 (logRVM_i)^2 + \varepsilon_i$$

a. Find an expression for the elasticity of total cost with respect to output. Does elastic-

[1] This exercise is modified and the data set is collected from the book—*Econometrics* written by Stephen J. Schmidt (McGraw-Hill, 2005).

ity appear to rise or fall as output rises?

$$elasticity = d(logTcost_i)/d(logRVM_i) = \beta_1 + 2\times\beta_2 logRVM_i$$

Elasticity will increase as output rises.

b. What is the estimated elasticity when RVM=5 000?

```
. reg  logTcost logRVM log2rvm

      Source |       SS       df       MS              Number of obs =     246
-------------+------------------------------           F(  2,   243) = 2899.07
       Model |  460.317879     2  230.158939           Prob > F      =  0.0000
    Residual |  19.2919139   243  .079390592           R-squared     =  0.9598
-------------+------------------------------           Adj R-squared =  0.9594
       Total |  479.609793   245  1.95759099           Root MSE      =  .28176

------------------------------------------------------------------------------
    logTcost |      Coef.   Std. Err.      t    P>|t|     [95% Conf. Interval]
-------------+----------------------------------------------------------------
      logRVM |   .8660641   .1248086     6.94   0.000     .6202194    1.111909
     log2rvm |   .0175937   .0086463     2.03   0.043     .0005625    .0346249
       _cons |    1.30154   .4443496     2.93   0.004     .4262717    2.176809
------------------------------------------------------------------------------
```

The estimated elasticity=0. 866 064 1+2×0. 017 593 7×(ln(5 000))=1. 165 762.

c. Test whether the elasticity is constant as output rises against the null hypothesis that it is changing (in either direction). What do you conclude?

H_0: $\beta_2=0$

H_a: $\beta_2\neq0$

```
. test  log2rvm=0

 ( 1)  log2rvm = 0

       F(  1,   243) =    4.14
            Prob > F =    0.0430
```

Since p-value=0. 043<α=5%, we reject H_0.

Conclusion: elasticity is not constant as output rises.

d. Find the point at which the estimated elasticity is equal to 1. Find a value of output for which the cost function has increasing returns to scale, and one for which it has decreasing returns to scale.

When the estimated elasticity=0. 866 064 1+2×0. 017 593 7×(ln RVM)=1, RVM= 44. 986 5.

When RVM is smaller than 44. 986 5, the cost function has increasing returns to scale.

When RVM is greater than 44. 986 5, the cost function has decreasing returns to scale.

(2) Open the file **wages1. dta.** Generate a quadratic term for *education* squared, and estimate the equation:

$$log\ Wages_i = \beta_0 + \beta_1\ education_i + \beta_2 education_i^2 + \varepsilon_i$$

a. Find an expression for the percentage increase in annual wage from a one-year increase in education. By what percentage does wage increase if one's education increases from 4 years to 5? By what percentage does wage increase if one's education increases from 13 years to 14? What is more valuable, the 5th year of a person's education or the 14th year?

```
. reg  logwage education education2

      Source |       SS       df       MS              Number of obs =     658
-------------+------------------------------           F(  2,   655) =   31.08
       Model |  65.6185343     2  32.8092672           Prob > F      =  0.0000
    Residual |  691.514955   655  1.05574802           R-squared     =  0.0867
-------------+------------------------------           Adj R-squared =  0.0839
       Total |  757.133489   657  1.15241018           Root MSE      =  1.0275

------------------------------------------------------------------------------
     logwage |      Coef.   Std. Err.      t    P>|t|     [95% Conf. Interval]
-------------+----------------------------------------------------------------
   education |  -.0004559   .0657499    -0.01   0.994     -.129562    .1286501
  education2 |   .0040407   .0026061     1.55   0.122    -.0010766    .0091579
       _cons |   9.174522   .4105623    22.35   0.000     8.368345    9.980699
```

According to the regression result:

$$\%\Delta \widehat{wages}/\Delta education = 100\hat{\beta}_1 + 200\hat{\beta}_2 education$$
$$= -0.045\ 59 + 0.808\ 14 education$$

If one's education increases from 4 years to 5, his wage will increase by

$-0.045\ 59+0.808\ 14\times4=3.186\ 97$ (%)

If one's education increases from 13 years to 14, his wage will increase by

$-0.045\ 59+0.808\ 14\times13=10.460\ 23$ (%)

Therefore, the 14th year of education is more valuable than the 5th year of education.

b. Test whether that expression is constant with respect to the amount of education or not. If it is not, does the return to education increase or decrease as the amount of education rises?

H_0: $\beta_2=0$

H_a: $\beta_2\neq0$

```
. test  education2=0

 ( 1)  education2 = 0

       F(  1,   655) =    2.40
            Prob > F =    0.1215
```

Since the p-value$=0.121\ 5>\alpha=5\%$, we do not reject H_0.

Conclusion: the expression is constant with respect to the amount of education.

c. Test whether $\beta_1=0$. Provide an economic interpretation of your finding.

H_0: $\beta_1=0$

H_a: $\beta_1\neq0$

```
. test  education=0

 ( 1)  education = 0

       F(  1,   655) =     0.00
            Prob > F =    0.9945
```

Since the p-value$=0.9945>\alpha=5\%$, we do not reject H_0.

Conclusion: β_1 is the return to education for a person who has none to begin with ($education=0$). We find that this increase is not statistically significantly different from 0.

d. Test the joint hypothesis that $\beta_1=0$ and $\beta_2=0$. Does education affect wages or not?

H_0: $\beta_1=0$, $\beta_2=0$

H_a: $\beta_1\neq0$, $\beta_2\neq0$

```
. test  education= education2=0

 ( 1)  education - education2 = 0
 ( 2)  education = 0

       F(  2,   655) =    31.08
            Prob > F =    0.0000
```

According to the test result, the p-value$=0.000<\alpha=0.05$, so we reject H_0, which means that β_1 and β_2 are jointly significant.

Conclusion: *education* matters but we can't say whether it is a linear or quadratic relationship.

第 6 章

进一步分析建模的不足之处

Ⅰ. 遗漏变量导致的估计偏差

根据第 5 章所学，我们将进一步讨论一些重要的建模问题，而这些问题往往会出现在实证分析里。在本章的第Ⅰ部分，我们一开始讨论的问题是遗漏变量的估计偏差问题。当多元回归模型遇到不合适的方程式而且不能正确解释因变量和自变量之间的关系时，这类问题往往会随之而来。

如我们所知，通常情况下，一个计量经济模型的建立取决于一个正式的经济模型、经济理论，甚至是直觉的存在。如果我们在方程式里包括了本不该属于此模型的变量，会产生什么结果？很容易证明，这种情况并不会导致 OLS 估计偏差的出现。这时，如果我们在方程式里遗漏了本该属于此模型的重要变量，又会出现什么结果呢？这里，我们通过下面的论证得知，如果一个关键的变量未能纳入回归模型，OLS 回归的估计量往往有偏差。

假如真正的模型是：

$$y=\beta_0+\beta_1 x_1+\beta_2 x_2+u$$

但是，我们忽略了 x_2，仅估计：

$$\tilde{y}=\tilde{\beta}_0+\tilde{\beta}_1 x_1$$

于是得：

$$\tilde{\beta}_1=\frac{\sum(x_{i1}-\bar{x}_1)y_i}{\sum(x_{i1}-\bar{x}_1)^2}$$

回忆一下，真正的模型里：

$$y_i=\beta_0+\beta_1 x_{i1}+\beta_2 x_{i2}+u_i$$

所以，分子转换为：

$$\sum(x_{i1}-\bar{x}_1)(\beta_0+\beta_1 x_{i1}+\beta_2 x_{i2}+u_i)=\beta_1\sum(x_{i1}-\bar{x}_1)^2+\beta_2\sum(x_{i1}-\bar{x}_1)x_{i2}$$
$$+\sum(x_{i1}-\bar{x}_1)u_i$$

因此，

$$\tilde{\beta}_1 = \beta_1 + \beta_2 \frac{\sum (x_{i1} - \overline{x}_1) x_{i2}}{\sum (x_{i1} - \overline{x}_1)^2} + \frac{\sum (x_{i1} - \overline{x}_1) u_i}{\sum (x_{i1} - \overline{x}_1)^2}$$

因为 $E(u_i)=0$，两边同时取期望值，我们得到：

$$E(\tilde{\beta}_1) = \beta_1 + \beta_2 \frac{\sum (x_{i1} - \overline{x}_1) x_{i2}}{\sum (x_{i1} - \overline{x}_1)^2}$$

考虑到 x_2 对 x_1 的回归：$\tilde{x}_2=\tilde{\delta}_0+\tilde{\delta}_1 x_1$，那么，

$$\tilde{\delta}_1 = \frac{\sum (x_{i1} - \overline{x}_1) x_{i2}}{\sum (x_{i1} - \overline{x}_1)^2}$$

故 $E(\tilde{\beta}_1)=\beta_1+\beta_2\tilde{\delta}_1$。

上述论证表明，如果我们忽视了本该属于此模型的某个重要变量的存在，那么 $\tilde{\beta}_1$ 的期望值取决于 β_1，β_2 和 $\tilde{\delta}_1$ 所取的数值。在公式里，$\tilde{\delta}_1$ 衡量 x_1 和 x_2 的相关关系。下面的表格总结了 OLS 估计量的偏差方向。

	Corr（x_1，x_2）>0	Corr（x_1，x_2）<0
$\beta_2>0$	正偏差	负偏差
$\beta_2<0$	负偏差	正偏差

简言之，如果 x_1 和 x_2 与 x_2 和 y 的相关关系是一致的，偏差则为正。如果 x_1 和 x_2 与 x_2 和 y 的相关关系不是一致的，偏差则为负。

注意：只有在下列两种情况下，偏差值是等于零的。

i）$\beta_2=0$，即 x_2 并不影响 y，不是真正属于该模型。

ii）x_1 和 x_2 不存在相关关系，即 $\tilde{\delta}_1$ 为零。

Ⅱ. 多重共线性的问题和解决方法

2.1 完全多重共线性

在计量经济学研究中，最基本的问题之一就是多重共线性的存在。究竟我们所指的多重共线性意味着什么？你是否还记得，在回归和分析 OLS 模型时，我们需要的重要假设中有一条是：解释变量不能是任何其他一个解释变量的完全线性函数（即没有完全多重共线性）。①

为了做一些有意义的多重共线性分析，请找到 **survey. dta** 并上传到 Stata。

假设我们想要通过过去一个月的数据预测你看电影的行为。一开始，我们不妨假设：

① 该练习受凯斯西储大学魏德海管理学院的 Eric Bettinger 的启发。数据通过作者计量经济课堂上的学生调查收集。

看电影的次数＝f(电影的知识程度)。我们试图检验你对电影感兴趣的程度是否会导致你看电影的实际次数的变化。

由于我们不可能直接观测并收集到衡量你的电影知识程度的数据，我们决定用下面的代理变量来替代衡量你的电影知识程度的变量，这些变量是："正确回答了第＃个问题"，而且它们都是虚拟变量，如果你正确回答了第＃个问题，相对应的代理变量数值为 1，否则为 0。更具体地说，该模型可以改写为：

看电影的次数＝f(正确回答了第一个问题,正确回答了第二个问题,正确回答了第三个问题,正确回答了第四个问题,正确回答了第五个问题,正确回答了第六个问题,回答问题的正确总数)

即＃ *movies*＝f($q1$，$q2$，$q3$，$q4$，$q5$，$q6$，*correct*)。

然后，我们采用线性回归，通过 Stata 的运行得到以下结果：

. gen *total*＝*theater*＋*tv*

. gen *correct*＝$q1+q2+q3+q4+q5+q6$

```
reg total q1 q2 q3 q4 q5 q6 correct

      Source |       SS       df       MS              Number of obs =      53
-------------+------------------------------           F(  6,    46) =    3.32
       Model |  97.6680072     6  16.2780012           Prob > F      =  0.0085
    Residual |  225.803691    46  4.90877589           R-squared     =  0.3019
-------------+------------------------------           Adj R-squared =  0.2109
       Total |  323.471698    52  6.22060958           Root MSE      =  2.2156

------------------------------------------------------------------------------
       total |      Coef.   Std. Err.      t    P>|t|     [95% Conf. Interval]
-------------+----------------------------------------------------------------
          q1 |    .612906   1.125354     0.54   0.589    -1.652314    2.878126
          q2 |  -1.959375   1.291024    -1.52   0.136    -4.558072    .6393213
          q3 |  -.4362873   1.318433    -0.33   0.742    -3.090156    2.217581
          q4 |   .1115949   1.907238     0.06   0.954    -3.727476    3.950666
          q5 |   .2526805   1.290547     0.20   0.846    -2.345056    2.850417
          q6 |  (dropped)
     correct |   .9601301   1.080071     0.89   0.379     -1.21394      3.1342
       _cons |   1.229942    .945136     1.30   0.200    -.6725181    3.132402
------------------------------------------------------------------------------
```

为什么我们得不到关于 $q6$ 的任何结果呢？

原因是完全多重共线性的存在。假如你仔细查找，会发现 *correct* 是 $q1$，$q2$，$q3$，$q4$，$q5$ 和 $q6$ 的完全线性组合——它只是其他 6 个解释变量的总和。这就是所谓的完全多重共线性。任何时候，假如某个解释变量是其他解释变量的线性组合，Stata 将自动去掉其中一个产生完全线性组合问题的解释变量。

假设我们认为去看电影的消费行为是性别的函数方程：

看电影的次数＝f(性别)

我们也可以写为：

看电影的次数＝f(男性,女性)

我们在 Stata 中回归上述模型：

```
gen female=1-male

reg total female male

      Source |       SS       df       MS              Number of obs =      53
-------------+------------------------------           F(  1,    51) =    0.00
       Model |  .025269542     1  .025269542           Prob > F      =  0.9499
    Residual |  323.446429    51  6.34208683           R-squared     =  0.0001
-------------+------------------------------           Adj R-squared = -0.0195
       Total |  323.471698    52  6.22060958           Root MSE      =  2.5184

------------------------------------------------------------------------------
       total |      Coef.   Std. Err.      t    P>|t|     [95% Conf. Interval]
-------------+----------------------------------------------------------------
      female |   .0446429   .7072442     0.06   0.950    -1.375209    1.464495
        male |  (dropped)
       _cons |     3.8125   .4451856     8.56   0.000     2.918753    4.706247
------------------------------------------------------------------------------
```

注意，Stata 在回归中去掉了“男性”变量。为什么？这仍是完全多重共线性的问题。在模型里，常数项的取值皆为 1，如果回答问题的人是男性，“男性”变量取值为 1，否则为零。“女性”变量取值则相反。如果你把“男性”变量和“女性”变量放在一起，它们的和永远是 1，正好是常数项的取值。因此，如果我们在模型里使用互斥的虚拟变量，完全多重共线性的问题会阻止我们使用每个虚拟变量。我们必须去掉其中任意一个虚拟变量（或去掉常数项）。为了加强理解，我们运行以下没有常数项的回归：

```
reg total female male, noconstant

      Source |       SS       df       MS              Number of obs =      53
-------------+------------------------------           F(  2,    51) =   61.30
       Model |  777.553571     2  388.776786           Prob > F      =  0.0000
    Residual |  323.446429    51  6.34208683           R-squared     =  0.7062
-------------+------------------------------           Adj R-squared =  0.6947
       Total |        1101    53  20.7735849           Root MSE      =  2.5184

------------------------------------------------------------------------------
       total |      Coef.   Std. Err.      t    P>|t|     [95% Conf. Interval]
-------------+----------------------------------------------------------------
      female |   3.857143    .549549     7.02   0.000     2.753877    4.960409
        male |     3.8125   .4451856     8.56   0.000     2.918753    4.706247
------------------------------------------------------------------------------
```

2.2 非完全多重共线性

迄今为止，我们讨论的是完全多重共线性。其解决方案很简单：只要去掉额外的解释变量即可。下面，我们要将注意力转向较不明显的非完全多重共线性的问题。也就是，解释变量之间具有高度相关性，但并不完全相关。事实上，两个变量之间相关性越大，我们就越难区分它们对被解释变量的影响，而且 OLS 估计参数的标准偏差将越大。

假设你要在以下两个模型里进行选择。

模型 A：

看电影的次数 $= f$(性别，正确回答了第一个问题，正确回答了第二个问题，正确回答了第三个问题，正确回答了第四个问题，正确回答了第五个问题，正确回答了第六个问题)

模型 B：

看电影的次数 $= f$(性别，回答问题的正确总数)

这两个模型哪一个是更好的选择？答案并不如模型 A 或模型 B 的方程式那么明确。我们不得不考虑一些实际问题，以获得更深的理解。我们先回归我们的模型：看电影的次数仅取决于对问题 6 回答的正确与否。

```
reg total q6

      Source |       SS       df       MS              Number of obs =      53
-------------+------------------------------           F(  1,    51) =    5.92
       Model |  33.6640058     1  33.6640058           Prob > F      =  0.0185
    Residual |  289.807692    51  5.68250377           R-squared     =  0.1041
-------------+------------------------------           Adj R-squared =  0.0865
       Total |  323.471698    52  6.22060958           Root MSE      =  2.3838

------------------------------------------------------------------------------
       total |      Coef.   Std. Err.      t    P>|t|     [95% Conf. Interval]
-------------+----------------------------------------------------------------
          q6 |   1.807692   .7426967     2.43   0.018     .3166665    3.298718
       _cons |        2.5   .6370974     3.92   0.000     1.220974    3.779026
------------------------------------------------------------------------------
```

在这个简单的模型里，最后一个问题（$q6$）具有很好的解释力。但是，我们可能会担心忽略了其他一些本应属于模型的解释变量。假设我们添加更多的解释变量，特别是关于回答问题 2、问题 3 和问题 4 的变量。

```
reg total q6 q2 q3 q4

      Source |       SS       df       MS              Number of obs =      53
-------------+------------------------------           F(  4,    48) =    2.28
       Model |  51.7286917     4  12.9321729           Prob > F      =  0.0739
    Residual |  271.743006    48  5.66131263           R-squared     =  0.1599
-------------+------------------------------           Adj R-squared =  0.0899
       Total |  323.471698    52  6.22060958           Root MSE      =  2.3794

------------------------------------------------------------------------------
       total |      Coef.   Std. Err.      t    P>|t|     [95% Conf. Interval]
-------------+----------------------------------------------------------------
          q6 |   .4750081   1.114083     0.43   0.672    -1.765006    2.715022
          q2 |  -.6028077   .7175667    -0.84   0.405    -2.045572    .8399569
          q3 |   .5823597   .6890101     0.85   0.402    -.802988     1.967707
          q4 |   1.424339   1.002281     1.42   0.162    -.5908817    3.439559
       _cons |   2.765649   .8464652     3.27   0.002     1.063717    4.467581
------------------------------------------------------------------------------
```

这回看来，回答问题 6 正确与否并不重要，因为它的 t 统计量已不再具有显著性。发生了什么事导致了这样的结果？答案在于不完全多重共线性的存在。从对问题 2、问题 3 和问题 4 的回答里所得到的信息有可能与问题 6 的回答所提供的信息是相同或相似的。当不完全共线性存在时，OLS 的估计参数的方差会被夸大，导致 t 统计量偏小，使 OLS 参数变得不具有显著性。

如果你看一下两种模型里关于 $q6$ 的标准偏差，就会发现它们是有变化的。在第一个模型中，标准偏差是 0.742 7，而在第二个模型中，标准偏差增加到 1.1。怎样识别不完全多重共线性？我们可以看看变量之间的相关系数。

```
. corr q6 q2 q3 q4
(obs=53)

             |       q6       q2       q3       q4
-------------+------------------------------------
          q6 |   1.0000
          q2 |  -0.1802   1.0000
          q3 |   0.0705   0.2305   1.0000
          q4 |   0.7396  -0.2034  -0.0222   1.0000
```

注意，第 4 个问题的答案（$q4$）和第 6 个问题的答案（$q6$）之间有很高的相关性（0.74）。当我们把 $q4$ 也包括在模型中时，它便试图重新解释 $q6$ 的一部分方差，从而减弱了 $q6$ 和被解释变量的关系。

如何检测多重共线性？

i）在一个有两个解释变量的模型里，我们可以画散点图。如果两个变量高度相关，在图上，大部分的点将沿着一条直线紧密地散布在直线周围。

ii）我们可以查看解释变量的相关系数。如果两个变量高度相关，相关系数将接近 1 或−1。

iii）以 x_k 为被解释变量，回归所有其他解释变量，从而得到 R_k^2。如果 $R_k^2=1$，我们有完全的多重共线性。如果 R_k^2 接近 1，我们有非完全的多重共线性。如果 R_k^2 接近 0，则不存在任何多重共线性的问题。

iv）我们可以检查“方差膨胀因素”（VIF）。在 Stata 中，键入“vif”来进行多重共线性的检验。该 VIF 的取值范围从 1.0 至无限大。VIF 值大于 10，表明多重共线性问题较为严重。1/VIF 的取值范围从 0.0 到 1.0，1.0 表示没有多重共线性问题。

如果不完全多重共线性的问题存在，那么我们如何解决它呢？

i）保留这些产生多重共线性问题的变量，但我们无法逐一解释其对被解释变量 y 的单独影响。例如，在 $y=\beta_0+\beta_1 x_1+\beta_2 x_2+\mu$ 里，x_1 和 x_2 高度相关。我们可以通过计算 $\Delta y=\beta_1\Delta x_1+\beta_2\Delta x_2$ 来测量它们对 y 的联合影响。

ii）去掉一个或多个导致多重共线性问题出现的变量。

iii）如果我们知道导致多重共线性问题出现的这些变量的具体线性函数方程，我们可以将这些变量合并在一起。例如，在 $y=\beta_0+\beta_1 x_1+\beta_2 x_2+\mu$ 里，x_1 和 x_2 高度相关。如果我们知道，$x_1=f(x_2)$，那么可以把 x_1 的方程式代入原来的模型，从而合并 x_1 和 x_2。

iv）收集更多数据，以增加样本大小，为此我们希望能够降低导致多重共线性问题出现的这些变量之间的相关系数。

Ⅲ. 附加上机操作练习

（1）打开数据文件 **schoolspend. dta**①，其中包含美国 50 个州的数据和 7 个变量：*totalspend* 是学区从幼儿园到 12 年级的教育总开销，单位是百万美元；*totalstateaid* 是州政府对学区提供的资助，单位为百万美元；*income* 是州总收入，单位为百万美元；*population* 是州总人口，单位为千人；*elderly*，*minority* 和 *schoolage* 分别是在州总人口中 65 岁及以上人口的比例，少数民族人口的比例和年龄为 6～17 岁的人口的比例。

a. 学校的支出是由收入以及当地和州政府的资助来决定的。如果有更多的州资助，当地官员可以在学校上投入更多钱，也可以减少当地收入，或者两者都施行。用经济模型表示如下：

$$totalspend=\beta_0+\beta_1 totalstateaid$$

β_1 的预期符号是什么？你觉得它不可能是什么值？

β_1 会是正的（或者等于 0），但不会是负的。如果学校收到更多州赞助，学校官员会加大学校开支。β_1 的值会小于等于 1，但不会大于 1，因为学校开支的增长不可能大于州赞助的增长。

b. 然而，我们知道大一些且富有一些的州更有可能会负担得起大笔的学校赞助。测试以下方程：

$$totalspend_i=\beta_0+\beta_1 totalstateaid_i+\beta_2\ income_i+\beta_3\ population_i+\varepsilon_i$$

其中有多少变量的系数是统计显著的？

```
. regress totalspend totalstateaid income population

      Source |       SS       df       MS              Number of obs =      50
-------------+------------------------------           F(  3,    46) =  219.42
       Model |  1.4782e+09     3   492734984           Prob > F      =  0.0000
    Residual |   103300792    46  2245669.38           R-squared     =  0.9347
-------------+------------------------------           Adj R-squared =  0.9304
       Total |  1.5815e+09    49  32275627.4           Root MSE      =  1498.6

------------------------------------------------------------------------------
  totalspend |      Coef.   Std. Err.      t    P>|t|     [95% Conf. Interval]
-------------+----------------------------------------------------------------
totalstate~d |  -.3285301   .3020649    -1.09   0.282    -.9365553    .2794951
      income |   .0229457   .0093498     2.45   0.018     .0041256    .0417658
  population |   .3469648   .3112457     1.11   0.271    -.2795403    .9734699
       _cons |  -11.87355   309.6011    -0.04   0.970    -635.0683    611.3212
------------------------------------------------------------------------------
```

① 该练习经过修改，数据集从下书获取：Stephen J. Schmidt，*Econometrics*（McGraw-Hill，2005）。

只有 *income* 的系数是统计显著的，因为它的 p 值=0.018<0.05。其他两个变量 *totalstateaid* 和 *population* 的 p 值都大于 0.05，所以它们不是统计显著的。

c. 检验 $\beta_3=0$ 的零假设。你是否拒绝该零假设？估计以下回归方程：

$$totalspend_i=\beta_0+\beta_1 totalstateaid_i+\beta_2 \ income_i+\varepsilon_i$$

你估计的 β_1 和 β_2 改变了多少？它们的标准差改变了多少？

H_0：$\beta_3=0$

H_a：$\beta_3\neq0$

```
. test  population=0

 ( 1)  population = 0

       F(  1,    46) =    1.24
            Prob > F =    0.2707
```

因为 p 值=0.271>0.05，我们不拒绝零假设，所以 *population* 的系数不是统计显著的。

```
. regress  totalspend totalstateaid income

      Source |       SS       df       MS              Number of obs =      50
-------------+------------------------------           F(  2,    47) =  326.81
       Model |  1.4754e+09     2   737707137           Prob > F      =  0.0000
    Residual |   106091471    47  2257265.34           R-squared     =  0.9329
-------------+------------------------------           Adj R-squared =  0.9301
       Total |  1.5815e+09    49  32275627.4           Root MSE      =  1502.4

------------------------------------------------------------------------------
  totalspend |      Coef.   Std. Err.      t    P>|t|     [95% Conf. Interval]
-------------+----------------------------------------------------------------
totalstate~d |  -.2886033   .3007074    -0.96   0.342    -.8935486    .3163419
      income |    .032104   .0044751     7.17   0.000     .0231013    .0411068
       _cons |    111.357   289.9391     0.38   0.703    -471.9252    694.6392
------------------------------------------------------------------------------
```

$\hat{\beta}_1$增加了 −0.288 603 3−(−0.328 530 1)=0.039 926 8，它的标准差的变化为 0.300 707 4−0.302 064 9=−0.001 357 5。

$\hat{\beta}_2$增加了 0.032 104−0.022 945 7=0.009 158 3，它的标准差的变化为 0.004 475 1−0.009 349 8=−0.004 874 7。

它们并没有变化太多，因此，*population* 不是一个模型中必需的变量。

d. 假设我们（不正确地）将 *income* 而不是 *population* 从模型中删除了。估计下面的方程：

$$totalspend_i=\beta_0+\beta_1 totalstateaid_i+\beta_3 population_i+\varepsilon_i$$

用回归结果检验 $\beta_3=0$ 的零假设。这次你发现了什么？

```
. regress totalspend totalstateaid population

      Source |       SS       df       MS              Number of obs =      50
-------------+------------------------------           F(  2,    47) =  294.63
       Model |  1.4647e+09     2   732339812           Prob > F      =  0.0000
    Residual |   116826121    47  2485662.15           R-squared     =  0.9261
-------------+------------------------------           Adj R-squared =  0.9230
       Total |  1.5815e+09    49  32275627.4           Root MSE      =  1576.6

------------------------------------------------------------------------------
  totalspend |      Coef.   Std. Err.      t    P>|t|     [95% Conf. Interval]
-------------+----------------------------------------------------------------
totalstate~d |  -.0650133   .2970396    -0.22   0.828      -.66258    .5325534
  population |   1.018143   .1563272     6.51   0.000     .7036533    1.332633
       _cons |  -115.4309   322.6852    -0.36   0.722    -764.5897    533.7279
------------------------------------------------------------------------------
```

H_0：$\beta_3=0$

H_a：$\beta_3\neq 0$

```
. test  population=0

 ( 1)  population = 0

       F(  1,     47) =   42.42
            Prob > F =    0.0000
```

因为 p 值=0.000<0.05，所以我们拒绝零假设。因此，*population* 的系数是统计显著的。

e. 计算出 *population* 和 *income* 之间的修正系数，并且画出两个变量的散点图。你为什么在两个回归中得出了不同的结果？有更多人口的州会在学校上支出更多吗，或者不是？简单解释原因。

```
. correlate  population income
(obs=50)

             | popula~n   income
-------------+------------------
  population |   1.0000
      income |   0.9922   1.0000
```

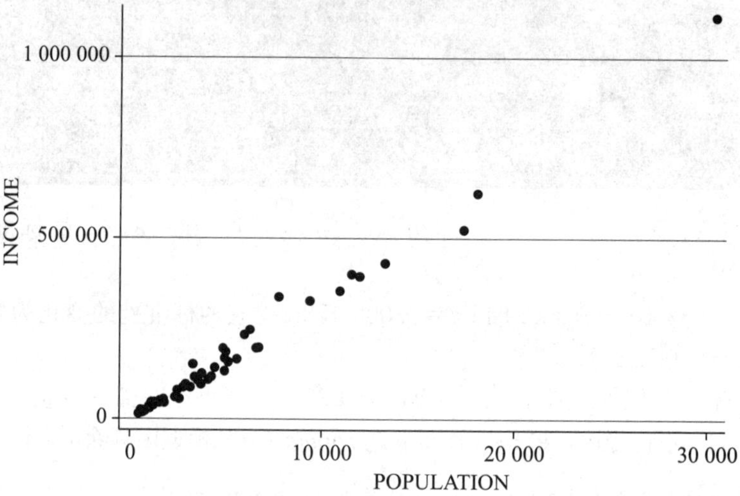

我们得出了不同结果是因为我们每次只用了 *income* 和 *population* 中的一个变量，并且它们是高度正相关的。如果我们同时使用这两个变量，模型就会有多重共线性的问题。通过删除 *income*，*population* 的系数变得统计显著了。同理，通过删除 *population*，*income* 的系数变得统计显著了。

根据最后的回归结果，$\hat{\beta}_3=1.018\,143$，表明当人口增加 1 000 人时，学校的平均支出会增加 1.018 143 百万美元。因此，有更多人口的州会在学校支出上花费更多的钱。

f. 假设我们没能控制住州面积这个变量，然后估计以下回归方程：

$$totalspend_i=\beta_0+\beta_1 totalstateaid_i+\varepsilon_i$$

检验 $\beta_1=0$ 的零假设。计算出 *totalstateaid*，*population* 和 *income* 之间的相关系数。

在这个例子中遗漏变量偏差是怎么影响估计 β_1 的？

```
. reg  totalspend totalstateaid

      Source |       SS       df       MS              Number of obs =      50
-------------+------------------------------           F(  1,    48) =  293.54
       Model |  1.3592e+09     1  1.3592e+09           Prob > F      =  0.0000
    Residual |   222262513    48  4630469.02           R-squared     =  0.8595
-------------+------------------------------           Adj R-squared =  0.8565
       Total |  1.5815e+09    49  32275627.4           Root MSE      =  2151.9

------------------------------------------------------------------------------
  totalspend |      Coef.   Std. Err.      t    P>|t|     [95% Conf. Interval]
-------------+----------------------------------------------------------------
totalstate~d |   1.803248   .1052493    17.13   0.000      1.59163    2.014866
       _cons |   939.0264   380.9753     2.46   0.017     173.0242    1705.029
------------------------------------------------------------------------------
```

H_0：$\beta_1=0$

H_a：$\beta_1\neq0$

```
. test  totalstateaid=0

 ( 1)  totalstateaid = 0

       F(  1,    48) =  293.54
            Prob > F =    0.0000
```

因为 p 值$=0.000<0.05$，所以我们拒绝零假设。因此 *totalstateaid* 是统计显著的。

```
. correlate  totalstateaid income population
(obs=50)

             | total~id   income popula~n
-------------+---------------------------
totalstate~d |   1.0000
      income |   0.9697   1.0000
  population |   0.9657   0.9922   1.0000
```

totalstateaid 和 *population* 之间的相关系数为 0.965 7，它和 *income* 之间的相关系数为0.969 7。这些系数都非常大，因此 *totalstateaid* 与 *population* 和 *income* 是高度相关的。将三个变量都包括在模型中会导致多重共线性的问题。将 *population* 和 *income* 删掉之后，*totalstateaid* 的系数变得统计显著了。

g. 做一个 F 检验来测试将 *income* 和 *population* 从回归模型中删掉是否可行。如果保持人口和州收入不变，州资助的增长会增加学校的开支吗？

```
. regress totalspend totalstateaid income population

      Source |       SS       df       MS              Number of obs =      50
-------------+------------------------------           F(  3,    46) =  219.42
       Model |  1.4782e+09     3   492734984           Prob > F      =  0.0000
    Residual |   103300792    46  2245669.38           R-squared     =  0.9347
-------------+------------------------------           Adj R-squared =  0.9304
       Total |  1.5815e+09    49  32275627.4           Root MSE      =  1498.6

------------------------------------------------------------------------------
  totalspend |      Coef.   Std. Err.      t    P>|t|     [95% Conf. Interval]
-------------+----------------------------------------------------------------
totalstate~d |  -.3285301   .3020649    -1.09   0.282    -.9365553    .2794951
      income |   .0229457   .0093498     2.45   0.018     .0041256    .0417658
  population |   .3469648   .3112457     1.11   0.271    -.2795403    .9734699
       _cons |  -11.87355   309.6011    -0.04   0.970    -635.0683    611.3212
------------------------------------------------------------------------------
```

```
. test  population= income=0

 ( 1)  population - income = 0
 ( 2)  population = 0

       F(  2,    46) =   26.49
            Prob > F =    0.0000
```

```
. test population=income

 ( 1)  - income + population = 0

       F(  1,    46) =    1.03
            Prob > F =    0.3158
```

根据第一个 F 检验，p 值$=0.000<0.05$，因此 *income* 和 *population* 是联合显著的。然而，在第二个 F 检验中，p 值$=0.315\ 8>0.05$，意味着它们对学校开支的作用相同。因此我们只能删除其中一个，不能将两个都删除。

根据 b 中的回归结果，当 *income* 和 *population* 保持不变时，州赞助上涨 1 单位，将会降低学校开支 0.328 530 1 单位，这与我们在 a 中的期望是相矛盾的。

（2）打开数据文件 **football. dta**[①]，其中包含有 30 个 NFL 队伍在 1997 赛季的样本数据并有四个变量：*attendance* 是该队伍在主场比赛中卖出的票的数量，*wins*，*losses* 和 *ties* 分别是 1997 赛季该队伍的胜场数量、败场数量和平局数量。

a. 卖出的票的数量由票的市场决定。假设买票者更想看一支赢了大部分比赛的球队而不是一支输了大部分比赛的球队。当一支球队的胜场数量增加时，它的需求曲线会如何变化？它的票的销售量（也就是出席情况）和票价会有什么变化？

需求曲线会向右移动，因为当一支球队的胜场数量增加时，会有更多的人想看他们的比赛。需求曲线向右移动后，该球队的票的销售量和票价都会增长。

b. 我们要用出场情况的数据来检验对于票的销售量的预测模型。考虑以下经济模型：

$$attendance=\beta_0+\beta_1 wins+\beta_2 losses+\beta_3 ties$$

β_1 的预期符号是什么？β_2 和 β_3 的预期符号是什么？

因为人们对胜场越多的队伍的票的需求越高，所以 β_1 应该是正的。相反，β_2 应该是负的，因为败场越多的队伍吸引的观众人数越少。对于平局越多的队伍，β_3 的预期符号为零。

c. 现在用 Stata 来估计以下回归方程：

$$attendance_i=\beta_0+\beta_1 wins_i+\beta_2 losses_i+\beta_3 ties_i+\varepsilon_i$$

发生了什么？为什么？（记住每支队伍在一个赛季中打 16 场比赛）

```
. reg  attendance wins losses ties
note: losses omitted because of collinearity

      Source |       SS       df       MS              Number of obs =      30
-------------+------------------------------           F(  2,    27) =    5.50
       Model |  5.6848e+10     2  2.8424e+10           Prob > F      =  0.0099
    Residual |  1.3956e+11    27  5.1688e+09           R-squared     =  0.2894
-------------+------------------------------           Adj R-squared =  0.2368
       Total |  1.9641e+11    29  6.7726e+09           Root MSE      =   71895

------------------------------------------------------------------------------
  attendance |      Coef.   Std. Err.      t    P>|t|     [95% Conf. Interval]
-------------+----------------------------------------------------------------
        wins |   12880.32   4593.183     2.80   0.009     3455.892    22304.76
      losses |  (omitted)
        ties |   74803.57   38681.87     1.93   0.064     -4565.08    154172.2
       _cons |   378352.3   39357.73     9.61   0.000     297596.9    459107.6
------------------------------------------------------------------------------
```

回归结果显示由于完全多重共线性的问题，$\hat{\beta}_2$ 被省略了。因为 $losses=16-wins-ties$，所以 *losses* 是完全取决于 *wins* 和 *ties* 的数量的。

---

① 该练习经过修改，数据集从下书获取：Stephen J. Schmidt，*Econometrics*（McGraw-Hill，2005）。

d. 用 Stata 估计以下回归方程：

$$attendance_i = \beta_0 + \beta_1 wins_i + \beta_2 ties_i + \varepsilon_i$$

如果一支队伍有 0 胜、0 平、16 负的记录，你预测它的观众出席情况会是怎样的？如果这支队伍多赢了一场比赛（并且少输了一场比赛），他们的观众出席情况增加多少？如果他们多打平一场比赛而不是输了呢？如果他们多打平一场比赛而不是赢了呢？

```
. reg   attendance wins ties

      Source |       SS       df       MS              Number of obs =      30
-------------+------------------------------           F(  2,    27) =    5.50
       Model |  5.6848e+10     2  2.8424e+10           Prob > F      =  0.0099
    Residual |  1.3956e+11    27  5.1688e+09           R-squared     =  0.2894
-------------+------------------------------           Adj R-squared =  0.2368
       Total |  1.9641e+11    29  6.7726e+09           Root MSE      =   71895

------------------------------------------------------------------------------
  attendance |      Coef.   Std. Err.      t    P>|t|     [95% Conf. Interval]
-------------+----------------------------------------------------------------
        wins |   12880.32   4593.183     2.80   0.009     3455.892    22304.76
        ties |   74803.57   38681.87     1.93   0.064     -4565.08    154172.2
       _cons |   378352.3   39357.73     9.61   0.000     297596.9    459107.6
------------------------------------------------------------------------------
```

如果 $wins=0$，$ties=0$ 并且 $losses=16$，那么出席的观众数量为 378 352.3 人。

如果一支球队多赢了一场比赛，观众数量会增加$\hat{\beta}_1=12\ 880.32$ 人。

如果一支球队多打平一场比赛而不是输了比赛，观众数量会增加$\hat{\beta}_2=74\ 803.57$ 人。

如果该球队多打平一场比赛而不是赢了比赛，观众的数量会增加$\hat{\beta}_2-\hat{\beta}_1=61\ 923.25$人。

e. 用 Stata 估计以下回归方程：

$$attendance_i = \beta_0 + \beta_1 losses_i + \beta_2 ties_i + \varepsilon_i$$

用估计结果回答 d 中相同的问题。你得到的结果相同还是不同？从原回归方程中删除 *wins* 或者 *losses* 有区别吗？

```
. reg   attendance losses ties

      Source |       SS       df       MS              Number of obs =      30
-------------+------------------------------           F(  2,    27) =    5.50
       Model |  5.6848e+10     2  2.8424e+10           Prob > F      =  0.0099
    Residual |  1.3956e+11    27  5.1688e+09           R-squared     =  0.2894
-------------+------------------------------           Adj R-squared =  0.2368
       Total |  1.9641e+11    29  6.7726e+09           Root MSE      =   71895

------------------------------------------------------------------------------
  attendance |      Coef.   Std. Err.      t    P>|t|     [95% Conf. Interval]
-------------+----------------------------------------------------------------
      losses |  -12880.32   4593.183    -2.80   0.009    -22304.76   -3455.892
        ties |   61923.24   38681.87     1.60   0.121     -17445.4    141291.9
       _cons |   584437.4   39357.73    14.85   0.000     503682.1    665192.8
------------------------------------------------------------------------------
```

如果 $wins=0$，$ties=0$ 和 $losses=16$，那么出席的观众数量为 $584\ 437.4-12\ 880.32\times 16=378\ 352.28$ 人。

如果一支球队多赢了一场比赛，观众数量会增加 $-\hat{\beta}_1=-(-12\ 880.32)=12\ 880.32$人。

如果一支球队多打平一场比赛而不是输了比赛，观众数量会增加$\hat{\beta}_2-\hat{\beta}_1=61\ 923.24+12\ 880.32=74\ 803.56$ 人。

如果该球队多打平一场比赛而不是赢了比赛，观众的数量会增加 $\hat{\beta}_2=61\ 923.24$ 人。

因此我们的结果与 d 中的结果一致，删除 *wins* 或者 *losses* 没有区别。

Chapter 6

Misspecification Analysis

Ⅰ. Omitted Variable Bias

Based on what we have learned in Chapter 5, we will further investigate some important specification issues that often arise in the empirical analysis. In this chapter, we begin, in this first section, by discussing the problem of omitted variable bias which occurs when a multiple regression model suffers from the misspecification of functional form and does not properly account for the relationship between the dependent variable and independent variables.

As we know, typically the formation of an econometric model begins from a formal economic model, economic theory, or even intuition. What happens if we include a variable in our specification that does not belong? It is very easy to prove that there is no effect on our parameter estimates and OLS remains unbiased. However, what happens if we exclude a variable from our specification that does belong? This time, we'd better go over the following proof in order to understand why OLS will usually be biased, if a key variable fails to enter the regression model.

Suppose the true model is given as:

$$y=\beta_0+\beta_1 x_1+\beta_2 x_2+u$$

but we estimate $\tilde{y}=\tilde{\beta}_0+\tilde{\beta}_1 x_1$, then:

$$\tilde{\beta}_1=\frac{\sum(x_{i1}-\bar{x}_1)y_i}{\sum(x_{i1}-\bar{x}_1)^2}$$

Recall the true model, so that:

$$y_i=\beta_0+\beta_1 x_{i1}+\beta_2 x_{i2}+u_i$$

so the numerator becomes:

$$\sum(x_{i1}-\bar{x}_1)(\beta_0+\beta_1 x_{i1}+\beta_2 x_{i2}+u_i)=\beta_1\sum(x_{i1}-\bar{x}_1)^2+\beta_2\sum(x_{i1}-\bar{x}_1)x_{i2}+\sum(x_{i1}-\bar{x}_1)u_i$$

As a result,

$$\tilde{\beta}_1 = \beta_1 + \beta_2 \frac{\sum (x_{i1} - \overline{x}_1) x_{i2}}{\sum (x_{i1} - \overline{x}_1)^2} + \frac{\sum (x_{i1} - \overline{x}_1) u_i}{\sum (x_{i1} - \overline{x}_1)^2}$$

since $E(u_i)=0$, taking expectations we have:

$$E(\tilde{\beta}_1) = \beta_1 + \beta_2 \frac{\sum (x_{i1} - \overline{x}_1) x_{i2}}{\sum (x_{i1} - \overline{x}_1)^2}$$

Consider the regression of x_2 on x_1:

$$\tilde{x}_2 = \tilde{\delta}_0 + \tilde{\delta}_1 x_1$$

then

$$\tilde{\delta}_1 = \frac{\sum (x_{i1} - \overline{x}_1) x_{i2}}{\sum (x_{i1} - \overline{x}_1)^2}$$

so $E(\tilde{\beta}_1)=\beta_1+\beta_2\tilde{\delta}_1$.

The above proof shows that if we ignore the existence of an important variable that is supposed to be included in the OLS regression model, the expected value of $\tilde{\beta}_1$ depends on the values taken by β_1, β_2, and $\tilde{\delta}_1$. Here, $\tilde{\delta}_1$ measures the correlation between x_1 and x_2. The following table summarizes the direction of bias:

	$\text{Corr}(x_1, x_2)>0$	$\text{Corr}(x_1, x_2)<0$
$\beta_2>0$	Positive bias	Negative bias
$\beta_2<0$	Negative bias	Positive bias

In short, if correlations between x_1, x_2 and y are in the same direction, bias will be positive. If correlations between x_1, x_2 and y are in the opposite direction, bias will be negative.

Note: only under the following two cases, bias is equal to zero.

i) $\beta_2=0$, that is x_2 doesn't really belong in the model.

ii) x_1 and x_2 are uncorrelated in the sample.

Ⅱ. Multicollinearity

2.1 Perfect Multicollinearity

One of the most basic problems in econometrics is the existence of multicollinearity in the regression. What exactly do we mean by multicollinearity? Remember that the assumption we want to focus on is: No explanatory variable is a perfect linear function of any other explanatory variables (no perfect multicollinearity). ①

To do some meaningful analysis of multicollinearity, please find and upload **survey. dta** onto Stata.

Suppose that we are trying to predict your movie-watching behavior over the past month. We might start by hypothesizing that: # *movies seen*=*f*(*gender*, *knowledge of movies*) . We are testing whether your interest leads to actual changes in the number of movies that you watch.

Since knowledge of movies is unobservable, we decide to proxy "knowledge" with the following variables where "answering question # right" is a dummy variable taking on the value of 1 if you were correct and 0 otherwise. More specifically, the model is rewritten as:

movies=*f*(*gender*, *answering question* 1 *right*, *answering question* 2 *right*, *answering question* 3 *right*, *answering question* 4 *right*, *answering question* 5 *right*, *answering question* 6 *right*, *total number correct*) .

We then use linear regression and get the following results in Stata:

. gen *total*=*theater*+*tv*

. gen *correct*=*q*1+*q*2+*q*3+*q*4+*q*5+*q*6

```
reg total q1 q2 q3 q4 q5 q6 correct

      Source |       SS       df       MS              Number of obs =      53
-------------+------------------------------           F(  6,    46) =    3.32
       Model |  97.6680072     6  16.2780012           Prob > F      =  0.0085
    Residual |  225.803691    46  4.90877589           R-squared     =  0.3019
-------------+------------------------------           Adj R-squared =  0.2109
       Total |  323.471698    52  6.22060958           Root MSE      =  2.2156

------------------------------------------------------------------------------
       total |      Coef.   Std. Err.      t    P>|t|     [95% Conf. Interval]
-------------+----------------------------------------------------------------
          q1 |    .612906   1.125354     0.54   0.589    -1.652314    2.878126
          q2 |  -1.959375   1.291024    -1.52   0.136    -4.558072    .6393213
          q3 |  -.4362873   1.318433    -0.33   0.742    -3.090156    2.217581
          q4 |   .1115949   1.907238     0.06   0.954    -3.727476    3.950666
          q5 |   .2526805   1.290547     0.20   0.846    -2.345056    2.850417
          q6 |  (dropped)
     correct |   .9601301   1.080071     0.89   0.379     -1.21394      3.1342
       _cons |   1.229942    .945136     1.30   0.200    -.6725181    3.132402
------------------------------------------------------------------------------
```

Why did no output appear for question 6?

The reason is perfect multicollinearity. If you notice, the total number correct is a perfect linear combination of the six quiz variables—it is just the sum of the other six variables. This is called perfect-multicollinearity. Anytime the explanatory variables are linear combinations of each other, the computer will exclude one automatically.

Suppose that we look at movie-going behavior as a function of gender alone: # *movies*=*f*(*gender*) . We could also write this as: # *movies*=*f*(*male*, *female*) .

Let's run this regression in Stata.

① This example is inspired by Eric Bettinger at Weatherhead School of Management, Case Western Reserve University. Data is collected from the student survey in my Econometrics class.

```
gen female=1-male
reg total female male

      Source |       SS       df       MS              Number of obs =      53
-------------+------------------------------           F(  1,    51) =    0.00
       Model |  .025269542     1  .025269542           Prob > F      =  0.9499
    Residual |  323.446429    51  6.34208683           R-squared     =  0.0001
-------------+------------------------------           Adj R-squared = -0.0195
       Total |  323.471698    52  6.22060958           Root MSE      =  2.5184

------------------------------------------------------------------------------
       total |      Coef.   Std. Err.      t    P>|t|     [95% Conf. Interval]
-------------+----------------------------------------------------------------
      female |   .0446429   .7072442     0.06   0.950    -1.375209    1.464495
        male |  (dropped)
       _cons |     3.8125   .4451856     8.56   0.000     2.918753    4.706247
------------------------------------------------------------------------------
```

Notice that it threw out the "male" variable. Why? It is perfectly collinear. The constant acts as a column of ones. Male is a one if you are a male and zero otherwise. Female is the opposite. If you add male and female together, you would get a variable of ones—which is the constant. As a result, if we are using mutually-exclusive dummy variables, perfect-multicollinearity prevents us from using each variable. We have to exclude one dummy variable category (or exclude the constant term).

Let's run the same regression as above without the constant term to reaffirm this point:

```
reg total female male, noconstant

      Source |       SS       df       MS              Number of obs =      53
-------------+------------------------------           F(  2,    51) =   61.30
       Model |  777.553571     2  388.776786           Prob > F      =  0.0000
    Residual |  323.446429    51  6.34208683           R-squared     =  0.7062
-------------+------------------------------           Adj R-squared =  0.6947
       Total |        1101    53  20.7735849           Root MSE      =  2.5184

------------------------------------------------------------------------------
       total |      Coef.   Std. Err.      t    P>|t|     [95% Conf. Interval]
-------------+----------------------------------------------------------------
      female |   3.857143    .549549     7.02   0.000     2.753877    4.960409
        male |     3.8125   .4451856     8.56   0.000     2.918753    4.706247
------------------------------------------------------------------------------
```

2. 2 Imperfect Multicollinearity

So far we have looked at perfect multicollinearity. Its solution was easy—just exclude the extra variable. Let's turn our attention to the less clear case—imperfect multicollinearity, where variables are highly, but not perfectly related. In fact, the more multicollinear two variables are, the harder it is to distinguish their effects on the dependent variable, the larger the standard errors of the estimates of their parameters will be.

Suppose we are deciding between these models:

Model A:

movies = *f*(*gender*, *answering question* 1 *right*, *answering question* 2 *right*, *answering question* 3 *right*, *answering question* 4 *right*, *answering question* 5 *right*, *answering question* 6 *right*),

or

Model B:

\# *movies*=*f*(*gender*, *total number correct*).

Which is the better model to choose? The answer is not as clear-cut as Model A or Model B. We will have to look into the actual questions to gain some insight. Let's start by looking at a model where we regress the total number of movies seen on responses to question 6 only.

```
reg total q6

      Source |       SS       df       MS              Number of obs =      53
-------------+------------------------------           F(  1,    51) =    5.92
       Model |  33.6640058     1  33.6640058           Prob > F      =  0.0185
    Residual |  289.807692    51  5.68250377           R-squared     =  0.1041
-------------+------------------------------           Adj R-squared =  0.0865
       Total |  323.471698    52  6.22060958           Root MSE      =  2.3838

------------------------------------------------------------------------------
       total |      Coef.   Std. Err.      t    P>|t|     [95% Conf. Interval]
-------------+----------------------------------------------------------------
          q6 |   1.807692   .7426967     2.43   0.018     .3166665    3.298718
       _cons |        2.5   .6370974     3.92   0.000     1.220974    3.779026
------------------------------------------------------------------------------
```

It appears in this simple model that the last question has good explanatory power in our model. But we may be worried that we have left out a number of other explanatory variables that belong. Suppose that we add a few more variables. In particular, we are going to add responses to questions 2, 3, and 4.

```
reg total q6 q2 q3 q4

      Source |       SS       df       MS              Number of obs =      53
-------------+------------------------------           F(  4,    48) =    2.28
       Model |  51.7286917     4  12.9321729           Prob > F      =  0.0739
    Residual |  271.743006    48  5.66131263           R-squared     =  0.1599
-------------+------------------------------           Adj R-squared =  0.0899
       Total |  323.471698    52  6.22060958           Root MSE      =  2.3794

------------------------------------------------------------------------------
       total |      Coef.   Std. Err.      t    P>|t|     [95% Conf. Interval]
-------------+----------------------------------------------------------------
          q6 |   .4750081   1.114083     0.43   0.672    -1.765006    2.715022
          q2 |  -.6028077   .7175667    -0.84   0.405    -2.045572    .8399569
          q3 |   .5823597   .6890101     0.85   0.402     -.802988    1.967707
          q4 |   1.424339   1.002281     1.42   0.162    -.5908817    3.439559
       _cons |   2.765649   .8464652     3.27   0.002     1.063717    4.467581
------------------------------------------------------------------------------
```

Now it appears that answers to question 6 are not as important. The *t*-stat is no longer significant. What happened? The answer is imperfect multicollinearity. Answers to questions 2, 3, and 4 are likely explaining the same information as the answer to question 6. When this imperfect multicollinearity exists, the variance of the coefficients is overstated, making the *t*-stats too small and making things look non-significant.

If we look at the standard errors on *q*6 in these two models, they change. In the first model, they are at 0.742 7 while in the second model they go up to 1.1. How can we see it? We can also look at the correlations between the included variables.

```
. corr q6 q2 q3 q4
(obs=53)

             |       q6       q2       q3       q4
-------------+------------------------------------
          q6 |   1.0000
          q2 |  -0.1802   1.0000
          q3 |   0.0705   0.2305   1.0000
          q4 |   0.7396  -0.2034  -0.0222   1.0000
```

Notice that the answers to question 4 have a high correlation (0.74) with the answers to question 6. When we include it, it "knocks out" our relationship with question 6 by trying to "reexplain" some of the variance.

How to detect multicollinearity?

i) In the case of two variables, we look at a scatter diagram. If two variables are highly correlated, they will be tightly grouped along a line in the plot.

ii) We can look at the correlation coefficient of the variables in question. If two variables are highly correlated, the correlation coefficient will be close to 1 or -1.

iii) Regress x_k on all other x variables in the model to get R_k^2. If $R_k^2=1$, there is perfect multicollinearity. If R_k^2 is close to 1, there is multicollinearity. If R_k^2 is close to 0, there is no problem of multicollinearity.

iv) We can examine the variance inflation factors (VIF). In Stata, type "vif" to test for multicollinearity. The VIF value ranges from 1.0 to infinity. VIFs greater than 10.0 are generally seen as indicative of severe multicollinearity. 1/VIF is tolerance which ranges from 0.0 to 1.0, with 1.0 being the absence of multicollinearity.

If the problem of multicollinearity exists, how do we fix the problem of imperfect multicollinearity?

i) Keep the variables in the equation, but we can't generalize about their separate effects. For instance, $y=\beta_0+\beta_1x_1+\beta_2x_2+\mu$, where x_1 and x_2 are highly correlated. We can measure their joint impact on y by computing $\Delta y=\beta_1\Delta x_1+\beta_2\Delta x_2$.

ii) Leave out one or more of the offending variables.

iii) Combine variables if we know their specific linear functional form. For instance, $y=\beta_0+\beta_1x_1+\beta_2x_2+\mu$, where x_1 and x_2 are highly correlated. If we know that $x_1=f(x_2)$, then we can combine x_1 and x_2 simply by plugging the function of x_1 into the original model.

iv) Collect more data to increase the sample size, then hopefully, we can decrease such a high correlation between the offending variables.

Ⅲ. Additional Computer Exercises

(1) Open the data file **schoolspend.dta**[①], which contains data on 50 U.S. states for seven variables: *totalspend* is the amount of money that school districts in the state spend on education from kindergarten through 12th grade, measured in millions of dollars; *totalstateaid* is the amount of money provided by the state to school districts, measured in millions of dollars; *income* is the total state income in millions of dollars; *population* is the total population of the state in thousands; and *elderly*, *minority*, and *schoolage* are the

---

① This exercise is modified and the data set is collected from the book—*Econometrics* written by Stephen J. Schmidt (McGraw-Hill, 2005).

fraction of the state's population that are 65 or over, members of ethnic minorities, and ages 6 to 17, respectively.

a. School spending decisions are made by school district officials, based on revenue raised locally and state aid. If more state aid is available, local officials could either spend more money on schools, cut back on local revenue, or do some of both. In an economic model of the form:

$$totalspend = \beta_0 + \beta_1 totalstateaid$$

What values would you expect β_1 to take, and what values would you expect it not to take?

β_1 is expected to be positive (or equal to 0), but not negative. As schools receive more state aid, the school officials will spend more money on schools, or they do not change spending on schools but cut back on local revenue, or both. Also, β_1 would be smaller than or equal to 1, not greater than 1, because school spending cannot increase by greater amount than the increased amount of state aid.

b. However, we also know that bigger and richer states will be able to afford to spend more money on school aid as well. Estimate the equation:

$$totalspend_i = \beta_0 + \beta_1 totalstateaid_i + \beta_2 income_i + \beta_3 population_i + \varepsilon_i$$

How many of the variables are statistically significant?

```
. regress totalspend totalstateaid income population

      Source |       SS           df       MS      Number of obs   =        50
-------------+----------------------------------   F(  3,      46)  =    219.42
       Model |  1.4782e+09         3   492734984   Prob > F        =    0.0000
    Residual |   103300792        46  2245669.38   R-squared       =    0.9347
-------------+----------------------------------   Adj R-squared   =    0.9304
       Total |  1.5815e+09        49  32275627.4   Root MSE        =    1498.6

------------------------------------------------------------------------------
  totalspend |      Coef.   Std. Err.      t    P>|t|     [95% Conf. Interval]
-------------+----------------------------------------------------------------
totalstate~d |  -.3285301   .3020649    -1.09   0.282    -.9365553    .2794951
      income |   .0229457   .0093498     2.45   0.018     .0041256    .0417658
  population |   .3469648   .3112457     1.11   0.271    -.2795403    .9734699
       _cons |  -11.87355   309.6011    -0.04   0.970    -635.0683    611.3212
------------------------------------------------------------------------------
```

According to the regression result, only *income* is statistically significant, since its p-value=0.018<5%. The other two variables, *totalstateaid* and *population*, have p-values greater than 5%. Therefore, we cannot reject the null hypothesis and conclude that they are not statistically significant.

c. Test the null hypothesis that $\beta_3 = 0$. Do you reject or fail to reject? Estimate the regression equation:

$$totalspend_i = \beta_0 + \beta_1 totalstateaid_i + \beta_2 income_i + \varepsilon_i$$

How much have your estimates of β_1 and β_2 changed? How much have their standard error changed?

$H_0: \beta_3=0$

$H_a: \beta_3\neq 0$

```
. test  population=0

 ( 1)  population = 0

       F(  1,    46) =    1.24
            Prob > F =    0.2707
```

Since the p-value$=0.271>a=5\%$, we do not reject H_0. Hence, *population* is not statistically significant.

```
. regress  totalspend totalstateaid income

      Source |       SS       df       MS              Number of obs =      50
-------------+------------------------------           F(  2,    47) =  326.81
       Model |  1.4754e+09     2   737707137           Prob > F      =  0.0000
    Residual |   106091471    47  2257265.34           R-squared     =  0.9329
-------------+------------------------------           Adj R-squared =  0.9301
       Total |  1.5815e+09    49  32275627.4           Root MSE      =  1502.4

------------------------------------------------------------------------------
  totalspend |      Coef.   Std. Err.      t    P>|t|     [95% Conf. Interval]
-------------+----------------------------------------------------------------
totalstate~d |  -.2886033   .3007074    -0.96   0.342    -.8935486    .3163419
      income |    .032104   .0044751     7.17   0.000     .0231013    .0411068
       _cons |    111.357   289.9391     0.38   0.703    -471.9252    694.6392
------------------------------------------------------------------------------
```

$\hat{\beta}_1$ increased by $-0.288\,603\,3-(-0.328\,530\,1)=0.039\,926\,8$, and its standard error changed by $0.300\,707\,4-0.302\,064\,9=-0.001\,357\,5$.

$\hat{\beta}_2$ increased by $0.032\,104-0.022\,945\,7=0.009\,158\,3$, and its standard error changed by $0.004\,475\,1-0.009\,349\,8=-0.004\,874\,7$.

They did not change a lot, so *population* is not a necessary variable in our model.

d. Suppose we (incorrectly) dropped *income* from the model instead of *population*. Estimate the equation:

$$totalspend_i=\beta_0+\beta_1 totalstateaid_i+\beta_3 population_i+\varepsilon_i$$

Use the results of this equation to test the null hypothesis that $\beta_3=0$. What do you find this time?

```
. regress totalspend totalstateaid population

      Source |       SS       df       MS              Number of obs =      50
-------------+------------------------------           F(  2,    47) =  294.63
       Model |  1.4647e+09     2   732339812           Prob > F      =  0.0000
    Residual |   116826121    47  2485662.15           R-squared     =  0.9261
-------------+------------------------------           Adj R-squared =  0.9230
       Total |  1.5815e+09    49  32275627.4           Root MSE      =  1576.6

------------------------------------------------------------------------------
  totalspend |      Coef.   Std. Err.      t    P>|t|     [95% Conf. Interval]
-------------+----------------------------------------------------------------
totalstate~d |  -.0650133   .2970396    -0.22   0.828      -.66258    .5325534
  population |   1.018143   .1563272     6.51   0.000     .7036533    1.332633
       _cons |  -115.4309   322.6852    -0.36   0.722    -764.5897    533.7279
------------------------------------------------------------------------------
```

$H_0: \beta_3=0$

$H_a: \beta_3\neq 0$

```
. test  population=0

 ( 1)  population = 0

       F(  1,    47) =   42.42
            Prob > F =    0.0000
```

Since p-value=0.000<5%, we reject H_0, so *population* is statistically significant.

e. Calculate the correction coefficient between *population* and *income*, and graph a scatterplot of the two variables. Why do you get different results in the two regressions? Do states with larger populations spend more on schooling, or not? Briefly explain why.

```
. correlate  population income
(obs=50)

             | popula~n   income
-------------+------------------
  population |   1.0000
      income |   0.9922   1.0000
```

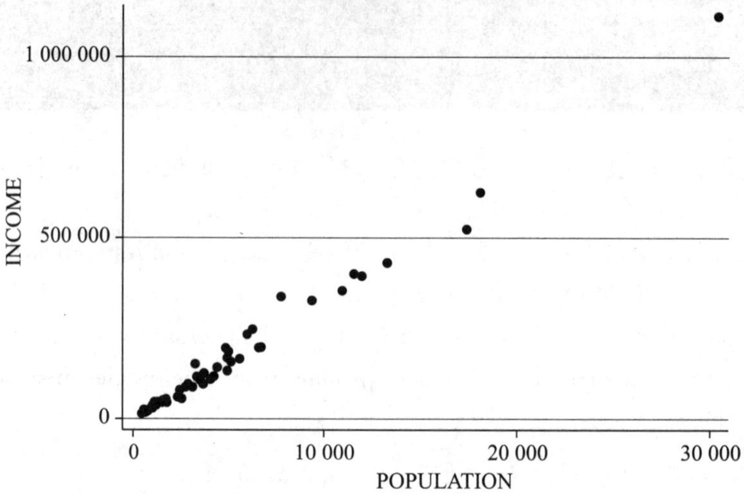

We get different results because we used only one variable between *income* and *population* each time, and they are highly positively correlated. Using both variables, our model has severe problem of multicollinearity. If we drop *income*, *population* then became statistically significant. If we drop *population*, *income* then became statistically significant.

According to the last regression result, $\hat{\beta}_3=1.018\ 143$, which indicates that when population increase by 1 unit, school spending increases by 1.018 143 units. So, states with larger populations spend more on schooling, which makes sense because states with larger population would have a larger number of students, and then require more schooling spending.

f. Suppose we had failed to control for the size of the state in our analysis at all, and estimated the regression:

$$totalspend_i=\beta_0+\beta_1 totalstateaid_i+\varepsilon_i$$

Estimate this equation and test whether $\beta_1=0$. Calculate the correlation coefficients between *totalstateaid* and *population* and *income*. How does omitted variable bias affect our estimate of β_1 in this case?

```
. reg totalspend totalstateaid

      Source |       SS       df       MS              Number of obs =      50
-------------+------------------------------           F(  1,    48) =  293.54
       Model |  1.3592e+09     1  1.3592e+09           Prob > F      =  0.0000
    Residual |   222262513    48  4630469.02           R-squared     =  0.8595
-------------+------------------------------           Adj R-squared =  0.8565
       Total |  1.5815e+09    49  32275627.4           Root MSE      =  2151.9

------------------------------------------------------------------------------
  totalspend |      Coef.   Std. Err.      t    P>|t|     [95% Conf. Interval]
-------------+----------------------------------------------------------------
totalstate~d |   1.803248   .1052493    17.13   0.000      1.59163    2.014866
       _cons |   939.0264   380.9753     2.46   0.017     173.0242    1705.029
------------------------------------------------------------------------------
```

$H_0: \beta_1=0$

$H_a: \beta_1\neq 0$

```
. test totalstateaid=0

 ( 1)  totalstateaid = 0

       F(  1,    48) =  293.54
            Prob > F =    0.0000
```

Since p-value$=0.000<5\%$, we reject H_0, so *totalstateaid* is statistically significant.

```
. correlate totalstateaid income population
(obs=50)

             | total~id   income popula~n
-------------+---------------------------
totalstate~d |   1.0000
      income |   0.9697   1.0000
  population |   0.9657   0.9922   1.0000
```

Totalstateaid has a 0.965 7 correlation coefficient with *population*, and has a 0.969 7 correlation coefficient with *income*. These are extremely high, so *totalstateaid* is highly correlated to *population* and *income*. Including all three variables in the model would cause multicollinearity problem. After dropping two of them, *population* and *income*, in this model, *totalstateaid* became statistically significant.

g. Perform an F test to test whether it is acceptable to drop both *income* and *population* from the original regression. Does an increase in state aid, holding population and state income constant, increase spending on schooling or not?

```
. regress totalspend totalstateaid income population

      Source |       SS       df       MS              Number of obs =      50
-------------+------------------------------           F(  3,    46) =  219.42
       Model |  1.4782e+09     3   492734984           Prob > F      =  0.0000
    Residual |   103300792    46  2245669.38           R-squared     =  0.9347
-------------+------------------------------           Adj R-squared =  0.9304
       Total |  1.5815e+09    49  32275627.4           Root MSE      =  1498.6

------------------------------------------------------------------------------
  totalspend |      Coef.   Std. Err.      t    P>|t|     [95% Conf. Interval]
-------------+----------------------------------------------------------------
totalstate~d |  -.3285301   .3020649    -1.09   0.282    -.9365553    .2794951
      income |   .0229457   .0093498     2.45   0.018     .0041256    .0417658
  population |   .3469648   .3112457     1.11   0.271    -.2795403    .9734699
       _cons |  -11.87355   309.6011    -0.04   0.970    -635.0683    611.3212
------------------------------------------------------------------------------
```

```
. test  population= income=0

 ( 1)  population - income = 0
 ( 2)  population = 0

       F(  2,    46) =   26.49
            Prob > F =    0.0000
```

```
. test population=income

 ( 1)  - income + population = 0

       F(  1,    46) =    1.03
            Prob > F =    0.3158
```

According to the first F-test, since p-value$=0.000<0.05$, so *income* and *population* jointly have significant effects on school spending. However, from the second F-test, we can see that p-value$=0.3158>0.05$, which means they have the same effects on school spending. So, we cannot drop both *income* and *population*, but we can drop one of them since they have the same effect.

According to the regression results in part b, holding *population* and *income* constant, a 1 unit increase in state aid will actually decrease school spending by $\hat{\beta}_1=0.3285301$ unit, which contradicts with our expectation in part a.

(2) Open the data file **football. dta**[①], which contains data on four variables measured on a sample of 30 NFL teams for the 1997 season: *attendance* is the number of tickets sold for the team's home games, and *wins*, *losses*, and *ties* are the team's number of wins, losses, and ties for the 1997 season, respectively.

a. The number of tickets sold is determined by the market for tickets. Assume that buyers have a higher demand to see a team that wins most of its games than they do to see a team that loses most of its games. When a team's number of wins increases, which way does its demand curve shift? What should happen to its ticket sales (that is, attendance) and ticket prices?

The demand curve would shift to the right, because as the team's number of wins increases, buyers will have a higher demand to watch the team's games. As the demand curve shifts to the right, both the team's equilibrium ticket sales and ticket price will increase.

b. We will use that data on attendance to test the model's prediction about ticket sales. Consider the economic model:

$$attendance=\beta_0+\beta_1 wins+\beta_2 losses+\beta_3 ties$$

What sign do you expect for β_1? What signs do you expect for β_2 and β_3?

Since people have a higher demand to see a team with more wins, the sign for β_1 is expected to be positive. Reversely, teams with a lot of losses are less likely to attract people to watch their games. Then, a negative sign for β_2 is expected. It follows that the sign for

① This exercise is modified and the data set is collected from the book—*Econometrics* written by Stephen J. Schmidt (McGraw-Hill, 2005).

β_3 is expected to be zero.

c. Now use Stata to estimate the regression equation:

$$attendance_i = \beta_0 + \beta_1 wins_i + \beta_2 losses_i + \beta_3 ties_i + \varepsilon_i$$

What happens, and why? (Remember that each team plays a total of 16 games in a season.)

```
. reg   attendance wins losses ties
note: losses omitted because of collinearity

      Source |       SS           df       MS      Number of obs   =        30
-------------+----------------------------------   F(  2,     27)  =      5.50
       Model |  5.6848e+10         2  2.8424e+10   Prob > F        =    0.0099
    Residual |  1.3956e+11        27  5.1688e+09   R-squared       =    0.2894
-------------+----------------------------------   Adj R-squared   =    0.2368
       Total |  1.9641e+11        29  6.7726e+09   Root MSE        =     71895

------------------------------------------------------------------------------
  attendance |      Coef.   Std. Err.      t    P>|t|     [95% Conf. Interval]
-------------+----------------------------------------------------------------
        wins |   12880.32   4593.183     2.80   0.009     3455.892    22304.76
      losses |  (omitted)
        ties |   74803.57   38681.87     1.93   0.064     -4565.08    154172.2
       _cons |   378352.3   39357.73     9.61   0.000     297596.9    459107.6
------------------------------------------------------------------------------
```

After regressing attendance on all three variables, it turns out that the estimated coefficient on *losses* is omitted because of perfect multicollinearity. We know that each team only plays 16 games in total. The regression omitted variable *losses* because it's dependent on the other two independent variables, *wins* and *ties*. That is, $losses = 16 - wins - ties$.

d. Instead, use Stata to estimate the equation:

$$attendance_i = \beta_0 + \beta_1 wins_i + \beta_2 ties_i + \varepsilon_i$$

What attendance do you predict a team would get if it had a record of 0 wins, 0 ties, and 16 losses? How much would attendance rise if it won an additional game (and therefore had one fewer loss)? How much would it rise if it tied one game instead of losing it? How much would attendance rise if it tied one game instead of winning it?

```
. reg   attendance wins ties

      Source |       SS           df       MS      Number of obs   =        30
-------------+----------------------------------   F(  2,     27)  =      5.50
       Model |  5.6848e+10         2  2.8424e+10   Prob > F        =    0.0099
    Residual |  1.3956e+11        27  5.1688e+09   R-squared       =    0.2894
-------------+----------------------------------   Adj R-squared   =    0.2368
       Total |  1.9641e+11        29  6.7726e+09   Root MSE        =     71895

------------------------------------------------------------------------------
  attendance |      Coef.   Std. Err.      t    P>|t|     [95% Conf. Interval]
-------------+----------------------------------------------------------------
        wins |   12880.32   4593.183     2.80   0.009     3455.892    22304.76
        ties |   74803.57   38681.87     1.93   0.064     -4565.08    154172.2
       _cons |   378352.3   39357.73     9.61   0.000     297596.9    459107.6
------------------------------------------------------------------------------
```

According to the regression result, if $wins = 0$, $ties = 0$ and $losses = 16$, then the attendance a team would get is 378 352.3 persons.

If the team won an additional game, the attendance would rise by $\hat{\beta}_1 = 12\ 880.32$ persons.

If the team tied one game instead of losing it, the attendance would rise by $\hat{\beta}_2 =$ 74 803. 57 persons.

If the team tied one game instead of winning it, the change in attendance would rise by $\hat{\beta}_2 - \hat{\beta}_1 = 61\ 923.25$ persons.

e. Suppose we instead used Stata to estimate the equation:

$$attendance_i = \beta_0 + \beta_1 losses_i + \beta_2 ties_i + \varepsilon_i$$

Use these estimates to answer the same questions as in part d. Do you get different answers, or the same answers? Does it matter whether you drop *wins* or *losses* from the original regression equation?

```
. reg attendance losses ties

      Source |       SS       df       MS              Number of obs =      30
-------------+------------------------------           F(  2,    27) =    5.50
       Model |  5.6848e+10     2  2.8424e+10           Prob > F      =  0.0099
    Residual |  1.3956e+11    27  5.1688e+09           R-squared     =  0.2894
-------------+------------------------------           Adj R-squared =  0.2368
       Total |  1.9641e+11    29  6.7726e+09           Root MSE      =   71895

------------------------------------------------------------------------------
  attendance |      Coef.   Std. Err.      t    P>|t|     [95% Conf. Interval]
-------------+----------------------------------------------------------------
      losses |  -12880.32   4593.183    -2.80   0.009    -22304.76   -3455.892
        ties |   61923.24   38681.87     1.60   0.121     -17445.4    141291.9
       _cons |   584437.4   39357.73    14.85   0.000     503682.1    665192.8
------------------------------------------------------------------------------
```

According to the regression results, if *wins*=0, *ties*=0 and *losses*=16, then the attendance a team would get is $584\ 437.4 - 12\ 880.32 \times 16 = 378\ 352.28$ persons.

If the team won an additional game, the attendance would rise by $-\hat{\beta}_1 = -(-12\ 880.32) =$ 12 880. 32 persons.

If the team tied one game instead of losing it, the attendance would rise by $\hat{\beta}_2 - \hat{\beta}_1 =$ $61\ 923.24 + 12\ 880.32 = 74\ 803.56$ persons.

If the team tied one game instead of winning it, the change in attendance would rise by $\hat{\beta}_2 = 61\ 923.24$ persons.

So, we get the same answers as those in part d. Dropping *wins* or *losses* from the original regression equation does not matter.

第 7 章

异方差问题的检验和解决方法

Ⅰ. 什么是异方差问题?

首先我们回忆一下同方差性的假设。它意味着对于每一个解释变量，随机误差项的条件方差是固定不变的。如果这一假设不成立，也就是说，如果根据每一个解释变量取值的不同，随机误差项的条件方差随之而有所不同，那么这些随机误差具有异方差性。

理论上，当随机误差项的条件方差随观测值的不同而有所变化时，异方差问题就会出现，现在的模型变成：

$$y_i = \beta_0 + \beta_1 x_i + \varepsilon_i$$

随机误差项的条件方差不再被假设为固定不变，即成为：

$$\mathrm{var}(\varepsilon_i) = \sigma_i^2$$

为什么我们会观测到异方差性?异方差问题最常出现在横截面数据模型里。我们考虑下面的例子。有 100 名学生报名参加打字班——其中一些学生先前有打字的经验，有些没有任何打字的经验。在第一堂课后，我们将会发现学生打字出现的错误数量非常分散。在最后一堂课后，这种分散将会变小。因此，误差方差不是固定的：它随着时间的增加而减小。

我们为什么要担心异方差问题?即使我们没有同方差假设，OLS 仍然是无偏一致的。但是，如果我们有异方差问题，估计值的标准差会有偏差。换句话说，OLS 不再是 BLUE。如果标准差有偏差，我们不能用通常的 t 统计，F 统计，或 LM 统计进行各种假设检验和推论。

Ⅱ. 如何检测异方差问题?

2.1 绘制图表

第一个检测异方差的简单方法就是画图。在 Stata 中，进行 OLS 回归之后，我们可以用“rvpplot”来检测异方差的问题。一般来说，当 x 值沿着 X 轴增加时，如果回归残差所形成的上下两条临界带越来越偏离（即变得更宽），误差项的方差也随之越来越大。另一方面，如果两条临界带越来越收敛（即变得更窄），误差项的方差也随之越来越小。如果两条临界带和 X 轴平行，我们则没有证据证明有异方差问题的存在。

例如，我们想研究两个变量之间的关系，在线性模型里，我们假定上司数目为 y 且被监督的工人数量为 x。

```
regress y x

      Source |       SS       df       MS              Number of obs =      27
-------------+------------------------------           F(  1,    25) =   86.54
       Model |  40862.6027     1  40862.6027           Prob > F      =  0.0000
    Residual |   11804.064    25   472.16256           R-squared     =  0.7759
-------------+------------------------------           Adj R-squared =  0.7669
       Total |  52666.6667    26  2025.64103           Root MSE      =  21.729

------------------------------------------------------------------------------
           y |      Coef.   Std. Err.      t    P>|t|     [95% Conf. Interval]
-------------+----------------------------------------------------------------
           x |   .1053611   .0113256     9.30   0.000     .0820355    .1286867
       _cons |   14.44806   9.562012     1.51   0.143    -5.245273    34.14139
------------------------------------------------------------------------------
```

在 Stata，回归之后，我们可以输入“rvpplot x”，我们便可以得到以下的图形：

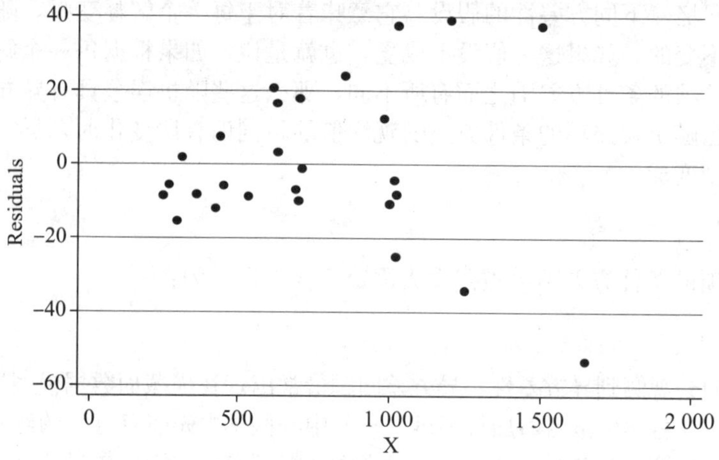

上述图表表明，回归残差的方差随着 x 值的增加而增加。当 x 值沿着 X 轴增加时，回归残差所形成的上下两条临界带变得越来越宽，由此指出了异方差问题的存在。

2.2 检验异方差

从本质内容上讲，我们试图检验：H_0：$\text{var}(u \mid x_1, x_2, \cdots, x_k)=\sigma^2$，这相当于检验 H_0：$E(u^2 \mid x_1, x_2, \cdots, x_k)=E(u^2)=\sigma^2$。如果 u^2 和某个解释变量 x_j 之间的关系是线性的，我们可以检验以下的线性约束条件：$u^2=d_0+d_1x_1+\cdots+d_kx_k+v$，这意味着我们想检验 H_0：$d_1=d_2=\cdots=d_k=0$。

i）Breusch-Pagan 检验。

该检验的基础思想是：$u^2=d_0+d_1x_1+\cdots+d_k x_k+v$。这意味着检验 H_0：$d_1=d_2=\cdots=d_k=0$。我们不能观测到总体误差项 u，但可以通过 OLS 回归所产生的残差项来估计它。在对所有的解释变量 x 回归残差项的平方，我们可以使用 R^2 来构造 F 检验。这里的 F 统计量是上述回归中所得到的用来检验总体显著性的 F 统计量，也就是，$F=[R^2/k]/[(1-R^2)/(n-k-1)]$，它服从自由度为 k 和 $n-k-1$ 的 F 分布。

ii）White 检验。

Breusch-Pagan 检验适用于发现的任何线性形式的异方差。White 检验借助解释变量 x 的平方项和解释变量之间的交叉乘积而允许非线性的存在。我们仍然可以使用 F 检验来检验是否所有的解释变量 x_j、解释变量的平方项 x_j^2 和解释变量之间的交叉乘积 x_jx_h 具有总体显著性。但是，这样做有可能很不方便。另一种 White 检验的替代形式源于：从 OLS 回归中得到的拟合值 $\hat{y}$ 是解释变量的函数，同时，$\hat{y}^2$ 是解释变量 x 的平方项和解释变量之间的交叉乘积的函数。因此，$\hat{y}$ 和 $\hat{y}^2$ 可以替代所有的解释变量 x_j、解释变量的平方项 x_j^2 和解释变量之间的交叉乘积 x_jx_h。我们可以用残差平方对 $\hat{y}$ 和 $\hat{y}^2$ 回归，并使用含有 R^2 的公式来计算 F 统计量。

注意：在 Stata 中，用 Breusch-Pagan 来检验异方差，我们可以输入“ hettest ”。如果采用 White 检验，在 Stata 中，我们可以输入“ whitetst”。

Ⅲ. 如何解决异方差问题

3.1　计算异方差稳健标准误

如上所述，当存在未知形式的异方差时，我们仍然可以使用 OLS 估计解释变量的系数，但我们需要修改 OLS 估计量的标准误，以进行 OLS 回归的假设推理。我们来考虑一个简单的线性回归模型，$y_i=\beta_0+\beta_1x_i+\mu_i$。如果误差方差取决于某个解释变量的特定值，那么 $\mathrm{Var}(\mu_i \mid x_i)=\sigma_i^2$。通过 OLS 回归，$\hat{\beta}_1=\beta_1+\dfrac{\sum_{i=1}^{n}(x_i-\bar{x})\mu_i}{\sum_{i=1}^{n}(x_i-\bar{x})^2}$，从而 $\mathrm{Var}(\hat{\beta}_1)=\left(\dfrac{1}{\sum_{i=1}^{n}(x_i-\bar{x})^2}\right)^2\sum_{i=1}^{n}(x_i-\bar{x})^2\sigma_i^2$。这才是考虑了异方差存在的正确的 OLS 方差公式。对上述公式求平方根便可以得出适当的标准误，称为异方差稳健标准误。这种方法可以推广到多元线性回归模型。只要我们修改了 OLS 估计值的标准误，我们就可以按通常方法来进行假设检验。

3.2　加权最小二乘估计

虽然我们可以随时计算异方差稳健标准误，如果我们知道异方差的具体形式，就可以得到比 OLS 回归更有效的估计值。其基本思路是我们通过加权最小二乘法将存在异方差的模型转换成一个同方差的模型。

i）异方差具有倍乘常数的形式。

假设异方差可以写为 $\mathrm{Var}(\mu \mid x)=\sigma^2h(x)$，其中的诀窍在于找出 $h(x)\equiv h_i$ 的构成。如果我们把整个方程式除以 $\sqrt{h_i}$，因为 h_i 是解释变量 x 的函数，那么 $E(\mu_i/\sqrt{h_i} \mid x)=0$，而且因为我们知道 $\mathrm{Var}(\mu \mid x)=\sigma^2h_i$，$\mathrm{Var}(\mu_i/\sqrt{h_i} \mid x)=\sigma^2$。通过这种方法，我们可以得到一个同方差的模型。例如，总体回归模型是：$y_i=\beta_0+\beta_1x_{i1}+\beta_2x_{i2}+\cdots+\beta_kx_{ik}+\mu_i$。如果

我们知道 $h(x)$ 是解释变量的具体函数，就可以把整个总体回归模型除以$\sqrt{h_i}$，那么我们可以得到 $y_i/\sqrt{h_i}=\beta_0/\sqrt{h_i}+\beta_1 x_{i1}/\sqrt{h_i}+\beta_2 x_{i2}/\sqrt{h_i}+\cdots+\beta_k x_{ik}/\sqrt{h_i}+\mu_i/\sqrt{h_i}$，或者 $y_i^*=\beta_0 x_{i0}^*+\beta_1 x_{i1}^*+\beta_2 x_{i2}^*+\cdots+\beta_k x_{ik}^*+\mu_i^*$。$\mu_i^*$ 的特性是：$E(\mu_i^* \mid x)=0$，而且 $\mathrm{Var}(\mu_i^* \mid x)=\sigma^2$。因此，模型就转换为具有同方差的模型。我们将 y^* 对 x_0^*，x_1^*，x_2^*，…，x_k^* 进行回归（这是个没有常数项的模型），便可以得到$\hat{\beta}_0$，$\hat{\beta}_1$，$\hat{\beta}_2$，…，$\hat{\beta}_k$。

ii）可行的 GLS 估计。

更为寻常的情况是你根本不知道异方差的确切形式。在这种情况下，需要对 $h(x_i)$ 进行估计。通常，我们首先建立一个相对灵活的模型，比如：$\mathrm{Var}(\mu \mid x)=\sigma^2\times\exp(d_0+d_1x_1+\cdots+d_kx_k)$。

因为我们不知道那些 d 系数的值，必须要估计它们。我们的假设意味着，$\mu^2=\sigma^2\exp(d_0+d_1x_1+\cdots+d_kx_k)v$，或者方程两边都取对数而转换为：$\log(\mu^2)=a_0+d_1x_1+\cdots+d_kx_k+e$，其中 e 和解释变量 x 不相关，互相独立。我们知道，$\hat{\mu}$ 是 μ 的估计，并且通过 OLS 可以得到。回归后，h 的估计值实际是 $\hat{h}=\exp(\hat{g})$，它的倒数就是我们需要的加权值。

总之，我们先回归最初的 OLS 模型，保存残差，计算残差平方，接着取对数。然后，我们会以 $\ln(\hat{\mu}^2)$ 为被解释变量对所有的解释变量进行回归并得到拟合值 $\hat{g}$。最后，我们以 $1/\exp(\hat{g})$ 作为加权值，以便运行加权最小二乘回归。

为了更好地理解上述讨论的理论和方法，接下来，我们一起讨论以下的上机练习。

Ⅳ. 上机操作练习

我们的课题是关于你是否加入了兄弟会。① 我们想要知道是否可以预测你的决定。请在 Stata 中打开 **fraternity. dta**。

我们从提出假设开始。我们认为加入兄弟会与你的兴趣和社交背景有关。确切地说，我们认为：*joining a fraternity or sorority*$=f($“*socialness*”，*academics*，*gender*，*athletics*$)$。我们用你在高三参加的跳舞次数来度量“*socialness*”。我们用你是否有奖学金来度量 *academics*。我们用高三参加的校运动代表队的数量来度量 *athletics*。*Gender* 是一个虚拟变量，1 代表男性，0 代表女性。

我们从用最小二乘法估计我们的模型开始：

```
reg fraternity dance  scholar m sports

      Source |       SS           df       MS      Number of obs   =       169
-------------+----------------------------------   F(  4,    164)  =     10.66
       Model |  6.30042284         4  1.57510571   Prob > F        =    0.0000
    Residual |  24.2321215       164  .147756839   R-squared       =    0.2064
-------------+----------------------------------   Adj R-squared   =    0.1870
       Total |  30.5325444       168  .181741336   Root MSE        =    .38439

------------------------------------------------------------------------------
  fraternity |      Coef.   Std. Err.      t    P>|t|     [95% Conf. Interval]
-------------+----------------------------------------------------------------
       dance |   .0515909   .0137505     3.75   0.000       .02444    .0787417
     scholar |   .2685093   .0732029     3.67   0.000     .1239677    .4130509
           m |   .0422289   .0954099     0.44   0.659    -.1461612    .2306189
      sports |   .0454733   .0315441     1.44   0.151    -.0168117    .1077583
       _cons |   -.211598   .0897179    -2.36   0.020     -.388749   -.034447
------------------------------------------------------------------------------
```

① 该练习受凯斯西储大学魏德海管理学院的 Eric Bettinger 的启发。数据通过作者计量经济课堂上的学生调查收集。

如你所知，异方差依然会产生无偏估计，但是它会导致标准误差错误。现在我们来考虑异方差的问题。

（1）用 Pagan 检验来检验模型是否有异方差。你的结果是什么？

```
reg  resid2 dance scholar m sports

    Source |       SS       df       MS              Number of obs =     169
-----------+------------------------------           F(  4,   164) =   10.31
     Model |  1.12246188     4  .280615471           Prob > F      =  0.0000
  Residual |  4.46386165   164  .027218669           R-squared     =  0.2009
-----------+------------------------------           Adj R-squared =  0.1814
     Total |  5.58632353   168  .033251926           Root MSE      =  .16498

------------------------------------------------------------------------------
    resid2 |      Coef.   Std. Err.      t    P>|t|     [95% Conf. Interval]
-----------+------------------------------------------------------------------
     dance |  -.0068588   .0059017    -1.16   0.247     -.018512    .0047944
   scholar |   .1520083   .0314187     4.84   0.000      .089971    .2140455
         m |   .0844698   .0409499     2.06   0.041     .0036128    .1653268
    sports |   .0045974   .0135387     0.34   0.735    -.0221353    .0313301
     _cons |  -.0263053   .0385069    -0.68   0.495    -.1023385    .0497279
------------------------------------------------------------------------------

test  dance scholar m sports

 ( 1)  dance = 0
 ( 2)  scholar = 0
 ( 3)  m = 0
 ( 4)  sports = 0

       F(  4,   164) =   10.31
            Prob > F =    0.0000
```

所发现的 p 值＝0.000 0，小于 5%，我们的结论是残差的方差和解释变量线性相关，因此模型中有异方差的问题。

（2）用 White 检验来检验异方差的问题。你的结果是什么？

```
reg  resid2  dance scholar m sports dance2  scholar2 sports2 dan_sch  dan_spo dan_m scho_m scho_spo m_spo

    Source |       SS       df       MS              Number of obs =     169
-----------+------------------------------           F( 12,   156) =    7.52
     Model |  2.04756395    12  .170630329           Prob > F      =  0.0000
  Residual |  3.53875958   156  .022684356           R-squared     =  0.3665
-----------+------------------------------           Adj R-squared =  0.3178
     Total |  5.58632353   168  .033251926           Root MSE      =  .15061

------------------------------------------------------------------------------
    resid2 |      Coef.   Std. Err.      t    P>|t|     [95% Conf. Interval]
-----------+------------------------------------------------------------------
     dance |  -.0132471    .030505    -0.43   0.665    -.0735032    .0470091
   scholar |   .0115863   .0799497     0.14   0.885    -.1463373    .1695099
         m |  -.0488983   .0929806    -0.53   0.600    -.2325617    .1347651
    sports |   .1594589   .0466906     3.42   0.001     .0672316    .2516863
    dance2 |   .0021141   .0023167     0.91   0.363     -.002462    .0066902
  scholar2 |  (dropped)
   sports2 |  -.0697491   .0118105    -5.91   0.000    -.0930783   -.0464199
   dan_sch |   .0016972   .0186449     0.09   0.928    -.0351319    .0385264
   dan_spo |  -.0016572   .0076767    -0.22   0.829    -.0168209    .0135065
     dan_m |   -.021674   .0312297    -0.69   0.489    -.0833617    .0400136
    scho_m |   .2255088   .0823848     2.74   0.007     .0627751    .3882424
  scho_spo |  -.0548485   .0414171    -1.32   0.187    -.1366592    .0269623
     m_spo |    .099716   .0548149     1.82   0.071    -.0085592    .2079912
     _cons |   .0129335   .0720826     0.18   0.858    -.1294503    .1553174
------------------------------------------------------------------------------
```

在回归结果里，我们发现 F 值等于 7.52，并且 p 值是 0.000 0。这些数据显示上述的用残差平方作为因变量的回归模型有整体显著性，即所有包含的解释变量联合显著。因此，所建模型有异方差的问题。

（3）如果模型有异方差，OLS 估计有偏差吗？OLS 标准误差呢？

OLS 估计没有偏差，但 OLS 标准误差有偏差。

（4）如果模型有异方差问题，你如何修正标准误差？展示你的 Stata 结果。

要解决异方差问题，我们要算出异方差稳健标准误。

```
. reg fraternity dance  scholar m sports, robust

Linear regression                               Number of obs =      169
                                                F(  4,   164) =    19.99
                                                Prob > F      =   0.0000
                                                R-squared     =   0.2064
                                                Root MSE      =   .38439

------------------------------------------------------------------------------
             |               Robust
  fraternity |      Coef.   Std. Err.      t    P>|t|     [95% Conf. Interval]
-------------+----------------------------------------------------------------
       dance |   .0515909   .0144806     3.56   0.000     .0229985    .0801833
     scholar |   .2685093   .0414281     6.48   0.000      .186708    .3503106
           m |   .0422289    .050127     0.84   0.401    -.0567487    .1412065
      sports |   .0454733   .0240031     1.89   0.060    -.0019216    .0928682
       _cons |   -.211598   .0433842    -4.88   0.000    -.2972615   -.1259344
------------------------------------------------------------------------------
```

（5）在修正异方差后，哪些变量是显著的？你的结果有改变吗？

首先，各系数都没有变。异方差不影响这些估计，但是影响标准误差。

其次，*dance* 的标准误差变大了。其他标准误差都变小了。

如果你注意到，在原来的估计中，我们没有发现 *sports* 有显著的影响。但是在我们修正标准误差后，*t* 值变大了，并且我们可以拒绝 *sports* 对加入兄弟会或姐妹会没有影响的假设。

（6）如果模型有异方差，你怎么用可行广义最小二乘法来得到更有效的估计？展示你的 Stata 结果。

在 Stata 中，输入下列代码：

```
. gen logu2=log (resid2)
. reg logu2  dance-sports
. predict ghat, xb
. gen hhat=exp (ghat)
. reg frat dance-sports [aw=1/hhat]
```

```
. reg frat dance-sports [aw = 1/hhat]
(sum of wgt is   7.6091e+03)

      Source |       SS       df       MS              Number of obs =     169
-------------+------------------------------           F(  4,   164) =   14.46
       Model |  1.68640976     4  .421602439           Prob > F      =  0.0000
    Residual |  4.78116763   164  .029153461           R-squared     =  0.2607
-------------+------------------------------           Adj R-squared =  0.2427
       Total |  6.46757739   168  .038497484           Root MSE      =  .17074

------------------------------------------------------------------------------
  fraternity |      Coef.   Std. Err.      t    P>|t|     [95% Conf. Interval]
-------------+----------------------------------------------------------------
       dance |   .0118176    .008586     1.38   0.171    -.0051358    .0287709
     scholar |   .2654755   .0393549     6.75   0.000     .1877679     .343183
           m |   .0025057    .031769     0.08   0.937    -.0602232    .0652346
      sports |   .0092227   .0142015     0.65   0.517    -.0188186    .0372641
       _cons |   -.035399    .025541    -1.39   0.168    -.0858306    .0150327
------------------------------------------------------------------------------
```

Ⅴ. 附加上机操作练习

请上传 **smoke. dta** 文件①，其中有六个变量：

cigs：每天抽烟的数量；

lincome：年收入；

cigpric：每包烟的价格（美分）；

educ：受教育时间；

age：年龄；

agesq：年龄的平方；

restaurn：二元变量，如果一个人住在禁止在餐馆中吸烟的州，变量值等于 1。

（1）用 OLS 方法估计以下方程：

$$cigs=\beta_0+\beta_1 lincome+\beta_2 cigpric+\beta_3 educ+\beta_4 age+\beta_5 agesq+\beta_6 restaurn+\mu$$

展示你的测试结果：

```
. regress cigs lincome cigpric educ age agesq restaurn

      Source |       SS       df       MS              Number of obs =     807
-------------+------------------------------           F(  6,   800) =    7.42
       Model |  8000.26634     6  1333.37772           Prob > F      =  0.0000
    Residual |  143753.416   800  179.691771           R-squared     =  0.0527
-------------+------------------------------           Adj R-squared =  0.0456
       Total |  151753.683   806  188.280003           Root MSE      =  13.405

------------------------------------------------------------------------------
        cigs |      Coef.   Std. Err.      t    P>|t|     [95% Conf. Interval]
-------------+----------------------------------------------------------------
     lincome |   .8764944   .7277844     1.20   0.229    -.5520983    2.305087
     cigpric |  -.0039872   .1009059    -0.04   0.968    -.2020588    .1940844
        educ |  -.5016556   .1670784    -3.00   0.003    -.8296195   -.1736917
         age |   .7705916   .1601228     4.81   0.000     .4562811    1.084902
       agesq |  -.0090225   .0017431    -5.18   0.000     -.012444   -.0056011
    restaurn |  -2.839908   1.110406    -2.56   0.011    -5.019562   -.6602539
       _cons |  -6.429084   8.681568    -0.74   0.459    -23.47043    10.61226
------------------------------------------------------------------------------
```

现在来考虑异方差的问题。

（2）用 Pagan 检验方法来检查你的模型中是否有异方差的问题。你的结果是什么？（列出整个 Pagan 检验的步骤。）

```
. predict residual, resid

. gen residual2=residual^2

. reg residual2 lincome cigpric educ age agesq restaurn

      Source |       SS       df       MS              Number of obs =     807
-------------+------------------------------           F(  6,   800) =    5.56
       Model |  4400738.75     6  733456.458           Prob > F      =  0.0000
    Residual |   105510512   800   131888.14           R-squared     =  0.0400
-------------+------------------------------           Adj R-squared =  0.0328
       Total |   109911251   806  136366.316           Root MSE      =  363.16

------------------------------------------------------------------------------
   residual2 |      Coef.   Std. Err.      t    P>|t|     [95% Conf. Interval]
-------------+----------------------------------------------------------------
     lincome |   24.49838   19.71703     1.24   0.214    -14.20485     63.2016
     cigpric |   1.254059   2.733728     0.46   0.647    -4.112069    6.620186
        educ |  -2.408043   4.526465    -0.53   0.595    -11.29319    6.477108
         age |   19.41574   4.338025     4.48   0.000     10.90049      27.931
       agesq |  -.2148287   .0472225    -4.55   0.000    -.3075233   -.1221341
    restaurn |  -71.42464   30.08297    -2.37   0.018    -130.4755   -12.37376
       _cons |   -460.294   235.1998    -1.96   0.051    -921.9757    1.387608
------------------------------------------------------------------------------
```

① 资料来源：http：//www. dartmouth. edu/～econ20pa/data1. html。

```
. test lincome cigpric educ age agesq restaurn

 ( 1)  lincome = 0
 ( 2)  cigpric = 0
 ( 3)  educ = 0
 ( 4)  age = 0
 ( 5)  agesq = 0
 ( 6)  restaurn = 0

       F(  6,   800) =    5.56
            Prob > F =    0.0000
```

由于 p 值=0.000 0<5%，我们拒绝零假设，所以模型中有异方差的问题。

用 Stata 指令"hettest"来检验你的测试结果。

```
Breusch-Pagan / Cook-Weisberg test for heteroskedasticity
         Ho: Constant variance
         Variables: fitted values of cigs

         chi2(1)      =    56.32
         Prob > chi2  =   0.0000
```

由于 p 值=0.000 0<0.05，所以我们拒绝零假设，我们的模型中有异方差的问题。

（3）你的模型有异方差问题吗？它会导致哪些结果？

根据 Pagan 检验的结果，p 值<0.05，所以我们的模型有异方差的问题。虽然有异方差的问题，但我们的 OLS 估计值依然是无偏并且一致的，但是估计值的标准误差是有偏的。因此，我们不能用 t 检验和 F 检验来进行统计推断。

（4）如果你的模型有异方差的问题，请用稳健标准误差来修正它。列出你的 Stata 修正结果。

```
. regress cigs lincome cigpric educ age agesq restaurn, robust

Linear regression                                      Number of obs =     807
                                                       F(  6,   800) =   10.79
                                                       Prob > F      =  0.0000
                                                       R-squared     =  0.0527
                                                       Root MSE      =  13.405

------------------------------------------------------------------------------
             |               Robust
        cigs |      Coef.   Std. Err.      t    P>|t|     [95% Conf. Interval]
-------------+----------------------------------------------------------------
     lincome |   .8764944   .5966207     1.47   0.142    -.2946326    2.047621
     cigpric |  -.0039872   .1059616    -0.04   0.970    -.2119828    .2040084
        educ |  -.5016556   .1623881    -3.09   0.002    -.8204126   -.1828985
         age |   .7705916   .1383231     5.57   0.000     .4990726    1.042111
       agesq |  -.0090225   .0014628    -6.17   0.000    -.0118939   -.0061512
    restaurn |  -2.839908   1.006094    -2.82   0.005    -4.814804   -.8650119
       _cons |  -6.429084   8.591874    -0.75   0.455    -23.29436     10.4362
------------------------------------------------------------------------------
```

（5）使用稳健标准误差的估计值的统计显著性与原来回归结果的统计显著性有什么不同？

与原回归估计的结果相比，系数和常数项都没有改变，但是 *cigpric* 的系数的标准误差增大了，而其他变量的系数的标准误差都下降了。尽管 *lincome* 的 p 值下降了，但是它依然是不显著的。同样的，*cigpric* 的系数仍是不显著的。与原来模型中一样，只有 *educ*，*age*，*agesq* 和 *restaurn* 是统计显著的。

（6）如果你的模型有异方差的问题，你如何用可行的 GLS 方法来获得更有效的估计？列出你的 Stata 结果。

（7）使用 FGLS 方法的估计值的统计显著性与原来回归结果的统计显著性有什么

```
. regress cigs lincome cigpric educ age agesq restaurn [aw = 1/hhat]
(sum of wgt is   2.0139e+01)

      Source |       SS       df       MS              Number of obs =     807
-------------+------------------------------           F(  6,   800) =   16.99
       Model |  10277.5487     6  1712.92479           Prob > F      =  0.0000
    Residual |  80656.8953   800  100.821119           R-squared     =  0.1130
-------------+------------------------------           Adj R-squared =  0.1064
       Total |   90934.444   806  112.821891           Root MSE      =  10.041

------------------------------------------------------------------------------
        cigs |      Coef.   Std. Err.      t    P>|t|     [95% Conf. Interval]
-------------+----------------------------------------------------------------
     lincome |    1.27258   .4353384     2.92   0.004     .4180396     2.12712
     cigpric |  -.0427271   .0782222    -0.55   0.585    -.1962721    .1108178
        educ |  -.4653066   .1205108    -3.86   0.000    -.7018613   -.2287519
         age |   .4854708   .0972053     4.99   0.000     .2946632    .6762785
       agesq |  -.0056657   .0009446    -6.00   0.000    -.0075198   -.0038115
    restaurn |  -3.480752   .7959342    -4.37   0.000    -5.043118   -1.918386
       _cons |  -3.647913   5.433727    -0.67   0.502    -14.31396    7.018132
------------------------------------------------------------------------------
```

不同?

系数和常数项都改变了。所有估计值的标准误差都减小了。

与原回归结果的估计值相比，*lincome* 的 p 值下降了许多，并且现在是统计显著的了。

cigpric 的 p 值也下降了，但它的估计系数依然不是统计显著的。

educ，*age*，*agesq* 和 *restaurn* 的系数依然是统计显著的。

(8) 使用 FGLS 方法的估计值的统计显著性与使用稳健标准误差的估计值的统计显著性有什么不同?

系数和常数项都改变了。FGLS 中的估计值的标准误差比稳健标准误差还要小。

lincome 的系数现在变为统计显著的了，因为它的 p 值在 FGLS 方法中下降了很多。

cigpric 的 p 值在 FGLS 方法中变小了，但在稳健标准误差回归中是增大的，不过它依然不是统计显著的。

educ，*age*，*agesq* 和 *restaurn* 的系数在两个模型中都是统计显著的。

Chapter 7

Heteroskedasticity

Ⅰ. What is Heteroskedasticity?

Recall the assumption of homoskedasticity implies that conditional on the explanatory variables, the variance of the unobserved errors is constant. If this is not true, that is, if the variance of the unobserved errors is different for different values of the x's, then the errors are heteroskedastic.

Mathematically, if heteroskedasticity occurs when the variance of the error terms differs across observations, the model now becomes:

$$y_i=\beta_0+\beta_1 x_i+\varepsilon_i$$

Variance of the errors is no longer assumed to be a constant, i. e. ,

$$\text{var}(\varepsilon_i)=\sigma_i^2$$

Why might we observe heteroskedasticity? Heteroskedasticity arises most often with cross-sectional data. Let's consider the following example. There are 100 students enrolled in a typing class—some of whom have typing experience and some of whom do not. After the first class there would be a great deal of dispersion in the number of typing mistakes. After the final class the dispersion would be smaller. Hence, the error variance is non-constant: it falls as time increases.

Why do we worry about heteroskedasticity? OLS is still unbiased and consistent, even if we do not assume homoskedasticity. The standard errors of the estimates are biased if we have heteroskedasticity. In other words, OLS is no longer BLUE. If the standard errors are biased, we cannot use the usual t statistics or F statistics or LM statistics for drawing inferences.

Ⅱ. How to Detect Heteroskedasticity

2.1 Plot a Graph

The first simple approach to detecting heteroskedasticity is plotting a graph. In Stata, after running OLS regression, we can use "rvpplot" to detect the problem of heteroskedasticity. In general, if the band within which the residuals lie diverges (i. e. becomes wider) as x increases, the error variance is also increasing with x. On the other hand, if the band converges (i. e. becomes narrower), the error variance decrease with x. If the band that contains the residual plots consists of two lines parallel to the X axis, there is no evidence of heteroskedasticity.

For example, suppose we decided to study the relationship between the two variables and a linear model was postulated between the number of supervisors (y) and the number of supervised workers (x).

```
regress y x

      Source |       SS       df       MS              Number of obs =      27
-------------+------------------------------           F(  1,    25) =   86.54
       Model |  40862.6027     1  40862.6027           Prob > F      =  0.0000
    Residual |   11804.064    25   472.16256           R-squared     =  0.7759
-------------+------------------------------           Adj R-squared =  0.7669
       Total |  52666.6667    26  2025.64103           Root MSE      =  21.729

------------------------------------------------------------------------------
           y |      Coef.   Std. Err.      t    P>|t|     [95% Conf. Interval]
-------------+----------------------------------------------------------------
           x |   .1053611   .0113256     9.30   0.000     .0820355    .1286867
       _cons |   14.44806   9.562012     1.51   0.143    -5.245273    34.14139
------------------------------------------------------------------------------
```

In Stata, after OLS regression, we can type "rvpplot x", and then we get the following graph:

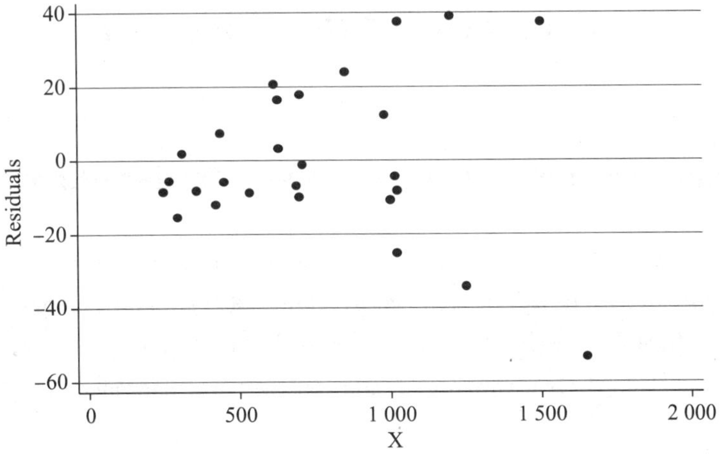

The above plot shows that the residual variance tends to increase with x. The residuals tend to lie in a band that diverges as one moves along the X axis. It reveals the presence of heteroskedasticity.

2.2 Testing for Heteroskedasticity

Essentially we want to test H_0: $\text{var}(u \mid x_1, x_2, \cdots, x_k)=\sigma^2$, which is equivalent to H_0: $E(u^2 \mid x_1, x_2, \cdots, x_k)=E(u^2)=\sigma^2$. If assuming the relationship between u^2 and x_j is linear, we can test a linear restriction for $u^2=d_0+d_1x_1+\cdots+d_kx_k+v$. This means testing H_0: $d_1=d_2=\cdots=d_k=0$.

i) The Breusch-Pagan Test.

The Breusch-Pagan Test: $u^2=d_0+d_1x_1+\cdots+d_kx_k+v$. This means testing H_0: $d_1=d_2=\cdots=d_k=0$. We do not observe the error, but can estimate it with the residuals from the OLS regression. After regressing the residuals squared on all of the x's, we can use the R^2 to form an F test. The F statistic is just the reported F statistic for overall significance of the regression, $F=[R^2/k]/[(1-R^2)/(n-k-1)]$, which is distributed $F_{k,n-k-1}$.

ii) The White Test.

The Breusch-Pagan test will detect any linear forms of heteroskedasticity. The White test allows for nonlinearities by using squares and crossproducts of all the x's. We still just use an F to test whether all the x_j, x_j^2, and x_jx_h are jointly significant. This can get to be pretty unwieldy. There is an alternate form of the White test. Consider that the fitted values from OLS, $\hat{y}$, are a function of all the x's, while $\hat{y}^2$ will be a function of the squares and crossproducts. Hence, $\hat{y}$ and $\hat{y}^2$ can proxy for all of the x_j, x_j^2, and x_jx_h. We, then, just need to regress the residuals squared on $\hat{y}$ and $\hat{y}^2$ and use the R^2 to form an F statistic.

Note: in Stata, to test for heteroskedasticity, for Pagan test, we can use "hettest". For White test, in Stata, we can use "whitetst".

Ⅲ. How to Fix the Problem of Heteroskedasticity

3.1 Calculate Heteroskedasticity-Robust Standard Error

As mentioned above, in case of heteroskedasticity of unknown form, we can still use OLS estimates for coefficients, but we need to adjust OLS standard errors in order to draw inferences from the OLS regression. Let us consider a simple linear regression model, where $y_i=\beta_0+\beta_1x_i+\mu_i$. If error variance depends on the particular value of x_i, $\text{Var}(\mu_i \mid x_i)=$

σ_i^2. Now, $\hat{\beta}_1 = \beta_1 + \dfrac{\sum_{i=1}^{n}(x_i - \bar{x})\mu_i}{\sum_{i=1}^{n}(x_i - \bar{x})^2}$, and thus $\mathrm{Var}(\hat{\beta}_1) = \left(\dfrac{1}{\sum_{i=1}^{n}(x_i - \bar{x})^2}\right)^2 \sum_{i=1}^{n}(x_i - \bar{x})^2\sigma_i^2$. This is the correct OLS variance formula in the presence of heteroskedasticity. The square root of the above formula gives the appropriate standard error, called a heteroskedasticity-robust standard error. This approach can be generalized to multiple linear regression models. Once we correct OLS variances, we can perform hypothesis tests in the usual manner.

3.2 Weighted Least Squares

While it's always possible to estimate robust standard errors for OLS estimates, if we know something about the specific form of heteroskedasticity, we can obtain more efficient estimates than OLS estimates. The basic idea is to transform the model into one that has homoskedastic errors by using the approach called weighted least squares.

1) Case of form being known up to a multiplicative constant.

Suppose heteroskedasticity can be modeled as $\mathrm{var}(\mu \mid x) = \sigma^2 h(x)$, where the trick is to figure out what $h(x) \equiv h_i$ looks like. If we divided our whole equation by $\sqrt{h_i}$, $E(\mu_i / \sqrt{h_i} \mid x) = 0$, because h_i is only a function of x; and $\mathrm{Var}(\mu_i / \sqrt{h_i} \mid x) = \sigma^2$, because we know $\mathrm{var}(\mu \mid x) = \sigma^2 h_i$. By doing so, we would have a model where the error is homoskedastic. For instance, population model is $y_i = \beta_0 + \beta_1 x_{i1} + \beta_2 x_{i2} + \cdots + \beta_k x_{ik} + \mu_i$. If we know that $h(x)$ is a specific function of the explanatory variables and $h(x)$ is positive, we can divide population model by $\sqrt{h_i}$. As a result, we have $y_i / \sqrt{h_i} = \beta_0 / \sqrt{h_i} + \beta_1 x_{i1} / \sqrt{h_i} + \beta_2 x_{i2} / \sqrt{h_i} + \cdots + \beta_k x_{ik} / \sqrt{h_i} + \mu_i / \sqrt{h_i}$ or $y_i^* = \beta_0 x_{i0}^* + \beta_1 x_{i1}^* + \beta_2 x_{i2}^* + \cdots + \beta_k x_{ik}^* + \mu_i^*$. The properties of μ_i^* are: $E(\mu_i^* \mid x) = 0$ and $\mathrm{Var}(\mu_i^* \mid x) = \sigma^2$. Thus the model has been transformed to have a homoskedastic error term. We just regress y^* on x_0^*, x_1^*, x_2^*, …, x_k^* without the constant term to get $\hat{\beta}_0$, $\hat{\beta}_1$, $\hat{\beta}_2$, …, $\hat{\beta}_k$.

2) Feasible GLS.

More typical is the case where you don't know the form of heteroskedasticity. In this case, you need to estimate $h(x_i)$. Typically, we start with the assumption of a fairly flexible model, such as:

$$\mathrm{Var}(\mu \mid x) = \sigma^2 \exp(d_0 + d_1 x_1 + \cdots + d_k x_k)$$

Since we don't know the d's, we must estimate them. Our assumption implies that $\mu^2 = \sigma^2 \exp(d_0 + d_1 x_1 + \cdots + d_k x_k) v$, or taking logs: $\log(\mu^2) = a_0 + d_1 x_1 + \cdots + d_k x_k + e$, where e has mean zero and is independent of x. Since we know that $\hat{\mu}$ is an estimate of μ, we can estimate this by OLS. After the regression, an estimate of h is obtained as $\hat{h} = \exp(\hat{g})$, and the inverse of this is our weight.

In summary, we run the original OLS model, save the residuals, $\hat{\mu}$, square them and take the log. Then, we regress $\ln(\hat{\mu}^2)$ on all of the independent variables to get the fitted values, $\hat{g}$. Finally, using $1/\exp(\hat{g})$ as the weight, we are able to run the weighted least square regression.

In order to better understand the above discussed theories and methods, next, let us move on and work on the following computer exercise.

Ⅳ. Computer Exercise

Our topic is whether or not you joined a fraternity. ①We want to see if we can predict your decision to join. Please find and upload **fraternity. dta** onto Stata.

Let's start by creating our hypotheses. We think that joining a fraternity has something to do with your interests and social background. Specifically, we think that *joining a fraternity or sorority*=*f* ("*socialness*", *academics*, *gender*, *athletics*) . We will measure "socialness" by the number of dances you attended during your senior year of high school. We will measure *academics* as whether or not you are on scholarship here. We will measure *athletics* as the number of varsity sport teams on which you played during your senior year. *Gender* is a dummy variable being one for men and zero for females.

We'll start by estimating our model with ordinary least squares.

```
reg fraternity dance  scholar m sports

      Source |       SS       df       MS              Number of obs =     169
-------------+------------------------------           F(  4,   164) =   10.66
       Model |  6.30042284     4  1.57510571           Prob > F      =  0.0000
    Residual |  24.2321215   164  .147756839           R-squared     =  0.2064
-------------+------------------------------           Adj R-squared =  0.1870
       Total |  30.5325444   168  .181741336           Root MSE      =  .38439

------------------------------------------------------------------------------
  fraternity |      Coef.   Std. Err.      t    P>|t|     [95% Conf. Interval]
-------------+----------------------------------------------------------------
       dance |   .0515909   .0137505     3.75   0.000       .02444    .0787417
     scholar |   .2685093   .0732029     3.67   0.000     .1239677    .4130509
           m |   .0422289   .0954099     0.44   0.659    -.1461612    .2306189
      sports |   .0454733   .0315441     1.44   0.151    -.0168117    .1077583
       _cons |   -.211598   .0897179    -2.36   0.020     -.388749    -.034447
------------------------------------------------------------------------------
```

As you may recall, heteroskedasticity still gives us unbiased estimates, but it makes our standard errors wrong. Now let's think about the problem of heteroskedasticity.

(1) Use Pagan test to check whether your model has the problem of heteroskedasticity. What is your result?

Reading the *p*-value=0. 000 0, which is less than 5%, we conclude that the variance of residuals is linearly correlated with the explanatory variables, thus there exists the problem of heteroskedasticity.

---

① This exercise is inspired by Eric Bettinger at Weatherhead School of Management, Case Western Reserve University. Data is collected from the student survey in my Econometrics class.

```
reg  resid2 dance scholar m sports

      Source |       SS       df       MS              Number of obs =     169
-------------+------------------------------           F(  4,   164) =   10.31
       Model |  1.12246188     4  .280615471           Prob > F      =  0.0000
    Residual |  4.46386165   164  .027218669           R-squared     =  0.2009
-------------+------------------------------           Adj R-squared =  0.1814
       Total |  5.58632353   168  .033251926           Root MSE      =  .16498

------------------------------------------------------------------------------
      resid2 |      Coef.   Std. Err.      t    P>|t|     [95% Conf. Interval]
-------------+----------------------------------------------------------------
       dance |  -.0068588   .0059017    -1.16   0.247     -.018512    .0047944
     scholar |   .1520083   .0314187     4.84   0.000      .089971    .2140455
           m |   .0844698   .0409499     2.06   0.041     .0036128    .1653268
      sports |   .0045974   .0135387     0.34   0.735    -.0221353    .0313301
       _cons |  -.0263053   .0385069    -0.68   0.495    -.1023385    .0497279
------------------------------------------------------------------------------

test  dance scholar m sports

 ( 1)  dance = 0
 ( 2)  scholar = 0
 ( 3)  m = 0
 ( 4)  sports = 0

       F(  4,   164) =   10.31
            Prob > F =    0.0000
```

(2) Use White test to check the problem of heteroskedasticity. What is your finding?

```
reg  resid2  dance scholar m sports dance2  scholar2 sports2 dan_sch  dan_spo dan_m scho_m scho_spo m_spo

      Source |       SS       df       MS              Number of obs =     169
-------------+------------------------------           F( 12,   156) =    7.52
       Model |  2.04756395    12  .170630329           Prob > F      =  0.0000
    Residual |  3.53875958   156  .022684356           R-squared     =  0.3665
-------------+------------------------------           Adj R-squared =  0.3178
       Total |  5.58632353   168  .033251926           Root MSE      =  .15061

------------------------------------------------------------------------------
      resid2 |      Coef.   Std. Err.      t    P>|t|     [95% Conf. Interval]
-------------+----------------------------------------------------------------
       dance |  -.0132471    .030505    -0.43   0.665    -.0735032    .0470091
     scholar |   .0115863   .0799497     0.14   0.885    -.1463373    .1695099
           m |  -.0488983   .0929806    -0.53   0.600    -.2325617    .1347651
      sports |   .1594589   .0466906     3.42   0.001     .0672316    .2516863
      dance2 |   .0021141   .0023167     0.91   0.363     -.002462    .0066902
    scholar2 |  (dropped)
     sports2 |  -.0697491   .0118105    -5.91   0.000    -.0930783   -.0464199
     dan_sch |   .0016972   .0186449     0.09   0.928    -.0351319    .0385264
     dan_spo |  -.0016572   .0076767    -0.22   0.829    -.0168209    .0135065
       dan_m |   -.021674   .0312297    -0.69   0.489    -.0833617    .0400136
      scho_m |   .2255088   .0823848     2.74   0.007     .0627751    .3882424
    scho_spo |  -.0548485   .0414171    -1.32   0.187    -.1366592    .0269623
       m_spo |    .099716   .0548149     1.82   0.071    -.0085592    .2079912
       _cons |   .0129335   .0720826     0.18   0.858    -.1294503    .1553174
------------------------------------------------------------------------------
```

From the regression results, we can find that the F statistic equals 10.31, and the associated p-value is 0.000 0. These figures show that the above regression model with the square of residuals as the dependent variable has overall significance, i.e., all the included explanatory variables are jointly significant. Hence, there exists the problem of heteroskedasticity.

(3) If your model has the problem of heteroskedasticity, are your OLS estimates biased? What about OLS standard errors?

OLS estimate are not biased, but OLS standard errors are biased.

(4) If your model has the problem of heteroskedasticity, how do you correct the standard errors? Show your Stata results.

To solve the problem of heteroskedasticity, we compute robust standard errors.

```
. reg fraternity dance  scholar m sports, robust

Linear regression                                      Number of obs =     169
                                                       F(  4,   164) =   19.99
                                                       Prob > F      =  0.0000
                                                       R-squared     =  0.2064
                                                       Root MSE      =  .38439

------------------------------------------------------------------------------
             |               Robust
  fraternity |      Coef.   Std. Err.      t    P>|t|     [95% Conf. Interval]
-------------+----------------------------------------------------------------
       dance |   .0515909   .0144806     3.56   0.000     .0229985    .0801833
     scholar |   .2685093   .0414281     6.48   0.000      .186708    .3503106
           m |   .0422289    .050127     0.84   0.401    -.0567487    .1412065
      sports |   .0454733   .0240031     1.89   0.060    -.0019216    .0928682
       _cons |   -.211598   .0433842    -4.88   0.000    -.2972615   -.1259344
------------------------------------------------------------------------------
```

(5) After correcting for heteroskedasticity, which variables are statistically significant? Are your results improved?

First, notice that the coefficients do not change. Heteroskedasticity does not affect those estimates. It only affects the standard errors.

Second, the standard error on *dance* goes up in the new estimates. The other standard errors actually decline.

If you notice, in our "old" estimates we did not find a significant effect of *sports*. After we correct the standard errors, our *t*-statistic is larger and we can reject the hypothesis that *sports* do not affect joining a fraternity or sorority.

(6) If your model has the problem of heteroskedasticity, how do you use feasible GLS method to get more efficient estimates? Show your Stata results.

In Stata, type the following codes:

. gen logu2=log (resid2)

. reg logu2 dance-sports

. predict ghat, xb

. gen hhat=exp (ghat)

. reg frat dance—sports [aw=1/hhat]

```
. reg frat dance-sports [aw = 1/hhat]
(sum of wgt is   7.6091e+03)

      Source |       SS       df       MS              Number of obs =     169
-------------+------------------------------           F(  4,   164) =   14.46
       Model |  1.68640976     4  .421602439           Prob > F      =  0.0000
    Residual |  4.78116763   164  .029153461           R-squared     =  0.2607
-------------+------------------------------           Adj R-squared =  0.2427
       Total |  6.46757739   168  .038497484           Root MSE      =  .17074

------------------------------------------------------------------------------
  fraternity |      Coef.   Std. Err.      t    P>|t|     [95% Conf. Interval]
-------------+----------------------------------------------------------------
       dance |   .0118176    .008586     1.38   0.171    -.0051358    .0287709
     scholar |   .2654755   .0393549     6.75   0.000     .1877679     .343183
           m |   .0025057    .031769     0.08   0.937    -.0602232    .0652346
      sports |   .0092227   .0142015     0.65   0.517    -.0188186    .0372641
       _cons |   -.035399    .025541    -1.39   0.168    -.0858306    .0150327
------------------------------------------------------------------------------
```

Ⅴ. Additional Computer Exercise

Please upload **smoke. dta.** [①]This file contains six variables:

cigs: the number of cigarettes smoked per day;

lincome: annual income;

cigpric: the per pack price of cigarettes (in cents);

educ: years of schooling;

age: measured in years;

agesq: age squared;

restaurn: binary indicator equal to one if the person resides in a state with restaurant smoking restriction.

(1) Estimate the equation by OLS:

$$cigs=\beta_0+\beta_1 lincome+\beta_2 cigpric+\beta_3 educ+\beta_4 age+\beta_5 agesq+\beta_6 restaurn+\mu$$

Show the estimation output:

```
. regress cigs lincome cigpric educ age agesq restaurn

      Source |       SS       df       MS              Number of obs =     807
-------------+------------------------------           F(  6,   800) =    7.42
       Model |  8000.26634     6  1333.37772           Prob > F      =  0.0000
    Residual |  143753.416   800  179.691771           R-squared     =  0.0527
-------------+------------------------------           Adj R-squared =  0.0456
       Total |  151753.683   806  188.280003           Root MSE      =  13.405

------------------------------------------------------------------------------
        cigs |      Coef.   Std. Err.      t    P>|t|     [95% Conf. Interval]
-------------+----------------------------------------------------------------
     lincome |   .8764944   .7277844     1.20   0.229    -.5520983    2.305087
     cigpric |  -.0039872   .1009059    -0.04   0.968    -.2020588    .1940844
        educ |  -.5016556   .1670784    -3.00   0.003    -.8296195   -.1736917
         age |   .7705916   .1601228     4.81   0.000     .4562811    1.084902
       agesq |  -.0090225   .0017431    -5.18   0.000     -.012444   -.0056011
    restaurn |  -2.839908   1.110406    -2.56   0.011    -5.019562   -.6602539
       _cons |  -6.429084   8.681568    -0.74   0.459    -23.47043    10.61226
------------------------------------------------------------------------------
```

Now let's think about heteroskedasticity.

(2) Use the Pagan test to check whether your model has the problem of heteroskedasticity. What is your result? (Show the whole procedure of conducting the Pagan test.)

p-value$=0.0000<0.05$, so we reject the null hypothesis, there is a problem of heteroskedasticity.

Use "hettest" to double check your test results.

p-value$=0.0000<0.05$, so we reject the null hypothesis and conclude that there is a problem of heteroskedasticity.

(3) Does your model have the problem of heteroskedasticity? What are the consequences?

According to the result of Pagan test, the p-value <0.05, so we reject the null hy-

① The data set is collected from http://www.dartmouth.edu/~econ20pa/data1.html.

```
. predict residual, resid

. gen residual2=residual^2

. reg residual2 lincome cigpric educ age agesq restaurn

      Source |       SS           df       MS            Number of obs   =       807
-------------+------------------------------------       F(  6,    800)  =      5.56
       Model |  4400738.75         6  733456.458         Prob > F        =    0.0000
    Residual |   105510512       800   131888.14         R-squared       =    0.0400
-------------+------------------------------------       Adj R-squared   =    0.0328
       Total |   109911251       806  136366.316         Root MSE        =    363.16

------------------------------------------------------------------------------
   residual2 |      Coef.   Std. Err.      t    P>|t|     [95% Conf. Interval]
-------------+----------------------------------------------------------------
     lincome |   24.49838   19.71703     1.24   0.214    -14.20485     63.2016
     cigpric |   1.254059   2.733728     0.46   0.647    -4.112069    6.620186
        educ |  -2.408043   4.526465    -0.53   0.595    -11.29319    6.477108
         age |   19.41574   4.338025     4.48   0.000     10.90049      27.931
       agesq |  -.2148287   .0472225    -4.55   0.000    -.3075233   -.1221341
    restaurn |  -71.42464   30.08297    -2.37   0.018    -130.4755   -12.37376
       _cons |   -460.294   235.1998    -1.96   0.051    -921.9757    1.387608
------------------------------------------------------------------------------
```

```
. test lincome cigpric educ age agesq restaurn

 ( 1)  lincome = 0
 ( 2)  cigpric = 0
 ( 3)  educ = 0
 ( 4)  age = 0
 ( 5)  agesq = 0
 ( 6)  restaurn = 0

       F(  6,   800) =     5.56
            Prob > F =    0.0000
```

```
Breusch-Pagan / Cook-Weisberg test for heteroskedasticity
         Ho: Constant variance
         Variables: fitted values of cigs

         chi2(1)      =    56.32
         Prob > chi2  =   0.0000
```

pothesis and the model has the problem of heteroskedasticity.

The consequences are that our OLS estimates are still unbiased and consistent, but the standard errors of the estimates are biased. Also we cannot use the usual t statistics or F statistics for drawing right inferences.

(4) If your model has the problem of heteroskedasticity, please correct for it to get the robust standard errors. Show your Stata results.

```
. regress cigs lincome cigpric educ age agesq restaurn, robust

Linear regression                                      Number of obs =     807
                                                       F(  6,   800) =   10.79
                                                       Prob > F      =  0.0000
                                                       R-squared     =  0.0527
                                                       Root MSE      =  13.405

------------------------------------------------------------------------------
             |               Robust
        cigs |      Coef.   Std. Err.      t    P>|t|     [95% Conf. Interval]
-------------+----------------------------------------------------------------
     lincome |   .8764944   .5966207     1.47   0.142    -.2946326    2.047621
     cigpric |  -.0039872   .1059616    -0.04   0.970    -.2119828    .2040084
        educ |  -.5016556   .1623881    -3.09   0.002    -.8204126   -.1828985
         age |   .7705916   .1383231     5.57   0.000     .4990726    1.042111
       agesq |  -.0090225   .0014628    -6.17   0.000    -.0118939   -.0061512
    restaurn |  -2.839908   1.006094    -2.82   0.005    -4.814804   -.8650119
       _cons |  -6.429084   8.591874    -0.75   0.455    -23.29436     10.4362
------------------------------------------------------------------------------
```

(5) How does the statistical significance of the estimates from the regression with the robust standard errors included compare with those from the original regression?

Compared with the estimates from the original regression result, the coefficients and the constant term do not change, but the standard error of *cigpric* goes up and all the other standard errors decline. Though p-values of *lincome* and the constant term go down, the parameter and the constant are still statistically insignificant. The p-value of *cigpric* goes up, but it's still statistically insignificant. Like the original regression model, only *educ*, *age*, *agesq* and *restaurn* are statistically significant.

(6) If your model has the problem of heteroskedasticity, how do you use feasible GLS method to get more efficient estimates? Show your Stata results.

```
. regress cigs lincome cigpric educ age agesq restaurn [aw = 1/hhat]
(sum of wgt is   2.0139e+01)

      Source |       SS       df       MS              Number of obs =     807
-------------+------------------------------           F(  6,   800) =   16.99
       Model |  10277.5487     6  1712.92479           Prob > F      =  0.0000
    Residual |  80656.8953   800  100.821119           R-squared     =  0.1130
-------------+------------------------------           Adj R-squared =  0.1064
       Total |   90934.444   806  112.821891           Root MSE      =  10.041

------------------------------------------------------------------------------
        cigs |      Coef.   Std. Err.      t    P>|t|     [95% Conf. Interval]
-------------+----------------------------------------------------------------
     lincome |    1.27258   .4353384     2.92   0.004     .4180396     2.12712
     cigpric |  -.0427271   .0782222    -0.55   0.585    -.1962721    .1108178
        educ |  -.4653066   .1205108    -3.86   0.000    -.7018613   -.2287519
         age |   .4854708   .0972053     4.99   0.000     .2946632    .6762785
       agesq |  -.0056657   .0009446    -6.00   0.000    -.0075198   -.0038115
    restaurn |  -3.480752   .7959342    -4.37   0.000    -5.043118   -1.918386
       _cons |  -3.647913   5.433727    -0.67   0.502    -14.31396    7.018132
------------------------------------------------------------------------------
```

(7) How does the statistical significance of the estimates from the FGLS method compare with those from the original regression?

The coefficients and the constant term have all changed. The standard errors for all estimates go down. Compared with the estimates from the original regression result, the p-value of *lincome* declines a lot, and is now statistically significant, so we can reject the null hypothesis and conclude that annual income does have significant impact on the number of cigarettes smoked per day. The p-value for *cigpric* also goes down a lot, but it is still statistically insignificant. The p-value for the constant increases a little bit and it's also insignificant. The p-values for *educ* and *restaurn* decline, and they together with *age* and *agesq* are still statistically significant like in the original model.

(8) How does the statistical significance of the estimates from the FGLS method compare with those from the regression with the robust standard errors included?

The coefficients and the constant term have all changed. The standard errors for all estimates from the FGLS method go down even more than they did in the robust regression model. Compared with the estimates from the regression with the robust standard errors included, the p-value of *lincome* declines even more, and is now statistically significant. The p-value for *cigpric* goes down unlike it goes up in the robust regression model, but it is still statistically insignificant. The p-values for *educ* and *restaurn* decline, and they together with *age* and *agesq* are still statistically significant like in the robust model.

第 8 章

自相关问题的检验和解决方法

Ⅰ. 什么是自相关问题?

我们最初的回归模型假设随机误差值之间是相互独立的。在大多数应用中，尤其涉及时间序列数据，例如宏观经济变量和金融变量，这种假设往往不再有效。这是因为这些数据往往具有一种“周期性”的特点。比如，今天下雨故而明天会下雨的可能性要比今天天晴故而明天会下雨的可能性更大。

当随机误差项在不同时间段彼此相关时，我们称这些随机误差是自相关，或者序列相关。最常见的问题是，随机误差的现期观测值与相邻时间段的观测值之间相关，但和远期时间段的观测值之间不是很相关。因此序列相关问题更会影响那些具有某种自然顺序特性的数据集。

在本章，我们将学习的重点集中于某一种特定类型的序列相关模型，称为一阶序列相关模型。基本上，这种模型意味着，现时间段的随机误差直接和下一个时间段的随机误差之间相关。理论上，如果一阶自相关存在，简单的线性模型便成为:

$$y_t=\beta_0+\beta_1 x_t+\varepsilon_t$$

而且:

$$\varepsilon_t=\rho\varepsilon_{t-1}+v_t, t=1,2,\cdots,n$$

其中，随机误差项 v_t 是随机变量，其均值为零，方差是 σ_v^2。

当自相关存在时，采用 OLS 回归会有什么后果呢? OLS 估计仍是无偏估计。然而，标准误的估计会有偏差。是否标准误的取值会被夸大或低估取决于自相关的性质。当自相关发生时，导致的结果是任何假设检验很有可能会得出错误的结论。换言之，OLS 不再是最佳线性无偏估计。因此，如果随机误差以一种模式而存在，这就意味着我们需要考虑另一种比 OLS 更为有效的回归方法。

Ⅱ. 如何检测自相关问题的存在

2.1　绘制图表

第一种用来检测自相关的简单方法是画图。我们逐一考虑以下三个图表。[①] 第一个图表显示了在一个简单的线性回归模型里 y 和 x 的散点图。显然，大多数点分散在拟合线周围，这表明了 y 和 x 存在线性关系。

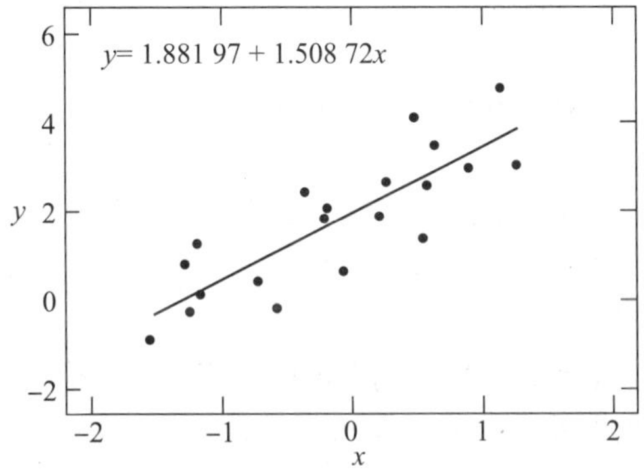

第二个图表显示了在不同观测值下相应的随机误差值，随机误差没有显示出明显的模式，反而是随机分布。

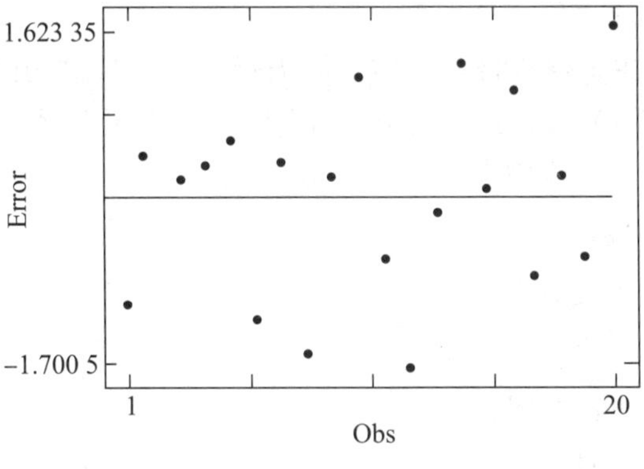

但是，有时候，随机误差会显示出明显的模式，它们之间相关，导致不同阶段的观测值之间相互依赖。

① 这三个图表 选自 Chapter 14. 3，*Statistics and Econometrics*：*Methods and Applications*，by Ashenfelter，Levine and Zimmerman，2003.

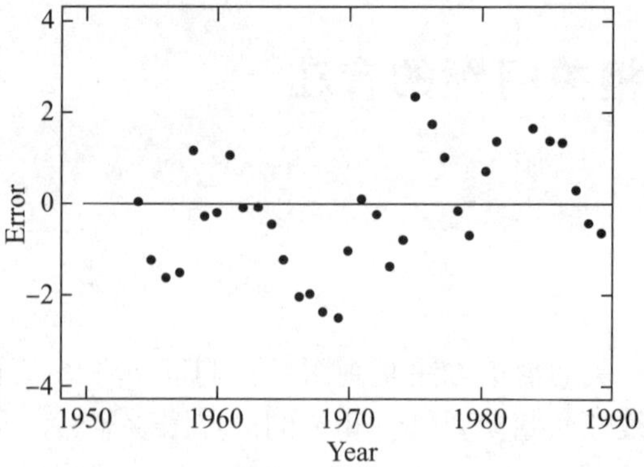

作为一个例子，最后一张图表显示了随机误差似乎不是随机的，而是遵循一种模式在变动。

2.2 检验自相关：Durbin－Watson 检验

Durbin－Watson 检验用来测试一阶序列相关是否存在。它提供了一种用来测试零假设 $\rho=0$ 的方法。备择假设可以是 $\rho\neq0$；$\rho>0$，即正序列相关；以及最常用的备择假设 $\rho<0$，即负序列相关。

在假设零假设正确的情况下，为了用 Durbin－Watson 检验一阶序列相关，我们期望 d 值接近 2。d 值越小，我们越有可能接受备择假设：

$$d=\frac{\sum_{t=2}^{n}e_t^2-2\sum_{t=2}^{n}e_te_{t-1}+\sum_{t=2}^{n}e_{t-1}^2}{\sum_{t=1}^{n}e_t^2}\approx1-2\hat{\rho}+1=2(1-\hat{\rho})$$

d 的样本分布取决于解释变量的取值。因为每一个计量模型问题有不同的解释变量，杜宾（Durbin）和沃森（Watson）推衍出了上限和下限的临界值。

杜宾和沃森制定了以下规则来检测正序列相关：

$$\begin{cases}d\leqslant d_l\rightarrow\text{拒绝零假设}\\ d_l<d<d_u\rightarrow\text{检验无定论}\\ d\geqslant d_u\rightarrow\text{不能拒绝零假设}\end{cases}$$

检验负序列相关的决策规则是：

$$\begin{cases}d\geqslant4-d_l\rightarrow\text{拒绝零假设}\\ 4-d_u<d<4-d_l\rightarrow\text{检验无定论}\\ d\leqslant4-d_u\rightarrow\text{不能拒绝零假设}\end{cases}$$

我们可以用双尾检验来检验是否我们事先相信有正或负序列相关存在，其相应的决策规则是：

$$\begin{cases}d\leqslant d_l\text{ 或者 }d\geqslant4-d_l\rightarrow\text{拒绝零假设}\\ d\geqslant d_u\text{ 或者 }d\leqslant4-d_u\rightarrow\text{不能拒绝零假设}\\ \text{否则，检验无定论}\end{cases}$$

Ⅲ. 如何解决自相关问题

我们用一阶序列相关模型来讨论这一问题。在这种模型中，任一时间段的随机误差是早期时间段的随机误差的函数。参数 ρ 衡量两个相邻误差的相关性。模型如下：

$$y_t=\beta_0+\beta_1 x_{1t}+\beta_2 x_{2t}+\cdots+\beta_k x_{kt}+\varepsilon_t$$

同时，ε_t 展示了随机误差之间跨时间段的相关性，写为：

$$\varepsilon_t=\rho\varepsilon_{t-1}+v_t,\ t=1,2,\cdots,n$$

广义差分法可以将有一阶序列相关特征的模型转换为随机误差之间不再相关。其方法就是，将原模型滞后一期并乘以参数 ρ，从而得到：

$$\rho y_{t-1}=\rho\beta_0+\rho\beta_1 x_{1(t-1)}+\rho\beta_2 x_{2(t-1)}+\cdots+\rho\beta_k x_{k(t-1)}+\rho\varepsilon_{t-1}$$

将上面的式子和原模型相减，得到：

$$\begin{aligned}y_t-\rho y_{t-1}&=(\beta_0-\rho\beta_0)+(\beta_1 x_{1t}-\rho\beta_1 x_{1(t-1)})+\cdots+(\beta_k x_{kt}-\rho\beta_k x_{k(t-1)})+(\varepsilon_t-\rho\varepsilon_{t-1})\\&=\beta_0(1-\rho)+\beta_1(x_{1t}-\rho x_{1(t-1)})+\cdots+\beta_k(x_{kt}-\rho x_{k(t-1)})+v_t\end{aligned}$$

这种变形所产生的残差如果满足经典回归的全部假定，运行广义差分模型：$y_t^*=\beta_0^*+\beta_1 x_{1t}^*+\beta_2 x_{2t}^*+\cdots+\beta_k x_{kt}^*+v_t$ 可以帮助我们得到原模型斜率参数的估计值。这一模型中 $\beta_0^*=\beta_0(1-\rho)$，$x_{it}^*=x_{it}-\rho x_{i(t-1)}$，等等。

转换后的模型可以通过 OLS 回归方法得到最佳线性无偏估计。但是，实施广义差分模型的实际困难是我们不知道参数 ρ 的值。我们可以通过以下两种方式来估计参数 ρ。

i）杜宾两步法。

我们将滞后被解释变量 y_{t-1} 移到广义差分模型的右边，可得到：$y_t=\rho y_{t-1}+(\beta_0-\rho\beta_0)+(\beta_1 x_{1t}-\rho\beta_1 x_{1(t-1)})+\cdots+(\beta_k x_{kt}-\rho\beta_k x_{k(t-1)})+v_t$。然后我们以 y_t 为被解释变量，y_{t-1}，x_{1t}，$x_{1(t-1)}$，x_{2t}，$x_{2(t-1)}$，$\cdots$，x_{kt}，$x_{k(t-1)}$ 为解释变量进行 OLS 回归，回归所得的 y_{t-1} 估计系数提供了参数 ρ 的估计值，我们可以采用此值进行广义差分模型的回归。

ii）Cochrane-Orcutt 方法。

第一步，我们估计原来的模型从而得到用来估计参数 ρ 的误差项。第二步，我们以从最初回归得来的误差项为被解释变量，该误差的滞后项为解释变量进行回归。这一回归的斜率参数的估计值提供了参数 ρ 的估计值。第三步，根据参数 ρ 的估计值 $\hat{\rho}$，我们估计广义差分模型，所得的估计系数可以生成一组新的误差项，我们由此再回到第二步。这一过程一直重复，直到我们知道参数 ρ 的估计值 $\hat{\rho}$ 几乎不再变化为止。

Ⅳ. 上机操作练习

现在，我们想探究一个简单的例子：流通中的真实货币（$M1$）如何随着联邦基金利率

（*FFR*）的变化而变化，而调整联邦基金利率是美联储调整货币政策最明显的手段之一。[①]

我们先从美联储直接下载 *M*1 和 *FFR* 的数据。请上传数据文件 **autocorr. dta**。我们有从 1959 年到 2002 年 3 月的每月数据的两个序列。

（1）基础的宏观经济知识告诉我们如果美联储想要减少流通的货币，它们会提高联邦资金利润。所以，如果我们运行下列回归测试：

$$\ln(M1)_t = a + b\times\ln(FFR)_t + c\times\ln(FFR)_{t-1} + d\times\ln(FFR)_{t-2} + e_t$$

我们期望 b，c 和 d 小于零。考虑到联邦资金利率可能会花一段时间才能影响货币供应量的事实，我们引入了联邦基金利率的滞后项。

在做回归测试之前，我们先输入以下 Stata 指令：

. gen lnm1=log(m1)

. gen lnffr=log(ffr)

. gen lnffr_1=log(ffr[_n-1])

. gen lnffr_2=log(ffr[_n-2])

```
reg lnm1 lnffr lnffr_1 lnffr_2

      Source |       SS       df       MS              Number of obs =     517
-------------+------------------------------           F(  3,   513) =    8.78
       Model |  15.4375148     3  5.14583827           Prob > F      =  0.0000
    Residual |  300.561504   513  .585889872           R-squared     =  0.0489
-------------+------------------------------           Adj R-squared =  0.0433
       Total |  315.999019   516    .6124012           Root MSE      =  .76543

------------------------------------------------------------------------------
        lnm1 |      Coef.   Std. Err.      t    P>|t|     [95% Conf. Interval]
-------------+----------------------------------------------------------------
       lnffr |  -.4382587   .4252217    -1.03   0.303    -1.273649    .3971314
     lnffr_1 |  -.0540469   .6416544    -0.08   0.933     -1.31464    1.206547
     lnffr_2 |    .820261   .4264712     1.92   0.055    -.0175839    1.658106
       _cons |   5.471954   .1276536    42.87   0.000     5.221166    5.722742
------------------------------------------------------------------------------
```

同期和上个月的系数是负的，p 值大于 5%，所以不显著。但在 10% 的显著性水平上，我们可以发现两个月以上的联邦资金利率的系数是正的并且显著的。

（2）如果我们观察回归测试的残差的图像，它们看起来像什么？我们需要担心跨时间的相关性吗？为什么？

在 Stata 中输入以下指令：

. gen obs=_n

. predict resid，resid

. graph twoway scatter resid obs

从图像中我们可以看出，残差显示出一个模式——它们随着时间增长。这代表它们在观测值之间是相互关联的，这造成了一个观测值之间不是互相独立的情况。

（3）当我们做 Durbin - Watson 检验时，得到了什么结果？

在 Stata 中输入：

. tsset obs

. dwstat

---

① 该练习受凯斯西储大学魏德海管理学院的 Eric Bettinger 的启发。资料来源：http：//connection. cwru. edu/econ326/mod8/C/autocorr. dta。

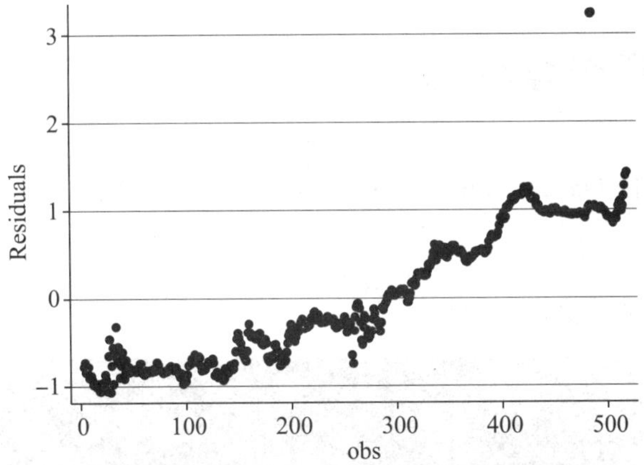


```
tsset obs
      time variable:  obs, 1 to 519
              delta:  1 unit


dwstat

Durbin-Watson d-statistic(  4,   517) =  .0417607
```

注意：Durbin-Watson 数值在 0～4 之间。如果它接近 0 或 4，我们就有上述问题。(我们需要 DW 值在 1.7～3.3 之间以确保在 99%的置信区间上没有问题。)

(4) 我们有自相关问题吗？自相关会影响 OLS 估计吗？标准误差呢？

从上述图表和 DW 检验中，我们可以得出有自相关问题的结论。尽管自相关不影响 OLS 估计，但它会造成 OLS 标准误差出现偏差。因此，OLS 不再是 BLUE。

(5) 我们如何修正自相关问题？

我们可以参考上述笔记里的公式。Stata 可以快速地帮我们解决这个问题。(展示回归结果。)

```
. prais lnm1 lnffr lnffr_1 lnffr_2, corc

Iteration 0:  rho = 0.0000
Iteration 1:  rho = 0.9814
Iteration 2:  rho = 0.9838
Iteration 3:  rho = 0.9840
Iteration 4:  rho = 0.9840
Iteration 5:  rho = 0.9840
Iteration 6:  rho = 0.9840

Cochrane-Orcutt AR(1) regression -- iterated estimates

      Source |       SS       df       MS              Number of obs =     516
-------------+------------------------------           F(  3,   512) =    0.14
       Model |  .008145938     3  .002715313           Prob > F      =  0.9346
    Residual |  9.77268111   512  .019087268           R-squared     =  0.0008
-------------+------------------------------           Adj R-squared = -0.0050
       Total |  9.78082705   515  .018991897           Root MSE      =  .13816

------------------------------------------------------------------------------
        lnm1 |      Coef.   Std. Err.      t    P>|t|     [95% Conf. Interval]
-------------+----------------------------------------------------------------
       lnffr |   -.048539   .0769635    -0.63   0.529    -.1997422    .1026641
     lnffr_1 |  -.0053187   .0777116    -0.07   0.945    -.1579916    .1473542
     lnffr_2 |   .0004847   .0767452     0.01   0.995    -.1502895    .1512589
       _cons |   6.392877   .4301668    14.86   0.000     5.547768    7.237986
-------------+----------------------------------------------------------------
         rho |   .9839764
------------------------------------------------------------------------------
Durbin-Watson statistic (original)    0.041761
Durbin-Watson statistic (transformed) 1.982308
```

(6) 我们的新发现是什么？自相关问题解决了吗？为什么？

在新的回归结果中，变形后的 DW 统计量是 1.98，它非常接近于 2，这表明自相关的问题已经被修正。

Ⅴ. 附加上机操作练习

（1）打开数据文件 **taxrcpt. dta**[①]，然后估计以下回归方程：

$$Receipts_t = \beta_0 + \beta_1 GDP_t + \varepsilon_t$$

标准误差和参数估计值是多少？

```
. reg  receipts gdp

      Source |       SS       df       MS              Number of obs =      36
-------------+------------------------------           F(  1,    34) =24742.45
       Model |  5593602.34     1  5593602.34           Prob > F      =  0.0000
    Residual |  7686.48413    34  226.073063           R-squared     =  0.9986
-------------+------------------------------           Adj R-squared =  0.9986
       Total |  5601288.83    35  160036.824           Root MSE      =  15.036

------------------------------------------------------------------------------
    receipts |      Coef.   Std. Err.      t    P>|t|     [95% Conf. Interval]
-------------+----------------------------------------------------------------
         gdp |   .1828322   .0011623   157.30   0.000       .18047    .1851943
       _cons |  -5.969813   4.182007    -1.43   0.163    -14.46867    2.529047
------------------------------------------------------------------------------
```

$\hat{\beta}_1$的值为 0.182 832 2，它的标准误差为 0.001 162 3。

$\hat{\beta}_0$的值为－5.969 813，它的标准误差为 4.182 007。

a. Durbin-Watson 统计量是多少？上下临界值是多少？你发现了正的自相关、负的自相关、没有自相关，还是在不确定的区域？

```
. tsset obs
        time variable:  obs, 1960 to 1995
                delta:  1 unit

. dwstat

Durbin-Watson d-statistic(  2,    36) =  .9206362
```

Durbin-Watson 统计量等于 0.920 636 2，从 Durbin-Watson 表格，我们可以找到上临界值为：$d_l=1.205$，下临界值为：$d_u=1.315$。

因为 Durbin-Watson 统计量等于 0.920 636 2$<d_l=1.205$，所以我们拒绝零假设，因此模型中有自相关的问题。

b. 在误差项中使用 AR(1) 来修正自相关问题，并重新估计回归方程。估计的参数值是增大了还是减小了？它们改变了很多还是与原来差不多？标准误差增大了还是减小了？它们改变了很多还是与原来差不多？

$\hat{\beta}_1$的值增加了 0.184 454 5－0.182 832 2＝0.001 622 3。它的值并没有改变很多。$\hat{\beta}_1$的标准误差增加了 0.002 280 1－0.001 162 3＝0.001 117 8，大约是原来的 0.001 117 8/0.001 162 3＝96.17%。因此它的标准误差增加了很多。

（2）打开数据文件 **macro. dta**[②]，其中包含 1947 年第一季度到 2001 年第四季度的季度消费额、GDP 和基本利率的观测值。

---

① 该练习经过修改，数据集从下书获取：Stephen J. Schmidt，*Econometrics*（McGraw-Hill，2005）。

② 同上。

```
. prais receipts gdp, corc

Iteration 0:  rho = 0.0000
Iteration 1:  rho = 0.5476
Iteration 2:  rho = 0.5708
Iteration 3:  rho = 0.5748
Iteration 4:  rho = 0.5756
Iteration 5:  rho = 0.5757
Iteration 6:  rho = 0.5757
Iteration 7:  rho = 0.5757
Iteration 8:  rho = 0.5757
Iteration 9:  rho = 0.5757

Cochrane-Orcutt AR(1) regression -- iterated estimates

      Source |       SS       df       MS              Number of obs =      35
-------------+------------------------------           F(  1,    33) = 6544.33
       Model |  1127510.45     1  1127510.45           Prob > F      =  0.0000
    Residual |  5685.51216    33  172.288247           R-squared     =  0.9950
-------------+------------------------------           Adj R-squared =  0.9948
       Total |  1133195.96    34  33329.2929           Root MSE      =  13.126

------------------------------------------------------------------------------
    receipts |      Coef.   Std. Err.      t    P>|t|     [95% Conf. Interval]
-------------+----------------------------------------------------------------
         gdp |   .1844545   .0022801    80.90   0.000     .1798156    .1890934
       _cons |  -9.926215   9.003204    -1.10   0.278    -28.24337     8.39094
-------------+----------------------------------------------------------------
         rho |   .5757425
------------------------------------------------------------------------------
Durbin-Watson statistic (original)    0.920636
Durbin-Watson statistic (transformed) 1.475558
```

a. 估计以下回归方程：

$$Consumption_t = \beta_0 + \beta_1 GDP_t + \beta_2 Primerate_t + \varepsilon_t$$

Durbin-Watson 统计量是多少？上下临界值是多少？你发现了正的自相关、负的自相关、没有自相关，还是在不确定的区域？

```
. reg  consumption gdp primerate

      Source |       SS       df       MS              Number of obs =     220
-------------+------------------------------           F(  2,   217) =       .
       Model |   876789728     2   438394864           Prob > F      =  0.0000
    Residual |  301260.067   217  1388.29524           R-squared     =  0.9997
-------------+------------------------------           Adj R-squared =  0.9997
       Total |   877090988   219  4004981.68           Root MSE      =   37.26

------------------------------------------------------------------------------
 consumption |      Coef.   Std. Err.      t    P>|t|     [95% Conf. Interval]
-------------+----------------------------------------------------------------
         gdp |   .6832974   .0009502   719.09   0.000     .6814246    .6851703
   primerate |   -12.7147   .7784773   -16.33   0.000    -14.24905   -11.18036
       _cons |   10.96344   5.524224     1.98   0.048     .0754326    21.85144
------------------------------------------------------------------------------
```

```
. gen index=_n

. tsset index
        time variable:  index, 1 to 220
                delta:  1 unit

. dwstat

Durbin-Watson d-statistic(  3,   220) =  .1975829
```

Durbin-Watson 统计量为 0.197 582 9。

上下临界值为：$d_l = 1.653$，$d_u = 1.693$。

因为 Durbin-Watson 统计量 $=0.197\ 582\ 9 < d_l = 1.653$，所以我们拒绝零假设。模型中有正的自相关问题。

b. 重新估计回归方程，这次将 AR(1) 的修正方法考虑进去。估计的 ρ 值是多少？

```
. prais  consumption gdp primerate, corc
Cochrane-Orcutt AR(1) regression -- iterated estimates

      Source |       SS       df       MS              Number of obs =     219
-------------+------------------------------           F(  2,   216) =  339.00
       Model |  160245.209     2  80122.6044           Prob > F      =  0.0000
    Residual |  51051.5146   216  236.349605           R-squared     =  0.7584
-------------+------------------------------           Adj R-squared =  0.7562
       Total |  211296.723   218  969.251025           Root MSE      =  15.374

------------------------------------------------------------------------------
 consumption |      Coef.   Std. Err.      t    P>|t|     [95% Conf. Interval]
-------------+----------------------------------------------------------------
         gdp |    .614386   .0236044    26.03   0.000     .5678615    .6609105
   primerate |  -5.635768   1.286981    -4.38   0.000    -8.172417   -3.099119
       _cons |   27672.98   10332.13     2.68   0.008     7308.284    48037.68
-------------+----------------------------------------------------------------
         rho |   .9998553
------------------------------------------------------------------------------
Durbin-Watson statistic (original)    0.197583
Durbin-Watson statistic (transformed) 2.106304
```

估计的 ρ 值是 0. 999 855 3。

c. 用一阶差分估计下面回归方程：

$$Consumption_t - Consumption_{t-1} = \beta_0 + \beta_1(GDP_t - GDP_{t-1}) + \beta_2(Primerate_t - Primerate_{t-1}) + \varepsilon_t$$

这个回归的 Durbin-Watson 统计量是多少？一阶差分解决了自相关的问题吗？

```
. gen condiff= consumption- consumption[_n-1]
(1 missing value generated)

. gen gdpdiff= gdp- gdp[_n-1]
(1 missing value generated)

. gen primdiff= primerate- primerate[_n-1]
(1 missing value generated)

. regress condiff gdpdiff primdiff

      Source |       SS       df       MS              Number of obs =     219
-------------+------------------------------           F(  2,   216) =  332.41
       Model |  156919.903     2  78459.9516           Prob > F      =  0.0000
    Residual |  50983.9246   216  236.036688           R-squared     =  0.7548
-------------+------------------------------           Adj R-squared =  0.7525
       Total |  207903.828   218  953.687284           Root MSE      =  15.363

------------------------------------------------------------------------------
     condiff |      Coef.   Std. Err.      t    P>|t|     [95% Conf. Interval]
-------------+----------------------------------------------------------------
     gdpdiff |   .6126927   .0237715    25.77   0.000     .5658388    .6595465
    primdiff |  -5.620563   1.286314    -4.37   0.000    -8.155898   -3.085229
       _cons |   4.058384   1.493332     2.72   0.007     1.115016    7.001752
------------------------------------------------------------------------------
```

```
. dwstat

Durbin-Watson d-statistic(  3,   219) =  2.103995
```

因为 Durbin-Watson 统计量为 2. 103 995$>d_u=1.693$，所以我们不拒绝零假设。模型中没有自相关的问题。

因此一阶差分能被用来解决自相关的问题。

Chapter 8

Autocorrelation

Ⅰ. What is Autocorrelation?

Our original regression model assumed that errors were independent of one another. In most applications involving time series data—e. g. macroeconomic and financial variables, this assumption is no longer valid. This is because this data is often of a "cyclical" nature. For example, the likelihood of tomorrow being rainy is greater if today is rainy than if today is sunny.

When errors associated with observations of different time periods are related to each other, we refer to the errors as being autocorrelated or serially correlated. Most often it's the case that errors associated with adjacent observations are correlated, and errors for observations which are "far apart" are not. Thus, serial correlation is only a concern for data sets exhibiting a natural ordering of some sort.

We will focus on a particular type of serial correlation, referred to as first order serial correlation. This basically means that errors in one time period are directly correlated with errors in the next time period. Mathematically, if first-order autocorrelation occurs, the simple linear model now becomes:

$y_t=\beta_0+\beta_1 x_t+\varepsilon_t$, and;

$\varepsilon_t=\rho\varepsilon_{t-1}+v_t$, $t=1, 2, \cdots, n$,

where, the v_t are uncorrelated random variables with mean zero and variance σ_v^2.

What are the consequences for OLS estimates in the presence of autocorrelation? When errors are autocorrelated, using OLS estimators result in unbiased estimators. However, the standard errors are estimated incorrectly. Whether the standard errors are overstated or understated depends on the nature of autocorrelation. Consequently, any hypothesis tests conducted could yield erroneous results. In other words, OLS is no longer BLUE. Hence, a pattern in the errors suggests another type of estimators that would be more efficient than OLS estimators.

Ⅱ. How to Detect Autocorrelation

2.1 Plot a Graph

The first simple approach to detecting autocorrelation is plotting a graph. Let us consider the following three graphs①, one by one. The first graph shows the scatter plot of y against x in a simple linear regression model. Clearly, most dots in the graph scatter around the fitted line, indicating that there is a linear relationship between y and x.

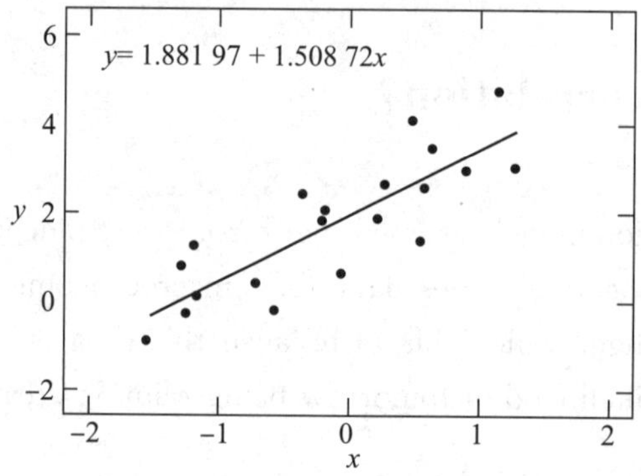

The second graph plots the errors for the different observations, which exhibit no obvious pattern—the errors seem random.

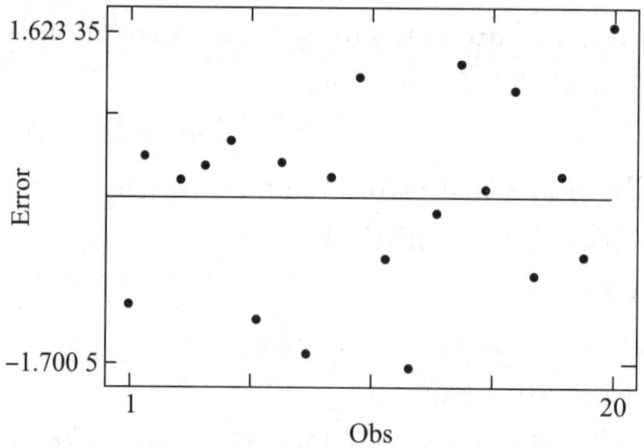

Sometimes, however, the errors follow a pattern—they are correlated across observations, creating a situation in which the observations are not independent with one another.

---

① These three graphs are selected from Chapter 14.3, *Statistics and Econometrics: Methods and Applications*, by Ashenfelter, Levine and Zimmerman, 2003.

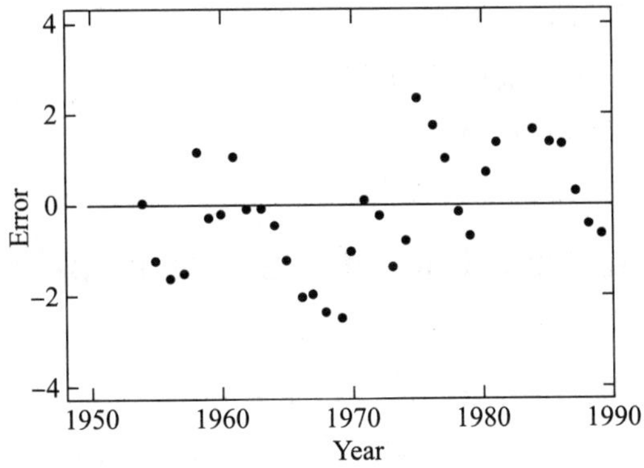

This last graph shows an example of residuals that do not seem to be random, but rather seem to follow a pattern.

2.2 Testing for Autocorrelation: The Durbin-Watson Test

The Durbin-Watson Test is a test for the presence of first-order serial correlation. It provides a way to test the null hypothesis that $\rho=0$. The alternative hypothesis can be $\rho\neq 0$; $\rho>0$: positive serial correlation; and the most likely alternative in economics $\rho<0$: negative serial correlation.

To test for positive serial correlation with the Durbin-Watson statistic, under the null we expect d to be near 2. The smaller d, the more likely the alternative hypothesis:

$$d=\frac{\sum_{t=2}^{n}e_t^2-2\sum_{t=2}^{n}e_te_{t-1}+\sum_{t=2}^{n}e_{t-1}^2}{\sum_{t=1}^{n}e_t^2}\approx 1-2\hat{\rho}+1=2(1-\hat{\rho})$$

The sampling distribution of d depends on the values of the explanatory variables. Since every problem has a different set of explanatory variables, Durbin and Watson derived upper and lower limits for the critical value of the test.

Durbin and Watson developed the following decision rule for detecting positive serial correlation:

$$\text{if}\begin{cases} d\leqslant d_l \rightarrow \text{reject } H_0 \\ d_l<d<d_u \rightarrow \text{test is inconclusive} \\ d\geqslant d_u \rightarrow \text{do not reject } H_0 \end{cases}$$

To test for negative serial correlation the decision rule is:

$$\text{if}\begin{cases} d\geqslant 4-d_l \rightarrow \text{reject } H_0 \\ 4-d_u<d<4-d_l \rightarrow \text{test is inconclusive} \\ d\leqslant 4-d_u \rightarrow \text{do not reject } H_0 \end{cases}$$

We can use a two-tailed test if there is no strong prior belief about whether there is positive or negative serial correlation—the decision rule is:

$$\text{if}\begin{cases} d\leqslant d_l \text{ or } d\geqslant 4-d_l \rightarrow \text{reject } H_0 \\ d\geqslant d_u \text{ or } d\leqslant 4-d_u \rightarrow \text{do not reject } H_0 \\ \text{otherwise, test is inconclusive} \end{cases}$$

Ⅲ. How to Fix the Problem of Autocorrelation

Let us consider a model of first-order serial correlation, where the correlation in the errors is such that the error in any period is a function of the error in the prior period. The parameter ρ measures the correlation in the error between adjacent observations. Model is shown below:

$$y_t=\beta_0+\beta_1 x_{1t}+\beta_2 x_{2t}+\cdots+\beta_k x_{kt}+\varepsilon_t$$

Meanwhile, ε_t captures the correlation in the errors across periods and is expressed as:

$$\varepsilon_t=\rho\,\varepsilon_{t-1}+v_t, t=1,2,\cdots,n$$

Quasi-differencing transforms a model characterized by first-order serial correlation so that the errors are no longer serially correlated. Lagging the original model by one period and multiplying each variable by ρ yields:

$$\rho y_{t-1}=\rho\beta_0+\rho\beta_1 x_{1(t-1)}+\rho\beta_2 x_{2(t-1)}+\cdots+\rho\beta_k x_{k(t-1)}+\rho\varepsilon_{t-1}$$

Subtracting this from the original model yields:

$$\begin{aligned} y_t-\rho y_{t-1}&=(\beta_0-\rho\beta_0)+(\beta_1 x_{1t}-\rho\beta_1 x_{1(t-1)})+\cdots+(\beta_k x_{kt}-\rho\beta_k x_{k(t-1)})+(\varepsilon_t-\rho\varepsilon_{t-1}) \\ &=\beta_0(1-\rho)+\beta_1(x_{1t}-\rho x_{1(t-1)})+\cdots+\beta_k(x_{kt}-\rho x_{k(t-1)})+v_t \end{aligned}$$

This transformation yields a residual that satisfies the usual requirements. Running the quasi-differenced model $y_t^*=\beta_0^*+\beta_1 x_{1t}^*+\beta_2 x_{2t}^*+\cdots+\beta_k x_{kt}^*+v_t$ yields estimates of the slope coefficients of the original model, where $\beta_0^*=\beta_0(1-\rho)$, $x_{it}^*=x_{it}-\rho\, x_{i(t-1)}$, and so forth.

OLS on the transformed model is BLUE. However, the practical difficulty of implementing the quasi-differenced model is we don't know ρ. Next, let us consider two ways that have been suggested to estimate ρ.

1) The Durbin Procedure.

If we take the lagged dependent variable y_{t-1} to the right-hand side of the quasi-difference model, we have:

$$y_t=\rho y_{t-1}+(\beta_0-\rho\beta_0)+(\beta_1 x_{1t}-\rho\beta_1 x_{1(t-1)})+\cdots+(\beta_k x_{kt}-\rho\beta_k x_{k(t-1)})+v_t$$

Then we run a regression of y_t on y_{t-1}, x_{1t}, $x_{1(t-1)}$, x_{2t}, $x_{2(t-1)}$, $\cdots$, x_{kt}, $x_{k(t-1)}$. The coefficient on x_{t-1} provides an estimate of ρ that might be used to form the variables used in the quasi-differenced regression.

2) The Cochrane-Orcutt Procedure.

First, we estimate the original model and the errors from the model are used to estimate ρ. Second, we regress the errors from the original regression on their lagged values. The slope coefficient of this regression provides an estimate of ρ. Third, given the estimate, $\hat{\rho}$, estimate the quasi-differenced model. Using the estimates of the coefficient generated by this estimation generates a new set of errors. Finally, the procedure then iterates and stops when the estimated $\hat{\rho}$ does not change by "much".

Ⅳ. Computer Exercise

Today, we want to look at a simple example of how actual money in circulation ($M1$) may change with changes to the Federal Funds Rate (FFR), one of the most visible tools of the FED in changing monetary policy. ①

We can first download data directly from the FED on $M1$ and FFR. Please upload the complete data file **autocorr. dta.** We have monthly data from 1959 to 2002: 3 for both series.

(1) Basic macroeconomics tells us that the FED will raise the federal funds rate if they want to decrease the amount of money in circulation. So if we run the following regression:

$$\ln(M1)_t = a + b\times\ln(FFR)_t + c\times\ln(FFR)_{t-1} + d\times\ln(FFR)_{t-2} + e_t$$

We expect that b, c, and d will be less than zero. We included some lags of FFR in order to take into account the fact that it may take some time for FFR to affect the money supply.

Before the regression, generate the following Stata codes:

. gen lnml=log(ml)

. gen lnffr=log(ffr)

. gen lnffr _ 1=log(ffr [_ n−1])

. gen lnffr _ 2=log(ffr [_ n−2])

```
reg lnm1 lnffr lnffr_1 lnffr_2

      Source |       SS       df       MS              Number of obs =     517
-------------+------------------------------           F(  3,   513) =    8.78
       Model |  15.4375148     3  5.14583827           Prob > F      =  0.0000
    Residual |  300.561504   513  .585889872           R-squared     =  0.0489
-------------+------------------------------           Adj R-squared =  0.0433
       Total |  315.999019   516    .6124012           Root MSE      =  .76543

------------------------------------------------------------------------------
        lnm1 |      Coef.   Std. Err.      t    P>|t|     [95% Conf. Interval]
-------------+----------------------------------------------------------------
       lnffr |  -.4382587   .4252217    -1.03   0.303    -1.273649    .3971314
     lnffr_1 |  -.0540469   .6416544    -0.08   0.933     -1.31464    1.206547
     lnffr_2 |    .820261   .4264712     1.92   0.055    -.0175839    1.658106
       _cons |   5.471954   .1276536    42.87   0.000     5.221166    5.722742
------------------------------------------------------------------------------
```

① This exercise is inspired by Eric Bettinger at Weatherhead School of Management, Case Western Reserve University. Data is collected from http: //connection. cwru. edu/econ326/mod8/C/autocorr. dta.

The coefficients on contemporaneous month and last month are negative and insignificant with p-values greater than 5%. But we can get a positive and significant coefficient on *FFR* from two months ago at 10% significance level.

(2) If we look at the plot of the residuals from this regression, what do they look like? Are we worried about correlation across time? Why?

In Stata, please type the following codes:

```
. gen obs= _n
. predict resid, resid
. graph twoway scatter resid obs
```

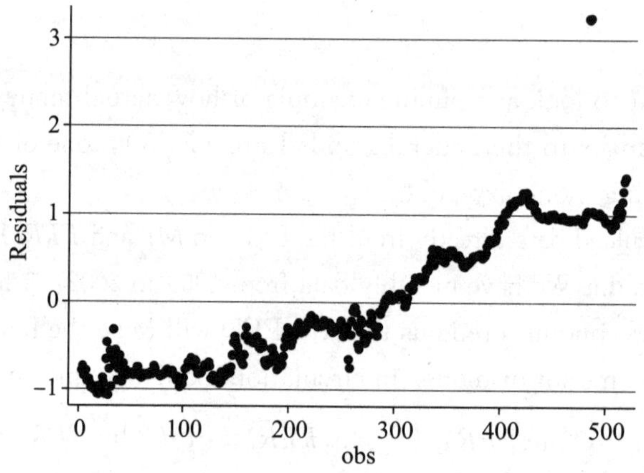

From the graph, the residuals display a pattern—they increase over the time period. This indicates that they are correlated across observations, creating a situation in which the observations are not independent of one another.

(3) When we perform a Durbin - Watson test, what do we get?

In Stata, type:

```
. tsset obs
. dwstat
```

```
tsset obs
       time variable:  obs, 1 to 519
               delta:  1 unit

dwstat

Durbin-Watson d-statistic(  4,    517) =  .0417607
```

Note: the Durbin-Watson varies between 0 and 4. If it is close to 0 or to 4, then we have a problem. (We would need a DW statistic between 1.7 and 3.3 to not have a problem over a 99 percent confidence interval.)

(4) Do we have the problem of autocorrelation? Does autocorrelation affect OLS estimates? What about standard errors?

From the above graph and the Durbin - Watson test, we conclude that we have the problem of autocorrelation. Although autocorrelation does not affect OLS estimates, it cause OLS standard errors biased. Hence, OLS is no longer BLUE.

(5) How do we fix the problem of autocorrelation?

We can review the notes for the class on the exact formulation. Stata does this for us fairly rapidly. (Show the regression results.)

```
. prais lnm1 lnffr lnffr_1 lnffr_2, corc

Iteration 0:   rho = 0.0000
Iteration 1:   rho = 0.9814
Iteration 2:   rho = 0.9838
Iteration 3:   rho = 0.9840
Iteration 4:   rho = 0.9840
Iteration 5:   rho = 0.9840
Iteration 6:   rho = 0.9840

Cochrane-Orcutt AR(1) regression -- iterated estimates

      Source |       SS       df       MS              Number of obs =     516
-------------+------------------------------           F(  3,   512) =    0.14
       Model |  .008145938     3  .002715313           Prob > F      =  0.9346
    Residual |  9.77268111   512  .019087268           R-squared     =  0.0008
-------------+------------------------------           Adj R-squared = -0.0050
       Total |  9.78082705   515  .018991897           Root MSE      =  .13816

------------------------------------------------------------------------------
        lnm1 |      Coef.   Std. Err.      t    P>|t|     [95% Conf. Interval]
-------------+----------------------------------------------------------------
       lnffr |   -.048539   .0769635    -0.63   0.529    -.1997422    .1026641
     lnffr_1 |  -.0053187   .0777116    -0.07   0.945    -.1579916    .1473542
     lnffr_2 |   .0004847   .0767452     0.01   0.995    -.1502895    .1512589
       _cons |   6.392877   .4301668    14.86   0.000     5.547768    7.237986
-------------+----------------------------------------------------------------
         rho |   .9839764
------------------------------------------------------------------------------
Durbin-Watson statistic (original)    0.041761
Durbin-Watson statistic (transformed) 1.982308
```

(6) What are our new findings? Has the problem of autocorrelation been corrected? Why?

From the new regression, the transformed Durbin-Watson statistic is 1.98. It is very close to 2, showing that the problem of autocorrelation has been corrected.

Ⅴ. Additional Computer Exercises

(1) Open the data file **taxrcpt. dta**[①], and then estimate the regression:

$$Receipts_t=\beta_0+\beta_1 GDP_t+\varepsilon_t$$

What are the values and standard errors of the parameter estimates?

```
. reg  receipts gdp

      Source |       SS       df       MS              Number of obs =      36
-------------+------------------------------           F(  1,    34) =24742.45
       Model |  5593602.34     1  5593602.34           Prob > F      =  0.0000
    Residual |  7686.48413    34  226.073063           R-squared     =  0.9986
-------------+------------------------------           Adj R-squared =  0.9986
       Total |  5601288.83    35  160036.824           Root MSE      =  15.036

------------------------------------------------------------------------------
    receipts |      Coef.   Std. Err.      t    P>|t|     [95% Conf. Interval]
-------------+----------------------------------------------------------------
         gdp |   .1828322   .0011623   157.30   0.000       .18047    .1851943
       _cons |  -5.969813   4.182007    -1.43   0.163    -14.46867    2.529047
------------------------------------------------------------------------------
```

① This exercise is modified and the data set is collected from the book—*Econometrics* written by Stephen J. Schmidt (McGraw-Hill, 2005).

The value of $\hat{\beta}_1$ is 0. 182 832 2 and its standard error is 0. 001 162 3.

The value of $\hat{\beta}_0$ is−5. 969 813 and its standard error is 4. 182 007.

a. What is the Durbin-Watson statistic? What are the upper and lower critical values? Do you find positive autocorrelation, negative autocorrelation, no autocorrelation, or are you in the uncertain region?

```
. tsset obs
        time variable:  obs, 1960 to 1995
                delta:  1 unit

. dwstat

Durbin-Watson d-statistic(  2,    36) =  .9206362
```

Durbin-Watson *d*-statistic (2, 36) =0. 920 636 2. From the Durbin-Watson Table, we can find the critical values are: d_l=1. 205, d_u=1. 315.

Since *d*-statistic=0. 920 636 2<d_l=1. 205, we reject the null hypothesis and conclude that there is a problem of positive serial correlation.

b. Re-estimate the equation using a correction for an AR(1) process in the error term. Have the estimated parameter values risen or fallen? Have they changed much, or are they about the same as before? Have the standard errors of the estimated parameters risen or fallen? Have they changed much, or are they about the same as before?

```
. prais receipts gdp, corc

Iteration 0:  rho = 0.0000
Iteration 1:  rho = 0.5476
Iteration 2:  rho = 0.5708
Iteration 3:  rho = 0.5748
Iteration 4:  rho = 0.5756
Iteration 5:  rho = 0.5757
Iteration 6:  rho = 0.5757
Iteration 7:  rho = 0.5757
Iteration 8:  rho = 0.5757
Iteration 9:  rho = 0.5757

Cochrane-Orcutt AR(1) regression -- iterated estimates

      Source |       SS       df       MS              Number of obs =      35
-------------+------------------------------           F(  1,    33) = 6544.33
       Model |  1127510.45     1  1127510.45           Prob > F      =  0.0000
    Residual |  5685.51216    33  172.288247           R-squared     =  0.9950
-------------+------------------------------           Adj R-squared =  0.9948
       Total |  1133195.96    34  33329.2929           Root MSE      =  13.126

------------------------------------------------------------------------------
    receipts |      Coef.   Std. Err.      t    P>|t|     [95% Conf. Interval]
-------------+----------------------------------------------------------------
         gdp |   .1844545   .0022801    80.90   0.000     .1798156    .1890934
       _cons |  -9.926215   9.003204    -1.10   0.278    -28.24337     8.39094
-------------+----------------------------------------------------------------
         rho |   .5757425
------------------------------------------------------------------------------
Durbin-Watson statistic (original)    0.920636
Durbin-Watson statistic (transformed) 1.475558
```

The value for $\hat{\beta}_1$ rises by 0. 184 454 5−0. 182 832 2=0. 001 622 3. The value for $\hat{\beta}_1$ hasn't changed much, it's still about the same as before. The standard error for $\hat{\beta}_1$ increases by 0. 002 280 1−0. 001 162 3=0. 001 117 8, and the rate of change is 0. 001 117 8/0. 001 162 3=96. 17%. So, it has changed a lot.

(2) Load the data file **macro. dta**[①], which contains quarterly observations on consumption, GDP, and the prime rate from the first quarter of 1947 to the fourth quarter of 2001.

a. Estimate the regression:

$$Consumption_t = \beta_0 + \beta_1 GDP_t + \beta_2 Primerate_t + \varepsilon_t$$

What is the Durbin-Watson statistic for this regression? Find the lower and upper critical values for the Durbin-Watson test. Does this regression have autocorrelation and, if so, is it positive or negative?

```
. reg consumption gdp primerate

      Source |       SS           df       MS      Number of obs   =       220
-------------+----------------------------------   F(  2,    217)  =         .
       Model |   876789728         2   438394864   Prob > F        =    0.0000
    Residual |  301260.067       217  1388.29524   R-squared       =    0.9997
-------------+----------------------------------   Adj R-squared   =    0.9997
       Total |   877090988       219  4004981.68   Root MSE        =     37.26

------------------------------------------------------------------------------
 consumption |      Coef.   Std. Err.      t    P>|t|     [95% Conf. Interval]
-------------+----------------------------------------------------------------
         gdp |   .6832974   .0009502   719.09   0.000     .6814246    .6851703
   primerate |   -12.7147   .7784773   -16.33   0.000    -14.24905   -11.18036
       _cons |   10.96344   5.524224     1.98   0.048     .0754326    21.85144
------------------------------------------------------------------------------
```

```
. gen index=_n

. tsset index
        time variable:  index, 1 to 220
                delta:  1 unit

. dwstat

Durbin-Watson d-statistic(  3,   220) =  .1975829
```

Durbin-Watson d-statistic (3, 220) $=0.197\,582\,9$.

The lower and upper bounds are: $d_l=1.653$, $d_u=1.693$.

Since d-statistic$=0.197\,582\,9<d_l=1.653$, we reject the null hypothesis. Hence, there is a problem of positive serial correlation.

b. Re-estimate the regression, including a correction for first-order autocorrelation. What is the estimated value of ρ?

The estimated value of ρ is $0.999\,855\,3$.

c. Estimate the regression in first differences:

$$Consumption_t - Consumption_{t-1} = \beta_0 + \beta_1 (GDP_t - GDP_{t-1}) + \beta_2 (Primerate_t - Primerate_{t-1}) + \varepsilon_t$$

---

① This exercise is modified and the data set is collected from the book—*Econometrics* written by Stephen J. Schmidt (McGraw-Hill, 2005).

```
. prais  consumption gdp primerate, corc
Cochrane-Orcutt AR(1) regression -- iterated estimates

      Source |       SS       df       MS              Number of obs =     219
-------------+------------------------------           F(  2,   216) =  339.00
       Model |  160245.209     2  80122.6044           Prob > F      =  0.0000
    Residual |  51051.5146   216  236.349605           R-squared     =  0.7584
-------------+------------------------------           Adj R-squared =  0.7562
       Total |  211296.723   218  969.251025           Root MSE      =  15.374

------------------------------------------------------------------------------
 consumption |      Coef.   Std. Err.      t    P>|t|     [95% Conf. Interval]
-------------+----------------------------------------------------------------
         gdp |    .614386   .0236044    26.03   0.000     .5678615    .6609105
   primerate |  -5.635768   1.286981    -4.38   0.000    -8.172417   -3.099119
       _cons |   27672.98   10332.13     2.68   0.008     7308.284    48037.68
-------------+----------------------------------------------------------------
         rho |   .9998553
------------------------------------------------------------------------------
Durbin-Watson statistic (original)    0.197583
Durbin-Watson statistic (transformed) 2.106304
```

What is the Durbin-Watson statistic for this regression? Has the first differencing dealt with the autocorrelation problem or not?

```
. gen condiff= consumption- consumption[_n-1]
(1 missing value generated)

. gen gdpdiff= gdp- gdp[_n-1]
(1 missing value generated)

. gen primdiff= primerate- primerate[_n-1]
(1 missing value generated)

. regress condiff gdpdiff primdiff

      Source |       SS       df       MS              Number of obs =     219
-------------+------------------------------           F(  2,   216) =  332.41
       Model |  156919.903     2  78459.9516           Prob > F      =  0.0000
    Residual |  50983.9246   216  236.036688           R-squared     =  0.7548
-------------+------------------------------           Adj R-squared =  0.7525
       Total |  207903.828   218  953.687284           Root MSE      =  15.363

------------------------------------------------------------------------------
     condiff |      Coef.   Std. Err.      t    P>|t|     [95% Conf. Interval]
-------------+----------------------------------------------------------------
     gdpdiff |   .6126927   .0237715    25.77   0.000     .5658388    .6595465
    primdiff |  -5.620563   1.286314    -4.37   0.000    -8.155898   -3.085229
       _cons |   4.058384   1.493332     2.72   0.007     1.115016    7.001752
------------------------------------------------------------------------------
```

```
. dwstat

Durbin-Watson d-statistic(  3,   219) =  2.103995
```

Since Durbin-Watson d-statistic $=2.103\ 995>d_u=1.693$, we do not reject the null hypothesis. Hence, there is no autocorrelation problem.

The first differencing can be used to fix the autocorrelation problem.

第 9 章

内生性问题和辅助变量

Ⅰ. 内生变量的问题

1.1 内生性的定义

如果一个自变量和误差项之间没有相关性，这一变量便是外生变量。相比之下，内生性是指一个自变量和误差项之间具有相关关系。从数学上来说，在一个回归方程 $y=\alpha+\beta_1x_1+\beta_2x_2+\cdots+\beta_kx_k+\mu$ 中，如果某个自变量 x_j 和随机误差 μ 之间相关，它就是内生变量。鉴于内生变量的存在，我们则需要处理内生性的问题。

为了增强对这个定义的理解，我们考虑一个工资模型[①]：

$$\log(wage)=\beta_0+\beta_1\,educ+\beta_2exper+\beta_3\,abil+u$$

我们主要关心的是 β_1 和 β_2 的估计。然而，我们知道，如果不能观测到 $abil$ 的数据，我们将会得到 β_1 和 β_2 的有偏估计（为什么？参见第 6 章所指出的遗漏变量会导致估计偏差的问题）。面临这样的现状，我们只能估计模型：

$$\log(wage)=\beta_0+\beta_1\,educ+\beta_2\,exper+v$$

由此所产生的主要的问题是，$educ$ 和 $exper$ 并非外生变量，或者它们具有内生性，也就是：$\mathrm{Cov}(educ,\ v)\neq0$，$\mathrm{Cov}(exper,\ v)\neq0$。

1.2 内生性的来源

i）遗漏变量。

如果依据数据建立起的真正模型是：

---

① 参考 Example 15.5，*Introductory Econometrics*：*A Modern Approach*，by Jeffrey Wooldridge，2006.

$$y=\alpha+\beta_1 x_1+\beta_2 x_2+\beta_3 x_3+\mu$$

但我们却估计模型：

$$y=\alpha+\beta_1 x_1+\beta_2 x_2+v$$

如果变量 x_1 和 x_3 具有相关关系，那么变量 x_1 将会是内生的。为什么？原因是误差项 v 是 μ 和 x_3 的函数。

如何处理遗漏变量的问题呢？我们可以采用如下几个办法。a）找出更多的数据，把每一个相互关联的变量包括在模型内。b）忽视它的存在这种方法只有在遗漏变量和其他变量之间不相关的情况下才可以采用。否则，系数估计将会有偏差，而且导致估计偏差过低或者过高。c）寻找代理变量。假设 y 是结果变量，x_3 是遗漏变量，z 是 x_3 的代理变量。那么代理变量需要具备什么性质？首先，代理变量应当和 x_3 密切相关。第二，代理变量必须是“多余的”（即可以忽略不计），从而使得 $E(y \mid x_1, x_2, x_3, z)=E(y \mid x_1, x_2, x_3)$。第三，在代理变量 z 存在的情况下，遗漏变量和其他每个回归变量之间不相关，即（$\text{corr}(x_3, x_j)=0 \mid z$）。

ii）测量误差。

如果依据数据建立起的真正模型是：

$$y=\alpha+\beta_1 x_1+\beta_2 x_2+\mu$$

但我们估计的模型是：

$$y=\alpha+\beta_1 x_1+\beta_2 x_2^*+\mu$$

其中，$x_2^*=x_2+\varphi$。

如果 φ 取决于 x_2，那么 x_2 将是内生变量。

例如：假设 x_2 用来测量医院规模（床位数），而且测量误差会随医院规模增大而增大。那么，当 x_2 增加时，φ 也随之增加。因而，μ 和 x_2 相关，造成了内生性问题的发生。重新安排方程，我们有：

$$y=\alpha+\beta_1 x_1+\beta_2 x_2^*+\mu$$
$$y=\alpha+\beta_1 x_1+\beta_2(x_2+\varphi)+\mu$$
$$y=\alpha+\beta_1 x_1+\beta_2 x_2+(\mu+\beta_2\varphi)$$

如果 φ 是 x_2 的函数，那么误差项和 x_2 相关，导致内生性。

如何处理测量误差呢？a）改进测量从而排除极端的异常值，或者得到更完整的数据。b）解释因测量误差所造成的影响程度很小，并通过外部数据来验证。c）解释测量误差和包括在模型里的变量不相关。

iii）联立性问题。

在联立方程组里，两个或两个以上的位于方程左边的变量同时是彼此的函数（也可以通过其他方式说明它们的关系）：

$$y_1=\alpha+\beta_1 x_1+\gamma_2 y_2+\varepsilon$$
$$y_2=\alpha+\gamma_1 x_1+\gamma_2 y_1+\varepsilon$$

为了解决这个联立性的问题，我们可以将这两个方程用“简化型”的方式改写为各个方程仅含一个内生变量（具体细节将在以后章节里讨论）。我们还可以使用辅助变量（IV）

的方法来解释这一问题。较笼统地说，只要回归变量 x 和随机误差之间有相关性，我们便可以考虑 IV 方法。

Ⅱ. 辅助变量（IV）估计法

在简单线性回归模型里：$y=\beta_0+\beta_1 x+u$，如果变量 z 是 x 的有效辅助变量，那么它必须符合下面的条件：

i）辅助变量必须是外生的，也就是 $\text{Cov}(z, u)=0$。

ii）辅助变量必须与内生变量 x 相关，也就是 $\text{Cov}(z, x)\neq 0$。

iii）辅助变量不应该进入最初的回归模型（即不能解释 y）。

我们可以使用常识和经济理论来决定是否 $\text{Cov}(z, u)=0$ 的假设有道理。我们可以通过回归 $x=\gamma_0+\gamma_1 z+v$ 来检验 H_0：$\gamma_1=0$，从而测试是否 $\text{Cov}(z, x)\neq 0$。有时我们将这一回归称为第一步回归。

注意：辅助变量和代理变量的关系。

在工资模型 $\log(wage)=\beta_0+\beta_1 educ+\beta_2 exper+\beta_3 abil+u$ 中，IQ 是不是教育变量的一个好的辅助变量呢？

如果 IQ 是 $abil$ 的代理变量，那么 $\text{Cov}(IQ, educ)=0$，而且 $\text{Cov}(IQ, abil)\neq 0$。那么，在模型 $\log(wage)=\beta_0+\beta_1 educ+\beta_2 exper+v$ 中，

（1）$\text{Cov}(IQ, v)\neq 0$，

（2）$\text{Cov}(IQ, educ)=0$。

结论：一个好的代理变量从来不是一个好的辅助变量，反之亦然！

2.1 简单回归模型中的辅助变量估计

对于 $y=\beta_0+\beta_1 x+u$ 的模型，同时假设 $\text{Cov}(z, y)=\beta_1\text{Cov}(z, x)+\text{Cov}(z, u)$，那么我们可以得到：$\beta_1=\text{Cov}(z, y)/\text{Cov}(z, x)$。故而，辅助变量法得到的 β_1 的估计值为：

$$\hat{\beta}_1=\frac{\sum(z_i-\bar{z})(y_i-\bar{y})}{\sum(z_i-\bar{z})(x_i-\bar{x})}$$

比较辅助变量估计和 OLS 估计，我们可以发现，在辅助估计情况下得到的标准误与 OLS 估计情况下得到的不同，往往会更大。辅助变量 z 和内生变量 x 越相关，通过辅助变量估计得到的标准误越小。如果 $\text{Cov}(x, u)\neq 0$，OLS 回归会有不一致的估计结果，但采用 IV 估计却会产生一致的估计结果。

2.2 多元回归模型中的辅助变量估计

IV 估计可扩展运用到多元回归模型。我们的问题是多元回归模型有可能包含多个内生变量。如果有多个内生变量，那么每一个内生变量至少需要一个辅助变量。假如结构模

型写为：$y_1=\beta_0+\beta_1 y_2+\beta_2 z_1+u_1$，其中 y_2 是内生的，z_1 是外生的。令 z_2 做辅助变量，故 $\mathrm{Cov}(z_2, u_1)=0$。而且 $y_2=p_0+p_1 z_1+p_2 z_2+v_2$，其中 $p_2\neq 0$。这种简化型方程式可以帮助我们回归以内生变量为被解释变量，外生变量为解释变量的模型。

注意：一个内生变量很有可能会有多个辅助变量。考虑我们最初的结构模型，并且 $y_2=p_0+p_1 z_1+p_2 z_2+p_3 z_3+v_2$。这里，我们假设 z_2 和 z_3 都是有效辅助变量：它们没有出现在结构模型里，并且与结构误差项 u_1 无关。

2.3 采用两阶段最小二乘法（2SLS）解释 IV 估计

两阶段最小二乘法（2SLS）可以被用来计算 IV 估计值。其方法如下：

第一阶段：把 x_2 作为所有其他变量和辅助变量（称为 z）的函数并进行回归预测：$x_2=a+g_1 x_1+g_2 z+n$。创建 x_2 的预测值，称之 x_2^p。

第二阶段：把 y 作为 x_2^p 和所有其他变量的函数并进行回归预测：$y=a+b_1 x_1+b_2 x_2^p+e$。

注意：我们需要调整标准误以考虑 x_2^p 是预测值这一事实。两阶段最小二乘估计只有在第二阶段的方程是线性的情况下才符合一致性要求。如果第二阶段的方程不是线性的，我们使用两阶段残差加入（2SRI）的方法。

其第一阶段仍然与两阶段最小二乘估计的第一阶段一样，并得到 $v=x_2-x_2^p$。

第二阶段：把 y 作为 x_1，x_2（不包括 x_2^p）和新残差项 v 的函数并进行回归预测：

$$y=f(a+b_1 x_1+b_2 x_2+b_3 v)+e$$

其中，$f(\cdot)$ 是非线性方程。如果第二阶段是线性的，那么 2SRI 和 2SLS 所得的结果应该是一样的。

Ⅲ. 内生性和辅助变量有效性的假设检验

3.1 内生性检验——Durbin-Wu-Hausman 检验

当解释变量都是外生变量时，2SLS 估计要比 OLS 估计的效率低（即有较大的方差）。因此，我们首先测试的是是否有内生性的存在。这一点很重要。原因是：为了避免使用 IV 估计时所需要的更大量的计算（因为两阶段估计要比一阶段估计更困难些），而且 IV 估计效率相对较低。

考虑如下模型：

$$y_1=\beta_0+\beta_1 y_2+\beta_2 z_1+\beta_3 z_2+\mu$$

其中，y_2 有可能是内生变量；z_3 和 z_4 是辅助变量。为了检验内生性的存在：

第 1 步：回归 $y_2=\gamma_0+\gamma_1 z_1+\gamma_2 z_2+\gamma_3 z_3+\gamma_4 z_4+v_2$ 以计算残差 $\hat{v}_2$。

第 2 步：回归 $y_1=\beta_0+\beta_1 y_2+\beta_2 z_1+\beta_3 z_2+\delta_1 \hat{v}_2+$误差。

第 3 步：检验 $\hat{v}_2$ 在后一种模式中的显著性。如果拒绝 H_0：$\delta_1=0$，我们就有证据表明，μ 和 v_2 是相关的，因此，y_2 是内生变量！

3.2　检验辅助变量的有效性

为了检验辅助变量的有效性，我们可以采取下面的步骤。

i）利用所有的辅助变量进行 2SLS 估计，并获得残差 $\hat{u}$。

ii）回归以残差 $\hat{u}$ 为被解释变量，所有的外生变量（即外生的解释变量和辅助变量）为解释变量的模型。

iii）考虑上述回归中度量总体显著性的 F 检验。零假设 H_0 可以解释为模型中的所有变量都是外生的。如果我们拒绝 H_0，那么至少有一个（或多个）变量不是外生的。

Ⅳ. 上机操作练习

我们考虑一个多元回归模型，并先使用 OLS 方法（我们有内生性的问题/遗漏变量偏差的问题）。

（1）在 Stata 中加载 **wage. dta**。[1] 然后，做如下回归：

```
reg lwage educ exper expersq

      Source |       SS       df       MS              Number of obs =     428
-------------+------------------------------           F(  3,   424) =   26.29
       Model |  35.0223023     3  11.6741008           Prob > F      =  0.0000
    Residual |  188.305149   424  .444115917           R-squared     =  0.1568
-------------+------------------------------           Adj R-squared =  0.1509
       Total |  223.327451   427  .523015108           Root MSE      =  .66642

------------------------------------------------------------------------------
       lwage |      Coef.   Std. Err.      t    P>|t|     [95% Conf. Interval]
-------------+----------------------------------------------------------------
        educ |   .1074896   .0141465     7.60   0.000     .0796837    .1352956
       exper |   .0415665   .0131752     3.15   0.002     .0156697    .0674633
     expersq |  -.0008112   .0003932    -2.06   0.040    -.0015841   -.0000382
       _cons |  -.5220407   .1986321    -2.63   0.009    -.9124668   -.1316145
------------------------------------------------------------------------------
```

在上图的回归模型中，我们怀疑 *educ* 是一个内生变量，因为受教育水平可能与一个人的自身能力相关，而这会被误差项捕捉到。因此 *educ* 可能会与误差项相关，并引起内生性问题。

（2）教育变量可能有许多辅助变量。检验母亲的受教育水平和父亲的受教育水平是否为好的辅助变量。

```
reg educ exper expersq motheduc fatheduc

      Source |       SS       df       MS              Number of obs =     753
-------------+------------------------------           F(  4,   748) =   66.52
       Model |  1025.94324     4   256.48581           Prob > F      =  0.0000
    Residual |  2884.0966    748  3.85574412           R-squared     =  0.2624
-------------+------------------------------           Adj R-squared =  0.2584
       Total |  3910.03984   752  5.19952106           Root MSE      =  1.9636

------------------------------------------------------------------------------
        educ |      Coef.   Std. Err.      t    P>|t|     [95% Conf. Interval]
-------------+----------------------------------------------------------------
       exper |    .085378   .0255485     3.34   0.001     .0352228    .1355333
     expersq |  -.0018564   .0008276    -2.24   0.025    -.0034812   -.0002317
    motheduc |   .1856173   .0259869     7.14   0.000     .1346014    .2366331
    fatheduc |   .1845745   .0244979     7.53   0.000     .1364817    .2326674
       _cons |   8.366716   .2667111    31.37   0.000     7.843125    8.890307
------------------------------------------------------------------------------

test motheduc fatheduc

 ( 1)  motheduc = 0
 ( 2)  fatheduc = 0

       F(  2,   748) =  124.76
            Prob > F =    0.0000
```

---

① 该练习基于下书中的薪酬案例：Jeffrey Wooldridge，*Introductory Econometrics*：*A Modern Approach*，2006。资料来源：http：//fmwww. bc. edu/ec-p/data/wooldridge/MROZ。

在这个回归中，我们用内生变量 *educ* 作为因变量，其他外生变量包括可能的辅助变量作为自变量。因为母亲和父亲的受教育水平联合显著，*educ* 有两个有效的辅助变量。

（3）检验辅助变量的外生性。

首先，我们用所有辅助变量评估一个完整的 2SLS 模型，并收集残差 $\hat{u}$。

```
. ivreg lwage (educ=motheduc fatheduc) exper expersq

Instrumental variables (2SLS) regression

      Source |       SS       df       MS              Number of obs =     428
-------------+------------------------------           F(  3,   424) =    8.14
       Model |  30.3074295     3  10.1024765           Prob > F      =  0.0000
    Residual |  193.020022   424   .4552359            R-squared     =  0.1357
-------------+------------------------------           Adj R-squared =  0.1296
       Total |  223.327451   427  .523015108           Root MSE      =  .67471

------------------------------------------------------------------------------
       lwage |      Coef.   Std. Err.      t    P>|t|     [95% Conf. Interval]
-------------+----------------------------------------------------------------
        educ |   .0613966   .0314367     1.95   0.051    -.0003945    .1231878
       exper |   .0441704   .0134325     3.29   0.001     .0177679    .0705729
     expersq |   -.000899   .0004017    -2.24   0.026    -.0016885   -.0001094
       _cons |   .0481003   .4003281     0.12   0.904    -.7387745    .8349751
------------------------------------------------------------------------------
Instrumented:  educ
Instruments:   exper expersq motheduc fatheduc
------------------------------------------------------------------------------
```

然后，我们用残差 $\hat{u}$ 对所有的外生变量（即外生变量和辅助变量）进行回归。

```
. predict resid, res
(325 missing values generated)

. reg resid exper expersq motheduc fatheduc

      Source |       SS       df       MS              Number of obs =     428
-------------+------------------------------           F(  4,   423) =    0.09
       Model |  .170502982     4  .042625746           Prob > F      =  0.9845
    Residual |  192.849518   423  .455909026           R-squared     =  0.0009
-------------+------------------------------           Adj R-squared = -0.0086
       Total |  193.020021   427   .45203752           Root MSE      =  .67521

------------------------------------------------------------------------------
       resid |      Coef.   Std. Err.      t    P>|t|     [95% Conf. Interval]
-------------+----------------------------------------------------------------
       exper |  -.0000183   .0133291    -0.00   0.999    -.0262179    .0261813
     expersq |   7.34e-07   .0003985     0.00   0.999    -.0007825     .000784
    motheduc |  -.0066065   .0118864    -0.56   0.579    -.0299704    .0167573
    fatheduc |   .0057823   .0111786     0.52   0.605    -.0161902    .0277547
       _cons |   .0109641   .1412571     0.08   0.938    -.2666892    .2886173
------------------------------------------------------------------------------
```

最后，我们用 F 检验来考虑回归的显著性。

```
. test exper expersq fatheduc motheduc

 ( 1)  exper = 0
 ( 2)  expersq = 0
 ( 3)  fatheduc = 0
 ( 4)  motheduc = 0

       F(  4,   423) =    0.09
            Prob > F =    0.9845
```

零假设可以被解释为模型中所有变量都是外生的。因为 p 值大于 5%，我们不拒绝零假设并且得出所有辅助变量都是外生的结论。

（4）做 Durbin-Wu-Hausman 检验来检验 *educ* 是不是内生的。

受教育水平的辅助变量有：父亲的受教育水平和母亲的受教育水平。我们先用所有的外生变量来运行一个简化型模型以检验 *educ* 的内生性。

```
reg educ exper expersq fatheduc motheduc

      Source |       SS       df       MS              Number of obs =     753
-------------+------------------------------           F(  4,   748) =   66.52
       Model |  1025.94324     4  256.48581            Prob > F      =  0.0000
    Residual |  2884.0966    748  3.85574412           R-squared     =  0.2624
-------------+------------------------------           Adj R-squared =  0.2584
       Total |  3910.03984   752  5.19952106           Root MSE      =  1.9636

------------------------------------------------------------------------------
        educ |      Coef.   Std. Err.      t    P>|t|     [95% Conf. Interval]
-------------+----------------------------------------------------------------
       exper |    .085378   .0255485     3.34   0.001     .0352228    .1355333
     expersq |  -.0018564   .0008276    -2.24   0.025    -.0034812   -.0002317
    fatheduc |   .1845745   .0244979     7.53   0.000     .1364817    .2326674
    motheduc |   .1856173   .0259869     7.14   0.000     .1346014    .2366331
       _cons |   8.366716   .2667111    31.37   0.000     7.843125    8.890307
------------------------------------------------------------------------------
```

然后，我们保存以上回归的残差，并命名为“residuals”。然后将残差加入到主要模型中，并用 OLS 估计模型。

```
predict residuals, resid

reg lwage educ exper expersq residuals

      Source |       SS       df       MS              Number of obs =     428
-------------+------------------------------           F(  4,   423) =   20.53
       Model |  36.3063711     4  9.07659278           Prob > F      =  0.0000
    Residual |  187.02108    423  .442130213           R-squared     =  0.1626
-------------+------------------------------           Adj R-squared =  0.1547
       Total |  223.327451   427  .523015108           Root MSE      =  .66493

------------------------------------------------------------------------------
       lwage |      Coef.   Std. Err.      t    P>|t|     [95% Conf. Interval]
-------------+----------------------------------------------------------------
        educ |   .0639033   .0292123     2.19   0.029     .0064841    .1213226
       exper |   .0463071   .0134368     3.45   0.001     .0198959    .0727183
     expersq |  -.0009444   .0004001    -2.36   0.019    -.0017308    -.000158
   residuals |   .0558771    .032788     1.70   0.089    -.0085706    .1203248
       _cons |  -.0114041   .3592486    -0.03   0.975    -.7175388    .6947307
------------------------------------------------------------------------------
```

然后，我们检验加入的残差的系数的显著性。

```
test residuals

( 1)  residuals = 0

       F(  1,   423) =    2.90
            Prob > F =    0.0891
```

在 10%的显著性水平上，较小的 p 值说明 OLS 不一致，并且 *educ* 是内生的。

（5）在 10%的显著性水平上要解决自生性的问题，我们用辅助变量法，其中父母的受教育水平是本人受教育水平的辅助变量。

```
ivreg lwage (educ = motheduc fatheduc) exper expersq

Instrumental variables (2SLS) regression

      Source |       SS       df       MS              Number of obs =     428
-------------+------------------------------           F(  3,   424) =    8.14
       Model |  30.3074295     3  10.1024765           Prob > F      =  0.0000
    Residual |  193.020022   424   .4552359            R-squared     =  0.1357
-------------+------------------------------           Adj R-squared =  0.1296
       Total |  223.327451   427  .523015108           Root MSE      =  .67471

------------------------------------------------------------------------------
       lwage |      Coef.   Std. Err.      t    P>|t|     [95% Conf. Interval]
-------------+----------------------------------------------------------------
        educ |   .0613966   .0314367     1.95   0.051    -.0003945    .1231878
       exper |   .0441704   .0134325     3.29   0.001     .0177679    .0705729
     expersq |   -.000899   .0004017    -2.24   0.026    -.0016885   -.0001094
       _cons |   .0481003   .4003281     0.12   0.904    -.7387745    .8349751
------------------------------------------------------------------------------
Instrumented:  educ
Instruments:   exper expersq motheduc fatheduc
------------------------------------------------------------------------------
```

Ⅴ. 附加上机操作练习

（1）打开数据文件 **fertile. dta**[①]，该文件包含关于 1988 年博茨瓦纳女性的数据。其中有孩子的数量、受教育时间、年龄、宗教和经济现状变量。

a）用 OLS 估计以下回归方程：

$$children=\beta_0+\beta_1 educ+\beta_2 age+\beta_3 age^2+u$$

并分析估计值。特别是在 *age* 不变的情况下，多一年的受教育时间对生育的估计影响是多少？如果 100 位女性都有多一年的受教育时间，她们会预期少生几个孩子？

```
. regress children educ age agesq

      Source |       SS       df       MS              Number of obs =    4361
-------------+------------------------------           F(  3,  4357) = 1915.20
       Model |  12243.0295     3  4081.00985           Prob > F      =  0.0000
    Residual |  9284.14679  4357  2.13085765           R-squared     =  0.5687
-------------+------------------------------           Adj R-squared =  0.5684
       Total |  21527.1763  4360  4.93742577           Root MSE      =  1.4597

------------------------------------------------------------------------------
    children |      Coef.   Std. Err.      t    P>|t|     [95% Conf. Interval]
-------------+----------------------------------------------------------------
        educ |  -.0905755   .0059207   -15.30   0.000     -.102183   -.0789679
         age |   .3324486   .0165495    20.09   0.000     .3000032     .364894
       agesq |  -.0026308   .0002726    -9.65   0.000    -.0031652   -.0020964
       _cons |  -4.138307   .2405942   -17.20   0.000    -4.609994    -3.66662
------------------------------------------------------------------------------
```

在 *age* 不变的情况下，多一年的受教育时间会导致少生 0.091 个孩子。对 100 位女性来说，她们总共会少生 9 个孩子。

b）*frsthalf* 是哑变量。如果一位女性是在 7 月份前出生的，那么变量等于 1。假设 *frsthalf* 与 a）中的误差项不相关，这表明 *frsthalf* 是 *educ* 的辅助变量的合理候选变量。（提示你需要做回归。）

educ 的简化型方程是：

$$educ=\alpha_0+\alpha_1 age+\alpha_2 age^2+\alpha_3 frsthalf+v$$

```
. regress educ age agesq frsthalf

      Source |       SS       df       MS              Number of obs =    4361
-------------+------------------------------           F(  3,  4357) =  175.21
       Model |  7238.42472     3  2412.80824           Prob > F      =  0.0000
    Residual |   60001.141  4357  13.7712052           R-squared     =  0.1077
-------------+------------------------------           Adj R-squared =  0.1070
       Total |  67239.5657  4360  15.4219187           Root MSE      =   3.711

------------------------------------------------------------------------------
        educ |      Coef.   Std. Err.      t    P>|t|     [95% Conf. Interval]
-------------+----------------------------------------------------------------
         age |  -.1079504   .0420402    -2.57   0.010    -.1903706   -.0255302
       agesq |  -.0005056   .0006929    -0.73   0.466    -.0018641    .0008529
    frsthalf |  -.8522854   .1128296    -7.55   0.000    -1.073489   -.6310821
       _cons |   9.692864   .5980686    16.21   0.000     8.520346    10.86538
------------------------------------------------------------------------------
```

并且我们需要保证 $\alpha_3\neq0$。从回归中我们得到 $\alpha_3=-0.852$ 且 s. e. $(\alpha_3)=0.113$。

因此，如果 *age* 不变，在一年的前半年中出生的女性会有少一年的受教育时间。α_3 的

① 资料来源：http：//fmwww. bc. edu/ec-p/data/wooldridge/fertile. dta。

p 值为 0.000，因此识别条件成立。

c）用 *frsthalf* 作为 *educ* 的辅助变量来估计 a）中的模型。与 a）中的 OLS 结果作比较。

```
. ivregress 2sls children age agesq (educ =frsthalf)

Instrumental variables (2SLS) regression          Number of obs =       4361
                                                  Wald chi2(3)  =    5300.22
                                                  Prob > chi2   =     0.0000
                                                  R-squared     =     0.5502
                                                  Root MSE      =       1.49

------------------------------------------------------------------------------
    children |      Coef.   Std. Err.      z    P>|z|     [95% Conf. Interval]
-------------+----------------------------------------------------------------
        educ |  -.1714989   .0531553    -3.23   0.001    -.2756813   -.0673165
         age |   .3236052   .0178514    18.13   0.000     .2886171    .3585934
       agesq |  -.0026723   .0002796    -9.56   0.000    -.0032202   -.0021244
       _cons |  -3.387805   .5478988    -6.18   0.000    -4.461667   -2.313943
------------------------------------------------------------------------------
Instrumented:  educ
Instruments:   age agesq frsthalf
```

现在估计的教育对于生育的影响变得更大了。在 *age* 不变的情况下，多一年受教育时间会导致少生 0.171 个孩子。

d）将二元变量 *electric*，*tv* 和 *bicycle* 加入模型中，并假设它们是外生的。用 OLS 和 2SLS 来估计回归方程并比较 *educ* 的系数。分析 *tv* 的系数并解释为什么电视的所有权对生育有消极作用。

当我们将 *electric*，*tv* 和 *bicycle* 加入模型中并用 OLS 来估计时，我们得到：

```
. regress children educ age agesq electric tv bicycle

      Source |       SS       df       MS              Number of obs =    4356
-------------+------------------------------           F(  6,  4349) =  984.92
       Model |  12387.1794     6  2064.5299            Prob > F      =  0.0000
    Residual |  9116.10133  4349  2.09613735           R-squared     =  0.5761
-------------+------------------------------           Adj R-squared =  0.5755
       Total |  21503.2808  4355  4.93760752           Root MSE      =  1.4478

------------------------------------------------------------------------------
    children |      Coef.   Std. Err.      t    P>|t|     [95% Conf. Interval]
-------------+----------------------------------------------------------------
        educ |  -.0767093   .0063526   -12.08   0.000    -.0891636    -.064255
         age |   .3402038   .0164417    20.69   0.000     .3079697    .3724379
       agesq |  -.0027081   .0002706   -10.01   0.000    -.0032385   -.0021777
    electric |  -.3027293   .0761869    -3.97   0.000    -.4520944   -.1533641
          tv |  -.2531443   .0914374    -2.77   0.006    -.4324082   -.0738803
     bicycle |    .317895   .0493661     6.44   0.000     .2211123    .4146778
       _cons |  -4.389784   .2403173   -18.27   0.000    -4.860928   -3.918639
------------------------------------------------------------------------------
```

采用 2SLS 来估计，我们得到：

```
. ivregress 2sls children age agesq electric tv bicycle (educ =frsthalf)

Instrumental variables (2SLS) regression          Number of obs =       4356
                                                  Wald chi2(6)  =    5539.15
                                                  Prob > chi2   =     0.0000
                                                  R-squared     =     0.5577
                                                  Root MSE      =     1.4777

------------------------------------------------------------------------------
    children |      Coef.   Std. Err.      z    P>|z|     [95% Conf. Interval]
-------------+----------------------------------------------------------------
        educ |  -.1639814   .0654742    -2.50   0.012    -.2923086   -.0356543
         age |   .3281451   .0190434    17.23   0.000     .2908207    .3654694
       agesq |  -.0027222   .0002763    -9.85   0.000    -.0032638   -.0021806
    electric |  -.1065314   .1658316    -0.64   0.521    -.4315553    .2184925
          tv |   -.002555    .209062    -0.01   0.990    -.4123089    .4071989
     bicycle |   .3320724    .051485     6.45   0.000     .2311636    .4329812
       _cons |  -3.591332   .6445703    -5.57   0.000    -4.854667   -2.327998
------------------------------------------------------------------------------
Instrumented:  educ
Instruments:   age agesq electric tv bicycle frsthalf
```

在两个估计中，将 *electric*，*tv* 和 *bicycle* 加入到模型中减少了 *educ* 的影响，但减少并不是很多。在 OLS 估计结果中，*tv* 的系数意味着在其他因素不变的情况下，有电视的家庭会比没有电视的家庭少生大概一个孩子。有没有电视这一变量可以用来替代很多其他因素，比如收入或者地理位置等。

有趣的是，当使用 IV 方法来估计时，电视拥有权的影响是统计不显著的。*Electric* 的系数也大大减小了。系数的大幅度减小显示出线性模型可能没能采用最好的函数形式。

（2）打开数据文件 **smoke. dta**。[①]

a）估计抽烟对年收入影响的模型如下：

$$\log(income)=\beta_0+\beta_1 cigs+\beta_2 educ+\beta_3 age+\beta_4 age^2+\mu_1$$

其中 *cigs* 是平均每天抽烟的数量。你怎么解释 β_1？

假设该方程表示了因果关系，那么如果一个人每天多抽一根烟，$100\times\beta_1$ 是收入百分比的大致变化量。

b）为了显示出香烟消费可能会由收入决定，香烟的需求方程如下：

$$cigs=\gamma_0+\gamma_1\log(income)+\gamma_2 educ+\gamma_3 age+\gamma_4 age^2+\gamma_5\log(cigpric)+\gamma_6 restaurn+\mu_2$$

其中 *cigpric* 是一包香烟的价格，*restaurn* 是一个二元变量，如果一个人住在餐馆禁止吸烟的州，那么该变量等于 1。假设这些变量是外生的，你期望 γ_5 和 γ_6 的符号是什么？

因为消费和价格是负相关的，我们期望 $\gamma_5\leqslant 0$。同样的，在其他因素相同的情况下，餐馆禁止吸烟会减少吸烟量，因此 $\gamma_6\leqslant 0$。

c）在什么假设下 a）中的收入方程可以被识别？

我们需要 γ_5 或者 γ_6 不等于零。也就是说，我们需要 *cigs* 方程中有至少一个外生变量，并且不是在 log(*income*) 方程中。

d）用 OLS 来估计收入方程并且讨论 β_1 的估计值。

```
. reg lincome cigs educ age agesq

      Source |       SS       df       MS              Number of obs =     807
-------------+------------------------------           F(  4,   802) =   39.61
       Model |  67.5412888     4  16.8853222           Prob > F      =  0.0000
    Residual |  341.854549   802  .426252555           R-squared     =  0.1650
-------------+------------------------------           Adj R-squared =  0.1608
       Total |  409.395838   806  .507935283           Root MSE      =  .65288

------------------------------------------------------------------------------
     lincome |      Coef.   Std. Err.      t    P>|t|     [95% Conf. Interval]
-------------+----------------------------------------------------------------
        cigs |   .0017306   .0017137     1.01   0.313    -.0016333    .0050945
        educ |   .0603606   .0078983     7.64   0.000     .0448567    .0758645
         age |   .0576908   .0076436     7.55   0.000      .042687    .0726946
       agesq |  -.0006306   .0000834    -7.56   0.000    -.0007943   -.0004669
       _cons |   7.795444   .1704271    45.74   0.000     7.460908    8.129979
------------------------------------------------------------------------------
```

cigs 的系数显示出吸烟导致收入上升，尽管该系数不是统计显著的。需要注意的是，OLS 忽略了收入和吸烟量之间的潜在的联立性。

e）估计 *cigs* 的简化方程。（这意味着用 *cigs* 回归所有外生变量。）log(*cigpric*) 和 *restaurn* 是显著的吗？

---

① 资料来源：http：//fmwww. bc. edu/ec-p/data/wooldridge/smoke. dta。

尽管 log(*cigpric*) 是非常不显著的，但是 *restaurn* 有期望的符号并且 t 统计量是−2.47。我们可以将 log(*cigpric*) 从分析中去除，但我们依然保留它。

```
. reg  cigs educ age agesq lcigpric restaurn

      Source |       SS       df       MS              Number of obs =     807
-------------+------------------------------           F(  5,   801) =    8.61
       Model |  7740.15214     5  1548.03043           Prob > F      =  0.0000
    Residual |  144013.531   801  179.792173           R-squared     =  0.0510
-------------+------------------------------           Adj R-squared =  0.0451
       Total |  151753.683   806  188.280003           Root MSE      =  13.409

------------------------------------------------------------------------------
        cigs |      Coef.   Std. Err.      t    P>|t|     [95% Conf. Interval]
-------------+----------------------------------------------------------------
        educ |  -.4501466   .1616396    -2.78   0.005    -.7674338   -.1328594
         age |    .822541   .1543224     5.33   0.000     .5196168    1.125465
       agesq |  -.0095903   .0016792    -5.71   0.000    -.0128864   -.0062942
    lcigpric |  -.3513161    5.76555    -0.06   0.951    -11.66869    10.96606
    restaurn |  -2.736389   1.109693    -2.47   0.014    -4.914639   -.5581394
       _cons |   1.580112   23.69558     0.07   0.947    -44.93266    48.09289
------------------------------------------------------------------------------
```

f）现在，用 2SLS 来估计收入方程。讨论 β_1 的估计值与 OLS 中的估计值。

```
. ivregress 2sls lincome educ age agesq (cigs = lcigpric restaurn)

Instrumental variables (2SLS) regression               Number of obs =     807
                                                       Wald chi2(4)  =   89.80
                                                       Prob > chi2   =  0.0000
                                                       R-squared     =       .
                                                       Root MSE      =  .87723

------------------------------------------------------------------------------
     lincome |      Coef.   Std. Err.      z    P>|z|     [95% Conf. Interval]
-------------+----------------------------------------------------------------
        cigs |  -.0421257   .0261371    -1.61   0.107    -.0933535     .009102
        educ |   .0396746   .0162305     2.44   0.015     .0078633    .0714859
         age |   .0938182   .0237794     3.95   0.000     .0472115    .1404249
       agesq |  -.0010508   .0002735    -3.84   0.000    -.0015868   -.0005148
       _cons |   7.780893   .2291541    33.95   0.000      7.33176    8.230027
------------------------------------------------------------------------------
Instrumented:  cigs
Instruments:   educ age agesq lcigpric restaurn
```

现在 *cigs* 的系数是负的并且在显著性水平为 10%的基础上几乎是统计显著的。其估计的影响很大：某人多抽一根烟会降低 4.2%的预测收入。

g）你认为香烟价格和餐馆禁止吸烟在收入方程式中是外生的吗？

州内的香烟价格和餐馆禁止吸烟是外生性的这一假设在收入方程中是有问题的。收入会根据地域不同而产生差异，餐馆吸烟禁令也是。也有可能在收入相对较低的州中，餐馆吸烟禁令实施的可能性会很小。

Chapter 9

Endogeneity and Instrumental Variable

Ⅰ. The Problem of Endogeneity

1.1 Definition of Endogeneity

An independent variable (x_j) is said to be exogenous if it is uncorrelated with the error term. In contrast, endogeneity means an independent variable (x_j) is endogenous if it is correlated with the error term. Mathematically, in a regression equation: $y=\alpha+\beta_1 x_1+\beta_2 x_2+\cdots+\beta_k x_k+\mu$, an independent variable x_j is endogenous if it is correlated with μ. Given the existence of endogenous variables, we must deal with the problem of endogeneity.

To understand this definition, let us start by considering a wage equation model[①]:

$$\log(wage)=\beta_0+\beta_1\, educ+\beta_2 exper+\beta_3\, abil+u$$

Our primary interest is in the estimation of β_1 and β_2. However, we know that if *abil* is not observed, we would obtain biased estimators of them (Why? See Omitted Variables Bias in Chapter 6). In practice, we can only estimate the model:

$$\log(wage)=\beta_0+\beta_1\, educ+\beta_2\, exper+v$$

Here, the main problem is that *educ* and *exper* are not exogenous, rather they are endogenous:

$$\mathrm{Cov}(educ, v)\neq 0,\ \mathrm{Cov}(exper, v)\neq 0$$

① See Example 15.5, *Introductory Econometrics: A Modern Approach*, by Jeffrey Wooldridge, 2006.

1.2 Sources of Endogeneity

i) Omitted variables.

If the true model underlying the data is:

$$y=\alpha+\beta_1 x_1+\beta_2 x_2+\beta_3 x_3+\mu$$

But we estimate the model:

$$y=\alpha+\beta_1 x_1+\beta_2 x_2+v$$

Then variable x_1 will be endogenous if it is correlated with x_3. Why? Because $v=f(\mu, x_3)$.

There are a few options for dealing with omitted variables: a) Find additional data so that every relevant variable is included. b) Ignore it—Acceptable only if the omitted variable is uncorrelated with all included variables; otherwise the coefficient estimates will be biased up or down. c) Find proxy variable. Suppose the following: y is the outcome; x_3 is the omitted variable; z is the proxy for x_3, what properties should the proxy z have? First, proxy z should be strongly correlated with x_3. Second, proxy z must be redundant (=ignorable), such that $E(y \mid x_1, x_2, x_3, z)=E(y \mid x_1, x_2, x_3)$. Third, omitted x_3 must be uncorrelated with other regressors conditional on z: $(\text{corr}(x_3, x_j)=0 \mid z)$ for each x_j.

ii) Measurement errors.

Suppose the true model underlying the data is:

$$y=\alpha+\beta_1 x_1+\beta_2 x_2+\mu$$

But we estimate the model:

$$y=\alpha+\beta_1 x_1+\beta_2 x_2^*+\mu$$

where $x_2^*=x_2+\varphi$.

Variable x_2 will be endogenous if φ depends on x_2.

For example: suppose that x_2 measures hospital size (number of beds), and that the measurement error is greater for larger hospitals. Then as x_2 grows, so does φ. Thus, μ is correlated with x_2, causing the problem of endogeneity. Rearranging the equation, we have:

$$y=\alpha+\beta_1 x_1+\beta_2 x_2^*+\mu$$
$$y=\alpha+\beta_1 x_1+\beta_2(x_2+\varphi)+\mu$$
$$y=\alpha+\beta_1 x_1+\beta_2 x_2+(\mu+\beta_2\varphi)$$

If $\varphi=f(x_2)$, then the error term is correlated with x_2, causing endogeneity.

How to deal with measurement errors? a) Improve measurement by refusing extreme outlier values or by requiring more complete data. b) Argue that the degree of error is small and use outside data for validation. c) Argue that the error term is uncorrelated with included variables.

iii) Simultaneity.

A system of simultaneous equations occurs when two or more left-hand side variables are functions of each other (there are other ways of stating it, too):

$$y_1 = \alpha + \beta_1 x_1 + \gamma_2 y_2 + \varepsilon$$
$$y_2 = \alpha + \gamma_1 x_1 + \gamma_2 y_1 + \varepsilon$$

To solve this problem of simultaneity, we can rewrite these two equations in "reduced form" as a single equation with an endogenous regressor (the detail will be discussed in a later chapter). We can also use the method of instrumental variables (IV). More generally, IV applies whenever a regressor x is correlated with the error term ε.

Ⅱ. Instrumental Variables (IV) Estimation

In the simple linear regression model, where $y=\beta_0+\beta_1 x+u$, in order for a variable, z, to serve as a valid instrument for x, the following must be true:

i) The instrument must be exogenous, that is, $\mathrm{Cov}(z, u)=0$.

ii) The instrument must be correlated with the endogenous variable x, that is, $\mathrm{Cov}(z, x)\neq 0$.

iii) The instrument should not enter the main equation (i. e., does not explain y).

We have to use common sense and economic theory to decide if it makes sense to assume $\mathrm{Cov}(z, u)=0$. We can test if $\mathrm{Cov}(z, x) \neq 0$ by just testing H_0: $\gamma_1=0$ in $x=\gamma_0+\gamma_1 z+v$. Sometimes we refer to this regression as the first-stage regression.

Note: IV v s. Proxy Variable.

Is *IQ* a good instrument for education in the model: $\log(wage)=\beta_0+\beta_1\, educ+\beta_2 exper+\beta_3\, abil+u$?

If *IQ* is a good proxy variable for *abil*, then $\mathrm{Cov}(IQ, educ)=0$ and $\mathrm{Cov}(IQ, abil)\neq 0$.

Then, in the model:

$$\log(wage)=\beta_0+\beta_1 educ+\beta_2 exper+v$$

(1) $\mathrm{Cov}(IQ, v) \neq 0$

(2) $\mathrm{Cov}(IQ, educ)=0$

Conclusion: a good proxy variable is never a good IV, and vice versa!

2.1 IV Estimation in the Simple Regression Case

For $y=\beta_0+\beta_1 x+u$, and given our assumptions: $\mathrm{Cov}(z,y) = \beta_1 \mathrm{Cov}(z,x) + \mathrm{Cov}(z, u)$, so $\beta_1=\mathrm{Cov}(z, y)/\mathrm{Cov}(z, x)$. Then the IV estimator for β_1 is:

$$\hat{\beta}_1 = \frac{\sum (z_i - \bar{z})(y_i - \bar{y})}{\sum (z_i - \bar{z})(x_i - \bar{x})}$$

Comparing IV versus OLS estimation, we find that the standard error in IV case differs from the OLS' . IV standard errors are larger. The stronger the correlation between z and x is, the smaller the IV standard errors are. However, IV is consistent, while OLS is inconsistent, when $\mathrm{Cov}(x, u) \neq 0$. What if our assumption that $\mathrm{Cov}(z, u)=0$ is false? The IV estimator will be inconsistent, too.

2.2 IV Estimation in the Multiple Regression Case

IV estimation can be extended to the multiple regression case. Our problem is that one or more of the variables are endogenous. We need an instrument for each endogenous variable. Write the structural model as $y_1=\beta_0+\beta_1 y_2+\beta_2 z_1+u_1$, where y_2 is endogenous and z_1 is exogenous. Let z_2 be the instrument, so $\mathrm{Cov}(z_2, u_1)=0$ and $y_2=p_0+p_1 z_1+p_2 z_2+v_2$, where $p_2 \neq 0$. This reduced form equation regresses the endogenous variable on all exogenous ones.

Note: It's possible to have multiple instruments. Consider our original structural model, and let $y_2=p_0+p_1 z_1+p_2 z_2+p_3 z_3+v_2$. Here we're assuming that both z_2 and z_3 are valid instruments—they do not appear in the structural model and are uncorrelated with the structural error term, u_1。

2.3 Interpretation as Two-Stage Least Squares (2SLS)

One computational method which can be used to calculate IV estimates is two-stage least-squares (2SLS). Two-stage least squares (2SLS) approach generally is taken as follows.

Stage 1:

Predict x_2 as a function of all other variables plus an IV (call it z):

$$x_2=a+g_1 x_1+g_2 z+n$$

Create predicted values of x_2—call them x_2^p.

Stage 2:

Predict y as a function of x_2^p and all other variables (but not z):

$$y=a+b_1 x_1+b_2 x_2^p+e$$

Note: adjust the standard errors to account for the fact that x_2^p is predicted. 2SLS is only consistent when the Stage 2 equation is linear. If Stage 2 is nonlinear, use the two-stage residual inclusion (2SRI) method:

Stage 1 as in 2SLS, leading to predicted x_2^p: develop residuals $v=x_2-x_2^p$.

Stage 2: Predict y as a function of x_1, x_2 (not x_2^p) and the new residuals v:

$$y=f(a+b_1 x_1+b_2 x_2+b_3 v)+e$$

where $f(\cdot)$ is a nonlinear function.

Note that if Stage 2 is linear, then 2SRI yields the same results as 2SLS.

Ⅲ. Hypothesis Testing for Endogeneity and Instrumental Variables

3.1 Testing for Endogeneity—Durbin-Wu-Hausman test

The 2SLS estimator is less efficient (i. e. larger variance) than the OLS' when the explanatory variables are exogenous. Therefore, it is important to test for endogeneity first, in order to avoid using an IV estimator that is both more computationally intensive (2 stages is more difficult than 1) and less efficient.

Consider the model:

$$y_1 = \beta_0 + \beta_1 y_2 + \beta_2 z_1 + \beta_3 z_2 + \mu$$

where y_2 is (possibly) endogenous; z_3 and z_4 are IVs.

In order to test for endogeneity:

Step 1: regress $y_2 = \gamma_0 + \gamma_1 z_1 + \gamma_2 z_2 + \gamma_3 z_3 + \gamma_4 z_4 + v_2$ to compute residuals $\hat{v}_2$.

Step 2: regress $y_1 = \beta_0 + \beta_1 y_2 + \beta_2 z_1 + \beta_3 z_2 + \delta_1 \hat{v}_2 + error$.

Step 3: Test for the significance of $\hat{v}_2$ in the latter model. If we reject H_0: $\delta_1 = 0$, then there is evidence that μ and v_2 are correlated, therefore y_2 is endogenous!

3.2 Testing for the Validity of the Instruments

To test for the validity of the instruments, we may follow the steps below.

i) Estimate the full 2SLS model with all IVs, obtain the residuals $\hat{u}$.

ii) Regress $\hat{u}$ on all exogenous variables (i. e. the exogenous variables and the IVs).

iii) Consider the F-test of significance of the regression. H_0 can be interpreted as exogeneity of all variables in the model. Then if we reject H_0, one (or more) of your IVs are not exogenous.

Ⅳ. Computer Exercise

We consider a multiple regression model and the OLS method is used first (we have the problem of endogeneity/ the problem of omitted variable bias).

(1) Please upload **wage. dta** onto Stata. [①]After that, run the following regression:

```
reg lwage educ exper expersq

      Source |       SS       df       MS              Number of obs =     428
-------------+------------------------------           F(  3,   424) =   26.29
       Model |  35.0223023     3  11.6741008           Prob > F      =  0.0000
    Residual |  188.305149   424  .444115917           R-squared     =  0.1568
-------------+------------------------------           Adj R-squared =  0.1509
       Total |  223.327451   427  .523015108           Root MSE      =  .66642

------------------------------------------------------------------------------
       lwage |      Coef.   Std. Err.      t    P>|t|     [95% Conf. Interval]
-------------+----------------------------------------------------------------
        educ |   .1074896   .0141465     7.60   0.000     .0796837    .1352956
       exper |   .0415665   .0131752     3.15   0.002     .0156697    .0674633
     expersq |  -.0008112   .0003932    -2.06   0.040    -.0015841   -.0000382
       _cons |  -.5220407   .1986321    -2.63   0.009    -.9124668   -.1316145
------------------------------------------------------------------------------
```

In the above regression model, we doubt that *educ* is an endogenous variable, since education level might be correlated with a person's inner ability which is captured in the error term. Hence *educ* is likely to be correlated with the error term, causing the problem of endogeneity.

(2) Education variable may have many instrumental variables. Test whether mother's education and father's education are good instrumental variables.

```
reg educ exper expersq motheduc fatheduc

      Source |       SS       df       MS              Number of obs =     753
-------------+------------------------------           F(  4,   748) =   66.52
       Model |  1025.94324     4   256.48581           Prob > F      =  0.0000
    Residual |   2884.0966   748  3.85574412           R-squared     =  0.2624
-------------+------------------------------           Adj R-squared =  0.2584
       Total |  3910.03984   752  5.19952106           Root MSE      =  1.9636

------------------------------------------------------------------------------
        educ |      Coef.   Std. Err.      t    P>|t|     [95% Conf. Interval]
-------------+----------------------------------------------------------------
       exper |    .085378   .0255485     3.34   0.001     .0352228    .1355333
     expersq |  -.0018564   .0008276    -2.24   0.025    -.0034812   -.0002317
    motheduc |   .1856173   .0259869     7.14   0.000     .1346014    .2366331
    fatheduc |   .1845745   .0244979     7.53   0.000     .1364817    .2326674
       _cons |   8.366716   .2667111    31.37   0.000     7.843125    8.890307
------------------------------------------------------------------------------

test motheduc fatheduc

 ( 1)  motheduc = 0
 ( 2)  fatheduc = 0

       F(  2,   748) =  124.76
            Prob > F =    0.0000
```

In this regression, we regress the endogenous variable—*educ* on all exogenous variables including the potential instrumental variables. Since mother's education and father's education are jointly significant, *educ* has two valid instrumental variables.

(3) Testing for the Exogeneity of the Instruments.

First, we estimate the full 2SLS model with all IVs, obtain the residuals $\hat{u}$.

① This exercise is based on the wage example in *Introductory Econometrics: A Modern Approach*, by Jeffrey Wooldridge, 2006. Data is collected from http://fmwww.bc.edu/ec-p/data/wooldridge/MROZ.

```
. ivreg lwage (educ=motheduc fatheduc) exper expersq

Instrumental variables (2SLS) regression

      Source |       SS       df       MS              Number of obs =     428
-------------+------------------------------           F(  3,   424) =    8.14
       Model |  30.3074295     3  10.1024765           Prob > F      =  0.0000
    Residual |  193.020022   424   .4552359            R-squared     =  0.1357
-------------+------------------------------           Adj R-squared =  0.1296
       Total |  223.327451   427  .523015108           Root MSE      =  .67471

------------------------------------------------------------------------------
       lwage |      Coef.   Std. Err.      t    P>|t|     [95% Conf. Interval]
-------------+----------------------------------------------------------------
        educ |   .0613966   .0314367     1.95   0.051    -.0003945    .1231878
       exper |   .0441704   .0134325     3.29   0.001     .0177679    .0705729
     expersq |   -.000899   .0004017    -2.24   0.026    -.0016885   -.0001094
       _cons |   .0481003   .4003281     0.12   0.904    -.7387745    .8349751
------------------------------------------------------------------------------
Instrumented:  educ
Instruments:   exper expersq motheduc fatheduc
------------------------------------------------------------------------------
```

Then, we regress $\hat{u}$ on all exogenous variables (i. e. the exogenous variables and the IVs).

```
. predict resid, res
(325 missing values generated)

. reg resid exper expersq motheduc fatheduc

      Source |       SS       df       MS              Number of obs =     428
-------------+------------------------------           F(  4,   423) =    0.09
       Model |  .170502982     4  .042625746           Prob > F      =  0.9845
    Residual |  192.849518   423  .455909026           R-squared     =  0.0009
-------------+------------------------------           Adj R-squared = -0.0086
       Total |  193.020021   427   .45203752           Root MSE      =  .67521

------------------------------------------------------------------------------
       resid |      Coef.   Std. Err.      t    P>|t|     [95% Conf. Interval]
-------------+----------------------------------------------------------------
       exper |  -.0000183   .0133291    -0.00   0.999    -.0262179    .0261813
     expersq |   7.34e-07   .0003985     0.00   0.999    -.0007825     .000784
    motheduc |  -.0066065   .0118864    -0.56   0.579    -.0299704    .0167573
    fatheduc |   .0057823   .0111786     0.52   0.605    -.0161902    .0277547
       _cons |   .0109641   .1412571     0.08   0.938    -.2666892    .2886173
------------------------------------------------------------------------------
```

Finally, we consider the F-test of significance of the regression.

```
. test exper expersq fatheduc motheduc

 ( 1)  exper = 0
 ( 2)  expersq = 0
 ( 3)  fatheduc = 0
 ( 4)  motheduc = 0

       F(  4,   423) =    0.09
            Prob > F =    0.9845
```

H_0 can be interpreted as exogeneity of all variables in the model. Since the p-value is greater than 5%, we do not reject H_0 and conclude that all of our IVs are exogenous.

(4) Perform a Durbin-Wu-Hausman test to test whether *educ* is endogenous.

Instrumental variables for education level are: father's education and mother's education. To test the endogeneity of *educ*, we first run a reduced form model, using all exogenous variables.

```
reg educ exper expersq fatheduc motheduc

      Source |       SS       df       MS              Number of obs =     753
-------------+------------------------------           F(  4,   748) =   66.52
       Model |  1025.94324     4  256.48581            Prob > F      =  0.0000
    Residual |  2884.0966    748  3.85574412           R-squared     =  0.2624
-------------+------------------------------           Adj R-squared =  0.2584
       Total |  3910.03984   752  5.19952106           Root MSE      =  1.9636

------------------------------------------------------------------------------
        educ |      Coef.   Std. Err.      t    P>|t|     [95% Conf. Interval]
-------------+----------------------------------------------------------------
       exper |    .085378   .0255485     3.34   0.001     .0352228    .1355333
     expersq |  -.0018564   .0008276    -2.24   0.025    -.0034812   -.0002317
    fatheduc |   .1845745   .0244979     7.53   0.000     .1364817    .2326674
    motheduc |   .1856173   .0259869     7.14   0.000     .1346014    .2366331
       _cons |   8.366716   .2667111    31.37   0.000     7.843125    8.890307
------------------------------------------------------------------------------
```

Then, we save the residual from the above regression. Call it "residuals". Then, include residuals in the main equation, and estimate the main equation by OLS.

```
predict residuals, resid

reg lwage educ exper expersq residuals

      Source |       SS       df       MS              Number of obs =     428
-------------+------------------------------           F(  4,   423) =   20.53
       Model |  36.3063711     4  9.07659278           Prob > F      =  0.0000
    Residual |  187.02108    423  .442130213           R-squared     =  0.1626
-------------+------------------------------           Adj R-squared =  0.1547
       Total |  223.327451   427  .523015108           Root MSE      =  .66493

------------------------------------------------------------------------------
       lwage |      Coef.   Std. Err.      t    P>|t|     [95% Conf. Interval]
-------------+----------------------------------------------------------------
        educ |   .0639033   .0292123     2.19   0.029     .0064841    .1213226
       exper |   .0463071   .0134368     3.45   0.001     .0198959    .0727183
     expersq |  -.0009444   .0004001    -2.36   0.019    -.0017308    -.000158
   residuals |   .0558771    .032788     1.70   0.089    -.0085706    .1203248
       _cons |  -.0114041   .3592486    -0.03   0.975    -.7175388    .6947307
------------------------------------------------------------------------------
```

Then, we test the significance of the coefficient of the added residual.

```
test residuals

 ( 1)  residuals = 0

       F(  1,   423) =    2.90
            Prob > F =    0.0891
```

At 10% significance level, the small p-value indicates that OLS is not consistent and educ is endogenous.

(5) To solve for the problem of endogeneity at 10% significance level, we turn to the IV approach, where father's education and mother's education are instrumental variables for education level.

```
ivreg lwage (educ = motheduc fatheduc) exper expersq

Instrumental variables (2SLS) regression

      Source |       SS       df       MS              Number of obs =     428
-------------+------------------------------           F(  3,   424) =    8.14
       Model |  30.3074295     3  10.1024765           Prob > F      =  0.0000
    Residual |  193.020022   424   .4552359            R-squared     =  0.1357
-------------+------------------------------           Adj R-squared =  0.1296
       Total |  223.327451   427  .523015108           Root MSE      =  .67471

------------------------------------------------------------------------------
       lwage |      Coef.   Std. Err.      t    P>|t|     [95% Conf. Interval]
-------------+----------------------------------------------------------------
        educ |   .0613966   .0314367     1.95   0.051    -.0003945    .1231878
       exper |   .0441704   .0134325     3.29   0.001     .0177679    .0705729
     expersq |   -.000899   .0004017    -2.24   0.026    -.0016885   -.0001094
       _cons |   .0481003   .4003281     0.12   0.904    -.7387745    .8349751
------------------------------------------------------------------------------
Instrumented:  educ
Instruments:   exper expersq motheduc fatheduc
------------------------------------------------------------------------------
```

Ⅴ. Additional Computer Exercises

(1) Open the data file named **fertile. dta**[①], which includes, for women in Botswana during 1988, information of number of children, years of education, age and religious and economic status variables.

a) Estimate this model by OLS:

$$children = \beta_0 + \beta_1 educ + \beta_2 age + \beta_3 age^2 + u$$

and then interpret the estimates. In particular, holding *age* fixed, what is the estimated effect of another year of education on fertility? If 100 women receive another year of education, how many fewer children are they expected to have?

```
. regress children educ age agesq

      Source |       SS       df       MS              Number of obs =    4361
-------------+------------------------------           F(  3,  4357) = 1915.20
       Model |  12243.0295     3  4081.00985           Prob > F      =  0.0000
    Residual |  9284.14679  4357  2.13085765           R-squared     =  0.5687
-------------+------------------------------           Adj R-squared =  0.5684
       Total |  21527.1763  4360  4.93742577           Root MSE      =  1.4597

------------------------------------------------------------------------------
    children |      Coef.   Std. Err.      t    P>|t|     [95% Conf. Interval]
-------------+----------------------------------------------------------------
        educ |  -.0905755   .0059207   -15.30   0.000     -.102183   -.0789679
         age |   .3324486   .0165495    20.09   0.000     .3000032     .364894
       agesq |  -.0026308   .0002726    -9.65   0.000    -.0031652   -.0020964
       _cons |  -4.138307   .2405942   -17.20   0.000    -4.609994    -3.66662
```

Another year of education, holding *age* fixed, results in about 0.091 fewer children. For a group of 100 women, if each gets another year of education, they collectively are predicted to have about nine fewer children.

b) *Frsthalf* is a dummy variable which equals to one if the woman was born during the first six months of the year. Assuming that *frsthalf* is uncorrelated with the error term from part a), show that *frsthalf* is reasonable IV candidate for *educ*. (Hint: You need to do a regression).

The reduced form for *educ* is:

$$educ = \alpha_0 + \alpha_1 age + \alpha_2 age^2 + \alpha_3 frsthalf + v$$

and we need $\alpha_3 \neq 0$. We obtain $\alpha_3 = -0.852$ and s. e. $(\alpha_3) = 0.113$.

Therefore, women born in the first half of the year are predicted to have almost one year less education, holding *age* fixed. The p-value of α_3 is 0.000, and so the identification condition holds.

c) Estimate the model from part a) by using *frsthalf* as an IV for *educ*. Compare the

① Data source: http: //fmwww. bc. edu/ec-p/data/wooldridge/fertile. dta.

estimated effect of education with the OLS estimate from part a).

```
. regress educ age agesq frsthalf

      Source |       SS       df       MS              Number of obs =    4361
-------------+------------------------------           F(  3,  4357) =  175.21
       Model |  7238.42472     3  2412.80824           Prob > F      =  0.0000
    Residual |   60001.141  4357  13.7712052           R-squared     =  0.1077
-------------+------------------------------           Adj R-squared =  0.1070
       Total |  67239.5657  4360  15.4219187           Root MSE      =   3.711

------------------------------------------------------------------------------
        educ |      Coef.   Std. Err.      t    P>|t|     [95% Conf. Interval]
-------------+----------------------------------------------------------------
         age |  -.1079504   .0420402    -2.57   0.010    -.1903706   -.0255302
       agesq |  -.0005056   .0006929    -0.73   0.466    -.0018641    .0008529
    frsthalf |  -.8522854   .1128296    -7.55   0.000    -1.073489   -.6310821
       _cons |   9.692864   .5980686    16.21   0.000     8.520346    10.86538
------------------------------------------------------------------------------
```

```
. ivregress 2sls children age agesq (educ =frsthalf)

Instrumental variables (2SLS) regression               Number of obs =    4361
                                                       Wald chi2(3)  = 5300.22
                                                       Prob > chi2   =  0.0000
                                                       R-squared     =  0.5502
                                                       Root MSE      =    1.49

------------------------------------------------------------------------------
    children |      Coef.   Std. Err.      z    P>|z|     [95% Conf. Interval]
-------------+----------------------------------------------------------------
        educ |  -.1714989   .0531553    -3.23   0.001    -.2756813   -.0673165
         age |   .3236052   .0178514    18.13   0.000     .2886171    .3585934
       agesq |  -.0026723   .0002796    -9.56   0.000    -.0032202   -.0021244
       _cons |  -3.387805   .5478988    -6.18   0.000    -4.461667   -2.313943
------------------------------------------------------------------------------
Instrumented:  educ
Instruments:   age agesq frsthalf
```

The estimated effect of education on fertility is now much larger. Another year of education, holding *age* fixed, results in about 0. 171 fewer children.

d) Add the binary variables *electric*, *tv*, and *bicycle* to the model and assume that these are exogenous. Estimate the equation by OLS and 2SLS and compare the estimated coefficients on *educ*. Interpret the coefficient on *tv* and explain why television ownership has a negative effect on fertility.

When we add *electric*, *tv*, and *bicycle* to the equation and estimate it by OLS we obtain:

```
. regress children educ age agesq electric tv bicycle

      Source |       SS       df       MS              Number of obs =    4356
-------------+------------------------------           F(  6,  4349) =  984.92
       Model |  12387.1794     6  2064.5299            Prob > F      =  0.0000
    Residual |  9116.10133  4349  2.09613735           R-squared     =  0.5761
-------------+------------------------------           Adj R-squared =  0.5755
       Total |  21503.2808  4355  4.93760752           Root MSE      =  1.4478

------------------------------------------------------------------------------
    children |      Coef.   Std. Err.      t    P>|t|     [95% Conf. Interval]
-------------+----------------------------------------------------------------
        educ |  -.0767093   .0063526   -12.08   0.000    -.0891636    -.064255
         age |   .3402038   .0164417    20.69   0.000     .3079697    .3724379
       agesq |  -.0027081   .0002706   -10.01   0.000    -.0032385   -.0021777
    electric |  -.3027293   .0761869    -3.97   0.000    -.4520944   -.1533641
          tv |  -.2531443   .0914374    -2.77   0.006    -.4324082   -.0738803
     bicycle |    .317895   .0493661     6.44   0.000     .2211123    .4146778
       _cons |  -4.389784   .2403173   -18.27   0.000    -4.860928   -3.918639
------------------------------------------------------------------------------
```

By 2SLS, we obtain:

```
. ivregress 2sls children age agesq electric tv bicycle (educ =frsthalf)

Instrumental variables (2SLS) regression          Number of obs =      4356
                                                   Wald chi2(6)  =   5539.15
                                                   Prob > chi2   =    0.0000
                                                   R-squared     =    0.5577
                                                   Root MSE      =    1.4777

    children       Coef.   Std. Err.      z    P>|z|     [95% Conf. Interval]

        educ   -.1639814   .0654742    -2.50   0.012    -.2923086   -.0356543
         age    .3281451   .0190434    17.23   0.000     .2908207    .3654694
       agesq   -.0027222   .0002763    -9.85   0.000    -.0032638   -.0021806
    electric   -.1065314   .1658316    -0.64   0.521    -.4315553    .2184925
          tv   -.002555     .209062    -0.01   0.990    -.4123089    .4071989
     bicycle    .3320724    .051485     6.45   0.000     .2311636    .4329812
       _cons   -3.591332   .6445703    -5.57   0.000    -4.854667   -2.327998

Instrumented:  educ
Instruments:   age agesq electric tv bicycle frsthalf
```

Adding *electric*, *tv*, and *bicycle* to the model reduces the estimated effect of *educ* in both cases, but not by too much. In the equation estimated by OLS, the coefficient on *tv* implies that, other factors fixed, for families that own a television will have about one fewer child than for families without a TV. Television ownership can be a proxy for different things, including income and perhaps geographic location.

Interestingly, the effect of TV ownership is statistically insignificant in the equation estimated by IV (even though we are not using an IV for *tv*). The coefficient on *electric* is also greatly reduced in magnitude in the IV estimation. The substantial drops in the magnitudes of these coefficients suggest that a linear model might not be the best functional form.

(2) Open the data file named **smoke. dta.** ①

a) A model to estimate the effects of smoking on annual income (perhaps through lost work days due to illness, or productivity effects) is:

$$\log(income)=\beta_0+\beta_1 cigs+\beta_2 educ+\beta_3 age+\beta_4 age^2+\mu_1$$

where *cigs* is number of cigarettes smoked per day, on average.

How do you interpret β_1?

Assuming the structural equation represents a causal relationship, $100\times\beta_1$ is the approximate percentage change in income if a person smokes one more cigarette per day.

b) To reflect the fact that cigarette consumption might be jointly determined with income, a demand for cigarettes equation is:

$$cigs=\gamma_0+\gamma_1\log(income)+\gamma_2 educ+\gamma_3 age+\gamma_4 age^2+\gamma_5\log(cigpric)$$
$$+\gamma_6 restaurn+\mu_2$$

where *cigpric* is the price of a pack of cigarettes (in cents), and *restaurn* is a binary variable equal to unity if the person lives in a state with restaurant smoking restrictions. Assuming these are exogenous to the individual, what signs would you expect for γ_5

① Data source: http: //fmwww. bc. edu/ec-p/data/wooldridge/smoke. dta.

and γ_6?

Since consumption and price are, ceteris paribus, negatively related, we expect $\gamma_5 \leqslant 0$ (allowing for $\gamma_5 = 0$). Similarly, everything else equal, restaurant smoking restrictions should reduce cigarette smoking, so $\gamma_6 \leqslant 0$.

c) Under what assumption is the income equation from part a) identified?

We need γ_5 or γ_6 to be different from zero. That is, we need at least one exogenous variable in the cigs equation that is not also in the log(*income*) equation.

d) Estimate the income equation by OLS and discuss the estimate of β_1.

```
. reg  lincome  cigs educ age agesq

      Source |       SS       df       MS              Number of obs =     807
-------------+------------------------------           F(  4,   802) =   39.61
       Model |  67.5412888     4  16.8853222           Prob > F      =  0.0000
    Residual |  341.854549   802  .426252555           R-squared     =  0.1650
-------------+------------------------------           Adj R-squared =  0.1608
       Total |  409.395838   806  .507935283           Root MSE      =  .65288

------------------------------------------------------------------------------
     lincome |      Coef.   Std. Err.      t    P>|t|     [95% Conf. Interval]
-------------+----------------------------------------------------------------
        cigs |   .0017306   .0017137     1.01   0.313    -.0016333    .0050945
        educ |   .0603606   .0078983     7.64   0.000     .0448567    .0758645
         age |   .0576908   .0076436     7.55   0.000      .042687    .0726946
       agesq |  -.0006306   .0000834    -7.56   0.000    -.0007943   -.0004669
       _cons |   7.795444   .1704271    45.74   0.000     7.460908    8.129979
------------------------------------------------------------------------------
```

The coefficient on *cigs* implies that cigarette smoking causes income to increase, although the coefficient is not statistically different from zero. Remember, OLS ignores potential simultaneity between income and cigarette smoking.

e) Estimate the reduced form for *cigs*. (Recall that this entails regressing *cigs* on all exogenous variables.) Are log(*cigpric*) and *restaurn* significant in the reduced form?

```
. reg  cigs educ age agesq lcigpric restaurn

      Source |       SS       df       MS              Number of obs =     807
-------------+------------------------------           F(  5,   801) =    8.61
       Model |  7740.15214     5  1548.03043           Prob > F      =  0.0000
    Residual |  144013.531   801  179.792173           R-squared     =  0.0510
-------------+------------------------------           Adj R-squared =  0.0451
       Total |  151753.683   806  188.280003           Root MSE      =  13.409

------------------------------------------------------------------------------
        cigs |      Coef.   Std. Err.      t    P>|t|     [95% Conf. Interval]
-------------+----------------------------------------------------------------
        educ |  -.4501466   .1616396    -2.78   0.005    -.7674338   -.1328594
         age |    .822541   .1543224     5.33   0.000     .5196168    1.125465
       agesq |  -.0095903   .0016792    -5.71   0.000    -.0128864   -.0062942
    lcigpric |  -.3513161    5.76555    -0.06   0.951    -11.66869    10.96606
    restaurn |  -2.736389   1.109693    -2.47   0.014    -4.914639   -.5581394
       _cons |   1.580112   23.69558     0.07   0.947    -44.93266    48.09289
------------------------------------------------------------------------------
```

While log (*cigpric*) is very insignificant, *restaurn* had the expected negative sign and a t statistic of about -2.47. We could drop log(*cigpric*) from the analysis but we leave it in.

f) Now, Estimate the income equation by 2SLS. Discuss how the estimate of β_1 compares with the OLS estimate.

```
. ivregress 2sls lincome educ age agesq (cigs = lcigpric restaurn)

Instrumental variables (2SLS) regression          Number of obs   =       807
                                                  Wald chi2(4)    =     89.80
                                                  Prob > chi2     =    0.0000
                                                  R-squared       =         .
                                                  Root MSE        =    .87723

------------------------------------------------------------------------------
     lincome |      Coef.   Std. Err.      z    P>|z|     [95% Conf. Interval]
-------------+----------------------------------------------------------------
        cigs |  -.0421257   .0261371    -1.61   0.107    -.0933535     .009102
        educ |   .0396746   .0162305     2.44   0.015     .0078633    .0714859
         age |   .0938182   .0237794     3.95   0.000     .0472115    .1404249
       agesq |  -.0010508   .0002735    -3.84   0.000    -.0015868   -.0005148
       _cons |   7.780893   .2291541    33.95   0.000      7.33176    8.230027
------------------------------------------------------------------------------
Instrumented:  cigs
Instruments:   educ age agesq lcigpric restaurn
```

Now the coefficient on *cigs* is negative and almost significant at the 10% level against a two-sided alternative. The estimated effect is very large: each additional cigarette someone smokes lowers predicted income by about 4.2%.

g) Do you think that cigarette prices and restaurant smoking restrictions are exogenous in the income equation?

Assuming that state level cigarette prices and restaurant smoking restrictions are exogenous in the income equation is problematical. Incomes are known to vary by region, as do restaurant smoking restrictions. It could be that in states where income is lower (after controlling for education and age), restaurant smoking restrictions are less likely to be in place.

第 10 章

虚拟自变量回归模型

Ⅰ. 虚拟变量

通常情况下，定性分析的信息会以二元形式出现，比如男性或女性，已婚或未婚，受过大学教育或没有受过大学教育，等等。这种定性分析的信息故而可以通过一个仅拥有 0 和 1 这两个数值的变量来解释，这一变量通常称为虚拟变量。显然，虚拟变量也称为二值变量。

如果我们收集到某个有定性信息的数据集，那么我们可以设立并使用下列虚拟变量，其中每一个虚拟变量只取 1 或 0 这两个数值。例如：

$$男性=\begin{cases}1,如果是男性\\0,如果不是男性\end{cases}，或已婚=\begin{cases}1,如果已婚\\0,如果未婚\end{cases}，等等。$$

因此，当我们浏览数据集时，我们可以看到：

人	男性	已婚
1	1	1
2	1	0
3	0	1

等等。

Ⅱ. 虚拟变量的应用

2.1　单一虚拟变量

如何在线性回归模型里使用虚拟变量？在本章中，我们将侧重于某些自变量（即解释变量）是虚拟变量的情况。我们考虑一个简单的模型，其解释变量包括一个连续变量（x）和一个虚拟变量（d）：$y=\beta_0+\delta_0 d+\beta_1 x+u$。这种模型可以用来解释截距的变化，因为：

如果 $d=0$，那么 $y=\beta_0+\beta_1 x+u$。

如果 $d=1$，那么 $y=(\beta_0+\delta_0)+\beta_1 x+u$。

注意，在上述模型里，$d=0$ 被视为基础组。

更具体地说，我们考虑一个工资方程①：

$$wage=\beta_0+\beta_1 edu+\delta_0 female+u$$

其中，女性 $=\begin{cases}1，如果是女性\\0，如果是男性\end{cases}$。

根据虚拟变量的特性，我们可以将上述的原始模型分为两个方程：

男性工资方程：$wage=\beta_0+\beta_1 edu+u$，

女性工资方程：$wage=\beta_0+\beta_1 edu+\delta_0+u$。

比较这两个方程，很明显，δ_0 衡量了男性工资和女性工资的差异。这可以通过下图来验证。

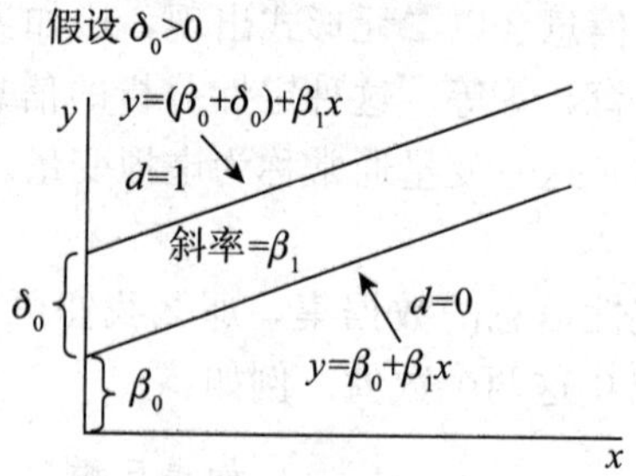

在上述模型里，我们选择以男性为基础组或基准组。β_0 是男性方程里的截距，而 $\beta_0+\delta_0$ 是女性方程里的截距。我们也可以选择以女性为基础组。关键问题在于在模型分析中，我们需要一直保持所选定的基础组。

只要工资方程满足所有 OLS 回归的必要条件，通过收集的数据，我们可以得到：

$$\widehat{wage}=\underset{(0.72)}{-1.27}-\underset{(0.26)}{1.85}female+\underset{(0.029)}{0.77}edu$$
$$n=500,R^2=0.4$$

衡量 $female$ 的系数表明了在同一教育水平下女性工人和男性工人平均每小时的工资差异。这里，工资差异为每小时平均 1.85 美元。

基于回归分析的结果，我们可以继续进行分析，以检验性别对于工资的影响效果是否显著。所设立的零假设和备择假设如下：

H_0：$\delta_0=0$ →在男女之间没有工资歧视

H_1：$\delta_0<0$ →在男女之间存在工资歧视

当零假设成立时，检验统计量是服从自由度为 $n-k-1$（此处 $k=2$）的 t 分布。如果显著性水平是 $\alpha=0.05$，从 t 分布表，我们可以查出自由度为（500－3）的临界值是－1.645。

① 参考 Example 7.1，*Introductory Econometrics*：*A Modern Approach*，by Jeffrey Wooldridge，2006.

然后，根据样本数据，对 δ_0 的最小二乘估计值是 -1.85，样本标准差是 0.26，相应的 t 值是 -7.115。由于 t 值 $=-7.115$ 小于临界值 $=-1.645$，因此我们拒绝零假设，并得出男女之间存在工资歧视的结论。

2.2　多个虚拟变量的使用

上述例子显示了我们该如何使用一个单一的虚拟变量。事实上，在同一模型里，我们可以使用多个虚拟变量来解释尽可能多的类别。假如在我们的数据里，每个人可能是高中辍学生、高中毕业生，或者是大学毕业生。要比较高中毕业生或者大学毕业生相对于高中辍学生的情况，我们要考虑 2 个虚拟变量：如果只是高中毕业生，$hsgrad=1$，否则为 0。如果是大学毕业生，$colgrad=1$，否则为 0。

我们再次回到工资方程，这一次，我们考虑多个虚拟变量：

$$\log(\widehat{wage})=\underset{(0.2)}{1.01}-\underset{(0.16)}{1.45}female+\underset{(0.001)}{0.09}edu+\underset{(0.001)}{0.05}married$$

$$n=500, R^2=0.45$$

在上面的例子中，婚姻系数表明了在教育水平和性别固定的情况下已婚和未婚工人的工资差别。更具体地说，该系数表明，在教育水平和性别固定的情况下，已婚工人要比未婚工人多获得 5%的工资。

注意，在上面的例子中，我们事先假定婚姻状况对工资的影响对女性和男性都是一样的。如果这一假设不成立，我们可能要考虑使用四组群体，如已婚男性、单身男性、已婚女性和单身女性。

总之，任何分类变量可以转变成一系列虚拟变量。但是，我们应该意识到虚拟变量陷阱的存在。由于基础组体现为模型的截距部分，如果我们有 n 个类别，我们应该只在模型里考虑 $n-1$ 个相关虚拟变量。否则，如下表所示，常数项和 n 个虚拟变量将完全共线。

个体	已婚男性	已婚女性	单身女性	单身男性	常数项
1	1	0	0	0	1
2	0	0	1	0	1
3	0	1	0	0	1

2.3　与虚拟变量有关的交互项

到目前为止，我们已学会使用虚拟变量来使截距发生变化。然而，我们还可以通过虚拟变量 d 和一个连续变量 x 之间的交互项来允许斜率参数的变化。从数学上来说，对于一个简单的模型：$y=\beta_0+\delta_0 d+\beta_1 x+\delta_1 d\times x+u$，我们可以考虑下面两种情况：

如果 $d=0$，那么 $y=\beta_0+\beta_1 x+u$。

如果 $d=1$，那么 $y=(\beta_0+\delta_0)+(\beta_1+\delta_1)x+u$。

比较这两种情况下 x 的系数，我们可以发现，δ_1 衡量斜率系数的变化。下图更加明确地证实了这一点。

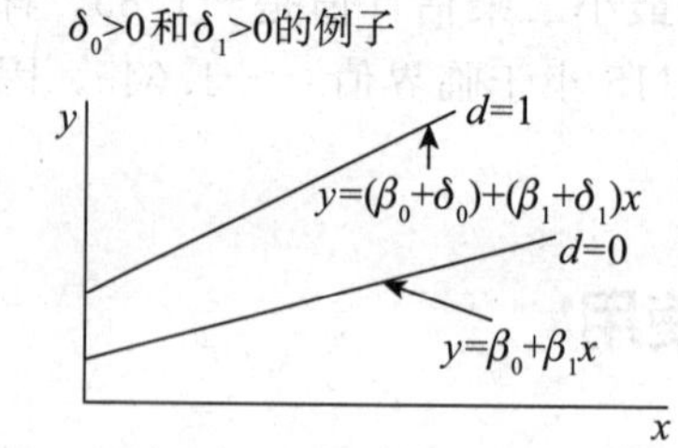

为了了解有关虚拟变量的交互项是如何起作用的，我们来比较以下三个工资方程：

模型 1：不考虑男性工人和女性工人的工资差别。

$$wage=\beta_0+\beta_1 edu+\mu$$

模型 2：考虑男性工人和女性工人的工资差别。

$$wage=\beta_0+\beta_1 edu+\delta_0 female+\mu$$

模型 3：考虑男性工人和女性工人工资方程里不同的截距和斜率。

$$wage=\beta_0+\beta_1 edu+\delta_0 female+\delta_1 female\times edu+\mu$$

对于第三个模型，因为$\frac{\Delta wage}{\Delta edu}=\beta_1+\delta_1 female$，如果想要研究男性工人和女性工人的教育收益是否一样，我们可以建立零假设为 H_0：$\delta_1=0$ 的检验。因为男性工人工资方程是 $wage=\beta_0+\beta_1 edu+\mu$，女性工人工资方程是 $wage=(\beta_0+\delta_0)+(\beta_1+\delta_1)edu+\mu$，如果要检验在相同的教育水平下男性工人和女性工人的工资是否相同，我们可以建立零假设为 H_0：$\delta_0=0$ 和 $\delta_1=0$ 的检验。

Ⅲ. 检验各组的差异——邹式检验法

回归函数在不同组是否不同的检验可以被看作是检验虚拟变量及其交互项是否具有联合显著性。故而，我们可以回归有交互项和没有交互项的受限模型和非受限模型来计算 F 统计量，但是这种计算可能会不方便。

$$F\equiv\frac{(SSR_r-SSR_{ur})/q}{SSR_{ur}/(n-k-1)},$$

其中 r 代表受限，ur 代表非受限。

另一种做法是采用邹式检验法。我们考虑回归模型为 $y=a+b\times x_1+c\times x_2+u$，根据两组数据，我们分别估计这两组数据的模型：

$y=a_1+b_1\times x_1+c_1\times x_2+u$　　第一组，

$y=a_2+b_2\times x_1+c_2\times x_2+u$　　第二组。

而且我们估计把两组数据合并起来的模型：

$y=a+b\times x_1+c\times x_2+u$　　两组合并。

在最后的回归里，我们假定 $a_1==a_2$，$b_1==b_2$，$c_1==c_2$。运用下面的公式进行邹式检验：

$$F=\frac{[SSR-(SSR_1+SSR_2)]}{SSR_1+SSR_2}\cdot\frac{[n-2(k+1)]}{k+1}$$

这个公式表明，我们不需要回归非受限模型（该模型包含与 k 个连续变量有关的交互项）来计算合适的 F 统计量，我们只需回归第一组里的受限模型，并获得 SSR_1，然后我们回归第二组里的受限模型，并获得 SSR_2。再将两组合并，回归合并模型得到 SSR，我们就可以计算 F 统计量。这种邹式检验法实际上只是一个简单的“限制性排除” F 检验，而且我们已经认识到，$SSR_{ur}=SSR_1+SSR_2$。

注意，在每组里，我们有 $k+1$ 个限制条件（斜率系数和截距）。因此，总的估计自由度为 $n-2k-2$。

Ⅳ. 上机操作练习

4.1　如何创建虚拟变量

有两种创建虚拟变量的方法：一种方法是使用“generate”指令，它可以一次创建一个虚拟变量；另一种方法是使用“tabulate”指令，它可以一次创建一整组辅助变量。

方法 1：使用“generate”指令。

```
input age

          age
1. 10
2. 20
3. 30
4. 40
5. 45
6. end
```

我们创建一个虚拟变量：如果被抽样人员小于 25 岁，虚拟变量值为 1。在 Stata 中，我们可以输入：

```
gen young = 0

replace young = 1 if age<25
(2 real changes made)

list young

     +-------+
     | young |
     |-------|
  1. |     1 |
  2. |     1 |
  3. |     0 |
  4. |     0 |
  5. |     0 |
     +-------+
```

注意：在 Stata 中，一个简单的方法是输入：gen young=(age<25)。

如果有一个字符串变量，我们要如何创建一个虚拟变量？我们可以在 Stata 中输入：

```
input str6 sex

          sex
1. female
2. male
3. male
4. female
5. male

gen female =0

replace female=1 if (sex == "female")
(2 real changes made)
```

方法 2：使用“tabulate”指令。

tabulate 和 generate（）选项可以创建一整组虚拟变量。

```
input group

       group
1. 1
2. 3
3. 2
4. 1
5. 2

tabulate group, gen(g)

      group |      Freq.     Percent        Cum.
------------+-----------------------------------
          1 |          2       40.00       40.00
          2 |          2       40.00       80.00
          3 |          1       20.00      100.00
------------+-----------------------------------
      Total |          5      100.00

list

     +-----------------------------------------------------------+
     | age   young      sex   female   group   g1   g2   g3 |
     |-----------------------------------------------------------|
  1. |  10       1   female        1       1    1    0    0 |
  2. |  20       1     male        0       3    0    0    1 |
  3. |  30       0     male        0       2    0    1    0 |
  4. |  40       0   female        1       1    1    0    0 |
  5. |  45       0     male        0       2    0    1    0 |
     +-----------------------------------------------------------+
```

你可以随意命名变量。如果我们输入了“tabulate group，gen（res）”，新的变量会被命名为 res1，res2 和 res3。

注意：“tabulate”可以被用在字符串变量上。例如：

```
input str9 result

        result
1. good
2. bad
3. good
4. excellent
5. bad

tabulate result, gen(res)

     result |      Freq.     Percent        Cum.
------------+-----------------------------------
        bad |          2       40.00       40.00
  excellent |          1       20.00       60.00
       good |          2       40.00      100.00
------------+-----------------------------------
      Total |          5      100.00

list res*

     +------------------------------------+
     |    result   res1   res2   res3 |
     |------------------------------------|
  1. |      good      0      0      1 |
  2. |       bad      1      0      0 |
  3. |      good      0      0      1 |
  4. | excellent      0      1      0 |
  5. |       bad      1      0      0 |
     +------------------------------------+
```

4.2 假设检验

请在 Stata 中打开 **wage1. dta**。[①] 请输入以下指令来学习如何使用另一种方法创建虚拟变量。

① 资料来源：http：//fmwww. bc. edu/ec-p/data/wooldridge/WAGE1. dta。

. gen male= （~female）

. gen single= （~married）

. gen marrmale= （married & ~female）

. gen marrfem= （married & female）

. gen singfem= （female & ~married）

. gen singmale= （~female & ~married）

我们来考虑以下模型：

```
gen femed = female*educ

reg lwage female educ femed

      Source |       SS       df       MS              Number of obs =     526
-------------+------------------------------           F(  3,   522) =   74.65
       Model |  44.531522     3  14.8438407            Prob > F      =  0.0000
    Residual |  103.79824   522  .198847202            R-squared     =  0.3002
-------------+------------------------------           Adj R-squared =  0.2962
       Total | 148.329762   525   .28253288            Root MSE      =  .44592

------------------------------------------------------------------------------
       lwage |      Coef.   Std. Err.      t    P>|t|     [95% Conf. Interval]
-------------+----------------------------------------------------------------
      female |  -.3600646   .1854296    -1.94   0.053    -.7243445    .0042153
        educ |   .0772279   .0089875     8.59   0.000     .0595718    .0948841
       femed |  -.0000641   .0145035    -0.00   0.996    -.0285565    .0284283
       _cons |   .8259547   .1180502     7.00   0.000     .5940427    1.057867
------------------------------------------------------------------------------
```

i）要测试男女的教育回报率是否相同，在做完回归检验后，我们可以输入：

```
test femed

( 1)  femed = 0

      F(  1,   522) =    0.00
           Prob > F =    0.9965
```

因为 p 值非常大，我们不能拒绝 *femed* 的系数是 0 的零假设，因此我们可以得出结论：男女的教育回报率是相同的。

ii）如何检测拥有相同教育背景的男女是否有相同的工资率。

在这个练习中，要检验男女的工资是否不同，我们可以使用邹氏检验。首先，我们分为两组将 *lwage* 对连续独立变量进行回归。

```
regress lwage educ if female ==1

      Source |       SS       df       MS              Number of obs =     252
-------------+------------------------------           F(  1,   250) =   56.55
       Model | 9.13742872     1  9.13742872            Prob > F      =  0.0000
    Residual | 40.3961831   250  .161584732            R-squared     =  0.1845
-------------+------------------------------           Adj R-squared =  0.1812
       Total | 49.5336118   251  .197345067            Root MSE      =  .40198

------------------------------------------------------------------------------
       lwage |      Coef.   Std. Err.      t    P>|t|     [95% Conf. Interval]
-------------+----------------------------------------------------------------
        educ |   .0771639   .0102613     7.52   0.000     .0569543    .0973735
       _cons |   .4658901   .1289047     3.61   0.000     .2120125    .7197676
------------------------------------------------------------------------------

reg lwage educ if female ==0

      Source |       SS       df       MS              Number of obs =     274
-------------+------------------------------           F(  1,   272) =   62.99
       Model | 14.6820937     1  14.6820937            Prob > F      =  0.0000
    Residual | 63.4020566   272  .233095796            R-squared     =  0.1880
-------------+------------------------------           Adj R-squared =  0.1850
       Total | 78.0841503   273  .286022529            Root MSE      =   .4828

------------------------------------------------------------------------------
       lwage |      Coef.   Std. Err.      t    P>|t|     [95% Conf. Interval]
-------------+----------------------------------------------------------------
        educ |   .0772279   .0097308     7.94   0.000     .0580707    .0963852
       _cons |   .8259547   .1278128     6.46   0.000     .5743265    1.077583
------------------------------------------------------------------------------
```

然后对于两组数据，我们将 *lwage* 对 *educ* 进行回归。

```
reg lwage educ

      Source |       SS       df       MS              Number of obs =     526
-------------+------------------------------           F(  1,   524) =  119.58
       Model |  27.5606296     1  27.5606296           Prob > F      =  0.0000
    Residual |  120.769132   524  .230475443           R-squared     =  0.1858
-------------+------------------------------           Adj R-squared =  0.1843
       Total |  148.329762   525   .28253288           Root MSE      =  .48008

------------------------------------------------------------------------------
       lwage |      Coef.   Std. Err.      t    P>|t|     [95% Conf. Interval]
-------------+----------------------------------------------------------------
        educ |   .0827444   .0075667    10.94   0.000     .0678796    .0976092
       _cons |   .5837726   .0973358     6.00   0.000     .3925562     .774989
------------------------------------------------------------------------------
```

在三个回归测试中，

$SSR=120.769\ 132$　　（来自两组结合的回归）

$SSR_1=40.396\ 183\ 1$　　（来自第一组的回归）

$SSR_2=63.402\ 056\ 6$　　（来自第二组的回归）

$k=1$　　（我们估计 1 个斜率系数）

$N_1=252$　　（来自第一组的回归）

$N_2=274$　　（来自第二组的回归）

因此，将以上数据代入公式中，我们得到：

$$\frac{\frac{120.769\ 132-(40.396\ 183\ 1+63.402\ 056\ 6)}{2}}{\frac{40.396\ 183\ 1+63.402\ 056\ 6}{252+274-2\times 2}}=\frac{\frac{16.970\ 892}{2}}{\frac{103.798\ 24}{522}}=42.673\ 199$$

在 Stata 中，我们可以输入：

```
test female femed

 ( 1)  female = 0
 ( 2)  femed = 0

       F(  2,   522) =   42.67
            Prob > F =    0.0000
```

因为 p 值小于 5%，我们拒绝 *female* 和 *femed* 的系数联合为 0 的零假设。因此，我们可以得出结论：相同教育背景的男性和女性的平均工资率不相同。

iii）我们可以检验一个更复杂的包含更多自变量（如工作经验和任期）的模型：

```
regress lwage female educ exper  tenure

      Source |       SS       df       MS              Number of obs =     526
-------------+------------------------------           F(  4,   521) =   84.07
       Model |  58.1853046     4  14.5463261           Prob > F      =  0.0000
    Residual |  90.1444572   521  .173021991           R-squared     =  0.3923
-------------+------------------------------           Adj R-squared =  0.3876
       Total |  148.329762   525   .28253288           Root MSE      =  .41596

------------------------------------------------------------------------------
       lwage |      Coef.   Std. Err.      t    P>|t|     [95% Conf. Interval]
-------------+----------------------------------------------------------------
      female |  -.3011459   .0372456    -8.09   0.000    -.3743158   -.2279759
        educ |   .0874623   .0069389    12.60   0.000     .0738307     .101094
       exper |   .0046294   .0016271     2.85   0.005     .0014328     .007826
      tenure |    .017367   .0029762     5.84   0.000     .0115201    .0232138
       _cons |   .5013479   .1019024     4.92   0.000     .3011579     .701538
------------------------------------------------------------------------------
```

要检验这个模型是否对男女都一样，我们可以输入：

```
gen femex = female*exper

gen femte = female * tenure

regress lwage female educ femed exper femex tenure femte

      Source |       SS       df       MS              Number of obs =     526
-------------+------------------------------           F(  7,   518) =   49.91
       Model |  59.7472642     7  8.53532345           Prob > F      =  0.0000
    Residual |  88.5824976   518  .171008683           R-squared     =  0.4028
-------------+------------------------------           Adj R-squared =  0.3947
       Total |  148.329762   525   .28253288           Root MSE      =  .41353

------------------------------------------------------------------------------
       lwage |      Coef.   Std. Err.      t    P>|t|     [95% Conf. Interval]
-------------+----------------------------------------------------------------
      female |   .0342173   .1993579     0.17   0.864     -.357432    .4258666
        educ |    .096264   .0090275    10.66   0.000     .0785289    .1139991
       femed |  -.0162279    .014157    -1.15   0.252    -.0440401    .0115844
       exper |    .008127   .0024097     3.37   0.001     .0033931     .012861
       femex |  -.0058595   .0032587    -1.80   0.073    -.0122613    .0005423
      tenure |   .0182129   .0036384     5.01   0.000      .011065    .0253608
       femte |  -.0079384   .0065482    -1.21   0.226    -.0208027    .0049258
       _cons |    .321899   .1346265     2.39   0.017     .0574178    .5863801
------------------------------------------------------------------------------
```

在将 *female* 和每个连续变量相乘后，我们将 *lwage* 对所有自变量和交互项进行回归，然后我们检验 *female* 和它的交互项的系数是不是都等于 0。

```
test female femed femex femte

 ( 1)  female = 0
 ( 2)  femed = 0
 ( 3)  femex = 0
 ( 4)  femte = 0

       F(  4,   518) =   18.82
            Prob > F =    0.0000
```

因为 p 值小于 5%，我们拒绝零假设，并且得出结论：男人和女人的工资模型不同。

V. 附加上机操作练习

打开数据文件 **ticket. dta**①，其中 *ticket*5 是个哑变量。假如有人愿意花 5 美元买电影票，*ticket*5 相应地取值为 1。同理，*ticket*10 是另外一个哑变量。假如有人愿意花 10 美元买电影票，*ticket*10 相应地取值为 1。

二元模型可以帮助我们模拟你有两个选择时的行为。例如，你买不买电影票？你今天去不去上学？你看不看电影？你吃不吃午饭？家长在不在学校当志愿者？在这个练习里，我们试图弄清楚什么因素会影响你买电影票的可能性。

因变量是你是否买电影票。我们有三个自变量：年龄、性别和你看过的朱莉娅·罗伯茨的电影的数量。

我们从简单线性回归开始。

$$ticket5 = a + b \times age + c \times male + d \times movies + e$$

① 该练习受凯斯西储大学魏德海管理学院的 Eric Bettinger 的启发。数据通过作者计量经济课堂上的学生调查收集。

使用 Stata，我们获得以下回归结果：

```
. reg ticket5 age male movies

      Source |       SS       df       MS              Number of obs =      30
-------------+------------------------------           F(  3,    26) =    8.13
       Model |  3.61352108     3  1.20450703           Prob > F      =  0.0006
    Residual |  3.85314559    26  .148197907           R-squared     =  0.4840
-------------+------------------------------           Adj R-squared =  0.4244
       Total |  7.46666667    29  .257471264           Root MSE      =  .38496

------------------------------------------------------------------------------
     ticket5 |      Coef.   Std. Err.      t    P>|t|     [95% Conf. Interval]
-------------+----------------------------------------------------------------
         age |   .0540832   .0417832     1.29   0.207    -.0318034    .1399698
        male |   .1732376   .1453926     1.19   0.244    -.1256211    .4720962
      movies |   .0784747    .018105     4.33   0.000     .0412593      .11569
       _cons |  -1.008443   .8485557    -1.19   0.245    -2.752674    .7357884
------------------------------------------------------------------------------
```

我们可以得到以下模型。

$$ticket5=-1.008\,443+0.054\,083\,2\times age+0.173\,237\,6\times male+0.078\,474\,7\times movies+e$$

因为因变量是二元的，所以如何解释这里的系数与以往方法有所不同。这里的回归系数实际上代表概率。用 *age* 来举例。如果你的年龄增加一岁，我们期望你会以 5.408 32％的概率更可能买票。如果你的年龄增加了两岁，我们期望你会以 10.816 64％的概率更可能买票。

对于性别来说，*male* 是一个二元变量。如果你是男性，它的取值为 1，如果你是女性，它的取值为 0。这也告诉我们男性与女性相比有 17.323 76％的概率更可能买电影票。

对于 *movies* 来说，你看过的她的每部电影增加了你买 5 美元电影票的可能性为 7.847 47％。

因此，这对你来说意味着什么？我们来探究这个模型如何预测你的行为。

常数项：−1.008 443

$0.054\,083\,2\times age$	（你的年龄＝22）
$0.173\,237\,6\times male$	（你的性别＝0）
$0.078\,474\,7\times movies$	（你看的电影数＝2）

对你来说，这些数值加起来是 0.338 336 8。这意味着我们预测出了你买电影票的概率是 33.833 68％。

我们可以通过查看每个人的预测值来检验这个模型是怎么运作的。举例来说，我们预测 4 号学生有 125.034 15％的几率买电影票。8 号学生有 138.009 63％的几率买电影票。注意，这些人的预测值很多是负的或大于 1 的。这是运用二元选择模型时常见的一个问题：我们可能会预测到某一事件发生的可能性大于 1。

我们来检验模型的拟合度。假设：如果你有超过 50％的几率会买票，你就真的会买电影票。

分析结果：

```
. predict predict5, xb

. gen predictbuy=0

. replace predictbuy=1 if predict5>0.5
(15 real changes made)

. tab  ticket5 predictbuy

           |      predictbuy
   ticket5 |         0          1 |     Total
-----------+----------------------+----------
         0 |        13          1 |        14
         1 |         2         14 |        16
-----------+----------------------+----------
     Total |        15         15 |        30
```

我们预测到 13 个人不会买票，事实上他们是没有买。我们预测到 14 个人会买，事实上他们买了。我们的这些预测是正确的。遗憾的是，我们预测到 2 个人不会买但他们实际上买了。我们也预测 1 个人会买，但实际上并没有买。

这 30 个人中，我们正确预测了 27 个人的行为。所以这一模型虽然有一定问题但还算是不错的预测模型。

Chapter 10

Models with Dummy Independent Variable

Ⅰ. Dummy Variables

Typically, qualitative information comes in binary form, such as male or female, married or single, college education or no college education, etc. This qualitative information can be captured by a zero-one variable, commonly called dummy variable. The dummy variable is also called binary variable, for obvious reasons.

If we have a data set on individuals, then we could use the following variables, each of which is a dummy variable that takes on either the value 1 or 0. For example:

$$male=\begin{cases}1, & \text{if are male}\\ 0, & \text{otherwise}\end{cases}, \text{ or } married=\begin{cases}1, & \text{if married}\\ 0, & \text{otherwise}\end{cases}, \text{ etc.}$$

Hence, if we browse the data set, we could see:

Person	Male	Married
1	1	1
2	1	0
3	0	1

etc.

Ⅱ. Application of Dummy Variables

2.1 Single Dummy Variable

How do we use a dummy variable in a linear regression model? In this chapter, we will focus on a dummy independent variable. Consider a simple model with one continuous variable (x) and one dummy variable (d): $y=\beta_0+\delta_0 d+\beta_1 x+u$. This can be interpreted as an intercept shift, since

If $d=0$, then $y=\beta_0+\beta_1 x+u$;

If $d=1$, then $y=(\beta_0+\delta_0)+\beta_1 x+u$.

Note, in the above model, the case of $d=0$ is the base group.

More specifically, consider a wage equation[①]:

$$wage=\beta_0+\beta_1 edu+\delta_0 female+u$$

where $female=\begin{cases}1, \text{ if person is female}\\0, \text{ if person is male}\end{cases}$.

Given the properties of a dummy variable, we can divide the above original model into two sub equations:

Male wage equation: $wage=\beta_0+\beta_1 edu+u$,

Female wage equation: $wage=\beta_0+\beta_1 edu+\delta_0+u$.

Comparing these two sub equations, obviously, δ_0 measures the difference in male and female wages. This can be verified by the following graph.

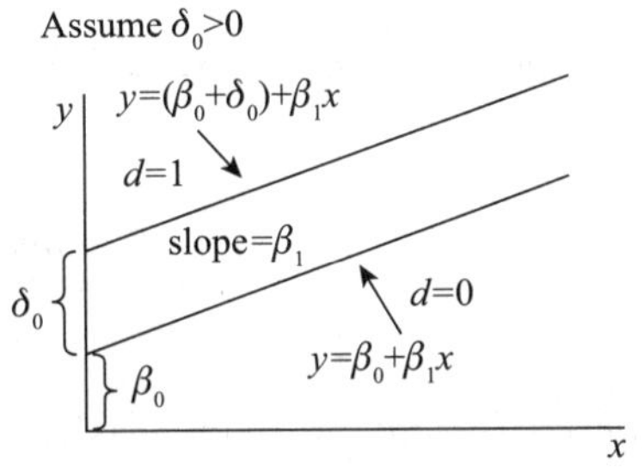

In the above case, we have chosen males as the base group or benchmark group. β_0 is the intercept for males, while $\beta_0+\delta_0$ is the intercept for females. We could choose females as base group too; hence, it is important to keep track of which group is the base group.

As long as the wage equation satisfies all of the necessary requirements for OLS regression, with collected data in hand, we could obtain:

$$\widehat{wage}=\underset{(0.72)}{-1.27}-\underset{(0.26)}{1.85}female+\underset{(0.029)}{0.77}edu$$

$$n=500, R^2=0.4$$

The coefficient on female measures the average difference in hourly wage of a female and a male, given the same level of education. In this case, the difference equals \$1.85 per hour.

Based on the regression results, we can go ahead to test whether the gender effect is statistically significant by setting up a null hypothesis against alternative hypothesis as follows:

---

① See Example 7.1, *Introductory Econometrics: A Modern Approach*, by Jeffrey Wooldridge, 2006.

H_0: $\delta_0=0\rightarrow$there is no wage discrimination between females and males

H_1: $\delta_0<0\rightarrow$there is a wage discrimination between females and males

The test statistic is t distributed with $n-k-1$ (here $k=2$) degrees of freedom if the null hypothesis is true. Let us select $\alpha=0.05$. Then, from the t table, we can read the critical value $t_c=-t_\alpha$ with (500−3) degrees of freedom=−1.645. Using the sample data, the least squares estimate of δ_0 is−1.85, with standard error=0.26. The value of the test statistic is −7.115. Since $t=-7.115<t_c=-1.645$, we reject the null hypothesis and conclude that there is a wage discrimination between females and males.

2.2 Multiple Categories

The last example shows us how to use a single dummy variable. In fact, we can use as many dummy variables as possible to control for something with multiple categories. Suppose everyone in our data is either a HS dropout, HS graduate only, or college graduate. To compare HS and college graduates to HS dropouts, include 2 dummy variables: *hsgrad*=1 if HS grad only, 0 otherwise; and *colgrad*=1 if college grad, 0 otherwise.

Once again, we go back to the wage equation, where there are a number of dummy variables:

$$\log(\widehat{wage})=\underset{(0.2)}{1.01}-\underset{(0.16)}{1.45}female+\underset{(0.001)}{0.09}edu+\underset{(0.001)}{0.05}married$$

$$n=500, R^2=0.45$$

In the above example, the coefficient on married shows the difference in wages between those who are married and those not married, holding education and gender fixed. More specifically, the coefficient on married indicates that holding education and gender constant, married people earn 5% more than single people.

Note that in the above example, the marriage premium is assumed to be the same for females and males. If this assumption does not hold, we may consider using four groups such as married males, single males, married females, and single females.

In short, any categorical variable can be turned into a set of dummy variables. However, we should be aware of a dummy variable trap. Because the base group is represented by the intercept, if there are n categories, there should be $n-1$ dummy variables included in the model. Otherwise, the constant term and n dummy variables would be perfectly collinear, as shown below.

Person	Married _ male	Married _ female	Single _ female	Single _ male	Constant
1	1	0	0	0	1
2	0	0	1	0	1
3	0	1	0	0	1

2.3 Interactions with Dummy Variables

So far, we have used dummy variables to allow for differences in intercept terms. However, we can also use them to allow for differences in slopes by considering interacting a dummy variable, d, with a continuous variable, x. Mathematically, in the simple model: $y=\beta_0+\delta_0 d+\beta_1 x+\delta_1 d\times x+u$, we can consider two sub-cases as follows:

If $d=0$, then $y=\beta_0+\beta_1 x+u$.

If $d=1$, then $y=(\beta_0+\delta_0)+(\beta_1+\delta_1)x+u$.

Comparing the coefficients on x in both cases, we can find that δ_1 measures a change in the slope. The following figure confirms this point more clearly.

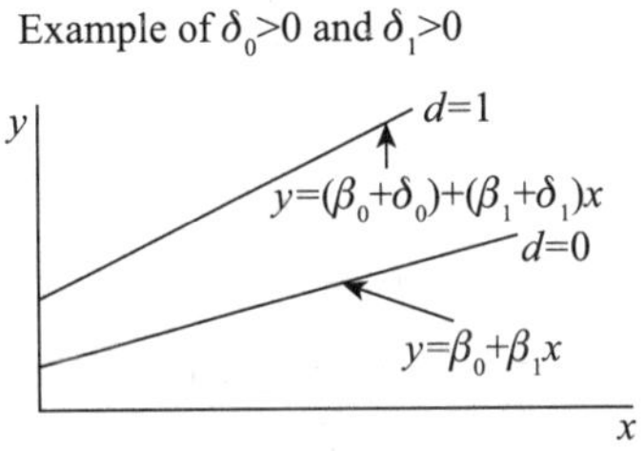

To understand how the interactions with dummies work in a model, let us compare the following three wage equations:

Model 1: assumes no difference in male and female wage.

$$wage=\beta_0+\beta_1 edu+\mu$$

Model 2: allows difference in intercepts for males and females.

$$wage=\beta_0+\beta_1 edu+\delta_0 female+\mu$$

Model 3: allows difference in intercepts and slopes for males and females.

$$wage=\beta_0+\beta_1 edu+\delta_0 female+\delta_1 female\times edu+\mu$$

In the third model, if we want to examine whether the return to education is the same for men as for women, we may set up the null hypothesis as H_0: $\delta_1=0$, since $\frac{\Delta wage}{\Delta edu}=\beta_1+\delta_1\ female$. If we want to check whether average wages are the same for men and women with identical levels of education, we may set up the null hypothesis as H_0: $\delta_0=0$ and $\delta_1=0$, since the male wage equation is $wage=\beta_0+\beta_1 edu+\mu$, while female wage equation is $wage=(\beta_0+\delta_0)+(\beta_1+\delta_1)edu+\mu$.

Ⅲ. Testing for Differences Across Groups—Chow Test

Testing whether a regression function is different for one group versus another can be thought of as simply testing for the joint significance of the dummy and its interactions with all other x variables. So, you can estimate the model with all the interactions and without and form an F statistic, but this can be unwieldy.

$$F=\frac{(SSR_r-SSR_{ur})/q}{SSR_{ur}/(n-k-1)},$$

where r is restricted and ur is unrestricted.

An alternative approach is to perform Chow-test. Consider the model: $y=a+b\times x_1+c\times x_2+u$, and say that we have two groups of data. We could estimate that model on the two groups separately:

$y=a_1+b_1\times x_1+c_1\times x_2+u$ for group 1,

$y=a_2+b_2\times x_1+c_2\times x_2+u$ for group 2,

and we could estimate a single, pooled regression:

$y=a+b\times x_1+c\times x_2+u$ for both groups.

In the last regression, we are asserting that $a_1==a_2$, $b_1==b_2$, and $c_1==c_2$. The formula for the "Chow test" of this constraint is:

$$F=\frac{[SSR-(SSR_1+SSR_2)]}{SSR_1+SSR_2}\cdot\frac{[n-2(k+1)]}{k+1}$$

It turns out we can compute the proper F statistic without running the unrestricted model with interactions with all k continuous variables. If we run the restricted model for group one to get SSR_1, then for group two to get SSR_2, and then we run the restricted model for all to get SSR, we can compute a F-statistic to perform the Chow test which is really just a simple F test for exclusion restrictions, since we've realized that $SSR_{ur}=SSR_1+SSR_2$.

Note, in each group, we have $k+1$ restrictions (each of the slope coefficients and the intercept), so the number of degrees of freedom is $n-2k-2$.

Ⅳ. Computer Exercise

4.1 How do we create dummy variables

There are two ways to create dummy variables: one is to use "generate", which creates one dummy variable at a time, the other is to use "tabulate", which creates a whole set of dummies at once.

Method 1 of 2: Use "generate".

```
input age

          age
1. 10
2. 20
3. 30
4. 40
5. 45
6. end
```

Let us generate a dummy variable taking on the value of 1 if the sampled persons are younger than 25. In Stata, we could type:

```
gen young = 0

replace young = 1 if age<25
(2 real changes made)

list young

      young
1.        1
2.        1
3.        0
4.        0
5.        0
```

Note: in Stata, an easier way to type would be: gen young= (age<25) .

If we have a string variable, how can we generate a dummy variable? We could type in Stata:

```
input str6 sex

          sex
1. female
2. male
3. male
4. female
5. male

gen female =0

replace female=1 if (sex == "female")
(2 real changes made)
```

Method 2 of 2: Use "tabulate".

Tabulate with the generate () option will generate a whole set of dummy variables.

```
input group

      group
1. 1
2. 3
3. 2
4. 1
5. 2

tabulate group, gen(g)

    group |      Freq.     Percent        Cum.
----------+-----------------------------------
        1 |          2       40.00       40.00
        2 |          2       40.00       80.00
        3 |          1       20.00      100.00
----------+-----------------------------------
    Total |          5      100.00

list

     age   young      sex   female   group   g1   g2   g3
1.    10       1   female        1       1    1    0    0
2.    20       1     male        0       3    0    0    1
3.    30       0     male        0       2    0    1    0
4.    40       0   female        1       1    1    0    0
5.    45       0     male        0       2    0    1    0
```

What you name the variable is up to you. If we had typed "tabulate group, gen (res)", the new variables would have been named res1, res2, and res3.

Note: "tabulate" can be used with string variables. For example:

```
input str9 result

        result
1.  good
2.  bad
3.  good
4.  excellent
5.  bad

tabulate result, gen(res)

     result |      Freq.     Percent        Cum.
------------+-----------------------------------
        bad |          2       40.00       40.00
  excellent |          1       20.00       60.00
       good |          2       40.00      100.00
------------+-----------------------------------
      Total |          5      100.00

list res*

     +----------------------------------------+
     |    result   res1   res2   res3 |
     |----------------------------------------|
1.   |      good      0      0      1 |
2.   |       bad      1      0      0 |
3.   |      good      0      0      1 |
4.   | excellent      0      1      0 |
5.   |       bad      1      0      0 |
     +----------------------------------------+
```

4.2 Hypothesis Test

Please upload **wage1.dta**[①] onto Stata. After that, run the following codes to learn how to generate dummy variables in another way.

. gen male= (~female)

. gen single= (~married)

. gen marrmale= (married & ~female)

. gen marrfem= (married & female)

. gen singfem= (female & ~married)

. gen singmale= (~female & ~married)

Let us consider the following model:

```
gen femed = female*educ

reg lwage female educ femed

      Source |       SS       df       MS              Number of obs =     526
-------------+------------------------------           F(  3,   522) =   74.65
       Model |  44.531522     3  14.8438407            Prob > F      =  0.0000
    Residual |  103.79824   522  .198847202            R-squared     =  0.3002
-------------+------------------------------           Adj R-squared =  0.2962
       Total | 148.329762   525   .28253288            Root MSE      =  .44592

------------------------------------------------------------------------------
       lwage |      Coef.   Std. Err.      t    P>|t|     [95% Conf. Interval]
-------------+----------------------------------------------------------------
      female |  -.3600646   .1854296    -1.94   0.053    -.7243445    .0042153
        educ |   .0772279   .0089875     8.59   0.000     .0595718    .0948841
       femed |  -.0000641   .0145035    -0.00   0.996    -.0285565    .0284283
       _cons |   .8259547   .1180502     7.00   0.000     .5940427    1.057867
------------------------------------------------------------------------------
```

① Data source: http: //fmwww.bc.edu/ec-p/data/wooldridge/WAGE1.dta.

i) To test whether the return to education is the same for men as for women, after the regression, you can type:

```
test femed

( 1)  femed = 0

      F(  1,   522) =    0.00
           Prob > F =    0.9965
```

Since the *p*-value is very large, we don't reject the null hypothesis that the coefficient on *femed* is 0, thus we conclude that the return to education is the same for men as for women.

ii) How to test average wage rates are the same for men and women with identical levels of education.

In this exercise, to test for the difference in wages between females and males, we can also turn to the Chow test. Firstly, we regress *lwage* on the continuous independent variables separately for two different groups.

```
regress lwage educ if female ==1

      Source |       SS       df       MS              Number of obs =     252
-------------+------------------------------           F(  1,   250) =   56.55
       Model |  9.13742872     1  9.13742872           Prob > F      =  0.0000
    Residual |  40.3961831   250  .161584732           R-squared     =  0.1845
-------------+------------------------------           Adj R-squared =  0.1812
       Total |  49.5336118   251  .197345067           Root MSE      =  .40198

------------------------------------------------------------------------------
       lwage |      Coef.   Std. Err.      t    P>|t|     [95% Conf. Interval]
-------------+----------------------------------------------------------------
        educ |   .0771639   .0102613     7.52   0.000     .0569543    .0973735
       _cons |   .4658901   .1289047     3.61   0.000     .2120125    .7197676
------------------------------------------------------------------------------

reg lwage educ if female ==0

      Source |       SS       df       MS              Number of obs =     274
-------------+------------------------------           F(  1,   272) =   62.99
       Model |  14.6820937     1  14.6820937           Prob > F      =  0.0000
    Residual |  63.4020566   272  .233095796           R-squared     =  0.1880
-------------+------------------------------           Adj R-squared =  0.1850
       Total |  78.0841503   273  .286022529           Root MSE      =   .4828

------------------------------------------------------------------------------
       lwage |      Coef.   Std. Err.      t    P>|t|     [95% Conf. Interval]
-------------+----------------------------------------------------------------
        educ |   .0772279   .0097308     7.94   0.000     .0580707    .0963852
       _cons |   .8259547   .1278128     6.46   0.000     .5743265    1.077583
------------------------------------------------------------------------------
```

Then, we regress *lwage* on *educ* for both groups.

```
reg lwage educ

      Source |       SS       df       MS              Number of obs =     526
-------------+------------------------------           F(  1,   524) =  119.58
       Model |  27.5606296     1  27.5606296           Prob > F      =  0.0000
    Residual |  120.769132   524  .230475443           R-squared     =  0.1858
-------------+------------------------------           Adj R-squared =  0.1843
       Total |  148.329762   525   .28253288           Root MSE      =  .48008

------------------------------------------------------------------------------
       lwage |      Coef.   Std. Err.      t    P>|t|     [95% Conf. Interval]
-------------+----------------------------------------------------------------
        educ |   .0827444   .0075667    10.94   0.000     .0678796    .0976092
       _cons |   .5837726   .0973358     6.00   0.000     .3925562     .774989
------------------------------------------------------------------------------
```

In these three regressions,

$SSR = 120.769\,132$ (from combined regression)

$SSR_1 = 40.396\,183\,1$ (from group 1 regression)

$SSR_2 = 63.402\,056\,6$ (from group 2 regression)

$k = 1$ (we estimate 1 slope coefficient)

$N_1 = 252$ (from group 1 regression)

$N_2 = 274$ (from group 2 regression)

So, plugging in, we get:

$$\frac{\dfrac{120.769\,132-(40.396\,183\,1+63.402\,056\,6)}{2}}{\dfrac{40.396\,183\,1+63.402\,056\,6}{252+274-2\times 2}}=\frac{\dfrac{16.970\,892}{2}}{\dfrac{103.798\,24}{522}}$$

$$=42.673\,199$$

In Stata, we can type:

```
test female femed

( 1)  female = 0
( 2)  femed = 0

      F(  2,   522) =   42.67
           Prob > F =    0.0000
```

Since the p-value is less than 5%, we reject the null hypothesis that both coefficients on *female* and *femed* are jointly equal to 0. Hence, we conclude that average wage rates are not the same for men and women with identical levels of education.

iii) For a more complicated model with more independent variables, such as working experience and tenure, we have:

```
regress lwage female educ exper  tenure

      Source |       SS       df       MS              Number of obs =     526
-------------+------------------------------           F(  4,   521) =   84.07
       Model |  58.1853046     4  14.5463261           Prob > F      =  0.0000
    Residual |  90.1444572   521  .173021991           R-squared     =  0.3923
-------------+------------------------------           Adj R-squared =  0.3876
       Total |  148.329762   525   .28253288           Root MSE      =  .41596

------------------------------------------------------------------------------
       lwage |      Coef.   Std. Err.      t    P>|t|     [95% Conf. Interval]
-------------+----------------------------------------------------------------
      female |  -.3011459   .0372456    -8.09   0.000    -.3743158   -.2279759
        educ |   .0874623   .0069389    12.60   0.000     .0738307     .101094
       exper |   .0046294   .0016271     2.85   0.005     .0014328     .007826
      tenure |    .017367   .0029762     5.84   0.000     .0115201    .0232138
       _cons |   .5013479   .1019024     4.92   0.000     .3011579     .701538
------------------------------------------------------------------------------
```

To test whether the model is different for males and females, we can type:

```
gen femex = female*exper

 gen femte = female * tenure

regress lwage female educ femed exper femex tenure femte

      Source |       SS       df       MS              Number of obs =     526
-------------+------------------------------           F(  7,   518) =   49.91
       Model |  59.7472642     7  8.53532345           Prob > F      =  0.0000
    Residual |  88.5824976   518  .171008683           R-squared     =  0.4028
-------------+------------------------------           Adj R-squared =  0.3947
       Total |  148.329762   525   .28253288           Root MSE      =  .41353

------------------------------------------------------------------------------
       lwage |      Coef.   Std. Err.      t    P>|t|     [95% Conf. Interval]
-------------+----------------------------------------------------------------
      female |   .0342173   .1993579     0.17   0.864     -.357432    .4258666
        educ |    .096264   .0090275    10.66   0.000     .0785289    .1139991
       femed |  -.0162279    .014157    -1.15   0.252    -.0440401    .0115844
       exper |    .008127   .0024097     3.37   0.001     .0033931     .012861
       femex |  -.0058595   .0032587    -1.80   0.073    -.0122613    .0005423
      tenure |   .0182129   .0036384     5.01   0.000      .011065    .0253608
       femte |  -.0079384   .0065482    -1.21   0.226    -.0208027    .0049258
       _cons |    .321899   .1346265     2.39   0.017     .0574178    .5863801
------------------------------------------------------------------------------
```

After multiplying *female* with each of the continuous variables, we regress *lwage* on all of the independent variables and the interaction terms, then we test whether the coefficients on *female* and its interactions are all equal to 0.

```
test female femed femex femte

 ( 1)  female = 0
 ( 2)  femed = 0
 ( 3)  femex = 0
 ( 4)  femte = 0

       F(  4,   518) =   18.82
            Prob > F =    0.0000
```

Since the p-value is less than 5%, we reject the null hypothesis, and conclude that the wage equation is different for men and women.

Ⅴ. Additional Computer Exercise

Open the data file named **ticket. dta**[①], where *ticket*5 is a dummy variable. It takes on the value of 1 if a person would like to pay $5 to buy a ticket. Similarly, *ticket*10 is another dummy variable with the value of 1 if a person would like to pay $10 for a ticket.

Binary models help us to model behavior when you have two choices. For example, do you buy the ticket or not? Do you go to class today or not? Do you see the movie or not? Do you eat lunch or not? Does a parent volunteer at school or not?

In this exercise, we want to figure out what affects your likelihood of buying a ticket.

The dependent variable is whether or not you bought a ticket. We have 3 candidate explanatory variables: age, gender, and the number of Julia Roberts' movies that you have seen.

---

① This exercise is inspired by Eric Bettinger at Weatherhead School of Management, Case Western Reserve University. Data is collected from a class survey.

Let's start with a simple linear regression.

$$ticket5 = a + b \times age + c \times male + d \times movies + e$$

Using Stata, we get:

```
. reg ticket5 age male movies

      Source |       SS       df       MS              Number of obs =      30
-------------+------------------------------           F(  3,    26) =    8.13
       Model |  3.61352108     3  1.20450703           Prob > F      =  0.0006
    Residual |  3.85314559    26  .148197907           R-squared     =  0.4840
-------------+------------------------------           Adj R-squared =  0.4244
       Total |  7.46666667    29  .257471264           Root MSE      =  .38496

------------------------------------------------------------------------------
     ticket5 |      Coef.   Std. Err.      t    P>|t|     [95% Conf. Interval]
-------------+----------------------------------------------------------------
         age |   .0540832   .0417832     1.29   0.207    -.0318034    .1399698
        male |   .1732376   .1453926     1.19   0.244    -.1256211    .4720962
      movies |   .0784747    .018105     4.33   0.000     .0412593      .11569
       _cons |  -1.008443   .8485557    -1.19   0.245    -2.752674    .7357884
------------------------------------------------------------------------------
```

By this point, we should be good at unpacking this.

$$ticket5 = -1.008\,443 + 0.054\,083\,2 \times age + 0.173\,237\,6 \times male + 0.078\,474\,7 \times movies + e$$

The coefficients in this case are different in their interpretation because the dependent variable is binary. The coefficients are actually probabilities in this case. For example, take *age*. If you were one year older, we would expect that you would be 5.408 32 percent more likely to have purchased the ticket. If you were two years older you would have been 10.816 64 percent more likely to have purchased the ticket.

As for *male*, *male* is a binary variable. It is a one if you are male and a zero if you are female. This also tells us that men are 17.323 76 percent more likely to buy a ticket than women.

Now, look at *movies*. Each movie of hers that you have seen increases your chances of buying a \$5 ticket by 7.847 47 percent.

So what does this mean for you? Let's figure out what the model predicts for you.

Constant term: −1.008 443

	$0.054\,083\,2 \times age$	(your age=22)
	$0.173\,237\,6 \times male$	(your gender=0)
	$0.078\,474\,7 \times movies$	(you saw 2 movies)

For you, this adds up to 0.338 336 8.

This means that we predicted a 33.833 68% chance that you purchased a ticket.

We can check how the model works by looking at the predicted values of everyone that we used in the estimation. For example, we predict that person 4 has a 125.034 15% chance of buying the ticket. Person 8 has a 138.009 63% chance of buying a ticket. Notice that predicted values for many of these people are negative or greater than one. This is one of the problems with binary choice models. We might wind up predicting something that is too likely or not.

Let's see how well our model fits. We will assume that if you are more than 50% likely to buy the ticket that you do. Let's compare how our predicted buying compares with actual behavior.

Results:

```
. predict predict5, xb

. gen predictbuy=0

. replace predictbuy=1 if predict5>0.5
(15 real changes made)

. tab  ticket5 predictbuy

           |      predictbuy
   ticket5 |         0          1 |     Total
-----------+----------------------+----------
         0 |        13          1 |        14
         1 |         2         14 |        16
-----------+----------------------+----------
     Total |        15         15 |        30
```

We predicted that 13 people would not buy who did not buy. We also predicted that 14 people would buy the ticket and they did. We got those right. Unfortunately, we predicted that 2 people would not buy and they did. We also predicted that 1 person would buy and they did not.

Of the 30 people, we predicted correctly for 27 people. Not bad.

第 11 章

虚拟因变量模型

Ⅰ. 线性概率模型

本章将介绍因变量是虚拟变量的模型。这方面的讨论是非常有用的，因为它能帮助我们解决那些以“是”或“否”作为答案的问题。例如：当我们在研究影响人们是否能完成高中学业的因素时，如果被观测的人是高中毕业生，可以让因变量取数值 1，否则因变量取数值 0。当我们衡量执行死刑时是否存在种族偏见时，如果被观测的杀人犯被处以死刑，我们可令因变量取数值 1，否则因变量取数值 0。解释变量可以是连续变量或虚拟变量。

因变量是虚拟变量的模型可采用如下形式：

$$y_i = \beta_0 + \beta_1 x_{1i} + \beta_2 x_{2i} + \cdots + \beta_k x_{ki} + \varepsilon_i$$

$$\text{其中 } y_i = \begin{cases} 1, & \text{如果是} \\ 0, & \text{否则} \end{cases}$$

对于这种模型的系数估计，我们可以采用 OLS 回归吗？如何解释回归系数呢？这些回归系数是无偏的吗？它们是有效的吗？

因变量是虚拟变量的模型称为线性概率模型。如果要掌握其属性，我们需注意以下几点：

(1) 由于误差均值为零，故 $E(y_i) = \beta_0 + \beta_1 x_{1i} + \beta_2 x_{2i} + \beta_3 x_{3i} + \cdots + \beta_k x_{ki}$。

(2) 如果 $p_i = \text{Prob}(y_i = 1), 1 - p_i = \text{Prob}(y_i = 0)$，那么 $E(y_i) = 1 \cdot p_i + 0 \cdot (1 - p_i) = p_i$。

该模型可写为：$p_i = \beta_0 + \beta_1 x_{1i} + \beta_2 x_{2i} + \beta_3 x_{3i} + \cdots + \beta_k x_{ki}$。

因此，斜率系数估计值显示了解释变量变化一个单位时对于 $y=1$ 的概率的影响。

由回归模型所得的预测值可以用来预测 $y=1$ 的概率。然而，这样的回归估计没有提供任何限制条件以保证预测值必须为正或小于 1。因为 $E(\varepsilon_i) = 0$，而且它们和解释变量不相关，OLS 估计量是无偏的。然而，随机误差会有异方差的问题。对于这个问题的解决，我们可以采用两个实际策略：利用 OLS 然后计算异方差稳健标准误，或者使用加权最小二乘法。

Ⅱ. Probit 和 Logit 模型

批评线性概率模型使用不恰当的另一个意见是，该模型假设 $y=1$ 的概率和解释变量之间是线性相关的。然而，它们之间有可能是非线性的关系。例如，非常穷的人或者非常富有的人的收入增加对于人们是否会购买汽车的概率不会有太大的影响，但是，对于其他收入群体而言，该影响往往大于零。Logit 和 Probit 模型是非线性的，并可以提供介于 0 和 1 之间的概率预测（如图 11—1 所示①）。

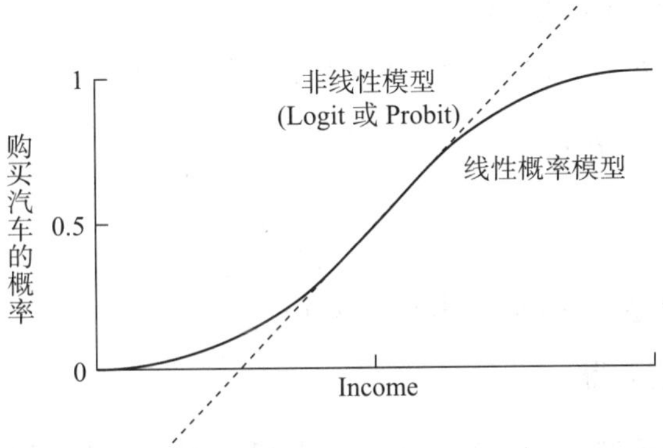

图 11—1

假设我们的虚拟变量依赖于无法观测到的效用指数，y^*。例如，y 是离散变量，如果有人购买了汽车，y 取 1，否则取 0。我们想象一个能反映个人买车愿望的连续变量 y^*。y^* 随着某些解释变量 x 的变化（比如收入）而连续地变化。

该模型可以正式写为：

$$y_i^* = \beta_0 + \beta_1 x_i + \varepsilon_i$$

如果效用指数足够高，被观测人将买车，那么：

$$y_i = 1, 若 y^* \geqslant 0$$

如果效用指数不是足够高，被观测人将不会买车，那么：

$$y_i = 0, 若 y^* < 0$$

基于这样的建模，我们定义：

$$\begin{aligned} p_i &= \mathrm{Prob}(y_i = 1) \\ &= \mathrm{Prob}(y_i^* \geqslant 0) \\ &= \mathrm{Prob}(\beta_0 + \beta_1 x_i + \varepsilon_i \geqslant 0) \\ &= \mathrm{Prob}(\varepsilon_i \geqslant -\beta_0 - \beta_1 x_i) \end{aligned}$$

① 该图选自 Chapter 16.3，*Statistics and Econometrics: Methods and Applications*，by Ashenfelter，Levine and Zimmerman，2003.

$$= 1 - F(-\beta_0 - \beta_1 x_i)\text{（其中 } F \text{ 是 } \varepsilon \text{ 的累积密度函数）}$$
$$= F(\beta_0 + \beta_1 x_i)\text{（如果 } F \text{ 是对称的）}$$

F 函数是误差项的累积密度函数。Probit 和 Logit 模型的基本区别就在于对 F 函数的选择不同。

其实，我们更感兴趣的是如何估计回归系数。通常情况下，我们采用最大似然估计法(MLE)。每个 y_i 的密度函数是 $f(y_i)=p_i^{y_i}(1-p_i)^{1-y_i}$。每个 y_i 要么取数值 1，要么取数值 0，而且，y_i 取 1 的概率是 $f(1)=p_i$，y_i 取 0 的概率是 $f(0)=(1-p_i)$。因此，似然估计方程为：

$$\begin{aligned} l &= f(y_1, y_2, \cdots, y_n) \\ &= f(y_1)f(y_2)\cdots f(y_n) \\ &= p_1^{y_1}(1-p_1)^{1-y_1}p_2^{y_2}(1-p_2)^{1-y_2}\cdots p_n^{y_n}(1-p_n)^{1-y_n} \\ &= \prod_{i=1}^{n} p_i^{y_i}(1-p_i)^{1-y_i} \end{aligned}$$

而且，

$$\ln l = \sum_{i=1}^{n} y_i \ln p_i + (1-y_i)\ln(1-p_i)$$

给定 $p_i = F(\beta_0 + \beta_1 x_i)$，得

$$\ln l = \sum_{i=1}^{n} y_i \ln F(\beta_0 + \beta_1 x_i) + (1-y_i)\ln(1-F(\beta_0+\beta_1 x_i))$$

备注：

似然比检验

在线性概率模型里，我们可以通过计算 F 统计量或 LM 统计量来检验排斥性限制条件。不同于线性概率模型，我们需要一种新的检验。最大似然估计（MLE）总是会产生一个对数似然值 L。正如我们以前所用的 F 检验，我们也需要估计受限模型和非受限模型，然后计算 $LR=2(L_{ur}-L_r) \sim \chi_q^2$。

拟合优度

在线性概率模型里，我们可以通过计算 R^2 来判断拟合优度。不同于线性概率模型，我们需要一种新的衡量拟合优度的方法。其中一种可行的方法是计算伪 R^2。这种方法是基于对数似然值并被定义为 $1-L_{ur}/L_r$。

2.1 Logit 回归模型

对于 Logit 模型，我们规定：

$$\text{Prob}(y_i=1)=F(\beta_0+\beta_1 x_i)=\frac{1}{1+e^{-(\beta_0+\beta_1 x_i)}}$$

当 $\beta_0+\beta_1 x_i \to -\infty$，$\text{Prob}(y_i=1)\to 0$。

当 $\beta_0+\beta_1 x_i \to \infty$，$\text{Prob}(y_i=1)\to 1$。

因此，Logit 模型的概率将介于 0 和 1 之间。

在线性概率模型里，回归系数测量的是在其他条件均相同的情况下解释变量的变化对于 $y=1$ 的概率的影响。在 Logit 模型里，

$$\frac{\partial \text{Prod}(y_i=1)}{\partial x_i}=\frac{\partial F(\beta_0+\beta_1 x_i)}{\partial x_i}=\frac{\beta_1 e^{-(\beta_0+\beta_1 x_i)}}{[1+e^{-(\beta_0+\beta_1 x_i)}]^2}$$

对于 Logit 模型，如何解释回归估计系数比较困难。但是，如果我们定义 $z_i=\beta_1+\beta_2 x_i$，Logit 模型可以重新整理以将"比值比"对数解释为 x 的线性函数。

$$p_i=\frac{e^{z_i}}{1+e^{z_i}}$$

$$\rightarrow 1-p_i=\frac{1}{1+e^{z_i}}$$

$$\rightarrow \ln\left(\frac{p_i}{1-p_i}\right)=\beta_1+\beta_2 x_i$$

因此，比值比（$P(y=1)$ /$P(y=0)$）的对数是 x 的线性函数。这样的整理有时会便于对回归估计系数进行解释。

另外，一条解释估计系数的经验法则是：将 Logit 回归估计系数除以 4，我们便可得到与线性概率模型估计系数近似的数值。

2.2　Probit 回归模型

在 Probit 模型，我们假定效用指数模型中的误差服从正态分布：$\varepsilon_i \sim N(0, \sigma^2)$，那么 $\text{Prob}(y_i=1)=F\left(\frac{\beta_0+\beta_1 x_i}{\sigma}\right)$，其中 F 是标准正态累积密度函数（c. d. f)。因此，

$$\text{Prob}(y_i=1)=F\left(\frac{\beta_0+\beta_1 x_i}{\sigma}\right)=\int_{-\infty}^{\frac{\beta_0+\beta_1 x_i}{\sigma}}\frac{1}{\sqrt{2\pi}}e^{-\frac{t^2}{2}}dt$$

计算上面方程的导数是比较复杂的：

$$\frac{\partial \text{Prob}(y_i=1)}{\partial x_i}=\frac{\partial F\left(\frac{\beta_0+\beta_1 x_i}{\sigma}\right)}{\partial x_i}=f\left(\frac{\beta_0+\beta_1 x_i}{\sigma}\right)\frac{\beta_1}{\sigma}$$

其中，f 是正态分布的密度函数。

用于解释 Probit 模型里估计系数的一条经验法则是：将 Probit 回归估计系数除以 2.5，我们便可得到与线性概率模型估计系数近似的数值。

Ⅲ. 上机操作练习①

在这个练习中，我们要通过测试一个二元响应模型来讨论什么因素决定了一个学生能

① 该练习基于 UCLA 的学术技术服务提供的 Stata 课堂笔记进行了修改。

否被研究生院录取。请在 Stata 中打开 **admission. dta**。[①] 这个数据集中有一个二元因变量叫作 *admit*。还有三个自变量：*gre*，*gpa* 和 *topnotch*。其中，*topnotch* 是一个哑变量，1 代表这所大学是顶尖学府，0 代表这所大学不是顶尖学府。

3.1 使用 Logit 模型

在运行 Logit 模型之前，我们最好检查一下是否有单元格是空白的或者数值非常小。如果有这种情况，我们运行 Logit 模型可能会有困难。

```
tab admit topnotch

           |       topnotch
     admit |         0          1 |     Total
-----------+----------------------+----------
         0 |       238         35 |       273
         1 |        97         30 |       127
-----------+----------------------+----------
     Total |       335         65 |       400
```

因为没有单元格是空白的或者数值太小，所以我们可以直接运行 Logit 模型。

```
. logit admit gre topnotch gpa

Iteration 0:   log likelihood = -249.98826
Iteration 1:   log likelihood = -239.17277
Iteration 2:   log likelihood = -239.06484
Iteration 3:   log likelihood = -239.06481

Logistic regression                               Number of obs   =        400
                                                  LR chi2(3)      =      21.85
                                                  Prob > chi2     =     0.0001
Log likelihood = -239.06481                       Pseudo R2       =     0.0437

------------------------------------------------------------------------------
       admit |      Coef.   Std. Err.      z    P>|z|     [95% Conf. Interval]
-------------+----------------------------------------------------------------
         gre |   .0024768   .0010702     2.31   0.021     .0003792    .0045744
    topnotch |   .4372236   .2918532     1.50   0.134    -.1347983    1.009245
         gpa |   .6675556   .3252593     2.05   0.040     .0300592    1.305052
       _cons |  -4.600814   1.096379    -4.20   0.000    -6.749678   -2.451949
------------------------------------------------------------------------------
```

在回归结果的上部，我们可以看到似然比的卡方值是 21.85，p 值是 0.000 1。这告诉我们这个模型整体上要比一个空的模型显著。在这个表格中，我们也可以看到 *gre* 和 *gpa* 是统计显著的，但是 *topnotch* 不显著。

对于系数的解释可能会比较别扭。例如，如果 *gre* 增加一单位，被研究生院录取的对数几率增加 0.002 5。因此，我们会希望将系数转化为指数，并且将它们作为比值比来解释。如果使用“or”这个选项，Stata 会帮助我们做这个运算，结果如下。

```
. logit , or

Logistic regression                               Number of obs   =        400
                                                  LR chi2(3)      =      21.85
                                                  Prob > chi2     =     0.0001
Log likelihood = -239.06481                       Pseudo R2       =     0.0437

------------------------------------------------------------------------------
       admit | Odds Ratio   Std. Err.      z    P>|z|     [95% Conf. Interval]
-------------+----------------------------------------------------------------
         gre |    1.00248   .0010729     2.31   0.021     1.000379    1.004585
    topnotch |   1.548402   .4519062     1.50   0.134     .8738922     2.74353
         gpa |   1.949466    .634082     2.05   0.040     1.030516    3.687881
------------------------------------------------------------------------------
```

现在我们可以说，如果 *gre* 上涨一单位，被研究生院录取的几率上涨 1.002 5 倍。

---

① 资料来源：http：//www. ats. ucla. edu/stat/stata/dae/probit. dta。

有时甚至比值比也很难被解释清楚。我们可以输入如下 Stata 指令来获得 x 对 $y=1$ 的概率的边际效应。

```
. mfx compute

Marginal effects after logit
      y  = Pr(admit) (predict)
         =  .3076378

variable      dy/dx    Std. Err.     z    P>|z|  [    95% C.I.   ]      X

     gre    .0005276     .00023    2.33   0.020   .000083  .000972   587.7
topnotch*   .0978326       .068    1.44   0.150  -.03545   .231115   .1625
     gpa    .1421872       .069    2.06   0.039   .006948  .277427  3.3899

(*) dy/dx is for discrete change of dummy variable from 0 to 1
```

另外，为了解释结果，我们也可以用预测的概率，因为有时它们比系数或比值比更容易理解。这可以由一组指令来完成，叫做“spost”，可以在使用之前下载。我们可以在 Stata 中输入“findit spostado”。

我们从“prtab”开始。这既可以被用于连续变量也可以被用于分类变量，而且它会显示出结果为 1 的预测概率，并适用于所有水平的指定的预测器。尽管 *topnotch* 并不是统计显著的，我们可以把它作为一个分类预测器。如下图所示，当 *gre* 和 *gpa* 保持它们的平均值不变的时候，如果大学是顶尖学府，预测的被录取概率为 0.39，如果不是顶尖学府，预测的被录取概率为 0.29。

```
. prtab topnotch

logit: Predicted probabilities of positive outcome for admit

 topnotch   Prediction

        0       0.2927
        1       0.3905

          gre   topnotch        gpa
x=      587.7      .1625     3.3899
```

```
. prtab gre

logit: Predicted probabilities of positive outcome for admit

      gre   Prediction

      220       0.1516
      300       0.1789
      340       0.1939
      360       0.2018
      380       0.2099
      400       0.2182
      420       0.2268
      440       0.2356
      460       0.2446
      480       0.2539
      500       0.2634
      520       0.2731
      540       0.2831
      560       0.2932
      580       0.3036
      600       0.3142
      620       0.3249
      640       0.3359
      660       0.3470
      680       0.3583
      700       0.3698
      720       0.3814
      740       0.3932
      760       0.4051
      780       0.4171
      800       0.4291

          gre   topnotch        gpa
x=      587.7      .1625     3.3899
```

在上图中，我们可以看到如果一个人的 GRE 成绩是 220 分，那么预测的他被录取的概率只有 0.15，但如果一个人的成绩是 800 分，那么这个概率会增加到 0.429（*gpa* 和 *topnotch* 都维持在它们的平均水平上不变）。

当 *gpa* 被设定为特定数值时，我们可以用“prvalue”指令来获取预测的概率。当一个人的 GPA 是 2 时，预测的被录取概率只有 0.149，被拒的概率为 0.85。当 GPA 是 3 时，预测的被录取概率为 0.255，被拒的概率为 0.745。当一个人的 GPA 是 4 时，预测的被录取概率为 0.40，被拒的概率为 0.6。

```
. prvalue , x(gpa=2)

logit: Predictions for admit

Confidence intervals by delta method

                              95% Conf. Interval
  Pr(y=1|x):        0.1494   [ 0.0310,    0.2679]
  Pr(y=0|x):        0.8506   [ 0.7321,    0.9690]

        gre  topnotch        gpa
x=    587.7     .1625          2

. prvalue , x(gpa=3)

logit: Predictions for admit

Confidence intervals by delta method

                              95% Conf. Interval
  Pr(y=1|x):        0.2551   [ 0.1893,    0.3209]
  Pr(y=0|x):        0.7449   [ 0.6791,    0.8107]

        gre  topnotch        gpa
x=    587.7     .1625          3

. prvalue , x(gpa=4)

logit: Predictions for admit

Confidence intervals by delta method

                              95% Conf. Interval
  Pr(y=1|x):        0.4004   [ 0.2973,    0.5034]
  Pr(y=0|x):        0.5996   [ 0.4966,    0.7027]
```

3.2 使用 Probit 模型

```
. probit admit gre topnotch gpa

Iteration 0:   log likelihood = -249.98826
Iteration 1:   log likelihood = -238.97735
Iteration 2:   log likelihood = -238.94339
Iteration 3:   log likelihood = -238.94339

Probit regression                          Number of obs   =        400
                                           LR chi2(3)      =      22.09
                                           Prob > chi2     =     0.0001
Log likelihood = -238.94339                Pseudo R2       =     0.0442

------------------------------------------------------------------------------
       admit |      Coef.   Std. Err.      z    P>|z|     [95% Conf. Interval]
-------------+----------------------------------------------------------------
         gre |   .0015244   .0006382     2.39   0.017     .0002736    .0027752
    topnotch |   .2730334   .1795984     1.52   0.128     -.078973    .6250398
         gpa |   .4009853   .1931077     2.08   0.038     .0225012    .7794694
       _cons |  -2.797884   .6475363    -4.32   0.000    -4.067032   -1.528736
------------------------------------------------------------------------------
```

注意，我们可以用 z 值和 Probit 指数来讨论系数。一个 GRE 是 0 分，GPA 是 0，并且读的不是顶尖学府的人的 z 值是−2.8。GRE 成绩每增加 1 分，z 值就会增加 0.001 524 4；

GPA 每增加一个绩点，Probit 指数增加 0.4。

用 z 值来描述结果可能对普通人来说不易理解。尽管我们不能得到比值比，但我们可以算出 x 对于概率 $y=1$ 的边际效应。

```
. mfx compute

Marginal effects after probit
      y  = Pr(admit) (predict)
         =  .30912718
------------------------------------------------------------------------------
variable |      dy/dx    Std. Err.     z    P>|z|  [    95% C.I.   ]      X
---------+--------------------------------------------------------------------
     gre |   .0005371      .00022    2.39   0.017   .000097  .000977   587.7
topnotch*|   .1000404      .06792    1.47   0.141  -.033089  .233169   .1625
     gpa |    .141291      .06794    2.08   0.038   .008122   .27446  3.3899
------------------------------------------------------------------------------
(*) dy/dx is for discrete change of dummy variable from 0 to 1
```

就像我们在 Logit 模型中做的一样，我们可以用“prtab”和“prvalue”指令来获得预测的概率。它们对于帮助我们解释结果非常有用。在这里就不重复演示了，读者可以稍后自己试验。

Ⅳ. 附加上机操作练习

（1）打开数据文件 **spread. dta**[①] 用于回答如下问题。

a）*favwin* 是二元变量，如果拉斯维加斯点扩散评分较高的队伍赢得了比赛，那么该变量取值为 1。估计被青睐的队伍获胜的概率，所用的线性概率模型如下所示：

$$P(favwin=1)=\beta_0+\beta_1 spread+u$$

如果 *spread* 含有所有相关信息，解释为什么我们会期望 $\beta_0=0.5$。

在每场比赛中，总有一个受观众喜欢和不受观众喜欢的队伍。*Spread* 用于衡量观众喜欢和不喜欢的队伍之间的差距。如果观众喜欢的队伍被判断为比不受喜欢的队伍好 5 分之多，那么 *spread* 就是 5。该模型试图预测偏爱的队伍赢得比赛的概率。如果 *spread* 包含了每个球队能否赢得比赛的所有信息，那么受偏爱的队伍能否获胜概率应是 50/50。也就是说，$\hat{\beta}_0$ 应等于 0.5。换另一种表述方式，如果 *spread* 为 0（如果没有喜不喜欢之说），那么任一队获胜的概率为 0.5。

b）用 OLS 估测 a）中的模型。检验 H_0：$\beta_0=0.5$。采用普通的标准差和异方差稳健标准差。

```
. regress favwin spread

      Source |       SS       df       MS              Number of obs =     553
-------------+------------------------------           F(  1,   551) =   68.57
       Model |  11.0636261     1  11.0636261           Prob > F      =  0.0000
    Residual |  88.9038241   551  .161349953           R-squared     =  0.1107
-------------+------------------------------           Adj R-squared =  0.1091
       Total |  99.9674503   552  .181100453           Root MSE      =  .40168

------------------------------------------------------------------------------
      favwin |      Coef.   Std. Err.      t    P>|t|     [95% Conf. Interval]
-------------+----------------------------------------------------------------
      spread |   .0193655   .0023386     8.28   0.000     .0147718    .0239593
       _cons |   .5769492   .0282345    20.43   0.000     .5214888    .6324097
------------------------------------------------------------------------------
```

① 资料来源：http://fmwww.bc.edu/ec-p/data/wooldridge/pntsprd.dta。

参考以上 Stata 结果中的 t 统计量，我们可以直接检验 H_0 为 $\beta_0=0$ 的假设。但是，这里我们要检验另一个不同的假设，即 $\beta_0=0.5$。我们为此需使用自己创造的 t 统计量。幸运的是，所有需要的信息都已给出。相关的 t 统计值是 $(0.5769-0.5)/0.0282=2.73$。基于此，在 5%的显著性水平上我们拒绝零假设。

```
. reg favwin spread, robust

Linear regression                               Number of obs =       553
                                                F(  1,   551) =    101.54
                                                Prob > F      =    0.0000
                                                R-squared     =    0.1107
                                                Root MSE      =    .40168

------------------------------------------------------------------------------
             |               Robust
      favwin |      Coef.   Std. Err.      t    P>|t|     [95% Conf. Interval]
-------------+----------------------------------------------------------------
      spread |   .0193655   .0019218    10.08   0.000     .0155905    .0231405
       _cons |   .5769492   .0316568    18.23   0.000     .5147664    .6391321
------------------------------------------------------------------------------
```

执行上述相同的步骤，但我们采用的是异方差稳健标准误差。所得的检验结果并没有因此而改变许多。

c）*spread* 是统计显著的吗？当 *spread*＝10 时，受偏爱的队伍获胜的估计概率是多少？

spread 是统计显著的（t 统计值＝8.28 或 10.08，这取决于我们是采用普通的标准差还是稳健的标准差）。当 *spread*＝10，受偏爱的队伍能赢的估计概率是 $0.577+0.0194\times10=0.771$。另外，我们也可以在 Stata 上计算所要的估计概率。Stata 的执行命令如下（我们采用普通标准差，即非稳健的标准误差）：

```
. reg favwin spread
. predict yhat
. sum yhat if spread==10
```

通过这些命令，我们就能确定受偏爱的队伍能赢的估计概率是 0.771。

d）现在，采用 Probit 模型来估计 $P(favwin=1)$。分析并检验截距为零的零假设。

```
. probit favwin spread

Iteration 0:   log likelihood = -302.74988
Iteration 1:   log likelihood = -264.91454
Iteration 2:   log likelihood = -263.56319
Iteration 3:   log likelihood = -263.56219
Iteration 4:   log likelihood = -263.56219

Probit regression                                 Number of obs   =        553
                                                  LR chi2(1)      =      78.38
                                                  Prob > chi2     =     0.0000
Log likelihood = -263.56219                       Pseudo R2       =     0.1294

------------------------------------------------------------------------------
      favwin |      Coef.   Std. Err.      z    P>|z|     [95% Conf. Interval]
-------------+----------------------------------------------------------------
      spread |    .092463   .0121811     7.59   0.000     .0685885    .1163374
       _cons |  -.0105926   .1037469    -0.10   0.919    -.2139329    .1927476
------------------------------------------------------------------------------
```

在 Probit 模型中，$P(favwin=1 \mid spread)=\Phi(\beta_0+\beta_1 spread)$，其中，$\Phi(\cdot)$ 代表标准累积分布函数，如果 $\beta_0=0$，那么 $P(favwin=1 \mid spread)=\Phi(\beta_1 spread)$，并且

$P(favwin=1 \mid spread=0)=\Phi(0)=0.5$。这是在线性概率模型中检验截距是否为 0.5 的相似形式。从上图中，我们可以看出测试 H_0：$\beta_0=0$ 的 t 统计量大概是 -0.102，所以我们不拒绝零假设。

e）用 Probit 模型来估计当 $spread=10$ 时受偏爱的队伍获胜的概率，并与 c）中的概率作比较。

当 $spread=10$ 时，Probit 模型估计的概率是 $\Phi[-0.0106+0.0925\times10]=\Phi(0.9144)\approx0.820$。这比 c）中的估计要大一些。

f）将 *favhome*，*fav25* 和 *und25* 加到 Probit 模型中，并用似然比检验测试这些变量的联合显著性。分析结果并且重点分析该 *spread* 方程是否将所有赛前观测的信息都包含进模型中。

```
. probit favwin spread favhome fav25 und25

Iteration 0:   log likelihood = -302.74988
Iteration 1:   log likelihood = -264.23393
Iteration 2:   log likelihood = -262.64279
Iteration 3:   log likelihood = -262.64177
Iteration 4:   log likelihood = -262.64177

Probit regression                                 Number of obs   =        553
                                                  LR chi2(4)      =      80.22
                                                  Prob > chi2     =     0.0000
Log likelihood = -262.64177                       Pseudo R2       =     0.1325

      favwin |      Coef.   Std. Err.      z    P>|z|     [95% Conf. Interval]
-------------+----------------------------------------------------------------
      spread |   .0878845   .0129491     6.79   0.000     .0625047    .1132642
     favhome |   .1485753   .1370571     1.08   0.278    -.1200517    .4172024
       fav25 |    .003068     .15869     0.02   0.985    -.3079587    .3140946
       und25 |  -.2198082   .2505842    -0.88   0.380    -.7109443    .2713278
       _cons |  -.0551801    .128763    -0.43   0.668    -.3075509    .1971907
```

当 *favhome*，*fav25* 和 *und25* 都加到 Probit 模型中后，对数似然值变为 -262.64。因此，似然比统计量是 $2[-262.64-(-263.56)]=2(263.56-262.64)=1.84$。$p$ 值大概是 0.61，因此 *favhome*，*fav25* 和 *und25* 是联合不显著的。当 *spread* 被控制后，其他因素对于预测结果没有作用。

（2）打开数据文件 **loanapp. dta**[①]，用于回答如下问题。

a）估计关于白人批准率的 Probit 模型。找到估计的白人和非白人的贷款批准率。这些与 OLS 模型的结果有什么不同？

因变量：*approve*	
自变量	系数（标准误差）
white	0.784 (0.087)
constant	0.547 (0.075)
观测值数目	1 989
对数似然值	−700.88
伪 R^2	0.053

① 资料来源：http：//fmwww. bc. edu/ec－p/data/wooldridge/loanapp. dta。

```
. probit approve white

Iteration 0:   log likelihood = -740.34659
Iteration 1:   log likelihood = -701.33221
Iteration 2:   log likelihood = -700.87747
Iteration 3:   log likelihood = -700.87744

Probit regression                                 Number of obs   =       1989
                                                  LR chi2(1)      =      78.94
                                                  Prob > chi2     =     0.0000
Log likelihood = -700.87744                       Pseudo R2       =     0.0533

------------------------------------------------------------------------------
     approve |      Coef.   Std. Err.      z    P>|z|     [95% Conf. Interval]
-------------+----------------------------------------------------------------
       white |   .7839465   .0867118     9.04   0.000     .6139946    .9538985
       _cons |   .5469463    .075435     7.25   0.000     .3990964    .6947962
------------------------------------------------------------------------------
```

sca z1= _ b [_ cons] + _ b [white] * 1

display normprob (z1)

. 90838786

sca z2= _ b [_ cons] + _ b [white] * 0

display normprob (z2)

. 70779219

```
. regress approve white

      Source |       SS       df       MS              Number of obs =    1989
-------------+------------------------------           F(  1,  1987) =  102.23
       Model |  10.4743407     1  10.4743407           Prob > F      =  0.0000
    Residual |   203.59303  1987  .102462521           R-squared     =  0.0489
-------------+------------------------------           Adj R-squared =  0.0485
       Total |  214.067371  1988  .107679764           Root MSE      =   .3201

------------------------------------------------------------------------------
     approve |      Coef.   Std. Err.      t    P>|t|     [95% Conf. Interval]
-------------+----------------------------------------------------------------
       white |   .2005957     .01984    10.11   0.000     .1616864     .239505
       _cons |   .7077922   .0182393    38.81   0.000     .6720221    .7435623
------------------------------------------------------------------------------
```

因为只有一个自变量，并且有两个值，所以只有两个不同的预测值：白人和非白人的贷款批准率的估计值。其中，非白人的批准率为 0.708，白人的批准率为 0.908。它们与 OLS 估计的结果相同。这是因为模型中的自变量是互斥的并且详尽的二元变量。那么，不管我们用线性概率模型，Probit 或者 Logit 模型预测概率都得到相同的结果。

b）现在，将变量 *hrat*，*obrat*，*loanprc*，*unem*，*male*，*married*，*dep*，*sch*，*cosign*，*chist*，*pubrec*，*mortlat*1，*mortlat*2 和 *vr* 加入到 Probit 模型中。有显著的证据证明对非白人的歧视吗？

```
. probit approve white hrat obrat loanprc unem male married dep sch cosign chist
> pubrec mortlat1 mortlat2 vr

Iteration 0:   log likelihood = -737.97933
Iteration 1:   log likelihood =  -603.5925
Iteration 2:   log likelihood = -600.27774
Iteration 3:   log likelihood = -600.27099
Iteration 4:   log likelihood = -600.27099

Probit regression                                 Number of obs   =       1971
                                                  LR chi2(15)     =     275.42
                                                  Prob > chi2     =     0.0000
Log likelihood = -600.27099                       Pseudo R2       =     0.1866

------------------------------------------------------------------------------
     approve |      Coef.   Std. Err.      z    P>|z|     [95% Conf. Interval]
-------------+----------------------------------------------------------------
       white |   .5202525   .0969588     5.37   0.000     .3302168    .7102883
        hrat |   .0078763   .0069616     1.13   0.258    -.0057682    .0215209
       obrat |  -.0276924   .0060493    -4.58   0.000    -.0395488    -.015836
     loanprc |  -1.011969   .2372396    -4.27   0.000     -1.47695   -.5469881
        unem |  -.0366849   .0174807    -2.10   0.036    -.0709464   -.0024234
        male |  -.0370014   .1099273    -0.34   0.736    -.2524549    .1784521
     married |   .2657469   .0942523     2.82   0.005     .0810159    .4504779
         dep |  -.0495756   .0390573    -1.27   0.204    -.1261266    .0269753
         sch |   .0146496   .0958421     0.15   0.879    -.1731974    .2024967
      cosign |   .0860713   .2457509     0.35   0.726    -.3955917    .5677343
       chist |   .5852812   .0959715     6.10   0.000     .3971805    .7733818
      pubrec |  -.7787405     .12632    -6.16   0.000    -1.026323   -.5311578
    mortlat1 |  -.1876237   .2531127    -0.74   0.459    -.6837153     .308468
    mortlat2 |  -.4943562   .3265563    -1.51   0.130    -1.134395    .1456823
          vr |  -.2010621   .0814934    -2.47   0.014    -.3607862    -.041338
       _cons |   2.062327   .3131763     6.59   0.000     1.448512    2.676141
------------------------------------------------------------------------------
```

在加入了更多自变量后，Probit 对于 *white* 的估计变为 0.520(s.e. ≈0.097)。因此，我们有非常显著的证据证明对非白人的歧视。

c）用 Logit 模型来估计 b）中的方程。与 Probit 估计中 *white* 的系数作比较。

```
. logit approve white hrat obrat loanprc unem male married dep sch cosign chist
> pubrec mortlat1 mortlat2 vr

Iteration 0:   log likelihood = -737.97933
Iteration 1:   log likelihood = -634.97536
Iteration 2:   log likelihood = -601.41194
Iteration 3:   log likelihood = -600.49724
Iteration 4:   log likelihood = -600.49616
Iteration 5:   log likelihood = -600.49616

Logistic regression                               Number of obs   =       1971
                                                  LR chi2(15)     =     274.97
                                                  Prob > chi2     =     0.0000
Log likelihood = -600.49616                       Pseudo R2       =     0.1863

------------------------------------------------------------------------------
     approve |      Coef.   Std. Err.      z    P>|z|     [95% Conf. Interval]
-------------+----------------------------------------------------------------
       white |   .9377643   .1729043     5.42   0.000      .598878     1.27665
        hrat |   .0132631   .0128802     1.03   0.303    -.0119816    .0385078
       obrat |  -.0530338   .0112803    -4.70   0.000    -.0751427   -.0309249
     loanprc |  -1.904951   .4604433    -4.14   0.000    -2.807404   -1.002499
        unem |  -.0665789   .0328086    -2.03   0.042    -.1308826   -.0022751
        male |  -.0663852   .2064292    -0.32   0.748    -.4709789    .3382086
     married |   .5032817   .1779983     2.83   0.005     .1544114     .852152
         dep |  -.0907336   .0733342    -1.24   0.216     -.234466    .0529989
         sch |   .0412287   .1784038     0.23   0.817    -.3084363    .3908938
      cosign |    .132059   .4460944     0.30   0.767    -.7422699    1.006388
       chist |   1.066577   .1712119     6.23   0.000     .7310075    1.402146
      pubrec |  -1.340665   .2173659    -6.17   0.000    -1.766694   -.9146358
    mortlat1 |  -.3098821     .46352    -0.67   0.504    -1.218365    .5986004
    mortlat2 |  -.8946755   .5685814    -1.57   0.116    -2.009075    .2197237
          vr |  -.3498279   .1537251    -2.28   0.023    -.6511237   -.0485322
       _cons |    3.80171   .5947074     6.39   0.000     2.636105    4.967315
------------------------------------------------------------------------------

.
```

当我们用 Logit 而不是 Probit 模型时，*white* 的系数（标准差）变为 0.938（0.173）。

d）你如何比较 Probit 和 Logit 模型中歧视的大小？

回忆我们先前所做，为了能比较 Probit 和 Logit 的估计值，我们可以将 Logit 的估计值乘以 0.625。缩放后的 Logit 系数变为 0.625×0.938≈0.586，与 Probit 的估计值非常接近。一个更好的比较方法是将其他自变量设置为有趣的值，比如它们样本的平均值，然后再比较预测的概率。

Chapter 11

Models with Dummy Dependent Variable

Ⅰ. Linear Probability Model

This chapter introduces models with a dummy variable as the dependent variable. They are very useful in that they allow us to address the questions for which there is a "yes" or "no" answer. Examples include: if you are studying factors that influence whether people complete high school. The dependent variable assumes the value 1 if the person graduates from high school and 0 otherwise. To measure whether there is a racial bias in the application of capital punishment, a researcher defines the dependent variable to be 1 if a murderer receives the death penalty and 0 otherwise. Explanatory variables may be continuous or dummy variables.

A dummy dependent variable model takes the form:

$$y_i=\beta_0+\beta_1 x_{1i}+\beta_2 x_{2i}+\cdots+\beta_k x_{ki}+\varepsilon_i$$

$$\text{where } y_i=\begin{cases}1, & \text{if yes}\\ 0, & \text{otherwise}\end{cases}$$

What if we estimated the slope coefficients of this model using OLS? What would the coefficients mean? Would they be unbiased? Are they efficient?

A regression model with a dummy dependent variable is a linear probability model. To see its properties, note the following:

(1) Since the mean error is zero, $E(y_i)=\beta_0+\beta_1 x_{1i}+\beta_2 x_{2i}+\beta_3 x_{3i}+\cdots+\beta_k x_{ki}$.

(2) If $p_i=\text{Prob}(y_i=1)$ and $1-p_i=\text{Prob}(y_i=0)$, then $E(y_i)=1\cdot p_i+0\cdot(1-p_i)=p_i$.

The model is $p_i=\beta_0+\beta_1 x_{1i}+\beta_2 x_{2i}+\beta_3 x_{3i}+\cdots+\beta_k x_{ki}$.

Thus, the estimated slope coefficients tell the impact of a unit change in that explanatory variable on the probability that $y=1$.

The predicted values from the regression model would provide predictions for the probability that $y=1$. However, nothing in the estimation strategy constrains the predictions from being negative or larger than 1. The OLS estimators are unbiased, since $E(\varepsilon_i)=0$ and they are uncorrelated with the explanatory variables. However, the errors are heteroskedastic. This suggests two empirical strategies: use OLS and then compute heteroskedasticity-robust standard errors, or use weighted least squares.

Ⅱ. Probit and Logit Models

Another criticism of the linear probability model is that the model assumes that the probability that $y=1$ is linearly related to the explanatory variables. However, the relation may be nonlinear. For example, increasing the income of the very poor or the very rich will probably have little effect on whether they buy an automobile, but it could have a nonzero effect on other income groups. Logit and probit models are nonlinear and provide predicted probabilities between 0 and 1 (as indicated by the following graph, figure 11—1[①]).

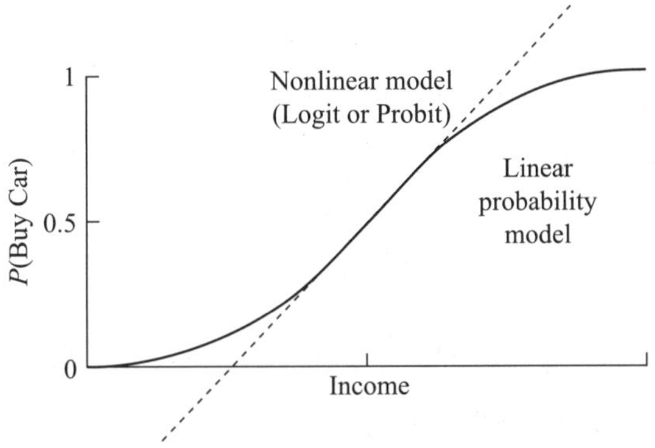

Figure 11—1

Suppose our underlying dummy dependent variable depends on an unobserved utility index, y^*. If y is discrete—taking on either the value 0 or 1 if someone buys a car, for instance, we can imagine a continuous variable y^* that reflects a person's desire to buy the car. y^* would vary continuously with some explanatory variable x, such as income.

The model is written formally as:

$$y_i^* = \beta_0 + \beta_1 x_i + \varepsilon_i$$

If the utility index is "high enough", a person will buy a car:

$$y_i = 1, \text{ if } y^* \geqslant 0$$

If the utility index is not "high enough", a person will not buy a car:

① This graph is selected from Chapter 16.3, *Statistics and Econometrics: Methods and Applications*, by Ashenfelter, Levine and Zimmerman, 2003.

$y_i=0$，if $y^*<0$

Based on this setup，we define：

$$
\begin{aligned}
p_i &= \text{Prob}(y_i=1)\\
&= \text{Prob}(y_i^* \geqslant 0)\\
&= \text{Prob}(\beta_0+\beta_1 x_i+\varepsilon_i \geqslant 0)\\
&= \text{Prob}(\varepsilon_i \geqslant -\beta_0-\beta_1 x_i)\\
&= 1-F(-\beta_0-\beta_1 x_i),\ \text{where } F \text{ is the c. d. f. for } \varepsilon\\
&= F(\beta_0+\beta_1 x_i),\ \text{if } F \text{ is symmetric}
\end{aligned}
$$

F is the cumulative density function（c. d. f. ）for the error term. This is where Logit and Probit models differ.

In fact，we are more interested in estimating the β's in the model. Typically this is done by using a maximum likelihood estimator（MLE）. Each outcome y_i has the density function $f(y_i)=p_i^{y_i}(1-p_i)^{1-y_i}$. Each y_i takes on either the value of 0 or 1 with probability $f(0)=(1-p_i)$ and $f(1)=p_i$. Hence，the likelihood function is：

$$
\begin{aligned}
l &= f(y_1, y_2, \cdots, y_n)\\
&= f(y_1)f(y_2)\cdots f(y_n)\\
&= p_1^{y_1}(1-p_1)^{1-y_1}p_2^{y_2}(1-p_2)^{1-y_2}\cdots p_n^{y_n}(1-p_n)^{1-y_n}\\
&= \prod_{i=1}^{n} p_i^{y_i}(1-p_i)^{1-y_i}
\end{aligned}
$$

and

$$
\ln l = \sum_{i=1}^{n} y_i \ln p_i + (1-y_i)\ln(1-p_i)
$$

which, given $p_i = F(\beta_0+\beta_1 x_i)$, gives

$$
\ln l = \sum_{i=1}^{n} y_i \ln F(\beta_0+\beta_1 x_i) + (1-y_i)\ln(1-F(\beta_0+\beta_1 x_i))
$$

Note：

The Likelihood Ratio Test

Unlike the linear probability model，where we can compute F statistics or LM statistics to test exclusion restrictions，we need a new type of test. Maximum likelihood estimation（MLE）will always produce a log-likelihood，L. Just as in an F test，you estimate the restricted and unrestricted models，then form $LR=2(L_{ur}-L_r) \sim \chi_q^2$.

Goodness of Fit

Unlike the linear probability model，where we can compute an R^2 to judge goodness of fit，we need new measures of goodness of fit. One possibility is a pseudo R^2 based on the log likelihood and defined as $1-L_{ur}/L_r$.

2.1 Logit Model

For the Logit model，we specify：

$$\text{Prob}(y_i=1)=F(\beta_0+\beta_1 x_i)=\frac{1}{1+e^{-(\beta_0+\beta_1 x_i)}}$$

$$\text{Prob}(y_i=1)\to 0 \text{ as } \beta_0+\beta_1 x_i\to-\infty$$

$$\text{Prob}(y_i=1)\to 1 \text{ as } \beta_0+\beta_1 x_i\to\infty$$

Thus, probabilities from the Logit model will be between 0 and 1.

With a linear probability model, an β estimate measures the *ceteris paribus* effect of a change in the explanatory variable on the probability that y equals 1. In the Logit model,

$$\frac{\partial \text{Prob}(y_i=1)}{\partial x_i}=\frac{\partial F(\beta_0+\beta_1 x_i)}{\partial x_i}=\frac{\beta_1 e^{-(\beta_0+\beta_1 x_i)}}{[1+e^{-(\beta_0+\beta_1 x_i)}]^2}$$

For a Logit model, a complication arises in interpreting the estimated β's. However, if we define $z_i=\beta_1+\beta_2 x_i$, the Logit model can be rearranged to express the log of "odds ratio" as a linear function of x:

$$p_i=\frac{e^{z_i}}{1+e^{z_i}}$$

$$\to 1-p_i=\frac{1}{1+e^{z_i}}$$

$$\to \ln\left(\frac{p_i}{1-p_i}\right)=\beta_1+\beta_2 x_i$$

So the log of odds ratio $(P(y=1)\ /P(y=0))$ is a linear function of x. This comes in handy sometimes.

A rule of thumb to interpret coefficient estimates is: divide a Logit coefficient by 4, then we will get an approximate linear probability model coefficient.

2.2 Probit Model

In the Probit model, we assume the error in the utility index model is normally distributed: $\varepsilon_i\sim N(0, \sigma^2)$, then:

$$\text{Prob}(y_i=1)=F\left(\frac{\beta_0+\beta_1 x_i}{\sigma}\right)$$

where F is the standard normal cumulative density function. Hence,

$$\text{Prob}(y_i=1)=F\left(\frac{\beta_0+\beta_1 x_i}{\sigma}\right)=\int_{-\infty}^{\frac{\beta_0+\beta_1 x_i}{\sigma}}\frac{1}{\sqrt{2\pi}}e^{-\frac{t^2}{2}}dt$$

Calculating the derivative is moderately complicated:

$$\frac{\partial \text{Prob}(y_i=1)}{\partial x_i}=\frac{\partial F\left(\frac{\beta_0+\beta_1 x_i}{\sigma}\right)}{\partial x_i}=f\left(\frac{\beta_0+\beta_1 x_i}{\sigma}\right)\frac{\beta_1}{\sigma}$$

where f is the density function of the normal distribution.

A rule of thumb to interpret coefficient estimates in the Probit model is: divide a Probit coefficient by 2.5, then we will get an approximate linear probability model coefficient.

Ⅲ. Computer Exercise[①]

In this exercise, we will estimate a binary response model to discuss what determines a student's chance to get into a graduate school. For our data analysis below, please upload **admission. dta**[②] into Stata. This data set has a binary dependent variable called *admit*. There are three independent variables: *gre*, *gpa* and *topnotch* which is a dummy variable in which 1 indicates that the undergraduate institution was "top notch" and 0 indicates that it was not.

3.1 Using the Logit Model

Before running Logit, we'd better check to see if any cells are empty or particularly small. If this occurs, we might have difficulty in running the Logit model.

```
tab admit topnotch

           |       topnotch
     admit |         0          1 |     Total
-----------+----------------------+----------
         0 |       238         35 |       273
         1 |        97         30 |       127
-----------+----------------------+----------
     Total |       335         65 |       400
```

Since none of the cells are too small or empty, we can go ahead and run our Logit model.

```
. logit admit gre topnotch gpa

Iteration 0:   log likelihood = -249.98826
Iteration 1:   log likelihood = -239.17277
Iteration 2:   log likelihood = -239.06484
Iteration 3:   log likelihood = -239.06481

Logistic regression                               Number of obs   =        400
                                                  LR chi2(3)      =      21.85
                                                  Prob > chi2     =     0.0001
Log likelihood = -239.06481                       Pseudo R2       =     0.0437

------------------------------------------------------------------------------
       admit |      Coef.   Std. Err.      z    P>|z|     [95% Conf. Interval]
-------------+----------------------------------------------------------------
         gre |   .0024768   .0010702     2.31   0.021     .0003792    .0045744
    topnotch |   .4372236   .2918532     1.50   0.134    -.1347983    1.009245
         gpa |   .6675556   .3252593     2.05   0.040     .0300592    1.305052
       _cons |  -4.600814   1.096379    -4.20   0.000    -6.749678   -2.451949
------------------------------------------------------------------------------
```

At the top of the output, we see that the likelihood ratio chi-square is 21.85 with the *p*-value of 0.0001. This shows us that our model as a whole fits significantly better than an empty model. In the table, we also see that both *gre* and *gpa* are statistically significant while *topnotch* is not.

The interpretation of the coefficients can be awkward. For example, for a one unit in-

① This exercise is modified based on the Stata class notes provided by UCLA Academic Technology Services.

② Data is collected from http://www.ats.ucla.edu/stat/stata/dae/probit.dta.

crease in *gre*, the log odds of being admitted to graduate school (vs. not being admitted) increases by 0.002 5. For this reason, we may prefer to exponentiate the coefficients and interpret them as odds-ratios. Stata will do this computation for us if we use the "or" option, illustrated below.

```
. logit , or

Logistic regression                               Number of obs   =        400
                                                  LR chi2(3)      =      21.85
                                                  Prob > chi2     =     0.0001
Log likelihood = -239.06481                       Pseudo R2       =     0.0437

------------------------------------------------------------------------------
       admit | Odds Ratio   Std. Err.      z    P>|z|     [95% Conf. Interval]
-------------+----------------------------------------------------------------
         gre |    1.00248   .0010729     2.31   0.021     1.000379    1.004585
    topnotch |   1.548402   .4519062     1.50   0.134     .8738922     2.74353
         gpa |   1.949466    .634082     2.05   0.040     1.030516    3.687881
------------------------------------------------------------------------------
```

Now we can say that for a one unit increase in *gre*, the odds of being admitted to graduate school (vs. not being admitted) increased by a factor of 1.002 5.

Even odds ratios can be hard to interpret. We can type the following Stata command to get the marginal effect of x's on probability of y that equals 1.

```
. mfx compute

Marginal effects after logit
      y  = Pr(admit) (predict)
         =  .3076378
------------------------------------------------------------------------------
variable |      dy/dx    Std. Err.     z    P>|z|  [    95% C.I.   ]      X
---------+--------------------------------------------------------------------
     gre |   .0005276      .00023    2.33   0.020   .000083  .000972    587.7
topnotch*|   .0978326        .068    1.44   0.150   -.03545  .231115    .1625
     gpa |   .1421872        .069    2.06   0.039   .006948  .277427   3.3899
------------------------------------------------------------------------------
(*) dy/dx is for discrete change of dummy variable from 0 to 1
```

Instead, we can also use predicted probabilities, which are sometimes easier to understand than the coefficients or odds ratios, in order to interpret our results. This can be done with a suite of commands, called "spost", which must be downloaded prior to their use. To do this, we can type "findit spostado" on the Stata command line.

We will start with "prtab". This can be used with either a continuous variable or a categorical variable and shows the predicted probability of the outcome being 1 for all levels of the specified predictor. Although *topnotch* is not statistically significant, we will use it as an example with a categorical predictor. As reported below, the predicted probability of being accepted into the graduate program is 0.39 if the undergraduate institution was "top notch" and 0.29 if it was not, while *gre* and *gpa* are held constant at their mean value.

```
. prtab topnotch

logit: Predicted probabilities of positive outcome for admit

----------------------
topnotch | Prediction
---------+------------
       0 |     0.2927
       1 |     0.3905
----------------------

          gre   topnotch        gpa
x=      587.7      .1625     3.3899
```

```
. prtab gre

logit: Predicted probabilities of positive outcome for admit

       gre   Prediction

       220     0.1516
       300     0.1789
       340     0.1939
       360     0.2018
       380     0.2099
       400     0.2182
       420     0.2268
       440     0.2356
       460     0.2446
       480     0.2539
       500     0.2634
       520     0.2731
       540     0.2831
       560     0.2932
       580     0.3036
       600     0.3142
       620     0.3249
       640     0.3359
       660     0.3470
       680     0.3583
       700     0.3698
       720     0.3814
       740     0.3932
       760     0.4051
       780     0.4171
       800     0.4291

           gre   topnotch        gpa
x=       587.7      .1625     3.3899
```

Above, we can see that the predicted probability of getting accepted is only 0.15 if one's GRE score is 220, but this predicted probability increases to 0.429 if one's GRE score is 800 (while *gpa* and *topnotch* are held constant at their mean, indicated at the end of the output).

```
. prvalue , x(gpa=2)

logit: Predictions for admit

Confidence intervals by delta method

                                 95% Conf. Interval
  Pr(y=1|x):          0.1494   [ 0.0310,    0.2679]
  Pr(y=0|x):          0.8506   [ 0.7321,    0.9690]

         gre   topnotch        gpa
x=     587.7      .1625          2

. prvalue , x(gpa=3)

logit: Predictions for admit

Confidence intervals by delta method

                                 95% Conf. Interval
  Pr(y=1|x):          0.2551   [ 0.1893,    0.3209]
  Pr(y=0|x):          0.7449   [ 0.6791,    0.8107]

         gre   topnotch        gpa
x=     587.7      .1625          3

. prvalue , x(gpa=4)

logit: Predictions for admit

Confidence intervals by delta method

                                 95% Conf. Interval
  Pr(y=1|x):          0.4004   [ 0.2973,    0.5034]
  Pr(y=0|x):          0.5996   [ 0.4966,    0.7027]
```

We can use the "prvalue" command to obtain the predicted probabilities when *gpa* is set to specific values: 2, 3 and 4. As you can see, when one's GPA is 2, the predicted probability of being accepted is only 0.149, and 0.85 of not being accepted. When GPA is 3, the probability of being accepted is 0.255, and 0.745 of not being accepted. When one's GPA is 4, the predicted probability of being accepted is 0.40, and 0.6 of not being accepted.

3.2 Using Probit Model

```
. probit admit gre topnotch gpa

Iteration 0:   log likelihood = -249.98826
Iteration 1:   log likelihood = -238.97735
Iteration 2:   log likelihood = -238.94339
Iteration 3:   log likelihood = -238.94339

Probit regression                                 Number of obs   =        400
                                                  LR chi2(3)      =      22.09
                                                  Prob > chi2     =     0.0001
Log likelihood = -238.94339                       Pseudo R2       =     0.0442

------------------------------------------------------------------------------
       admit |      Coef.   Std. Err.      z    P>|z|     [95% Conf. Interval]
-------------+----------------------------------------------------------------
         gre |   .0015244   .0006382     2.39   0.017     .0002736    .0027752
    topnotch |   .2730334   .1795984     1.52   0.128    -.078973     .6250398
         gpa |   .4009853   .1931077     2.08   0.038     .0225012    .7794694
       _cons |  -2.797884   .6475363    -4.32   0.000    -4.067032   -1.528736
------------------------------------------------------------------------------
```

Please note that the coefficients can be discussed in terms of either z-scores or Probit index. These are equivalent terms. The z-score of a person with a zero GRE score and zero GPA at a non-topnotch school is about −2.8. For each point of increase in GRE score, the z-score is increased by 0.001 524 4; for each point of increase in GPA, the Probit index increases by 0.4.

Describing the results in terms of z-scores may not be the simplest metric for your audience to understand. We can compute the marginal effects of x's on the probability of $y=1$, even though we can't get odds ratios.

```
. mfx compute

Marginal effects after probit
      y  = Pr(admit) (predict)
         =  .30912718
------------------------------------------------------------------------------
variable |      dy/dx    Std. Err.     z    P>|z|  [    95% C.I.   ]      X
---------+--------------------------------------------------------------------
     gre |   .0005371      .00022    2.39   0.017   .000097  .000977   587.7
topnotch*|   .1000404      .06792    1.47   0.141  -.033089  .233169   .1625
     gpa |    .141291      .06794    2.08   0.038   .008122   .27446  3.3899
------------------------------------------------------------------------------
(*) dy/dx is for discrete change of dummy variable from 0 to 1
```

Just like what we did in the Logit model, we can also use "prtab" and "prvalue" commands to obtain predicted probabilities, which are often useful for helping to tell the "story" of our results. To skip iteration, you may try it on your own later on.

Ⅳ. Additional Computer Exercises

(1) Open the data file named **spread. dta**[①] for the following questions.

a) The variable *favwin* is a binary variable if the team favored by the Las Vegas point spread wins. A linear probability model to estimate the probability that the favored team wins is:

$$P(favwin=1)=\beta_0+\beta_1 spread+u$$

Explain why, if the spread incorporates all relevant information, we expect $\beta_0=0.5$.

In every game, there is a favorite and an underdog. The *spread* is an expression of the gap between the favorite and the underdog. If the favorite is judged to be 5 points better than the underdog, then the spread is 5. The model is attempting to predict the probability that the favored team wins a game. If the *spread* incorporates all information relevant to whether or not a team wins the game, then the probability of the favorite winning by more or less than the *spread* should be 50/50. That is, $\hat{\beta}_0$ should be equal to 0. 5. Said another way, if the *spread* was 0 (if there was no favorite), then the probability of either team winning is 0. 5.

b) Estimate the model from part a) by OLS. Test H_0: $\beta_0=0.5$ against a two-sided alternative. Use both the usual and heteroskedasticity—robust standard errors.

```
. regress favwin spread

      Source |       SS       df       MS              Number of obs =     553
-------------+------------------------------           F(  1,   551) =   68.57
       Model |  11.0636261     1  11.0636261           Prob > F      =  0.0000
    Residual |  88.9038241   551  .161349953           R-squared     =  0.1107
-------------+------------------------------           Adj R-squared =  0.1091
       Total |  99.9674503   552  .181100453           Root MSE      =  .40168

------------------------------------------------------------------------------
      favwin |      Coef.   Std. Err.      t    P>|t|     [95% Conf. Interval]
-------------+----------------------------------------------------------------
      spread |   .0193655   .0023386     8.28   0.000     .0147718    .0239593
       _cons |   .5769492   .0282345    20.43   0.000     .5214888    .6324097
------------------------------------------------------------------------------
```

If we consult the *t*-statistic printed out by Stata, we can directly evaluate the hypothesis H_0: $\beta_0=0$. But let's test a different hypothesis. We have to make our own *t*-statistic for that hypothesis. Luckily, all the necessary information is printed out for me. The relevant *t*-statistic is given by (0. 576 9−0. 5)/0. 028 2=2. 73. Based on this *t*-statistic, we would reject the null at the $\alpha=0.05$ level.

```
. reg favwin spread, robust

Linear regression                                      Number of obs =     553
                                                       F(  1,   551) =  101.54
                                                       Prob > F      =  0.0000
                                                       R-squared     =  0.1107
                                                       Root MSE      =  .40168

------------------------------------------------------------------------------
             |               Robust
      favwin |      Coef.   Std. Err.      t    P>|t|     [95% Conf. Interval]
-------------+----------------------------------------------------------------
      spread |   .0193655   .0019218    10.08   0.000     .0155905    .0231405
       _cons |   .5769492   .0316568    18.23   0.000     .5147664    .6391321
------------------------------------------------------------------------------
```

① This data set is collected from http: //fmwww. bc. edu/ec—p/data/wooldridge/pntsprd. dta.

Performing the exact same procedure with the heteroskedasticity—robust standard errors does not change things much.

c) Is *spread* statistically significant? What is the estimated probability that the favored team wins when $spread=10$?

spread is statistically significant (t-statistic$=8.28$ or 10.08 depending on whether robust standard errors are used or not). The estimated probability that the favored team wins when $spread=10$ is obtained by $0.577+0.0194\times10=0.771$. Alternatively, we can have Stata do the work for us. The following are the commands we have Stata do the work for us (we do this with the regular, i. e. non-robust, standard errors):

```
. reg favwin spread
. predict yhat
. sum yhat if spread==10
```

Using these commands, we can determine that the predicted probability of the favorite winning when the *spread* is 10 points is equal to 0.771.

d) Now, estimate a Probit model for $P(favwin=1)$. Interpret and test the null hypothesis that the intercept is zero.

```
. probit favwin spread

Iteration 0:   log likelihood = -302.74988
Iteration 1:   log likelihood = -264.91454
Iteration 2:   log likelihood = -263.56319
Iteration 3:   log likelihood = -263.56219
Iteration 4:   log likelihood = -263.56219

Probit regression                          Number of obs   =        553
                                           LR chi2(1)      =      78.38
                                           Prob > chi2     =     0.0000
Log likelihood = -263.56219                Pseudo R2       =     0.1294

      favwin |      Coef.   Std. Err.      z    P>|z|     [95% Conf. Interval]
      spread |    .092463    .0121811    7.59   0.000     .0685885    .1163374
       _cons |  -.0105926    .1037469   -0.10   0.919    -.2139329    .1927476
```

In the Probit model, $P(favwin=1\mid spread)=\Phi(\beta_0+\beta_1 spread)$, where $\Phi(\cdot)$ denotes the standard normal cdf, if $\beta_0=0$ then $P(favwin=1\mid spread)=\Phi(\beta_1 spread)$ and, in particular, $P(favwin=\beta_1\mid spread=0)=\Phi(0)=0.5$. This is the analog of testing whether the intercept is 0.5 in the LPM. From the Table, the t statistic for testing H_0: $\beta_0=0$ is only about-0.102, so we do not reject H_0.

e) Use the Probit model to estimate the probability that the favored team wins when $spread=10$. Compare this with the linear probability model from part c).

When $spread=10$ the predicted response probability from the estimated Probit model is $\Phi[-0.0106+0.0925\times10]=\Phi(0.9144)\approx0.820$. This is somewhat above the estimate for the LPM.

f) Add the variables *favhome*, *fav25* and *und25* to the Probit model and test joint significance of these variables using the likelihood ratio test. Interpret this result, focusing on the equation of whether the spread incorporates all observable information prior to a game.

```
. probit favwin spread favhome fav25 und25

Iteration 0:   log likelihood = -302.74988
Iteration 1:   log likelihood = -264.23393
Iteration 2:   log likelihood = -262.64279
Iteration 3:   log likelihood = -262.64177
Iteration 4:   log likelihood = -262.64177

Probit regression                          Number of obs   =        553
                                           LR chi2(4)      =      80.22
                                           Prob > chi2     =     0.0000
Log likelihood = -262.64177                Pseudo R2       =     0.1325

------------------------------------------------------------------------------
      favwin |      Coef.   Std. Err.      z    P>|z|     [95% Conf. Interval]
-------------+----------------------------------------------------------------
      spread |   .0878845   .0129491     6.79   0.000     .0625047    .1132642
     favhome |   .1485753   .1370571     1.08   0.278    -.1200517    .4172024
       fav25 |    .003068     .15869     0.02   0.985    -.3079587    .3140946
       und25 |  -.2198082   .2505842    -0.88   0.380    -.7109443    .2713278
       _cons |  -.0551801    .128763    -0.43   0.668    -.3075509    .1971907
------------------------------------------------------------------------------
```

When *favhome*, *fav*25, and *und*25 are added to the Probit model, the value of the log likelihood becomes−262. 64. Therefore, the likelihood ratio statistic is 2 [−262. 64−(−263. 56)] =2(263. 56 − 262. 64) = 1. 84. The *p*-value is about 0. 61, so *favhome*, *fav*25, and *und*25 are jointly very insignificant. Once spread is controlled for, these other factors have no additional power for predicting the outcome.

(2) Open the data file named **loanapp. dta**[①]for the following questions.

a) Estimate a Probit model of *approve* on *white*. Find the estimated probability of loan approval for both whites and nonwhites. How do these compare with the linear probability estimates?

Dependent Variable: *approve*	
Independent Variable	Coefficient (Standard Error)
white	0. 784 (0. 087)
constant	0. 547 (0. 075)
Number of Observations	1 989
Log Likelihood Value	−700. 88
Pseudo *R*-Squared	0. 053

① Data source: http: //fmwww. bc. edu/ec−p/data/wooldridge/loanapp. dta.

```
. probit approve white

Iteration 0:   log likelihood = -740.34659
Iteration 1:   log likelihood = -701.33221
Iteration 2:   log likelihood = -700.87747
Iteration 3:   log likelihood = -700.87744

Probit regression                               Number of obs   =       1989
                                                LR chi2(1)      =      78.94
                                                Prob > chi2     =     0.0000
Log likelihood = -700.87744                     Pseudo R2       =     0.0533

     approve |      Coef.   Std. Err.      z    P>|z|     [95% Conf. Interval]

       white |   .7839465   .0867118     9.04   0.000     .6139946    .9538985
       _cons |   .5469463    .075435     7.25   0.000     .3990964    .6947962
```

sca z1= _b [_cons] + _b [white] * 1

display normprob (z1)

.90838786

sca z2= _b [_cons] + _b [white] * 0

display normprob (z2)

.70779219

```
. regress approve white

      Source |       SS       df       MS              Number of obs =    1989
                                                       F(  1,  1987) =  102.23
       Model |  10.4743407     1  10.4743407           Prob > F      =  0.0000
    Residual |   203.59303  1987  .102462521           R-squared     =  0.0489
                                                       Adj R-squared =  0.0485
       Total |  214.067371  1988  .107679764           Root MSE      =   .3201

     approve |      Coef.   Std. Err.      t    P>|t|     [95% Conf. Interval]

       white |   .2005957     .01984    10.11   0.000     .1616864     .239505
       _cons |   .7077922   .0182393    38.81   0.000     .6720221    .7435623
```

As there is only one explanatory variable that takes on just two values, there are only two different predicted values: the estimated probabilities of loan approval for white and nonwhite applicants. These are 0.708 for nonwhites and 0.908 for whites. These are identical to the fitted values from the linear probability model. This must always be the case when the independent variables in a binary response model are mutually exclusive and exhaustive binary variables. Then, the predicted probabilities, whether we use the LPM, probit, or logit models, are simply the cell frequencies. (In other words, 0.708 is the proportion of loans approved for nonwhites and 0.908 is the proportion approved for whites.)

b) Now, add the variables *hrat*, *obrat*, *loanprc*, *unem*, *male*, *married*, *dep*, *sch*, *cosign*, *chist*, *pubrec*, *mortlat1*, *mortlat2*, and *vr* to the Probit model. Is there statistically significant evidence of discrimination against nonwhites?

```
. probit approve white hrat obrat loanprc unem male married dep sch cosign chist
> pubrec mortlat1 mortlat2 vr

Iteration 0:   log likelihood = -737.97933
Iteration 1:   log likelihood =  -603.5925
Iteration 2:   log likelihood = -600.27774
Iteration 3:   log likelihood = -600.27099
Iteration 4:   log likelihood = -600.27099

Probit regression                                 Number of obs   =       1971
                                                  LR chi2(15)     =     275.42
                                                  Prob > chi2     =     0.0000
Log likelihood = -600.27099                       Pseudo R2       =     0.1866

------------------------------------------------------------------------------
     approve |      Coef.   Std. Err.      z    P>|z|     [95% Conf. Interval]
-------------+----------------------------------------------------------------
       white |   .5202525   .0969588     5.37   0.000     .3302168    .7102883
        hrat |   .0078763   .0069616     1.13   0.258    -.0057682    .0215209
       obrat |  -.0276924   .0060493    -4.58   0.000    -.0395488    -.015836
     loanprc |  -1.011969   .2372396    -4.27   0.000     -1.47695   -.5469881
        unem |  -.0366849   .0174807    -2.10   0.036    -.0709464   -.0024234
        male |  -.0370014   .1099273    -0.34   0.736    -.2524549    .1784521
     married |   .2657469   .0942523     2.82   0.005     .0810159    .4504779
         dep |  -.0495756   .0390573    -1.27   0.204    -.1261266    .0269753
         sch |   .0146496   .0958421     0.15   0.879    -.1731974    .2024967
      cosign |   .0860713   .2457509     0.35   0.726    -.3955917    .5677343
       chist |   .5852812   .0959715     6.10   0.000     .3971805    .7733818
      pubrec |  -.7787405     .12632    -6.16   0.000    -1.026323   -.5311578
    mortlat1 |  -.1876237   .2531127    -0.74   0.459    -.6837153     .308468
    mortlat2 |  -.4943562   .3265563    -1.51   0.130    -1.134395    .1456823
          vr |  -.2010621   .0814934    -2.47   0.014    -.3607862    -.041338
       _cons |   2.062327   .3131763     6.59   0.000     1.448512    2.676141
------------------------------------------------------------------------------
```

With the set of controls added, the Probit estimate on *white* becomes about 0.520(s. e. ≈ 0.097). Therefore, there is still very strong evidence of discrimination against nonwhites.

c) Estimate the model from part b) by Logit. Compare the coefficient on *white* to the Probit estimate.

```
. logit approve white hrat obrat loanprc unem male married dep sch cosign chist
> pubrec mortlat1 mortlat2 vr

Iteration 0:   log likelihood = -737.97933
Iteration 1:   log likelihood = -634.97536
Iteration 2:   log likelihood = -601.41194
Iteration 3:   log likelihood = -600.49724
Iteration 4:   log likelihood = -600.49616
Iteration 5:   log likelihood = -600.49616

Logistic regression                               Number of obs   =       1971
                                                  LR chi2(15)     =     274.97
                                                  Prob > chi2     =     0.0000
Log likelihood = -600.49616                       Pseudo R2       =     0.1863

------------------------------------------------------------------------------
     approve |      Coef.   Std. Err.      z    P>|z|     [95% Conf. Interval]
-------------+----------------------------------------------------------------
       white |   .9377643   .1729043     5.42   0.000      .598878     1.27665
        hrat |   .0132631   .0128802     1.03   0.303    -.0119816    .0385078
       obrat |  -.0530338   .0112803    -4.70   0.000    -.0751427   -.0309249
     loanprc |  -1.904951   .4604433    -4.14   0.000    -2.807404   -1.002499
        unem |  -.0665789   .0328086    -2.03   0.042    -.1308826   -.0022751
        male |  -.0663852   .2064292    -0.32   0.748    -.4709789    .3382086
     married |   .5032817   .1779983     2.83   0.005     .1544114     .852152
         dep |  -.0907336   .0733342    -1.24   0.216     -.234466    .0529989
         sch |   .0412287   .1784038     0.23   0.817    -.3084363    .3908938
      cosign |    .132059   .4460944     0.30   0.767    -.7422699    1.006388
       chist |   1.066577   .1712119     6.23   0.000     .7310075    1.402146
      pubrec |  -1.340665   .2173659    -6.17   0.000    -1.766694   -.9146358
    mortlat1 |  -.3098821     .46352    -0.67   0.504    -1.218365    .5986004
    mortlat2 |  -.8946755   .5685814    -1.57   0.116    -2.009075    .2197237
          vr |  -.3498279   .1537251    -2.28   0.023    -.6511237   -.0485322
       _cons |    3.80171   .5947074     6.39   0.000     2.636105    4.967315
------------------------------------------------------------------------------

.
```

When we use Logit instead of Probit, the coefficient (standard error) on *white* becomes 0.938 (0.173).

d) How would you compare the size of the discrimination effect between Probit and Logit?

Recall that, to make Probit and Logit estimates roughly comparable, we can multiply the Logit estimates by 0.625. The scaled Logit coefficient becomes $0.625 \times 0.938 \approx 0.586$, which is reasonably close to the Probit estimate. A better comparison would be to compare the predicted probabilities by setting the other controls at interesting values, such as their average values in the sample.

第 12 章

面板数据模型

Ⅰ. 面板数据的作用

1.1 什么是面板数据?

迄今为止，我们集中于横截面数据的学习。在横截面数据里，每一个观测单元代表的是某个实体（通常指个体）在某一特定时间点上的信息。然而，研究者们有时会遇到另外一种类型的数据。面板数据提供的是某个实体（如个人、国家或其他实体）在一段时间内的信息。面板数据的基本格式如下：

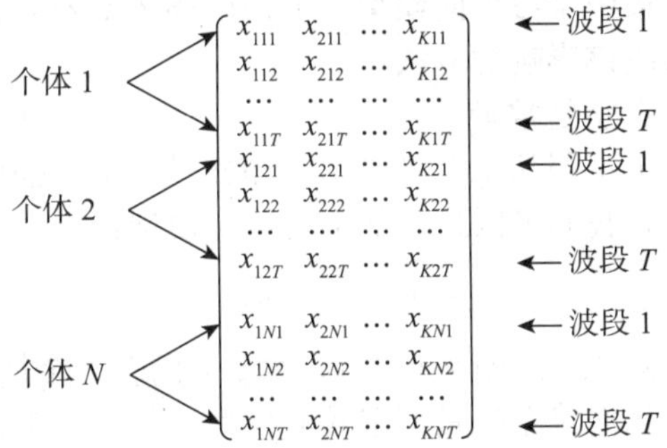

1.2 不可观测的异质性

面板数据有助于我们意识到模型里很可能存在不可观测的异质性问题。什么是不可观测的异质性？假设我们的数据包含了关于 N 个个体在 T 年里的信息。完整的数据集有 $N \times T$ 个观测值。假设我们要估计一个以 y 为因变量而 x 为自变量的标准回归模型，但是模型里往往存在着一些无法观测到的故而也无法控制的具有个体特性的影响因素。通过我们以前学到的知识，如果某些与解释变量或被解释变量相关的变量被忽视掉，OLS 是会有偏差的。例如，我们要研究吸烟对癌症发病率的影响。我们可能还需要考虑一些相关的因素，如饮酒、饮食的选择等。然而，许多个体特征是无法观测到的，例如热情，承担风险的愿望。这些影响因素被称为无法观测的异质性，它们因人而异。要解决这个问题，我们可以建立一个误差组合模型。该模型如下：

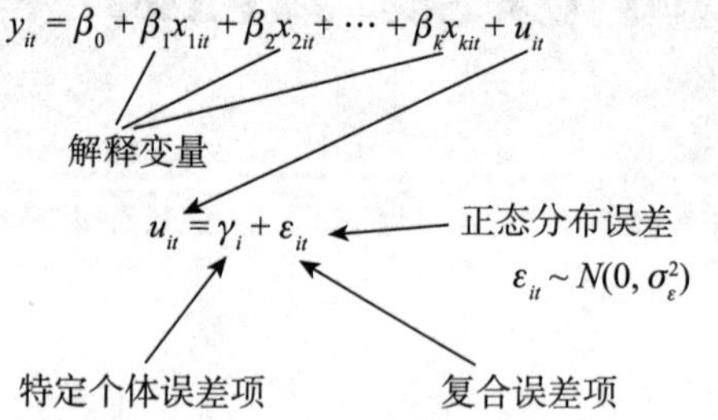

在面板数据模型里，误差项是三个组成部分的总和（在双向模型里）或两个组成部分的总和（在单向模型里）。双向模型假设误差项包括个体特征的影响因素、时间影响因素和额外的异质项。在单向模型里，只包括个体特征的影响因素和额外的异质项。

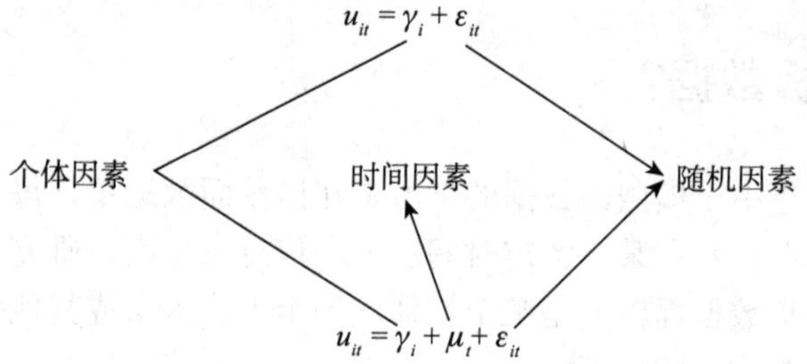

在本章中，我们主要集中学习单向模型。上面的图表显示，γ_i代表个体特征的影响因素。通常，我们有两种解决该影响的方法：

（1）固定影响——假定 γ_i是常量。

（2）随机影响——假定 γ_i服从某一种概率分布并且是随机抽取的。

鉴于这两种解决方案，我们可以采用如下的特定模型：

$$y_{it}=\beta_0+\gamma_i+\beta_1x_{1it}+\beta_2x_{2it}+\cdots+\beta_kx_{kit}+u_{it}$$

其中，y_{it}代表了在个体 i 和时间 t 上因变量的取值；γ_i代表了个体特征的影响因素。因此，如果 γ_i被视为常数，那么我们建立的是固定效应模型。如果 γ_i被视为随机变量，那么我们建立的是随机效应模型。

Ⅱ. 面板回归模型

2.1 固定效应模型

在固定效应模型里，对于第 i 个被观测的个体，我们视 γ_i为常数：

$$y_{it}=(\beta_0+\gamma_i)+\beta_1 x_{1it}+\beta_2 x_{2it}+\cdots+\beta_k x_{kit}+u_{it}$$

虽然 γ_i 是常数项的一部分，却因个体而异。

在固定效应模型，我们需假设个体的独特属性并不是随机变化的结果。事实上，每个个体的特性会因个体而异，而且对个体而言具有固定性和长期性。如果这一假设是正确的，我们能够使用面板数据来估计模型中变量的无偏斜率系数。

为了消除不可观测的异质性所带来的潜在偏差，对于样本里每个被观测的个体而言，固定影响因素就像虚拟变量一样会导致截距上下移动变化。基于此特征，我们可以采用两种方法来估计固定效应模型。

ⅰ）一阶差分方法。

第一种方法使用来自每一个被观测的个体在两个不同时期里的数据。对于每个时期，我们有两个不同的回归模型：

$$y_{i(t-1)}=\beta_0+\gamma_i+\beta_1 x_{1i(t-1)}+\beta_2 x_{2i(t-1)}+\cdots+\beta_k x_{ki(t-1)}+\varepsilon_{i(t-1)}$$
$$y_{it}=\beta_0+\gamma_i+\beta_1 x_{1it}+\beta_2 x_{2it}+\cdots+\beta_k x_{kit}+\varepsilon_{it}$$

除了衡量个体特性的固定效应的变量外，在第一个和第二个方程里所有其他变量都包含时间下标。将第一个和第二个方程相减，

$$\Delta y_i=\beta_1\Delta x_{1i}+\beta_2\Delta x_{2i}+\cdots+\beta_k\Delta x_{ki}+\Delta\varepsilon_i$$

将两个不同时间段的变量进行一阶差分，可以解决不可观察的异质性问题。因为每个个体在一段时间内的固定特性可以通过一阶差分消除掉。当该模型的所有假设成立时，所估计的斜率系数不会有遗漏变量导致的估计偏差问题。

ⅱ）平均偏差方法。

第二种方法使用来自同一个体的多个时期的数据。这个方法首先采用的是最初的回归方程：

$$y_{it}=\beta_0+\gamma_i+\beta_1 x_{1it}+\beta_2 x_{2it}+\cdots+\beta_k x_{kit}+\varepsilon_{it}$$

然后通过取每个变量的均值，将原方程修改为：

$$\bar{y}_{i.}=\beta_0+\gamma_i+\beta_1\bar{x}_{1i.}+\beta_2\bar{x}_{2i.}+\cdots+\beta_k\bar{x}_{ki.}+\bar{\varepsilon}_{i.}$$

第二个方程仍包含着衡量个体特性的固定效应的变量 γ_i，这是因为一个常数的均值仍然是常数。将第一个方程和第二个方程相减：

$$y_{it}-\bar{y}_{i.}=\beta_1(x_{1it}-\bar{x}_{1i.})+\cdots+\beta_k(x_{kit}-\bar{x}_{ki.})+(\varepsilon_{it}-\bar{\varepsilon}_{i.})$$

只要所有不包括在模型变量里的个体特性随时间固定不变，该模型的参数估计不会产生遗漏变量导致的偏差问题。

注意：通过采用平均偏差并运用最小二乘法来估计：$y_{it}-\bar{y}_{i.}=\beta_1(x_{1it}-\bar{x}_{1i.})+\cdots+\beta_k(x_{ki.}-\bar{x}_{i.})+(\varepsilon_{it}-\bar{\varepsilon}_{i.})$，我们可以得到固定效应估计量或称为“组内”估计量。所谓的“组内”估计是因为它依赖于个体的内部变异，而不是个体与个体之间的变异。由此，还有另一种估计量的存在也并不奇怪。例如：估计 $y_{it}-\bar{y}_{.t}=\beta_1(x_{1it}-\bar{x}_{1.t})+\cdots+\beta_k(x_{kit}-\bar{x}_{k.t})+(\varepsilon_{it}-\bar{\varepsilon}_{.t})$ 可以得到“组间”估计量。随机效应模型是一个固定效应（“组内”）估计和“组间”估计的组合：

$$(y_{it}-\bar{y}_{i.}-\bar{y}_{t}-\bar{y})=\beta_1(x_{1it}-\bar{x}_{1i.}-\bar{x}_{1.t}-\bar{x}_1)+\cdots+\beta_k(x_{kit}-\bar{x}_{ki.}-\bar{x}_{k.t}-\bar{x}_k)$$
$$+(\varepsilon_{it}-\bar{\varepsilon}_{i.}-\bar{\varepsilon}_{.t}-\bar{\varepsilon})$$

2.2 随机效应模型

有些人在某一特定方面和其他人相比总是有不同之处，这一方面可以解释为固定影响。然而，我们还有另一种模型可以用来描述不同个体之间的特征区别。假设个体特性这一影响因素并不是一个常数，对于每个个体而言其特性随时间变迁而随机变化。这种变化可视为回归模型的残差中除标准误这一项之外的另一个组成要素。因而，对于每个特定的个体，残差在如下模型里将包含 $\gamma_i+\varepsilon_{it}$：

$$y_{it}=\beta_0+\beta_1 x_{1it}+\beta_2 x_{2it}+\cdots+\beta_k x_{kit}+\gamma_i+\varepsilon_{it}$$

在这个模型中，γ_i 被视为一个随机变量，而不是一个常数。对于不同的个体，它的效应可以解释为截距的变化。但这些变化的差异随被观测个体的不同而随机分布。该模型最直接的扩展就是包括一个随机时间成分 γ_s。

在随机效应模型中，对于残差的这一部分 γ_i，通常我们假设：

ⅰ）对于被观测的个体 i，γ_i 的方差是固定的，也就是，对于被观测的个体 i，$\mathrm{Var}(\gamma_i)=\sigma_\gamma$。

ⅱ）在不同的被观测的个体 i 和 j 之间，γ_i 和 γ_j 的残差的协方差为零，也就是 $\mathrm{Cov}(\gamma_i, \gamma_j)=0$，$\forall i\neq j$。

ⅲ）残差中反映个体特性的组成部分和任何一个解释变量不相关，也就是 $\mathrm{Cov}(\gamma_i, X_{jt})=0$，$\forall i$，$j$ 和 t。

根据这些假设，尽管存在不可观测的异质性，由于模型的残差和任何一个解释变量不相关，OLS 回归仍是无偏的，即 $\mathrm{Cov}(\gamma_i+\varepsilon_{it}, X_{jt})=0$，$\forall i$，$j$ 和 t。但是，模型可能会有序列相关问题。

在样本中，对于 N 个观测个体而言，残差之间相关系数不为零：$\mathrm{Cov}(\gamma_i+\varepsilon_{it}, \gamma_i+\varepsilon_{is})\neq 0$，$s\neq t$。如果序列相关存在，用 OLS 公式计算回归系数的标准误将会产生不正确的估计，因此 OLS 不再是 BLUE。解决方案之一是采用广义最小二乘法（GLS）。

2.3 固定效应或随机效应?

这两种模型对于个体特性有非常不同的假设。因此，当选择模型时，我们需要意识到如何从这两种模型选择出合适的模型。

我们可以通过假设检验来选择合适的面板模型。在下面的上机操作练习里，我们将会讲解如何使用 Hausman 检验比较和选择固定效应模型或随机效应模型。另外，许多研究人员根据他们的直觉来选择使用的模型。如果我们收集到一个国家所有州的数据，直觉告诉我们使用固定效应模型可能比较明智。如果我们仅有不完整的数据，选择会变得比较困难。以下是一些建议：

ⅰ）如果 T（时间序列数据的数量）很大且 N（横截面单元的数量）很小，使用固定效应模型或随机效应模型进行参数估计很可能没有多大的区别。基于计算方便，固定效应模型可能更可取些。

ⅱ）当 N 很大且 T 很小时，如果我们坚定地认为横截面数据的个体不是从大样本里随机抽取的，固定效应模型较适当。如果横截面数据的个体被视为随机抽样，那么随机效应模型较适当。

ⅲ）如果误差项里的某个组成部分和一个或多个自变量相关，固定效应模型可能更适当。

ⅵ）如果 N 很大且 T 很小，并且随机效应模型的所有假设成立，随机效应模型的参数估计要比固定效应模型的参数估计更有效。

Ⅲ. 上机操作练习

在这个练习中，我们需要增加数据集的存储量，因为我们会用到一个较大的数据集，名为 **woman. dta**[①]，上传该数据集。我们要将存储量增加到 10MB。在 Stata 中，输入“set mem 10m”。

（1）建立新变量。

我们的目的是将女性工资的对数对下列变量进行回归：

grade＝受教育年限；

age＝女性的年龄；

age2＝年龄的平方；

ttl _ exp＝工作的总年限；

ttl _ exp2＝工作总年限的平方；

tenure＝在最近的工作中工作的年限；

tenure2＝上一个变量的平方；

black＝哑变量，如果女性是黑人，值为 1，否则，值为 0；

not _ smsa＝哑变量，如果女性住在乡下，值为 1，否则，值为 0；

south＝哑变量，如果女性住在南部的州，值为 1，否则，值为 0。

（2）面板数据的描述统计指标。

现在，必须指示 Stata 我们有一个面板数据集。输入 tsset 指令：“tsset idcode year”。

注意：在上个指令中，*idcode* 是一个用来区分我们数据集中个体的变量。*Year* 是一个区分时间段的变量。

在 Stata 中，与面板数据有关的指令总是以 xt 为字头。我们可以打开帮助文件来浏览这些指令。

```
. help xt
```

在进行估计之前，我们最好像往常一样描述并总结数据集。Stata 有专门描述和总结面板数据集的指令。

---

① 资料来源：http：//www. stata—press. com/data/r8/xtdatasmpl。

. xtdes

. xtsum

注意："xtdes" 允许我们观察数据的规律，比如在不同时间段中有不同规律的观测值的个体数量。在该例中，我们有不平衡的面板数据，因为不是所有个体在每年都有观测值。"xtsum" 指令给我们提供了数据集中变量的描述性统计数据，并考虑了整体的、组间的、组内的变化。整体是指整个数据集。组间的是指每个个体在不同时间段的平均值的变化。组内的是指每个个体与各自平均值的偏差的变化。

我们可能也对将面板数据的制表指令应用在一个变量上感兴趣。比如，应用在变量 *black* 上，为了得到一个单向表，我们可以使用以下指令：

. xttab black

(3) 面板数据分析。

现在我们来学习面板数据的估计指令。

ⅰ) 混合最小二乘估计回归。

我们要运行的第一种回归是混合最小二乘估计回归。这只是简单地将最小二乘回归应用到整个数据集上。然而，这个回归不考虑我们在不同时间段有不同个体，并且也不考虑数据集的面板特征。

```
reg ln_wage grade age* ttl_exp* tenure* black not_smsa south

      Source |       SS       df       MS              Number of obs =   12293
-------------+------------------------------           F( 10, 12282) =  687.96
       Model |  1171.8669     10  117.18669           Prob > F      =  0.0000
    Residual | 2092.10451  12282  .170339074           R-squared     =  0.3590
-------------+------------------------------           Adj R-squared =  0.3585
       Total | 3263.97141  12292  .265536236           Root MSE      =  .41272

------------------------------------------------------------------------------
     ln_wage |      Coef.   Std. Err.      t    P>|t|     [95% Conf. Interval]
-------------+----------------------------------------------------------------
       grade |    .066003   .0015684    42.08   0.000     .0629288    .0690772
         age |  -.0037805   .0127087    -0.30   0.766    -.0286916    .0211305
        age2 |  -.0000653   .0001795    -0.36   0.716    -.0004172    .0002865
     ttl_exp |   .0380632   .0038826     9.80   0.000     .0304528    .0456737
    ttl_exp2 |  -.0001812   .0001869    -0.97   0.332    -.0005476    .0001852
      tenure |   .0351204   .0026324    13.34   0.000     .0299604    .0402803
     tenure2 |  -.0013263   .0001686    -7.87   0.000    -.0016568   -.0009958
       black |  -.0886489   .0088517   -10.01   0.000    -.1059995   -.0712983
    not_smsa |  -.1929917   .0084369   -22.87   0.000    -.2095293   -.1764541
       south |  -.0898548    .008044   -11.17   0.000    -.1056222   -.0740873
       _cons |   .8159543   .2218402     3.68   0.000     .3811126    1.250796
------------------------------------------------------------------------------
```

注意：在之前的指令中，我们没有输入"age age2"。我们只需要输入"age *"。当输入这个指令时，我们是在指示 Stata 将所有以 age 开头的变量包括在回归中。

ⅱ) 固定效应估计和随机效应估计（Hausman 检验）。

在面板数据的实证研究中，我们总是关心在两个回归中如何做选择。这个选择是关于固定效应估计和随机效应估计。

为了估计的一致性，如果误差项与自变量无关，我们应该使用随机效应模型，因为它是一个关于组间和组内估计的加权平均。但是，如果个体的效应或者时间效应与自变量相关，那么个体或时间效应必须用哑变量来评估以便解决内生性问题。

首先，我们要做一个固定效应回归，然后是随机效应回归，之后我们会用 Hausman 检验来检验应该用哪一个模型，并且该检验结果经常展示出来以便于证明我们的选择。

下面来做固定效应回归：

```
. xtreg ln_wage grade age* ttl_exp* tenure* black not_smsa south, fe

Fixed-effects (within) regression               Number of obs      =     12293
Group variable: idcode                          Number of groups   =      3456

R-sq:  within  = 0.0916                         Obs per group: min =         1
       between = 0.2631                                        avg =       3.6
       overall = 0.2141                                        max =         6

                                                F(8,8829)          =    111.28
corr(u_i, Xb)  = 0.0279                         Prob > F           =    0.0000

------------------------------------------------------------------------------
     ln_wage |      Coef.   Std. Err.      t    P>|t|     [95% Conf. Interval]
-------------+----------------------------------------------------------------
       grade |  (dropped)
         age |   .0009433   .0116222     0.08   0.935    -.0218389    .0237254
        age2 |  -.0002997   .0001562    -1.92   0.055    -.0006058    6.44e-06
     ttl_exp |   .0588723   .0070158     8.39   0.000     .0451196    .0726249
    ttl_exp2 |  -.0002974   .0002084    -1.43   0.154     -.000706    .0001112
      tenure |   .0224444   .0026359     8.52   0.000     .0172775    .0276112
     tenure2 |  -.0012442    .000175    -7.11   0.000    -.0015873   -.0009011
       black |  (dropped)
    not_smsa |  -.0768878   .0218558    -3.52   0.000    -.1197303   -.0340454
       south |   -.059834   .0221643    -2.70   0.007    -.1032813   -.0163868
       _cons |    1.59244   .2060833     7.73   0.000     1.188469    1.996412
-------------+----------------------------------------------------------------
     sigma_u |  .41275024
     sigma_e |  .27600537
         rho |  .69100986   (fraction of variance due to u_i)
------------------------------------------------------------------------------
F test that all u_i=0:     F(3455, 8829) =     5.39          Prob > F = 0.0000
```

现在，来做随机效应回归：

```
. xtreg ln_wage grade age* ttl_exp* tenure* black not_smsa south, re

Random-effects GLS regression                   Number of obs      =     12293
Group variable: idcode                          Number of groups   =      3456

R-sq:  within  = 0.0880                         Obs per group: min =         1
       between = 0.4190                                        avg =       3.6
       overall = 0.3567                                        max =         6

Random effects u_i ~ Gaussian                   Wald chi2(10)      =   3377.50
corr(u_i, X)       = 0 (assumed)                Prob > chi2        =    0.0000

------------------------------------------------------------------------------
     ln_wage |      Coef.   Std. Err.      z    P>|z|     [95% Conf. Interval]
-------------+----------------------------------------------------------------
       grade |   .0643748   .0024985    25.77   0.000     .0594779    .0692717
         age |   .0049517   .0102755     0.48   0.630    -.0151878    .0250913
        age2 |  -.0002152   .0001451    -1.48   0.138    -.0004997    .0000692
     ttl_exp |   .0416154    .003821    10.89   0.000     .0341263    .0491045
    ttl_exp2 |   -.000144   .0001747    -0.82   0.410    -.0004864    .0001984
      tenure |   .0290022   .0023756    12.21   0.000      .024346    .0336583
     tenure2 |   -.001279   .0001566    -8.17   0.000     -.001586   -.0009721
       black |  -.0756085   .0143898    -5.25   0.000     -.103812    -.047405
    not_smsa |  -.1638295   .0120031   -13.65   0.000    -.1873552   -.1403039
       south |  -.0777664    .011514    -6.75   0.000    -.1003333   -.0551994
       _cons |   .6828395   .1818643     3.75   0.000     .3263922    1.039287
-------------+----------------------------------------------------------------
     sigma_u |  .31839394
     sigma_e |  .27600537
         rho |  .57095246   (fraction of variance due to u_i)
------------------------------------------------------------------------------
```

然后，我们对随机效应回归做 Hausman 检验。当我们做 Hausman 检验时，检验的是假设第一个模型为真的零假设。(在这个例子中，第一个模型是随机效应。) 接着我们要对固定效应模型进行检验。为了完成这个检验，我们做的最后一个回归需要是随机效应回归。要做的第一件事是将该回归的结果存档。我们用“estimates store”指令来完成。注意，我们必须命名存储的结果。下面，我们要做固定效应模型的回归（替代假设）。因为我们已经做过固定效应的回归并且观察了结果，因而可以在指令前直接用“quietly”选项来运行。这个选项可以用在任何 Stata 指令中，可以让 Stata 运行指令但不在结果窗口中显示结果。最后，我们做 Hausman 检验，并使用假设随机效应模型为真的零假设。

```
est store re

quietly xtreg ln_wage grade age* ttl_exp* tenure* black not_smsa south, fe

hausman . re

                 ---- Coefficients ----
             |      (b)          (B)            (b-B)     sqrt(diag(V_b-V_B))
             |       .           re          Difference          S.E.
-------------+----------------------------------------------------------------
         age |   .0009433     .0049517       -.0040085        .0054304
        age2 |  -.0002997    -.0002152       -.0000845        .0000577
     ttl_exp |   .0588723     .0416154        .0172569         .005884
    ttl_exp2 |  -.0002974     -.000144       -.0001534        .0001137
      tenure |   .0224444     .0290022       -.0065578         .001142
     tenure2 |  -.0012442     -.001279        .0000349        .0000782
    not_smsa |  -.0768878    -.1638295        .0869417        .0182647
       south |   -.059834    -.0777664        .0179323         .018939
------------------------------------------------------------------------------
                          b = consistent under Ho and Ha; obtained from xtreg
           B = inconsistent under Ha, efficient under Ho; obtained from xtreg

    Test:  Ho:  difference in coefficients not systematic

                  chi2(8) = (b-B)'[(V_b-V_B)^(-1)](b-B)
                          =       89.49
                Prob>chi2 =      0.0000
```

在该例中，我们应该拒绝随机效应模型，因为 Hausman 检验的 p 值小于 5%，并且这是应该选择固定效应模型的证据。

ⅲ）其他回归方法。

如果我们想运行带有稳健标准误差的固定效应模型，可以使用以下指令：

. areg ln _ wage grade age * ttl _ exp * tenure * black not _ smsa south，absorb（idcode）robust

我们可能想对面板数据进行最大似然估计，可以输入：

. xtreg ln _ wage grade age * ttl _ exp * tenure * black not _ smsa south，mle

Ⅳ）时间哑变量。

当我们做面板数据的实证研究时，经常讨论将时间效应（时间哑变量）纳入固定效应模型中。

为了达到这个目的，我们先创建时间哑变量。

. tab year，g（y）

为了对将时间哑变量纳入固定效应模型中进行检验，我们首先运行一个包含时间哑变量的固定效应模型，然后使用“testparm”指令。

```
. xtreg ln_wage grade age* ttl_exp* tenure* black not_smsa south y*, fe

Fixed-effects (within) regression               Number of obs      =     12293
Group variable: idcode                          Number of groups   =      3456

R-sq:  within  = 0.0956                         Obs per group: min =         1
       between = 0.2449                                        avg =       3.6
       overall = 0.1956                                        max =         6

                                                F(13,8824)         =     71.76
corr(u_i, Xb)  = -0.0620                        Prob > F           =    0.0000

------------------------------------------------------------------------------
     ln_wage |      Coef.   Std. Err.      t    P>|t|     [95% Conf. Interval]
-------------+----------------------------------------------------------------
       grade |  (dropped)
         age |    .055874   .0170351     3.28   0.001     .0224812    .0892668
        age2 |  -.0005845   .0001664    -3.51   0.000    -.0009106   -.0002584
     ttl_exp |   .0669626   .0072187     9.28   0.000     .0528122     .081113
    ttl_exp2 |  -.0004821   .0002105    -2.29   0.022    -.0008947   -.0000695
      tenure |   .0216011   .0026419     8.18   0.000     .0164223    .0267798
     tenure2 |  -.0011873   .0001752    -6.78   0.000    -.0015308   -.0008439
       black |  (dropped)
    not_smsa |  -.0773324   .0218221    -3.54   0.000    -.1201088   -.0345561
       south |  -.0594989   .0221376    -2.69   0.007    -.1028938    -.016104
        year |  -.0410534   .0136193    -3.01   0.003    -.0677504   -.0143563
          y1 |  (dropped)
          y2 |  -.0299615   .0087471    -3.43   0.001    -.0471079   -.0128151
          y3 |  -.0337915   .0089443    -3.78   0.000    -.0513245   -.0162586
          y4 |  -.0176105   .0090619    -1.94   0.052     -.035374     .000153
          y5 |  -.0198696   .0094037    -2.11   0.035    -.0383031   -.0014362
          y6 |  (dropped)
       _cons |   81.44174   26.59399     3.06   0.002     29.31133    133.5721
-------------+----------------------------------------------------------------
     sigma_u |  .41811501
     sigma_e |  .27547309
         rho |  .69731259   (fraction of variance due to u_i)
------------------------------------------------------------------------------
F test that all u_i=0:     F(3455, 8824) =     5.42          Prob > F = 0.0000
```

现在我们对时间哑变量进行检验，并设定零假设为时间哑变量不是联合显著的。

```
testparm y*

( 1)  year = 0
( 2)  y1 = 0
( 3)  y2 = 0
( 4)  y3 = 0
( 5)  y4 = 0
( 6)  y5 = 0
( 7)  y6 = 0
      Constraint 2 dropped
      Constraint 7 dropped

      F(  5,  8824) =    7.83
           Prob > F =    0.0000
```

我们拒绝时间哑变量不是联合显著的零假设（p 值小于 5%），并且应该将时间效应纳入固定效应回归中。

如果将时间哑变量纳入回归可以允许我们在个体效应中使用随机效应模型，结果会怎么样？首先，我们要做一个包含时间哑变量的随机效应回归，然后我们使用“xttest0”指令来检验随机效应。

```
 xtreg ln_wage grade age* ttl_exp* tenure* black not_smsa south y*, re
note: y1 dropped because of collinearity
note: y6 dropped because of collinearity

Random-effects GLS regression                   Number of obs      =     12293
Group variable: idcode                          Number of groups   =      3456

R-sq:  within  = 0.0912                         Obs per group: min =         1
       between = 0.4189                                        avg =       3.6
       overall = 0.3571                                        max =         6

Random effects u_i ~ Gaussian                   Wald chi2(15)      =   3413.59
corr(u_i, X)       = 0 (assumed)                Prob > chi2        =    0.0000

     ln_wage       Coef.   Std. Err.      z    P>|z|     [95% Conf. Interval]

       grade    .0640186   .0025003    25.60   0.000     .0591181    .0689192
         age    .0273925   .0111443     2.46   0.014       .00555     .049235
        age2   -.0004727   .0001546    -3.06   0.002    -.0007756   -.0001698
     ttl_exp    .0446606   .0038673    11.55   0.000     .0370808    .0522405
    ttl_exp2   -.0002213   .0001761    -1.26   0.209    -.0005664    .0001238
      tenure    .0285262   .0023793    11.99   0.000     .0238629    .0331895
     tenure2   -.0012561   .0001568    -8.01   0.000    -.0015634   -.0009487
       black   -.0746025   .0144026    -5.18   0.000     -.102831    -.046374
    not_smsa   -.1638432   .0120005   -13.65   0.000    -.1873637   -.1403227
       south   -.0782872   .0115163    -6.80   0.000    -.1008588   -.0557156
        year   -.0076007   .0025611    -2.97   0.003    -.0126204   -.0025811
          y2   -.0320497   .0084826    -3.78   0.000    -.0486753   -.0154242
          y3   -.0358153   .0085202    -4.20   0.000    -.0525146   -.0191161
          y4   -.0183633   .0083179    -2.21   0.027     -.034666   -.0020606
          y5   -.0255666   .0083462    -3.06   0.002    -.0419249   -.0092083
       _cons    15.30293   5.014625     3.05   0.002      5.47445    25.13142
```

现在，我们使用“xttest0”指令并设定零假设为随机效应。

```
. xttest0

Breusch and Pagan Lagrangian multiplier test for random effects

        ln_wage[idcode,t] = Xb + u[idcode] + e[idcode,t]

        Estimated results:
                         |       Var     sd = sqrt(Var)
                ---------+-----------------------------
                 ln_wage |   .2655362       .5153021
                       e |   .0758854       .2754731
                       u |   .1015094       .3186053

        Test:   Var(u) = 0
                             chi2(1) =  5697.66
                         Prob > chi2 =     0.0000
```

随机效应的零假设被拒绝（p 值小于 5%），所以我们应该用包含时间效应的固定效应模型。

Ⅳ. 附加上机操作练习

这个问题用到了 **murder. dta**[①]，其中包含了 1987 年、1990 年和 1993 年各州谋杀率的数据。假设研究人员对于死刑是否有威慑性感兴趣，在我们开始做练习前，先看一看数据中有哪些变量，并且它们代表了什么。

. use murder，clear

. desc

```
Contains data from murder.dta
  obs:           153
 vars:            13                          13 Sep 2000 15:34
 size:         5,049 (99.9% of memory free)

              storage  display     value
variable name   type   format      label      variable label

id              byte   %9.0g                  state identifier
state           str2   %9s                    postal code
year            byte   %9.0g                  87, 90, or 93
mrdrte          float  %9.0g                  murders per 100,000 population
exec            byte   %9.0g                  total executions, past 3 years
unem            float  %9.0g                  annual unem. rate
d90             byte   %9.0g                  =1 if year == 90
d93             byte   %9.0g                  =1 if year == 93
cmrdrte         float  %9.0g                  mrdrte - mrdrte[t-1]
cexec           byte   %9.0g                  exec - exec[t-1]
cunem           float  %9.0g                  unem - unem[t-1]
cexec_1         byte   %9.0g                  cexec[t-1]
cunem_1         float  %9.0g                  cunem[t-1]

Sorted by:
```

. sum

Variable	Obs	Mean	Std. Dev.	Min	Max
id	153	26	14.76794	1	51
state	0				
year	153	90	2.457534	87	93
mrdrte	153	8.070588	9.192867	.8	78.5
exec	153	1.228758	3.791432	0	34
unem	153	5.973203	1.680617	2.2	12
d90	153	.3333333	.4729527	0	1
d93	153	.3333333	.4729527	0	1
cmrdrte	102	.8421568	4.290271	-2.6	41.6
cexec	102	.1862745	2.950853	-11	23
cunem	102	.0058823	1.658272	-5.8	3.6
cexec_1	51	-.2745098	2.191606	-11	5
cunem_1	51	-.8862745	1.7339	-5.8	3.1

a）假设一个研究员将谋杀率建模为一个失业率和过去三年处决人数的函数。根据这个简单的模型，做 Hausman 检验，并且决定固定效应模型是否更合适。注意，要检验的零假设是什么。

要做 Hausman 检验，我们需要先估计随机效应模型，然后再使用“hausman”命令：

. xtreg mrdrte unem exec，i（id）fe

① 资料来源：http：//fmwww. bc. edu/ec—p/data/wooldridge/murder. dta。

```
Fixed-effects (within) regression               Number of obs      =       153
Group variable: id                              Number of groups   =        51

R-sq:  within  = 0.0047                         Obs per group: min =         3
       between = 0.0007                                        avg =       3.0
       overall = 0.0002                                        max =         3

                                                F(2,100)           =      0.24
corr(u_i, Xb)  = -0.0635                        Prob > F           =    0.7909

------------------------------------------------------------------------------
      mrdrte |      Coef.   Std. Err.      t    P>|t|     [95% Conf. Interval]
-------------+----------------------------------------------------------------
        unem |    .095914   .2800721     0.34   0.733    -.4597411    .6515692
        exec |  -.1140743   .1800836    -0.63   0.528    -.4713551    .2432065
       _cons |   7.637844   1.684436     4.53   0.000     4.295971    10.97972
-------------+----------------------------------------------------------------
     sigma_u |   8.788124
     sigma_e |   3.612922
         rho |  .85542114   (fraction of variance due to u_i)
------------------------------------------------------------------------------
F test that all u_i=0:     F(50, 100) =    16.46            Prob > F = 0.0000
```

. estimates store fixed

. xtreg mrdrte unem exec, i (id) re

```
Random-effects GLS regression                   Number of obs      =       153
Group variable: id                              Number of groups   =        51

R-sq:  within  = 0.0015                         Obs per group: min =         3
       between = 0.0732                                        avg =       3.0
       overall = 0.0433                                        max =         3

Random effects u_i ~ Gaussian                   Wald chi2(2)       =      0.90
corr(u_i, X)       = 0 (assumed)                Prob > chi2        =    0.6369

------------------------------------------------------------------------------
      mrdrte |      Coef.   Std. Err.      z    P>|z|     [95% Conf. Interval]
-------------+----------------------------------------------------------------
        unem |   .2560543   .2708762     0.95   0.345    -.2748532    .7869619
        exec |  -.0351956   .1619968    -0.22   0.828    -.3527036    .2823124
       _cons |   6.584371   2.001338     3.29   0.001     2.661819    10.50692
-------------+----------------------------------------------------------------
     sigma_u |  8.1923983
     sigma_e |   3.612922
         rho |  .83717807   (fraction of variance due to u_i)
------------------------------------------------------------------------------
```

. estimates store random

. hausman fixed random

```
                 ---- Coefficients ----
             |      (b)          (B)            (b-B)     sqrt(diag(V_b-V_B))
             |     fixed        random       Difference          S.E.
-------------+----------------------------------------------------------------
        unem |    .095914     .2560543       -.1601403        .0711792
        exec |  -.1140743    -.0351956       -.0788787        .0786584
------------------------------------------------------------------------------
                           b = consistent under Ho and Ha; obtained from xtreg
            B = inconsistent under Ha, efficient under Ho; obtained from xtreg

    Test:  Ho:  difference in coefficients not systematic

                  chi2(2) = (b-B)'[(V_b-V_B)^(-1)](b-B)
                          =        6.79
                Prob>chi2 =      0.0336
```

p 值等于 0.034，这表明我们可以拒绝零假设。这里的零假设是任何未观测到的效应都与 *unem* 和 *exec* 不相关。从技术上讲，我们想检验系数差异是否为系统性的，其实所检验的是相同的事情。为什么？因为 Hausman 检验背后的思想是在零假设下（未观测到的效应与 x 不相关）两个不同的估计量都是一致的（这个例子中是随机效应和固定效应）。如果它们都是一致的，我们可以期望在估计量中只有随机的变化。如果这里有系统性的差异，我们必须拒绝零假设并得出结论：未观测到的效应与 x 相关。

b）考虑一个固定效应模型的替代模型——一阶差分。估计这个模型，调整标准差来应对异方差问题。因为每个州有两个观测值，在一阶差分模型的误差中可能依然有序列相关。做一个简单的序列相关检验。这个模型中有这个问题吗？

一阶差分模型是另一个去除相关的未观测效应的方法：

. reg cmrdrte cunem cexec，robust

```
Linear regression                                      Number of obs =     102
                                                       F(  2,     99) =    8.93
                                                       Prob > F      =  0.0003
                                                       R-squared     =  0.0090
                                                       Root MSE      =  4.3139

------------------------------------------------------------------------------
             |               Robust
     cmrdrte |      Coef.   Std. Err.      t    P>|t|     [95% Conf. Interval]
-------------+----------------------------------------------------------------
       cunem |  -.0447929   .1346571    -0.33   0.740    -.3119818    .2223961
       cexec |  -.1313545   .0311427    -4.22   0.000    -.1931484   -.0695606
       _cons |   .8668883    .429753     2.02   0.046      .014165    1.719612
------------------------------------------------------------------------------
```

要做一个序列相关的检验，我们需要得到残差和它的滞后项。我们在得出滞后项的时候需要小心，要确定数据是用“by id:”排序的以避免使用前一个州的残差。

. predict uhat，resid

. sort id year

. by id：gen uhat _ 1=uhat [_ n−1]

. reg uhat uhat _ 1，robust

```
Linear regression                                      Number of obs =      51
                                                       F(  1,     49) =    1.19
                                                       Prob > F      =  0.2798
                                                       R-squared     =  0.0028
                                                       Root MSE      =   1.071

------------------------------------------------------------------------------
             |               Robust
        uhat |      Coef.   Std. Err.      t    P>|t|     [95% Conf. Interval]
-------------+----------------------------------------------------------------
      uhat_1 |   .0094241   .0086225     1.09   0.280    -.0079035    .0267518
       _cons |  -.4596857   .1506809    -3.05   0.004    -.7624903   -.1568811
------------------------------------------------------------------------------
```

因为滞后项的系数不是显著地异于零，我们不能拒绝没有序列相关的零假设。注意，我做了异方差的稳健修正，但是结果并没有改变。

c）根据以上结果，你能得出关于死刑的威慑性的什么结论？

随机效应模型显示出没有显著的威慑性影响，但一阶差分模型显示有影响。因为 Hausman 检验说明未观测到的效应是一个问题，所以一阶差分模型更理想。因此，一个州每次死刑执行都会减少 0.13%的谋杀率。虽然这个效应很小，但依然很显著。

Chapter 12

Panel Data

Ⅰ. The Role of Panel Data

1.1 What is Panel Data?

Thus far we have concentrated on cross-sectional data, where a unit of observation may represent some entity (typically an individual) at a particular point in time. However, one other type of data is sometimes available to researchers. Panel data provide information for particular entities (like individuals, countries, or others) over a period of time. The Basic Data Structure generally takes the following format:

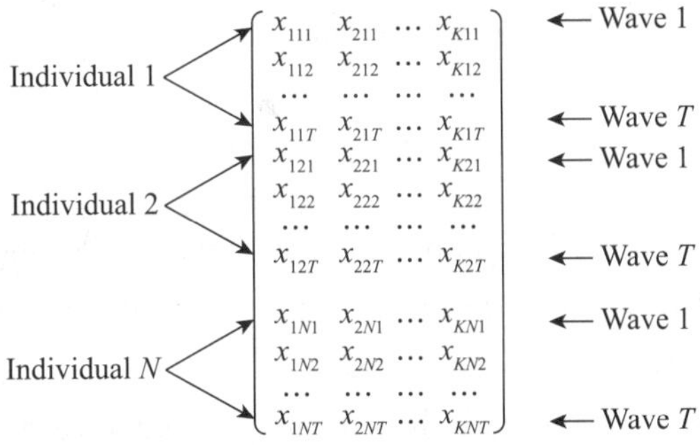

1.2 Unobservable Heterogeneity

Panel data allow us to formally recognize the possible existence of unobservable heterogeneity in our model. What is unobservable heterogeneity? Suppose we have data on N individuals over a period of T years. The complete dataset includes $N \times T$ observations. Suppose we want to estimate a standard regression model of y on a number (k) of x variables. But there exists an individual-specific component that cannot be controlled because it is not observed. As we have learned, OLS is biased if a variable is omitted that is related to the dependent variable and is related to an included explanatory variable. For example, if we wish to study the impact of cigarette smoking on the incidence of cancer, we may also need to examine related factors, such as drinking and diet choices. However, many individual characteristics are not observed, e. g. enthusiasm, willingness to take risks. These vary across individuals-described as unobserved heterogeneity. To solve this issue, we can develop an error components model as follows.

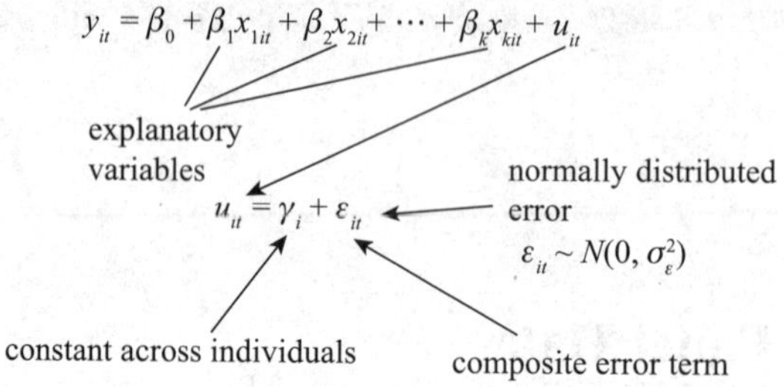

In panel data, the error term can be the result of the sum of three components (in the twoway model) or just two (in the oneway model). The twoway model assumes the error term as having a specific individual term effect, a specific time effect and an additional idiosyncratic term. In the oneway model, we only have the specific individual effect and an additional idiosyncratic term.

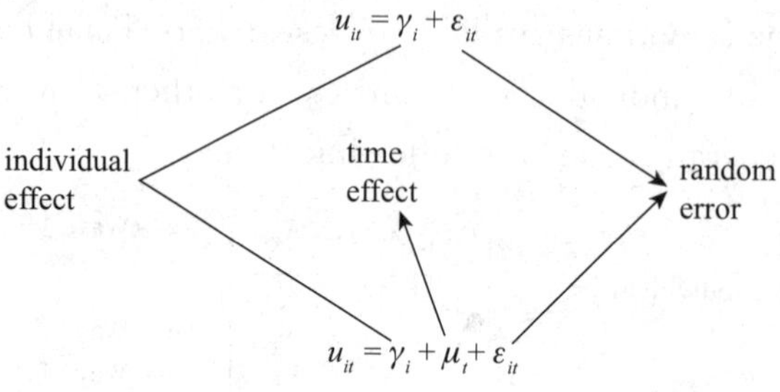

In this chapter, we mainly focus on the oneway model. As shown in the above figure, γ_i measures individual effects. There are two options for the treatment of individual effects:

(1) Fixed effects—assume γ_i is constant.

(2) Random effects—assume γ_i is drawn independently from some probability distribution.

Given each of these two solutions, we can specify the model to take the form:

$$y_{it}=\beta_0+\gamma_i+\beta_1 x_{1it}+\beta_2 x_{2it}+\cdots+\beta_k x_{kit}+u_{it}$$

where y_{it} represents the value of the dependent variable for individual i at time t; γ_i represents the individual-specific component. Hence, if γ_i is treated as a constant, then we have a fixed effects model. If γ_i is treated as a random variable, then we have a random effects model.

Ⅱ. Panel Regression Models

2.1 The Fixed Effects Model

For a fixed effects model, we treat γ_i as a constant for each individual:

$$y_{it} = (\beta_0 + \gamma_i) + \beta_1 x_{1it} + \beta_2 x_{2it} + \cdots + \beta_k x_{kit} + u_{it}$$

γ_i is now a part of the constant term, but varies by individuals.

In the fixed effects model, we need to assume that that unique attributes of individuals are not the result of random variation. Indeed, they represent fixed, longstanding differences.

If this assumption is accurate, panel data enables us to estimate unbiased slope coefficients for the included variables.

To eliminate the potential bias brought about by unobservable heterogeneity, the fixed effect acts like a dummy variable, shifting the intercept up or down for each individual in the sample. Based on this feature, we may consider two approaches to estimate a fixed effects model.

ⅰ) First Difference Approach.

The first approach uses data from two separate periods for the same individual. We specify two separate regression models for each period:

$$y_{i(t-1)} = \beta_0 + \gamma_i + \beta_1 x_{1i(t-1)} + \beta_2 x_{2i(t-1)} + \cdots + \beta_k x_{ki(t-1)} + \varepsilon_{i(t-1)}$$
$$y_{it} = \beta_0 + \gamma_i + \beta_1 x_{1it} + \beta_2 x_{2it} + \cdots + \beta_k x_{kit} + \varepsilon_{it}$$

All variables in the first and second equations contain time subscripts, except for the individual fixed effect. Subtracting the second equation from the first yields:

$$\Delta y_i = \beta_1 \Delta x_{1i} + \beta_2 \Delta x_{2i} + \cdots + \beta_k \Delta x_{ki} + \Delta\varepsilon_i$$

Taking the difference in variables between one period and the next solves the unobservable heterogeneity problem, because the characteristics of an individual that are fixed over time disappear. When the assumptions of this model hold, the remaining slope coefficients will not be subject to the omitted-variable bias.

ⅱ) Deviations from Means.

A second approach uses data from multiple periods for the same individual. Start with the same basic regression equation:

$$y_{it} = \beta_0 + \gamma_i + \beta_1 x_{1it} + \beta_2 x_{2it} + \cdots + \beta_k x_{kit} + \varepsilon_{it}$$

Modify it by taking the mean of each variable:

$$\bar{y}_{i.} = \beta_0 + \gamma_i + \beta_1 \bar{x}_{1i.} + \beta_2 \bar{x}_{2i.} + \cdots + \beta_k \bar{x}_{ki.} + \bar{\varepsilon}_{i.}$$

The second equation contains the same individual fixed effect, γ_i, because the mean of a constant is a constant. Subtracting the second equation from the first yields:

$$y_{it} - \bar{y}_{i.} = \beta_1 (x_{1it} - \bar{x}_{1i.}) + \cdots + \beta_k (x_{kit} - \bar{x}_{ki.}) + (\varepsilon_{it} - \bar{\varepsilon}_{i.})$$

Estimates of the parameters of this model can be obtained with no omitted-variable bias, provided it is a valid assumption that all individual characteristics not explicitly included are constant over time.

Note: taking deviations from individual means and applying least squares to estimate $y_{it} - \bar{y}_{i.} = \beta_1 (x_{1it} - \bar{x}_{1i.}) + \cdots + \beta_k (x_{kit} - \bar{x}_{ki.}) + (\varepsilon_{it} - \bar{\varepsilon}_{i.})$, we can get either fixed-effects or "within" estimators. The reason why it is called the "within" estimator is because it relies on variations within individuals rather than between individuals. Not surprisingly, there is another type of estimator that uses only information on individual means from the model $y_{it} - \bar{y}_{.t} = \beta_1 (x_{1it} - \bar{x}_{1.t}) + \cdots + \beta_k (x_{kit} - \bar{x}_{k.t}) + (\varepsilon_{it} - \bar{\varepsilon}_{.t})$. This is known as the "between" estimator. The Random Effects model is a combination of the Fixed Effects ("within") estimator and the "between" estimator:

$$(y_{it} - \bar{y}_{i.} - \bar{y}_t - \bar{y}) = \beta_1 (x_{1it} - \bar{x}_{1i.} - \bar{x}_{1.t} - \bar{x}_1) + \cdots + \beta_k (x_{kit} - \bar{x}_{ki.} - \bar{x}_{k.t} - \bar{x}_k) + (\varepsilon_{it} - \bar{\varepsilon}_{i.} - \bar{\varepsilon}_{.t} - \bar{\varepsilon})$$

2.2 Random Effects Models

Some individuals always have outcomes that differ from others in a specific way—captured by the individual fixed effect. However, an alternative framework could be used to characterize differences across individuals. Suppose the individual-specific component was not a constant, but each individual's realization of a random variable was specific to him or her. It may be considered an element of the model's residual in addition to the standard error term in the regression model. Hence, the residual for a particular individual would take the form $\gamma_i + \varepsilon_{it}$ in the following model:

$$y_{it} = \beta_0 + \beta_1 x_{1it} + \beta_2 x_{2it} + \cdots + \beta_k x_{kit} + \gamma_i + u_{it}$$

In this model γ_i is treated as a random variable, not a constant. Effects can still be interpreted as shifts in the intercept for different individuals. But the difference is those shifts are randomly distributed across individuals. A straightforward extension of this model could include a random time component, γ_s.

For this part of the residual, in the random effects model, we commonly assume:

ⅰ) Constant variance for different individuals, i. e., $\mathrm{Var}(\gamma_i) = \sigma_\gamma$ for all i.

ⅱ) Covariance of these residuals across individuals is zero, i. e., $\mathrm{Cov}(\gamma_i, \gamma_j) = 0$, $\forall i \neq j$.

iii) Individual component of the residual is uncorrelated with any of the included explanatory variables, i. e., $\mathrm{Cov}(\gamma_i, X_{jt})=0$, $\forall i$, j, and t.

Under these assumptions, despite the presence of unobservable heterogeneity, OLS is not biased because the residual for the model is uncorrelated with any of the explanatory variables: $\mathrm{Cov}(\gamma_i+\varepsilon_{it}, X_{jt})=0$, $\forall i$, j, and t. However, serial correlation can be a problem.

For the N observations for each individual in the sample, there is a non-zero correlation in the residuals: $\mathrm{Cov}(\gamma_i+\varepsilon_{it}, \gamma_i+\varepsilon_{is})\neq 0$ for $s\neq t$. If serial correlation does exist, OLS formulas for computing standard errors of regression coefficients yield incorrect estimates, and hence OLS is no longer BLUE. The solution involves an estimation procedure, called as generalized least squares (GLS).

2.3 Fixed Effects or Random Effects?

These two types of panel models make very different assumptions about the individual-specific component. Hence, we need to recognize which model is more appropriate when choosing between the models.

We can turn to hypothesis tests. In the next section, we will discuss how to use a Hausman test to choose the right panel model. Alternatively, many researchers use their intuition regarding which model to use. When we have data on all states in the country, intuition tells us that a fixed effects specification probably is sensible. With individual data the choice is more difficult. Here are several suggestions:

i) If T (the number of time series data) is large and N (the number of cross-sectional units) is small, there is likely to be little difference in the values of the parameters estimated by the fixed effects model (FEM) and random effects model (REM). Based on computational convenience, FEM may be preferable.

ii) When N is large and T is small, and if we strongly believe that the cross-sectional units are not random drawing from a larger sample, FEM is appropriate. If the units are regarded as random drawings, REM is appropriate.

iii) If the individual error component and one or more independent variables are correlated, FEM is appropriate.

iv) If N is large and T is small, and if the assumptions underlying REM hold, REM estimators are more efficient than the FEM estimators.

Ⅲ. Computer Exercise

In this exercise, we need to increase the size of memory allocated to the dataset, because we will use a much larger dataset than in previous exercises. We are going to allocate

10 megabits to the dataset. In Stata, type "set mem 10m". Please upload **woman. dta**[①]into Stata as usual.

(1) Generate New Variables.

Our purpose is to run regressions of the logarithm of women's wages on the following variables:

grade=number of years studying;

age=woman's age;

age2=square of woman's age;

ttl _ exp=total number of years working;

ttl _ exp2=square of the previous variable;

tenure=number of years working in the last job;

tenure2=square of the previous variable;

black=dummy variable equal to 1 if the woman is black; 0 otherwise;

not _ smsa=dummy variable equal to one if the woman lives in a rural area; 0 otherwise;

south=dummy variable equal to one if the woman lives in a southern state; 0 otherwise.

(2) Descriptive Statistics for Panel Data.

Now, we have to instruct Stata that we have a panel dataset. We do it with the command "tsset".

. tsset idcode year

Note: in the last command, *idcode* is the variable that identifies individuals in our dataset. *Year* is the variable that identifies time periods.

The commands referring to panel data in Stata almost always start with the prefix "xt". We can check for these commands by calling the help file for "xt".

. help xt

Before we perform estimations, we'd better describe and summarize the dataset as usual. Stata has specific commands for describing and summarizing panel datasets.

. xtdes

. xtsum

Please note that "xtdes" permits us to observe the pattern of the data, like the number of individuals with different patterns of observations across time periods. In our case, we have an unbalanced panel because not all individuals have observations for all years. The "xtsum" command gives us general descriptive statistics of the variables in the dataset, considering the overall, the between and the within variations. Overall refers to the whole dataset. Between refers to the variation of the means to each individual (across time periods). Within refers to the variation of the deviation from the respective mean to each indi-

---

① Data is collected from http: //www. stata—press. com/data/r8/xtdatasmpl.

vidual.

We may also be interested in applying the panel data tabulate command to a variable; for instance, to the variable *black*, in order to obtain a one-way table.

. xttab black

(3) Panel Regression Analysis.

Let's now turn to estimation commands for panel data.

ⅰ) Pooled OLS regression.

The first type of regression that we are going to run is a pooled OLS regression. It is simply an OLS regression applied to the whole dataset. However, this regression does not consider that we have different individuals across time periods, and does not consider the panel nature of the dataset, either.

```
reg ln_wage grade age* ttl_exp* tenure* black not_smsa south

      Source |       SS       df       MS              Number of obs =   12293
-------------+------------------------------           F( 10, 12282) =  687.96
       Model |   1171.8669    10   117.18669           Prob > F      =  0.0000
    Residual |  2092.10451 12282  .170339074           R-squared     =  0.3590
-------------+------------------------------           Adj R-squared =  0.3585
       Total |  3263.97141 12292  .265536236           Root MSE      =  .41272

------------------------------------------------------------------------------
     ln_wage |      Coef.   Std. Err.      t    P>|t|     [95% Conf. Interval]
-------------+----------------------------------------------------------------
       grade |    .066003   .0015684    42.08   0.000     .0629288    .0690772
         age |  -.0037805   .0127087    -0.30   0.766    -.0286916    .0211305
        age2 |  -.0000653   .0001795    -0.36   0.716    -.0004172    .0002865
     ttl_exp |   .0380632   .0038826     9.80   0.000     .0304528    .0456737
    ttl_exp2 |  -.0001812   .0001869    -0.97   0.332    -.0005476    .0001852
      tenure |   .0351204   .0026324    13.34   0.000     .0299604    .0402803
     tenure2 |  -.0013263   .0001686    -7.87   0.000    -.0016568   -.0009958
       black |  -.0886489   .0088517   -10.01   0.000    -.1059995   -.0712983
    not_smsa |  -.1929917   .0084369   -22.87   0.000    -.2095293   -.1764541
       south |  -.0898548    .008044   -11.17   0.000    -.1056222   -.0740873
       _cons |   .8159543   .2218402     3.68   0.000     .3811126    1.250796
------------------------------------------------------------------------------
```

Note: In the previous command, we do not need to type "age age2". We just need to type "age * ". When we do this, we are instructing Stata to include all the variables starting with the expression age to be included in the regression.

ⅱ) Fixed Effects Models v. s. Random Effects Models (Hausman Test).

In empirical work in panel data, we are always concerned with choosing between two alternative regressions. This choice is between fixed effects estimation and random effects estimation.

In order for consistent estimation, if the error term is not correlated with the independent variables, the random effects model should be used because it is a weighted average of between and within estimation. But, if there is correlation between the individual and/or time effects and the independent variables, then the individual and/or time effects must be estimated as dummy variables in order to solve for the endogeneity problem.

First, we will run a fixed effects regression, then a random effects regression, and afterwards we will want to test for which model to use via a Hausman test, which should usually be reported in order to justify our choice among the two models.

Let's run a fixed effects regression:

```
. xtreg ln_wage grade age* ttl_exp* tenure* black not_smsa south, fe

ixed-effects (within) regression               Number of obs      =     12293
roup variable: idcode                           Number of groups   =      3456

-sq:  within  = 0.0916                          Obs per group: min =         1
      between = 0.2631                                         avg =       3.6
      overall = 0.2141                                         max =         6

                                                F(8,8829)          =    111.28
orr(u_i, Xb)  = 0.0279                          Prob > F           =    0.0000

------------------------------------------------------------------------------
     ln_wage |      Coef.   Std. Err.      t    P>|t|     [95% Conf. Interval]
-------------+----------------------------------------------------------------
       grade |  (dropped)
         age |   .0009433   .0116222     0.08   0.935    -.0218389    .0237254
        age2 |  -.0002997   .0001562    -1.92   0.055    -.0006058    6.44e-06
     ttl_exp |   .0588723   .0070158     8.39   0.000     .0451196    .0726249
    ttl_exp2 |  -.0002974   .0002084    -1.43   0.154     -.000706    .0001112
      tenure |   .0224444   .0026359     8.52   0.000     .0172775    .0276112
     tenure2 |  -.0012442    .000175    -7.11   0.000    -.0015873   -.0009011
       black |  (dropped)
    not_smsa |  -.0768878   .0218558    -3.52   0.000    -.1197303   -.0340454
       south |   -.059834   .0221643    -2.70   0.007    -.1032813   -.0163868
       _cons |    1.59244   .2060833     7.73   0.000     1.188469    1.996412
-------------+----------------------------------------------------------------
     sigma_u |  .41275024
     sigma_e |  .27600537
         rho |  .69100986   (fraction of variance due to u_i)
------------------------------------------------------------------------------
 test that all u_i=0:     F(3455, 8829) =     5.39           Prob > F = 0.0000
```

Now, run a random effects regression:

```
. xtreg ln_wage grade age* ttl_exp* tenure* black not_smsa south, re

andom-effects GLS regression                    Number of obs      =     12293
roup variable: idcode                           Number of groups   =      3456

-sq:  within  = 0.0880                          Obs per group: min =         1
      between = 0.4190                                         avg =       3.6
      overall = 0.3567                                         max =         6

andom effects u_i ~ Gaussian                    Wald chi2(10)      =   3377.50
orr(u_i, X)       = 0 (assumed)                 Prob > chi2        =    0.0000

------------------------------------------------------------------------------
     ln_wage |      Coef.   Std. Err.      z    P>|z|     [95% Conf. Interval]
-------------+----------------------------------------------------------------
       grade |   .0643748   .0024985    25.77   0.000     .0594779    .0692717
         age |   .0049517   .0102755     0.48   0.630    -.0151878    .0250913
        age2 |  -.0002152   .0001451    -1.48   0.138    -.0004997    .0000692
     ttl_exp |   .0416154    .003821    10.89   0.000     .0341263    .0491045
    ttl_exp2 |   -.000144   .0001747    -0.82   0.410    -.0004864    .0001984
      tenure |   .0290022   .0023756    12.21   0.000      .024346    .0336583
     tenure2 |   -.001279   .0001566    -8.17   0.000     -.001586   -.0009721
       black |  -.0756085   .0143898    -5.25   0.000     -.103812    -.047405
    not_smsa |  -.1638295   .0120031   -13.65   0.000    -.1873552   -.1403039
       south |  -.0777664    .011514    -6.75   0.000    -.1003333   -.0551994
       _cons |   .6828395   .1818643     3.75   0.000     .3263922    1.039287
-------------+----------------------------------------------------------------
     sigma_u |  .31839394
     sigma_e |  .27600537
         rho |  .57095246   (fraction of variance due to u_i)
------------------------------------------------------------------------------
```

Next, let's perform the Hausman test for random effects. When we run a Hausman test, we are testing the null hypothesis that assumes as true the first model that we run. (In our case the first model is random effects). Then we are going to test against the alternative of a fixed effects model. In order to do this, the last regression that we performed was the random effects one. The first thing to do is to save the results of that regression. We do it with the "estimates store" command. Note that we must give a name to the results that we are saving. Next, we run the fixed effects model (which is the alternative hypothesis). Because we have already run the fixed effects model and observed the results, we can just run it with the "quietly" option before the command, which can be used for any command in Stata, in order for Stata to perform a command without showing the results in the results window. Finally, we perform the Hausman test which assumes as true the null hypothesis of a random effects model.

```
est store re
quietly xtreg ln_wage grade age* ttl_exp* tenure* black not_smsa south, fe
hausman . re

                 ---- Coefficients ----
             |      (b)          (B)            (b-B)     sqrt(diag(V_b-V_B))
             |       .           re          Difference          S.E.
-------------+----------------------------------------------------------------
         age |   .0009433     .0049517       -.0040085        .0054304
        age2 |  -.0002997    -.0002152       -.0000845        .0000577
     ttl_exp |   .0588723     .0416154        .0172569         .005884
    ttl_exp2 |  -.0002974     -.000144       -.0001534        .0001137
      tenure |   .0224444     .0290022       -.0065578         .001142
     tenure2 |  -.0012442     -.001279        .0000349        .0000782
    not_smsa |  -.0768878    -.1638295        .0869417        .0182647
       south |   -.059834    -.0777664        .0179323         .018939
------------------------------------------------------------------------------
                           b = consistent under Ho and Ha; obtained from xtreg
            B = inconsistent under Ha, efficient under Ho; obtained from xtreg

    Test:  Ho:  difference in coefficients not systematic

                  chi2(8) = (b-B)'[(V_b-V_B)^(-1)](b-B)
                          =       89.49
                Prob>chi2 =      0.0000
```

In our case, we should reject the random effects model because the p-value of the Hausman test is lower than 5%, which is evidence to choose the fixed effects model.

ⅲ) Other Estimation Methods.

If we want a fixed effects model with robust standard errors, we can use the following command:

. areg ln _ wage grade age * ttl _ exp * tenure * black not _ smsa south, absorb (idcode) robust

We may be interested in running a maximum likelihood estimation in panel data. We would type:

. xtreg ln _ wage grade age * ttl _ exp * tenure * black not _ smsa south, mle

ⅳ) Time Dummies.

When we do empirical work in panel data, we often debate between the inclusion of time effects (time dummies) in our fixed effects model.

In order to do this, let's first generate our time dummies.

. tab year, g (y)

In order to perform the test for the inclusion of time dummies in our fixed effects regression, first we run fixed effects including the time dummies and then we apply the "testparm" command.

```
. xtreg ln_wage grade age* ttl_exp* tenure* black not_smsa south y*, fe

Fixed-effects (within) regression               Number of obs      =     12293
Group variable: idcode                          Number of groups   =      3456

R-sq:  within  = 0.0956                         Obs per group: min =         1
       between = 0.2449                                        avg =       3.6
       overall = 0.1956                                        max =         6

                                                F(13,8824)         =     71.76
corr(u_i, Xb)  = -0.0620                        Prob > F           =    0.0000

------------------------------------------------------------------------------
     ln_wage |      Coef.   Std. Err.      t    P>|t|     [95% Conf. Interval]
-------------+----------------------------------------------------------------
       grade |  (dropped)
         age |    .055874   .0170351     3.28   0.001     .0224812    .0892668
        age2 |  -.0005845   .0001664    -3.51   0.000    -.0009106   -.0002584
     ttl_exp |   .0669626   .0072187     9.28   0.000     .0528122     .081113
    ttl_exp2 |  -.0004821   .0002105    -2.29   0.022    -.0008947   -.0000695
      tenure |   .0216011   .0026419     8.18   0.000     .0164223    .0267798
     tenure2 |  -.0011873   .0001752    -6.78   0.000    -.0015308   -.0008439
       black |  (dropped)
    not_smsa |  -.0773324   .0218221    -3.54   0.000    -.1201088   -.0345561
       south |  -.0594989   .0221376    -2.69   0.007    -.1028938    -.016104
        year |  -.0410534   .0136193    -3.01   0.003    -.0677504   -.0143563
          y1 |  (dropped)
          y2 |  -.0299615   .0087471    -3.43   0.001    -.0471079   -.0128151
          y3 |  -.0337915   .0089443    -3.78   0.000    -.0513245   -.0162586
          y4 |  -.0176105   .0090619    -1.94   0.052     -.035374     .000153
          y5 |  -.0198696   .0094037    -2.11   0.035    -.0383031   -.0014362
          y6 |  (dropped)
       _cons |   81.44174   26.59399     3.06   0.002     29.31133    133.5721
-------------+----------------------------------------------------------------
     sigma_u |  .41811501
     sigma_e |  .27547309
         rho |  .69731259   (fraction of variance due to u_i)
------------------------------------------------------------------------------
F test that all u_i=0:     F(3455, 8824) =     5.42          Prob > F = 0.0000
```

Now we apply the test for time dummies, which assumes the null hypothesis that the time dummies are not jointly significant.

```
testparm y*

( 1)  year = 0
( 2)  y1 = 0
( 3)  y2 = 0
( 4)  y3 = 0
( 5)  y4 = 0
( 6)  y5 = 0
( 7)  y6 = 0
      Constraint 2 dropped
      Constraint 7 dropped

      F(  5,  8824) =    7.83
           Prob > F =    0.0000
```

We reject the null hypothesis that the time dummies are not jointly significant (the p-value smaller than 5%), and as a consequence our fixed effects regression should include time effects.

What if the inclusion of time dummies in our regression would permit us to use a random effects model in the individual effects? First, we will run random effects regression including our time dummies, and then we will apply the "xttest0" command to test for random effects in this case.

```
 xtreg ln_wage grade age* ttl_exp* tenure* black not_smsa south y*, re
ote: y1 dropped because of collinearity
ote: y6 dropped because of collinearity

andom-effects GLS regression                    Number of obs      =     12293
roup variable: idcode                           Number of groups   =      3456

-sq:  within  = 0.0912                          Obs per group: min =         1
      between = 0.4189                                         avg =       3.6
      overall = 0.3571                                         max =         6

andom effects u_i ~ Gaussian                    Wald chi2(15)      =   3413.59
orr(u_i, X)       = 0 (assumed)                 Prob > chi2        =    0.0000

------------------------------------------------------------------------------
     ln_wage |      Coef.   Std. Err.      z    P>|z|     [95% Conf. Interval]
-------------+----------------------------------------------------------------
       grade |   .0640186   .0025003    25.60   0.000     .0591181    .0689192
         age |   .0273925   .0111443     2.46   0.014       .00555     .049235
        age2 |  -.0004727   .0001546    -3.06   0.002    -.0007756   -.0001698
     ttl_exp |   .0446606   .0038673    11.55   0.000     .0370808    .0522405
    ttl_exp2 |  -.0002213   .0001761    -1.26   0.209    -.0005664    .0001238
      tenure |   .0285262   .0023793    11.99   0.000     .0238629    .0331895
     tenure2 |  -.0012561   .0001568    -8.01   0.000    -.0015634   -.0009487
       black |  -.0746025   .0144026    -5.18   0.000     -.102831    -.046374
    not_smsa |  -.1638432   .0120005   -13.65   0.000    -.1873637   -.1403227
       south |  -.0782872   .0115163    -6.80   0.000    -.1008588   -.0557156
        year |  -.0076007   .0025611    -2.97   0.003    -.0126204   -.0025811
          y2 |  -.0320497   .0084826    -3.78   0.000    -.0486753   -.0154242
          y3 |  -.0358153   .0085202    -4.20   0.000    -.0525146   -.0191161
          y4 |  -.0183633   .0083179    -2.21   0.027     -.034666   -.0020606
          y5 |  -.0255666   .0083462    -3.06   0.002    -.0419249   -.0092083
       _cons |   15.30293   5.014625     3.05   0.002      5.47445    25.13142
------------------------------------------------------------------------------
```

Now we apply the "xttest0" command which assumes the null hypothesis of random effects.

```
. xttest0

Breusch and Pagan Lagrangian multiplier test for random effects

        ln_wage[idcode,t] = Xb + u[idcode] + e[idcode,t]

        Estimated results:
                         |       Var     sd = sqrt(Var)
                ---------+-----------------------------
                 ln_wage |   .2655362       .5153021
                       e |   .0758854       .2754731
                       u |   .1015094       .3186053

        Test:   Var(u) = 0
                             chi2(1) =  5697.66
                         Prob > chi2 =     0.0000
```

The null hypothesis of random effects is once again rejected (the p-value smaller than 5%), thus we should use a fixed effects model with time effects.

Ⅳ. Additional Computer Exercise

This problem uses **murder. dta**[①]which contains state-level data on murder rates in 1987, 1990 and 1993. It assumes a researcher is interested in whether the death penalty serves as a deterrent. Take a close look at what variables are in the dataset and what their meanings are before getting started.

. use murder, clear

. desc

```
Contains data from murder.dta
  obs:           153
 vars:            13                          13 Sep 2000 15:34
 size:         5,049 (99.9% of memory free)

              storage  display     value
variable name   type   format      label      variable label

id              byte   %9.0g                  state identifier
state           str2   %9s                    postal code
year            byte   %9.0g                  87, 90, or 93
mrdrte          float  %9.0g                  murders per 100,000 population
exec            byte   %9.0g                  total executions, past 3 years
unem            float  %9.0g                  annual unem. rate
d90             byte   %9.0g                  =1 if year == 90
d93             byte   %9.0g                  =1 if year == 93
cmrdrte         float  %9.0g                  mrdrte - mrdrte[t-1]
cexec           byte   %9.0g                  exec - exec[t-1]
cunem           float  %9.0g                  unem - unem[t-1]
cexec_1         byte   %9.0g                  cexec[t-1]
cunem_1         float  %9.0g                  cunem[t-1]

Sorted by:
```

. sum

Variable	Obs	Mean	Std. Dev.	Min	Max
id	153	26	14.76794	1	51
state	0				
year	153	90	2.457534	87	93
mrdrte	153	8.070588	9.192867	.8	78.5
exec	153	1.228758	3.791432	0	34
unem	153	5.973203	1.680617	2.2	12
d90	153	.3333333	.4729527	0	1
d93	153	.3333333	.4729527	0	1
cmrdrte	102	.8421568	4.290271	-2.6	41.6
cexec	102	.1862745	2.950853	-11	23
cunem	102	.0058823	1.658272	-5.8	3.6
cexec_1	51	-.2745098	2.191606	-11	5
cunem_1	51	-.8862745	1.7339	-5.8	3.1

a) Suppose that a researcher is modeling the murder rate simply as a function of the unemployment rate and the number of executions in the past 3 years. Based on this simple model, carry out a Hausman test to determine whether a fixed effect model is preferred. Make clear what the null hypothesis being tested is.

① Data source: http: //fmwww. bc. edu/ec—p/data/wooldridge/murder. dta.

To do a Hausman test, we need to estimate the random effects model and use *hausman* afterward:

. xtreg mrdrte unem exec, i (id) fe

```
Fixed-effects (within) regression               Number of obs      =       153
Group variable: id                              Number of groups   =        51

R-sq:  within  = 0.0047                         Obs per group: min =         3
       between = 0.0007                                        avg =       3.0
       overall = 0.0002                                        max =         3

                                                F(2,100)           =      0.24
corr(u_i, Xb)  = -0.0635                        Prob > F           =    0.7909

      mrdrte        Coef.   Std. Err.      t    P>|t|     [95% Conf. Interval]

        unem      .095914   .2800721     0.34   0.733    -.4597411    .6515692
        exec    -.1140743   .1800836    -0.63   0.528    -.4713551    .2432065
       _cons     7.637844   1.684436     4.53   0.000     4.295971    10.97972

     sigma_u    8.788124
     sigma_e    3.612922
         rho   .85542114   (fraction of variance due to u_i)

F test that all u_i=0:     F(50, 100) =    16.46             Prob > F = 0.0000
```

. estimates store fixed

. xtreg mrdrte unem exec, i (id) re

```
Random-effects GLS regression                   Number of obs      =       153
Group variable: id                              Number of groups   =        51

R-sq:  within  = 0.0015                         Obs per group: min =         3
       between = 0.0732                                        avg =       3.0
       overall = 0.0433                                        max =         3

Random effects u_i ~ Gaussian                   Wald chi2(2)       =      0.90
corr(u_i, X)       = 0 (assumed)                Prob > chi2        =    0.6369

      mrdrte        Coef.   Std. Err.      z    P>|z|     [95% Conf. Interval]

        unem     .2560543   .2708762     0.95   0.345    -.2748532    .7869619
        exec    -.0351956   .1619968    -0.22   0.828    -.3527036    .2823124
       _cons     6.584371   2.001338     3.29   0.001     2.661819    10.50692

     sigma_u   8.1923983
     sigma_e    3.612922
         rho   .83717807   (fraction of variance due to u_i)
```

. estimates store random

. hausman fixed random

```
                 ---- Coefficients ----
             |      (b)          (B)            (b-B)     sqrt(diag(V_b-V_B))
             |     fixed        random       Difference          S.E.

        unem |     .095914     .2560543       -.1601403        .0711792
        exec |   -.1140743    -.0351956       -.0788787        .0786584

                           b = consistent under Ho and Ha; obtained from xtreg
            B = inconsistent under Ha, efficient under Ho; obtained from xtreg

    Test:  Ho:  difference in coefficients not systematic

                  chi2(2) = (b-B)'[(V_b-V_B)^(-1)](b-B)
                          =        6.79
                Prob>chi2 =      0.0336
```

The p-value implies we can reject the null hypothesis at the 0.034 level. The null hypothesis in this case is that any unobserved effect is uncorrelated with *unem* and *exec*. Technically, the test is for whether the difference in coefficients is systematic, but this is the same thing. Why? Because the idea behind a Hausman test is that under the null hypothesis (in this case the unobserved effect is uncorrelated with x's) 2 different estimators are both consistent (in this case random effects and fixed effects). If they are both consistent, we would expect only random variation in the estimates. If there is a systematic difference, we must reject the null hypothesis and conclude that the unobserved effect is correlated with the x's.

b) Consider an alternative to the fixed effect model—first differences. Estimate this model, adjusting the standard errors for possible heteroskedasticity. Because there are still 2 observations per state, there may still be serial correlation in the errors of this first differenced model. Do a simple test for serial correlation. Does there appear to be a problem?

A first difference model is another way of removing the correlated unobserved effect:

. reg cmrdrte cunem cexec, robust

```
Linear regression                                      Number of obs =     102
                                                       F(  2,     99) =    8.93
                                                       Prob > F      =  0.0003
                                                       R-squared     =  0.0090
                                                       Root MSE      =  4.3139

------------------------------------------------------------------------------
             |               Robust
     cmrdrte |      Coef.   Std. Err.      t    P>|t|     [95% Conf. Interval]
-------------+----------------------------------------------------------------
       cunem |  -.0447929   .1346571    -0.33   0.740    -.3119818    .2223961
       cexec |  -.1313545   .0311427    -4.22   0.000    -.1931484   -.0695606
       _cons |   .8668883    .429753     2.02   0.046      .014165    1.719612
------------------------------------------------------------------------------
```

To do a serial correlation test, we need to get the residual and its lag. We need to be careful in computing the lag to make sure the data is sorted and to use "by id:" to avoid using the previous state's residual.

. predict uhat, resid

. sort id year

. by id: gen uhat_1=uhat [_n−1]

. reg uhat uhat_1, robust

```
Linear regression                                      Number of obs =      51
                                                       F(  1,     49) =    1.19
                                                       Prob > F      =  0.2798
                                                       R-squared     =  0.0028
                                                       Root MSE      =   1.071

------------------------------------------------------------------------------
             |               Robust
        uhat |      Coef.   Std. Err.      t    P>|t|     [95% Conf. Interval]
-------------+----------------------------------------------------------------
      uhat_1 |   .0094241   .0086225     1.09   0.280    -.0079035    .0267518
       _cons |  -.4596857   .1506809    -3.05   0.004    -.7624903   -.1568811
------------------------------------------------------------------------------
```

Since the coefficient on the lagged residual is not significantly different from zero, we cannot reject the null hypothesis of no serial correlation. Note that I did a heteroskedasticity robust test, but the result is the same without that correction.

c) Based on the above, what would you conclude about the possible deterrent effects of the death penalty?

While the random effects model showed no significant deterrent effect, the first difference model did. Since the Hausman test implied that unobserved effects were a problem, the first difference model should be preferred. Thus, it appears that every execution in a state reduces its murder rate by 0.13 percentage points. This is very small, but is a significant effect.

第 13 章

联立方程组模型

Ⅰ. 联立方程组模型的建立

1.1 结构式方程组和简化式方程组

本章要讨论的问题是我们感兴趣的且需要估计的方程在一组联立线性方程组中。我们来考虑如下一个简单的凯恩斯模型：

$$\text{结构式方程组}\begin{cases} c_t=\alpha+\beta Y_t+\varepsilon_t & (1)\\ Y_t=c_t+I_t & (2)\end{cases}$$

其中，C_t是时期 t 的消费支出，

Y_t是时期 t 的收入，

I_t是时期 t 的投资，

ε_t是随机误差，其均值为零而方差固定，

α 和 β 是结构参数。

在这个例子中，我们看到两个方程共同形成一个联立方程结构式，用来分析经济的运行情况。在这里，我们的目标是估计 α 和 β，并对这些结构参数进行统计分析。

该模型包含两个变量：C_t 和 Y_t。它们相互依赖——消费影响收入，同时收入影响消费。正如我们过去所学，受模型内部因素影响的变量是内生变量。在联立方程组模型里，有多少个内生变量就应该有多少个联立方程式。受模型外部因素影响的变量是外生变量。投资（I_t）是模型里唯一的外生变量。

内生变量被表示为仅仅是外生变量的函数，这样的方法往往很有效。因此，我们把 C_t 和 Y_t 写成 I_t 的方程。要做到这一点，我们将方程（1）代入方程（2），同样，方程（2）代入方程（1）。新的方程被称为简化式方程：

$$\text{简化式方程组}\begin{cases} c_t=\dfrac{\alpha}{1-\beta}+\dfrac{\beta}{1-\beta}I_t+\dfrac{1}{1-\beta}\varepsilon_t & (3)\\ Y_t=\dfrac{\alpha}{1-\beta}+\dfrac{1}{1-\beta}I_t+\dfrac{1}{1-\beta}\varepsilon_t & (4)\end{cases}$$

简化式方程组里的系数称为影响乘数。方程（3）里的投资系数就是众所周知的乘数。投资增长一美元会导致收入增加一美元，这又导致了消费量增加一美元，从而导致收入增加 β 美元，进而导致消费增加 β^2 美元。如果我们计算由此产生的无限几何级数，来自每一个“回合”的影响是：

$$
\begin{aligned}
&\beta+\beta^2+\beta^3+\beta^4+\cdots\\
=&\beta(1+\beta+\beta^2+\beta^3+\cdots)\\
=&\frac{\beta}{1-\beta}
\end{aligned}
$$

对于联立方程组模型，采用 OLS 回归往往是不恰当的。因为在这个例子中 $\mathrm{Cov}(Y_t，\varepsilon_t)\neq 0$。因此，内生变量和误差项之间有相关性，这就违反了 OLS 回归所必须遵循的假设，从而导致估计偏差。如果我们放弃用 OLS 估计方程（1）而是用 OLS 估计简化式方程（3），我们的做法将是适当的，因为在投资在模型里是外生变量的假设下，投资变量和误差项不相关。

1.2　识别问题

估计简化式模型的好处在于 OLS 将提供无偏估计。然而，它并不能直接提供结构参数的估计。只有在某些情况下，我们可以通过简化式估计量来恢复与之相关的结构参数。在很多时候，我们会遇到识别问题。

什么是识别问题？通过以下两个方程组成的结构模型，我们来讨论识别问题的存在：

$$
\text{结构式方程组}\begin{cases}Y_1=\beta_1Y_2+\beta_2X_1+\beta_3X_2 & (5)\\ Y_2=\gamma_1Y_1+\gamma_2X_1+\gamma_3X_2 & (6)\end{cases}
$$

其中，Y_1 和 Y_2 是内生变量，X_1 和 X_2 是外生变量。

在此，方程组里不包含误差项，我们的目的是为了强调识别问题本质上不是统计问题。这是一个逻辑问题而且必须在估计之前合理地解决。求解简化式方程组，我们可以得到：

$$
\text{简化式方程组}\begin{cases}Y_1=\dfrac{\beta_1\gamma_2+\beta_2}{1-\beta_1\gamma_1}X_1+\dfrac{\beta_1\gamma_3+\beta_3}{1-\beta_1\gamma_1}X_2 & (7)\\[2ex] Y_2=\dfrac{\beta_2\gamma_1+\gamma_2}{1-\beta_1\gamma_1}X_1+\dfrac{\beta_3\gamma_1+\gamma_3}{1-\beta_1\gamma_1}X_2 & (8)\end{cases}
$$

上述方程也可以写为：

$$
\text{简化式方程组}\begin{cases}Y_1=\Pi_{11}X_1+\Pi_{12}X_2 & (9)\\ Y_2=\Pi_{21}X_1+\Pi_{22}X_2 & (10)\end{cases}
$$

其中，$\Pi_{11}=\dfrac{\beta_1\gamma_2+\beta_2}{1-\beta_1\gamma_1}$，$\Pi_{12}=\dfrac{\beta_1\gamma_3+\beta_3}{1-\beta_1\gamma_1}$，$\Pi_{21}=\dfrac{\beta_2\gamma_1+\gamma_2}{1-\beta_1\gamma_1}$，和 $\Pi_{22}=\dfrac{\beta_3\gamma_1+\gamma_3}{1-\beta_1\gamma_1}$。

既使我们知道这 4 个简化式参数 Π_{11}，Π_{12}，Π_{21} 和 Π_{22}，用这 4 个估计值来求解结构模型里的 6 个结构式参数也是不容乐观的。一般情况下，我们不能用 4 个方程求解 6 个未知数。也就是说，在这个例子中，我们有识别问题。我们能从简化式系数值推断结构方程中的系数值吗？如果可以，那么这一结构方程被识别。如果结构方程不能被识别，我们不能采用间接最小二乘法来估计它。

间接最小二乘法是估计简化式模型并恢复结构参数的过程。假设方程（9）和方程（10）里的Π_{11}，Π_{12}，Π_{21}和Π_{22}是已知的。如果方程（9）和方程（10）代入方程（5）替代Y_1和Y_2：

$$(\Pi_{11}-\beta_1\Pi_{21}-\beta_2)X_1+(\Pi_{12}-\beta_1\Pi_{22}-\beta_3)X_2=0 \tag{11}$$

上述式子必须满足所有的X_1和X_2取值。假设$X_1=1$和$X_2=0$,那么：

$$(\Pi_{11}-\beta_1\Pi_{21}-\beta_2)1=0 \tag{12}$$

如果$X_1=0$和$X_2=1$，那么：

$$(\Pi_{12}-\beta_1\Pi_{22}-\beta_3)1=0 \tag{13}$$

我们能够用方程（12）和方程（13）求解方程（5）中的结构式参数吗？答案是：不可能，因为我们有两个方程，但是有三个未知数。

案例 1：结构式方程（5）不能被识别。需要被确认的结构式参数比确定它们的方程组要多。

案例 2：如案例 1 所提，相对于简化式参数，需估计的结构式参数太多。如果可以事先加入一些限制结构式方程的条件，就可以减少需估计的结构式参数。假设我们认为$\beta_3=0$。方程（12）和方程（13）被简化为：

$$(\Pi_{11}-\beta_1\Pi_{21}-\beta_2)1=0$$
$$(\Pi_{12}-\beta_1\Pi_{22})1=0$$
（这一假设将导致两个方程和两个未知数的结果）

案例 3：如果我们加入另一个限制条件——$\beta_3=0$和$\beta_2=0$，那么方程（5）只有一个未知的结构式参数β_1。我们在结构式方程里加入的事先限制条件比需要识别的限制条件多，那么方程（5）被过度识别。

1.3 识别的阶条件

在上述三种情况下，我们可以找到一定的规律。在案例 1 中，被排除出方程的外生变量比包括在方程中的内生变量少。没有外生变量被排除出方程（5），但方程（5）的右侧有一个内生变量。在案例 2 中，有一个外生变量被排除出方程（5），而且方程（5）有一个内生变量。故而方程（5）被完全识别。在案例 3 中，两个外生变量没有被包括在方程（5）中，而方程（5）的右侧有一个内生变量。方程（5）被过度识别。

通过上面的规律，我们可以得出如下用于判别方程是否被识别的规则，即所谓的阶条件。

设X=联立方程组模型中的外生变量从某一个特定方程里被排除掉的数量。

设N=位于该特定方程的右侧的内生变量的数量。

如果$X<N$，该方程不能被识别。

如果$X=N$，该方程被完全识别。

如果$X>N$，该方程被过度识别。

Ⅱ. 估计联立方程组模型

2.1 完全识别的方程：间接最小二乘估计

当联立方程组模型里的一个方程被完全识别，结构式参数和简化式参数之间就存在一对一的相互关系。我们可以通过一种独特的方法用简化式方程来求解结构式方程的参数。用于简化式方程的 OLS 方法称为间接最小二乘。这种方法给出的简化式参数估计具有一致性，然而，我们面临的困难是如何用简化式方程组来一一求解出结构式方程组里的结构式参数值。

2.2 过度识别的方程：两阶段最小二乘估计

我们考虑下列联立线性方程组：

$$Y_{1t}=\beta_{10}+\beta_{11}Y_{2t}+\gamma_{11}X_{1t}+\gamma_{21}X_{2t}+\mu_{1t} \tag{14}$$

$$Y_{2t}=\beta_{20}+\beta_{21}Y_{1t}+\mu_{2t} \tag{15}$$

运用阶条件，我们可以很容易地发现，方程（14）不能被识别，因而我们没有办法估计结构式参数。方程（15）是被过度识别，因此我们有多种方式来估计结构式参数。由于误差项和位于方程式右边的内生变量之间有相关性，我们不能使用 OLS 来估计方程（15）。在这种情况下，可能的解决办法是使用辅助变量。正如我们以前学到的，一个适当的辅助变量将与 Y_{1t} 相关但与 u_{2t} 无关。

两阶段最小二乘估计（2SLS）背后的逻辑是：假设我们能发现一个变量，它是 X_1 和 X_2 的最优线性组合，而且它和 Y_{1t} 有最大的相关性。以 Y_{1t} 为被解释变量，X_1 和 X_2 为解释变量的 OLS 回归将产生这两个外生变量的线性组合，以及最大的 R^2 值。按照这一逻辑，在第一阶段，我们使用 OLS 估计简化式方程，并从估计中得到预测值。在第二阶段，我们使用内生变量的预测值替代该内生变量，并用 OLS 估计替代后的方程。

注意：如果方程能被完全识别，2SLS 回归所提供的估计值将与间接最小二乘法提供的估计值是相同的。

2.3 Hausman 检验

如果我们怀疑位于方程式右边的变量是内生的，如何通过检验证实我们的怀疑是正确的？Hausman[①] 建议：如果位于方程式右边的变量是外生的，那么通过比较，两种估计方法所得估计应该都是一致的。如果位于方程式右边的变量是内生的，那么两种估计方法中

---

① Hausman, J. A. (1978), "Specification Tests in Econometrics," *Econometrica*, Vol. 46, No. 6. (Nov., 1978), pp. 1251−1271.

只有一种是一致的。因此，我们可以看一下两种估计之间的差异是否大到足以证明内生性是一个严重问题。

方程式右边的变量是：		
估计量	内生的	外生的
OLS	不一致估计	一致且有效估计
IV	一致估计	一致但非有效估计

根据上面的表格所示[①]，如果被怀疑的位于方程式右边的变量是外生的，OLS 估计值（但它们的标准误相对较小）应该和使用辅助变量的估计值相似。如果被怀疑的位于方程式右边的变量是内生的，那么这两种估计方法应该产生不同的估计值。

为了运行 Hausman 检验，我们进行一个多元回归：该模型的自变量是内生变量 x 和误差项。这一误差项是从以 x 为因变量，其辅助变量为自变量的回归中得到的。然后，我们检验该误差项的系数是否为零。如果我们能拒绝它是零，便可得出这样的结论：内生性会造成问题。

Ⅲ. 上机操作练习[②]

松露是美食爱好者的心头好。它们是长在地下的可食用真菌。我们来考虑一个松露的供求模型：

需求：$q_t=\alpha_1+\alpha_2 p_t+\alpha_3 ps_t+\alpha_4 di_t+\varepsilon_t^d$

供应：$q_t=\beta_1+\beta_2 p_t+\beta_3 pf_t+\varepsilon_t^s$

在需求等式中，

q=时间 t 时在一个特定的法国市场中松露的交易数量，

p=松露的市场价，

ps=松露的替代品的市场价，

di=人均可支配收入。

供应等式包含了市场价和供应数量，并且也包括了 pf=生产要素的价格，在这个例子中是搜索过程中使用的松露的每小时租赁价格。

在这个模型中，我们假设 p 和 q 是内生变量。外生变量是 ps，pf 和 di。

3.1 识别

在考虑估计之前，我们先来检查一下每个等式的识别情况。识别等式的法则是为了识

① 这一表格选自 Chapter 15.6.3，*Statistics and Econometrics*：*Methods and Applications*，by Ashenfelter，Levine and Zimmerman，2003.

② 该练习有过修改，相关数据基于下书 14.7 节中的例子：*Undergraduate Econometrics*，2nd Edition，Hill，Griffiths，and Judge，2001。

别出等式，在一个有 M 个等式的系统中，每个等式至少要省略 $M-1$ 个变量。

可以识别需求等式吗？为什么？

$X=1$，被排除的外生变量，

$N=1$，包含的内生变量。

当 $N=X$ 时，结构式方程可以被识别。

可以识别供给等式吗？为什么？

$X=2$，被排除的外生变量，

$N=1$，包含的内生变量。

当 $X>N$ 时，结构式方程是过度识别的。

现在我们得出结论：系统中的每个等式都是识别的或过度识别的，因此可以用 2SLS 来估计。

3.2　简化式方程

简化式方程可以将每个内生变量 p 和 q 用外生变量 ps，di，pf，截距变量和误差项来表示。

$$q_t=\pi_{11}+\pi_{21}ps_t+\pi_{31}di_t+\pi_{41}pf_t+\upsilon_{t1}$$

$$p_t=\pi_{12}+\pi_{22}ps_t+\pi_{32}di_t+\pi_{42}pf_t+\upsilon_{t2}$$

我们可以用 OLS 来估计以上等式吗？为什么？

答：可以，因为每个简化式方程都没有内生性问题。只要它满足了所有必需要求，我们就可以用 OLS 来估计以上等式。

请在 Stata 中打开名为 **truffle. dta**[①] 的数据文件。然后，在 Stata 中输入以下指令。

```
reg q ps di pf

      Source |       SS       df       MS              Number of obs =      30
-------------+------------------------------           F(  3,    26) =   19.97
       Model |  430.382636     3  143.460879           Prob > F      =  0.0000
    Residual |  186.754175    26  7.18285287           R-squared     =  0.6974
-------------+------------------------------           Adj R-squared =  0.6625
       Total |  617.136811    29  21.2805797           Root MSE      =  2.6801

------------------------------------------------------------------------------
           q |      Coef.   Std. Err.      t    P>|t|     [95% Conf. Interval]
-------------+----------------------------------------------------------------
          ps |    .656402   .1425376     4.61   0.000     .3634118    .9493922
          di |   .2167156   .0700474     3.09   0.005     .0727312    .3607001
          pf |  -.5069824   .1212616    -4.18   0.000    -.7562393   -.2577255
       _cons |     7.8951   3.243421     2.43   0.022     1.228152    14.56205
------------------------------------------------------------------------------

predict qhat, xb
```

在上图中，我们可以看到估计系数是统计显著的，所以我们可以得出结论：外生变量影响松露的交易数量。另一方面，$R^2=0.697$ 并且整体 F 统计量是 19.97，p 值小于 5%。所以，我们可以得出简化式方程整体显著的结论。

在 Stata 中，输入以下指令。

在下图中，我们可以看到估计系数是统计显著的，因此我们得出结论：外生变量对市场价格有影响。另一方面，$R^2=0.889$ 并且整体 F 统计量是 69.19，p 值小于 0.000 1。所以我们可以得出这个模型有统计显著的解释力的结论。

---

① 资料来源：*Undergraduate Econometrics*，2nd Edition，Hill，Griffiths，and Judge，2001。

```
reg p ps di pf

      Source |       SS       df       MS              Number of obs =      30
-------------+------------------------------           F(  3,    26) =   69.19
       Model |  1003.86396     3  334.621321           Prob > F      =  0.0000
    Residual |  125.744143    26  4.83631318           R-squared     =  0.8887
-------------+------------------------------           Adj R-squared =  0.8758
       Total |  1129.60811    29  38.9520036           Root MSE      =  2.1992

------------------------------------------------------------------------------
           p |      Coef.   Std. Err.      t    P>|t|     [95% Conf. Interval]
-------------+----------------------------------------------------------------
          ps |   .5693824   .1169602     4.87   0.000     .3289672    .8097976
          di |   .2534164   .0574779     4.41   0.000     .1352689    .3715638
          pf |   .4513019   .0995021     4.54   0.000     .2467725    .6558314
       _cons |  -10.83747   2.661412    -4.07   0.000    -16.30808   -5.366864
------------------------------------------------------------------------------

 predict phat
option xb assumed; fitted values)
```

3.3 间接最小二乘法

$$\hat{q}_t = \hat{\pi}_{11} + \hat{\pi}_{21} ps_t + \hat{\pi}_{31} di_t + \hat{\pi}_{41} pf_t + \upsilon_{t1}$$

$$= 7.895 + 0.66 ps_t + 0.22 di_t - 0.51 pf_t$$

$$\hat{p}_t = \hat{\pi}_{12} + \hat{\pi}_{22} ps_t + \hat{\pi}_{32} di_t + \hat{\pi}_{42} pf_t$$

$$= -10.837 + 0.569 ps_t + 0.253 di_t + 0.451 pf_t$$

将上面两个等式替换到已经被完全识别的需求等式中，我们可以求出估计的结构参数：

$\hat{\alpha}_1 = -4.35$　　　$\hat{\alpha}_2 = -1.13$

$\hat{\alpha}_3 = 1.304$　　　$\hat{\alpha}_4 = 0.502\,5$

注意，不能用间接最小二乘法来估计一个过度识别的等式。为了解决这个问题，我们用 2SLS 方法。

3.4 两阶段最小二乘估计

简化式方程被用来获取 $\hat{p}$，然后在 2SLS 模型的第二阶段中被用来取代供应和需求等式右侧的变量 p。

2SLS 的结果可以通过输入以下指令获得。

```
. ivreg  q (p=phat) ps di

Instrumental variables (2SLS) regression

      Source |       SS       df       MS              Number of obs =      30
-------------+------------------------------           F(  3,    26) =    5.90
       Model | -14.7802477     3 -4.92674922           Prob > F      =  0.0033
    Residual |  631.917058    26  24.3045022           R-squared     =       .
-------------+------------------------------           Adj R-squared =       .
       Total |  617.136811    29  21.2805797           Root MSE      =    4.93

------------------------------------------------------------------------------
           q |      Coef.   Std. Err.      t    P>|t|     [95% Conf. Interval]
-------------+----------------------------------------------------------------
           p |  -1.123377    .494255    -2.27   0.032    -2.139333   -.1074214
          ps |   1.296033   .3551932     3.65   0.001     .5659232    2.026143
          di |   .5013978   .2283556     2.20   0.037     .0320062    .9707893
       _cons |  -4.279472   5.543884    -0.77   0.447    -15.67509    7.116145
------------------------------------------------------------------------------
Instrumented:  p
Instruments:   ps di phat
------------------------------------------------------------------------------
```

注意，价格的系数是负的，显示出随着市场价的上涨，松露的需求量会下降，就像需求定律预测的那样。报告的标准误差是通过 Stata 的 2SLS 获得的。它们及其 t 值在大样本中都是有效的。p 值显示出估计的需求曲线的斜率是显著异于 0 的。松露的替代品的价格上涨会导致松露的需求量上涨。最后，收入的效应是积极的，显示出松露是普通商品。综上所述，这些变量都有统计显著的系数，所以对松露需求量都有影响。

```
. ivreg q (p=phat) pf

Instrumental variables (2SLS) regression

      Source |       SS       df       MS              Number of obs =      30
-------------+------------------------------           F(  2,    27) =   95.26
       Model |  556.582222     2  278.291111           Prob > F      =  0.0000
    Residual |  60.5545883    27  2.24276253           R-squared     =  0.9019
-------------+------------------------------           Adj R-squared =  0.8946
       Total |  617.136811    29  21.2805797           Root MSE      =  1.4976

------------------------------------------------------------------------------
           q |      Coef.   Std. Err.      t    P>|t|     [95% Conf. Interval]
-------------+----------------------------------------------------------------
           p |   1.013945   .0747587    13.56   0.000     .8605525    1.167337
          pf |  -1.000909    .082528   -12.13   0.000    -1.170243   -.831576
       _cons |    20.0328   1.223115    16.38   0.000     17.52318    22.54243
------------------------------------------------------------------------------
Instrumented:  p
Instruments:   pf phat
------------------------------------------------------------------------------
```

正如预测的一样，松露的价格上涨使松露供应量也上涨。寻找松露的猪的租赁费用上涨，松露的供应量降低。这些变量都有统计显著的系数估计。

3.5　Hausman 检验

我们可以用 Stata 的 hausman 指令来检验 ivreg 和 OLS 估计之间的差距是不是足够大，因此可以证明 OLS 估计不一致。

要使用 Hausman 检验，我们需要完成以下步骤：

(1) 获取一个无论假设是否为真都是一致的估计；

(2) 用“estimates store”来保存估计结果并合理命名；

(3) 获取一个在我们要检验的假设中有效（且一致）的估计，并且在其他情况下不一致；

(4) 用“estimates store”保存估计结果并合理命名；

(5) 用“hausman”来做检验。

在 Stata 中输入以下指令来完成该检验。

```
. quietly ivreg q (p=phat) ps di
. estimates store ivreg
. quietly reg q p ps di
. estimates store ols
```

```
. hausman ivreg . , constant sigmamore

Note: the rank of the differenced variance matrix (1) does not equal the number of coefficients being tested (4); be
      sure this is what you expect, or there may be problems computing the test.  Examine the output of your
      estimators for anything unexpected and possibly consider scaling your variables so that the coefficients are on
      a similar scale.

                 ---- Coefficients ----
             |      (b)          (B)            (b-B)     sqrt(diag(V_b-V_B))
             |     ivreg         ols         Difference          S.E.
-------------+----------------------------------------------------------------
           p |   -1.123377     .0698861       -1.193263        .2591631
          ps |    1.296033     .7100395        .5859937        .1272711
          di |    .5013978     .0076445        .4937532        .1072375
       _cons |   -4.279472     1.091044       -5.370516        1.166415
------------------------------------------------------------------------------
                           b = consistent under Ho and Ha; obtained from ivreg
            B = inconsistent under Ha, efficient under Ho; obtained from regress

    Test:  Ho:  difference in coefficients not systematic

                  chi2(1) = (b-B)'[(V_b-V_B)^(-1)](b-B)
                          =       21.20
                Prob>chi2 =      0.0000
```

因为 p 值小于 5%，所以我们拒绝零假设，得出结论：ivreg 和 OLS 估计之间有差别，并且 OLS 估计不一致。

Ⅳ. 附加上机操作练习

考虑如下由两个方程组成的联立方程模型并用它来研究美国的农业劳动力市场：

$$\ln(L_i)=\beta_0+\beta_1\ln(W_i)+\beta_2\ln(Land_i)+\beta_3\ln(RE_i)+\beta_4\ln(Othexp_i)+\beta_5\ln(Sch_i)+\varepsilon_i \qquad (*)$$

$$\ln(W_i)=\alpha_0+\alpha_1\ln(L_i)+\alpha_2\ln(Sch_i)+\alpha_3\ln(Othwag_i)+\mu_i \qquad (**)$$

其中，L＝劳动力（州农业劳动力的总人日）；

W＝工资（每小时年均复合农场工资）；

RE＝研究和推广服务支出（用于创新的代理变量）；

$Land$＝耕地存量土地价值；

$Othexp$＝非人工营业支出；

Sch＝农村男性正规教育年限的中值；

$Othwag$＝工匠、工头等的替代工资（加权平均）。

a）哪些变量是外生的，哪些是内生的？

L 和 W 是内生的。其他变量都是外生的。

b）解析出（即通过代数）两个简化式方程。

$\ln(L)$ 的简化方程是：

$$\ln(L_i)=\frac{1}{1-a_1}b_0+\frac{a_0b_1}{1-a_1}+\left(\frac{a_2b_1+b_5}{1-a_1}\right)\ln(Sch_i)+\frac{a_3b_1}{1-a_1}\ln(Othwag_i)+\frac{b_2}{1-a_1}\ln(Land_i)+\frac{b_3}{1-a_1}\ln(RE_i)+\frac{b_4}{1-a_1}\ln(Othexp_i)+\frac{b_1e_2+e_1}{1-a_1}$$

ln(W) 的简化方程是：

$$\ln(W_i)=\frac{1}{1-b_1}a_0+\frac{a_1b_0}{1-b_1}+\left(\frac{a_1b_5+a_2}{1-b_1}\right)\ln(Sch_i)+\frac{a_3}{1-b_1}\ln(Othwag_i)$$

$$+\frac{a_1b_2}{1-b_1}\ln(Land_i)+\frac{a_1b_3}{1-b_1}\ln(RE_i)+\frac{a_3}{1-b_1}\ln(Othexp_i)+\frac{a_1e_1+e_2}{1-b_1}$$

c) 利用阶条件来证明式（∗）是被完全识别的，而式（∗∗）是过度识别的。

方程式（∗）是被完全识别的，因为方程式（∗∗）中只有一个外生变量不在方程式（∗）中。方程式（∗∗）是被过度识别的，因为方程式（∗）中有三个外生变量不在方程式（∗∗）中。

d) 使用数据文件 **labor. dta**。[1] 用 OLS 方法估计方程式（∗）和方程式（∗∗）。用两阶段最小二乘法估计方程式（∗）和方程式（∗∗）。比较两种方法的估计结果。你是否认为 OLS 方法相对而言较为不合适？

OLS 对这些方程的估计：

. regress lnlabor lnwage lnland lnre lnothexp lnsch

Source	SS	df	MS		
				Number of obs =	39
				F(5, 33) =	45.12
Model	11.0167377	5	2.20334753	Prob > F =	0.0000
Residual	1.61159521	33	.048836218	R-squared =	0.8724
				Adj R-squared =	0.8530
Total	12.6283329	38	.332324549	Root MSE =	.22099

lnlabor	Coef.	Std. Err.	t	P>|t|	[95% Conf.	Interval]
lnwage	-1.105774	.2893065	-3.82	0.001	-1.694373	-.517176
lnland	.3118018	.0837263	3.72	0.001	.1414594	.4821441
lnre	.4446036	.1140206	3.90	0.000	.2126269	.6765803
lnothexp	.2645385	.1127825	2.35	0.025	.0350808	.4939961
lnsch	-.2623222	.6082036	-0.43	0.669	-1.499722	.9750773
_cons	.8757252	1.943497	0.45	0.655	-3.078349	4.8298

. regress lnwage lnlabor lnsch lnothwag

Source	SS	df	MS		
				Number of obs =	39
				F(3, 35) =	46.92
Model	1.871368	3	.623789334	Prob > F =	0.0000
Residual	.465284236	35	.013293835	R-squared =	0.8009
				Adj R-squared =	0.7838
Total	2.33665224	38	.061490848	Root MSE =	.1153

lnwage	Coef.	Std. Err.	t	P>|t|	[95% Conf.	Interval]
lnlabor	-.0109471	.0340323	-0.32	0.750	-.0800364	.0581422
lnsch	1.164415	.2384458	4.88	0.000	.6803442	1.648486
lnothwage	.4682868	.1323288	3.54	0.001	.1996451	.7369286
_cons	-2.972985	.6356697	-4.68	0.000	-4.263463	-1.682507

两阶段最小二乘法估计：

. regress lnlabor lnwage lnland lnre lnothexp lnsch (lnland lnre lnothexp lnsch lnothwag)

[1] 数据集取自下书的第 15 章：*Statistics and Econometrics: Methods and Applications*，by Ashenfelter，Levine and Zimmerman，2003。

```
Instrumental variables (2SLS) regression

      Source |       SS       df       MS              Number of obs =      39
-------------+------------------------------           F(  5,    33) =   41.63
       Model |  10.9478902     5  2.18957803           Prob > F      =  0.0000
    Residual |  1.68044271    33  .050922506           R-squared     =  0.8669
-------------+------------------------------           Adj R-squared =  0.8468
       Total |  12.6283329    38  .332324549           Root MSE      =  .22566

------------------------------------------------------------------------------
     lnlabor |      Coef.   Std. Err.      t    P>|t|     [95% Conf. Interval]
-------------+----------------------------------------------------------------
      lnwage |  -1.449278   .6012275    -2.41   0.022    -2.672485   -.2260714
      lnland |   .3286769   .0892823     3.68   0.001     .1470308    .5103231
        lnre |   .4687022   .1220887     3.84   0.001     .2203109    .7170935
    lnothexp |   .2497877    .117341     2.13   0.041     .0110556    .4885198
       lnsch |   .3420969   1.111155     0.31   0.760    -1.918564    2.602758
       _cons |  -.8591309   3.306457    -0.26   0.797    -7.586169    5.867907
------------------------------------------------------------------------------
```

. regress lnwage lnlabor lnsch lnothwag (lnsch lnothwag lnland lnre lnothexp)

```
Instrumental variables (2SLS) regression

      Source |       SS       df       MS              Number of obs =      39
-------------+------------------------------           F(  3,    35) =   44.97
       Model |  1.84881748     3  .616272493           Prob > F      =  0.0000
    Residual |  .487834759    35  .013938136           R-squared     =  0.7912
-------------+------------------------------           Adj R-squared =  0.7733
       Total |  2.33665224    38  .061490848           Root MSE      =  .11806

------------------------------------------------------------------------------
      lnwage |      Coef.   Std. Err.      t    P>|t|     [95% Conf. Interval]
-------------+----------------------------------------------------------------
     lnlabor |   .0333775   .0384072     0.87   0.391    -.0445932    .1113482
       lnsch |   1.234335    .245481     5.03   0.000     .7359817    1.732687
   lnothwage |   .4643323   .1355053     3.43   0.002      .189242    .7394226
       _cons |  -3.576787   .6870601    -5.21   0.000    -4.971593   -2.181981
------------------------------------------------------------------------------
```

OLS 和 2SLS 的估计值相差不多，尤其是将 2SLS 估计值的较大标准差考虑进去之后。尽管因为内生性问题，OLS 不是估计这个问题的一个合适的方法，但在实践中，用 2SLS 方法纠正这个问题并没有使结果改变太多。

Chapter 13

Simultaneous Model

Ⅰ. The Setup of a Simultaneous Equations Model

1.1 Structural and Reduced-Form Equations

This chapter considers the situation where the equation we are interested in is embedded in a system of simultaneous linear equations. Consider the following simple Keynesian model:

$$\text{Structural Equations}\begin{cases} c_t=\alpha+\beta Y_t+\varepsilon_t & (1)\\ Y_t=c_t+I_t & (2)\end{cases}$$

where C_t is consumption expenditures in time period t,

Y_t is income in period t,

I_t is investment in period t,

ε_t is an error term with mean zero and constant variance,

α and β are structural parameters.

In this example, the two equations provide a structure for how the economy functions. Here, our goal is to provide estimates for α and β, and conduct statistical inferences for structural parameters.

This model contains two dependent variables: C_t and Y_t. They are jointly dependent—consumption affects income and income affects consumption. As we have learned, variables determined within the context of the model are endogenous variables. In the simultaneous model, there must be as many equations as there are endogenous variables. Variables determined outside the context of the model are exogenous variables. Investment (I_t) is the only exogenous variable in the model.

It is often useful to express endogenous variables so that they are functions only of exogenous variables. Thus, we would like to express C_t and Y_t as functions of I_t. To do so, we substitute equation (1) into equation (2) and, similarly, equation (2) into equation (1). The new equations are called the reduced-form equations:

$$\text{Reduced-Form Equations}\begin{cases} c_t = \dfrac{\alpha}{1-\beta} + \dfrac{\beta}{1-\beta} I_t + \dfrac{1}{1-\beta} \varepsilon_t & (3) \\ Y_t = \dfrac{\alpha}{1-\beta} + \dfrac{1}{1-\beta} I_t + \dfrac{1}{1-\beta} \varepsilon_t & (4) \end{cases}$$

Coefficients on reduced-form equations are called impact multipliers. From equation (3), the coefficient on investment is the well-known multiplier. A dollar increase in investment leads to a dollar increase in income which, in turn, leads to a dollar increase in consumption, which leads to a β dollar increase in income, which leads to a β^2 dollar increase in consumption. Tracing out the resulting infinite geometric series, the effects from each "round" are:

$$\begin{aligned} & \beta + \beta^2 + \beta^3 + \beta^4 + \cdots \\ = & \beta(1 + \beta + \beta^2 + \beta^3 + \cdots) \\ = & \frac{\beta}{1-\beta} \end{aligned}$$

In the context of simultaneous equations, usually it is not appropriate to use OLS to estimate structural parameters, because, as in this example, $\mathrm{Cov}(Y_t, \varepsilon_t) \neq 0$. Hence, there is a correlation between the endogenous variable and the error term. This violates the maintained assumption of the OLS regression model and would induce a bias. Suppose, rather than estimating equation (1) using OLS, we estimate the reduced-form equation (3) using OLS. This would be appropriate since investment and the error term are uncorrelated by the assumption that investment is exogenous.

1.2 Identification Problem

There are advantages to estimating a reduced-form model in that OLS will provide unbiased estimates. However, it does not provide direct estimates of the structural parameters. Only under certain circumstances we can "unscramble" the reduced-form estimates to recover the associated structural parameters. Very often, we have the identification problem.

What is the identification problem? Using the following two-equation structural model, we will develop the identification problem:

$$\text{Structual Equations}\begin{cases} Y_1 = \beta_1 Y_2 + \beta_2 X_1 + \beta_3 X_2 & (5) \\ Y_2 = \gamma_1 Y_1 + \gamma_2 X_1 + \gamma_3 X_2 & (6) \end{cases}$$

where Y_1, Y_2 are endogenous variables, X_1, X_2 are exogenous variables.

The equations do not contain an error term in order to emphasize the point that the identification problem is not statistical in nature. It is a logical problem and must be resolved logically prior to estimation. Solving for the reduced-form equations results in:

$$\text{Reduced-form Equations}\begin{cases} Y_1=\dfrac{\beta_1\gamma_2+\beta_2}{1-\beta_1\gamma_1}X_1+\dfrac{\beta_1\gamma_3+\beta_3}{1-\beta_1\gamma_1}X_2 & (7)\\ Y_2=\dfrac{\beta_2\gamma_1+\gamma_2}{1-\beta_1\gamma_1}X_1+\dfrac{\beta_3\gamma_1+\gamma_3}{1-\beta_1\gamma_1}X_2 & (8)\end{cases}$$

which are usually written as

$$\text{Reduced-form Equations}\begin{cases} Y_1=\Pi_{11}X_1+\Pi_{12}X_2 & (9)\\ Y_2=\Pi_{21}X_1+\Pi_{22}X_2 & (10)\end{cases}$$

where $\Pi_{11}=\dfrac{\beta_1\gamma_2+\beta_2}{1-\beta_1\gamma_1}$, $\Pi_{12}=\dfrac{\beta_1\gamma_3+\beta_3}{1-\beta_1\gamma_1}$, $\Pi_{21}=\dfrac{\beta_2\gamma_1+\gamma_2}{1-\beta_1\gamma_1}$, and $\Pi_{22}=\dfrac{\beta_3\gamma_1+\gamma_3}{1-\beta_1\gamma_1}$.

Even if we knew the four reduced-form parameters Π_{11}, Π_{12}, Π_{21}, Π_{22}, we should not be very optimistic about using these four numbers to solve for the six structural parameters in the structural model. Generally one cannot solve four equations for six unknowns. That is to say, in this example, we have the identification problem. Can the values of the coefficients of a particular structural equation be deduced from the reduced-form coefficients? If yes, then that particular structural equation is identified. If a model is not identified, it cannot be estimated by indirect least squares.

Indirect least squares is the process of estimating the reduced-form model and recovering the structural parameters. Suppose Π_{11}, Π_{12}, Π_{21}, Π_{22} from equations (9) and (10) are known. If equations (9) and (10) are substituted into equation (5) for Y_1 and Y_2:

$$(\Pi_{11}-\beta_1\Pi_{21}-\beta_2)X_1+(\Pi_{12}-\beta_1\Pi_{22}-\beta_3)X_2=0 \tag{11}$$

which must hold for all values of X_1 and X_2. Suppose $X_1=1$ and $X_2=0$, then:

$$(\Pi_{11}-\beta_1\Pi_{21}-\beta_2)1=0 \tag{12}$$

If $X_1=0$ and $X_2=1$, then:

$$(\Pi_{12}-\beta_1\Pi_{22}-\beta_3)1=0 \tag{13}$$

Can equations (12) and (13) be solved for the structural parameters in equation (5)?

Answer: No—there are two equations with three unknowns.

Case 1: Structural equation (5) is not identified. There are more structural coefficients to determine than the equations with which to determine them.

Case 2: With Case 1 there were too many structural parameters to estimate relative to the number of reduced-form parameters. Imposing more *a priori* restrictions on the structural model can reduce the number of structural coefficients needed to be identified. Suppose we believe $\beta_3=0$. Equations (12) and (13) simplify to:

$$\begin{matrix}(\Pi_{11}-\beta_1\Pi_{21}-\beta_2)1=0\\ (\Pi_{12}-\beta_1\Pi_{22})1=0\end{matrix}$$, results in two equations with two unknowns.

Case 3: If we impose another restriction—$\beta_3=0$ and $\beta_2=0$, then equation (5) should have one unknown structural parameter, β_1. We have more *a priori* restrictions on the structural model than needed for identification. Thus, equation (5) is overidentified.

1.3 The Order Condition for Identification

A pattern exists in the three cases. In Case 1, fewer exogenous variables were excluded from the equation than endogenous variables included. There were no exogenous variables excluded from equation (5) and there was one endogenous variable included on the right-hand side of equation (5). In Case 2, one exogenous variable was not included in equation (5) and one endogenous variable was included on the right-hand side of equation (5). Equation (5) was exactly identified. In Case 3, two exogenous variables were not included in equation (5) and one endogenous variable was included on the right-hand side of equation (5). Equation (5) was overidentified.

This pattern suggests a rule for deciding whether an equation is identified, called the order condition.

Let X= the number of exogenous variables in the system of equations that are excluded from a particular equation.

Let N= the number of endogenous variables included on the right-hand side of a particular equation.

If $X < N$, the equation is not identified.

If $X = N$, the equation is exactly identified.

If $X > N$, the equation is overidentified.

Ⅱ. Estimating a Simultaneous Equations Model

2.1 Exactly Identified Equations: Indirect Least Squares

When an equation is exactly identified, a one-to-one correspondence exists between the structural and the reduced-form parameters. A unique way exists to unscramble the reduced-form equation to solve for the structural parameters of an equation. OLS on a reduced-form equation is called indirect least squares. It gives consistent estimates of the reduced-form parameters; however, the difficulty is we must be able to solve the reduced-form equations for unique values of the structural parameters.

2.2 Overidentified Equations: Two-Stage Least Squares

Consider the following simultaneous linear equations:

$$Y_{1t} = \beta_{10} + \beta_{11} Y_{2t} + \gamma_{11} X_{1t} + \gamma_{21} X_{2t} + \mu_{1t} \tag{14}$$

$$Y_{2t} = \beta_{20} + \beta_{21} Y_{1t} + \mu_{2t} \tag{15}$$

By applying the order condition, we can easily find that Equation (14) is not identified and there is no way to estimate the structural parameters. Equation (15) is overidentified and hence there are multiple ways to estimate the structural parameters. We cannot use OLS to estimate equation (15), because of the correlation between the error term and the right-hand side endogenous variable. A possible solution in this context is to use an instrumental variable. As we learned before, an appropriate instrumental variable would be correlated with Y_{1t} and uncorrelated with u_{2t}.

The logic behind the two-stage least squares estimator (2SLS) is: suppose we found a variable that was an optimal linear combination of X_1 and X_2 and it maximized the correlation with Y_{1t}. The OLS regression of Y_{1t} on X_1 and X_2 would produce the linear combination of the two exogenous variables that maximizes the R^2. Following this logic, on stage 1, we estimate the reduced-form equations using OLS and take the predicted values from that estimation. On stage 2, we use the predicted value of the endogenous variable in place of the endogenous variable and estimate the resulting equation using OLS.

Note: Estimates provided by 2SLS will be identical to those provided by indirect least squares when the equation is exactly identified.

2.3 Hausman Specification Test

If we suspect a right-hand side variable in an equation is endogenous, how might we test whether this is the case? Hausman① suggests comparing two estimators for which both of the estimators are consistent if the right-hand side variable being considered is exogenous. Only one of the estimators is consistent if the variable is endogenous, hence we can ask whether the difference between the two estimators is large enough to suggest that endogeneity is a severe problem. ②

	Right-hand side variable is:	
Estimator	Endogenous	Exogenous
OLS	Inconsistent estimates	Consistent and efficient estimates
Instrumental variable	Consistent estimates	Consistent but inefficient estimates

If the suspected right-hand side variable is exogenous, the OLS estimators should be similar (but with smaller standard errors) to the instrumental variable's estimators. If the suspected variable is endogenous, then the two estimators should yield different estimates.

To apply the Hausman test for endogeneity, we run a multiple regression model: the

① Hausman, J. A. (1978), "Specification Tests in Econometrics," *Econometrica*, Vol. 46, No. 6. (Nov., 1978), pp. 1251—1271.

② This table is selected from Chapter 15. 6. 3, *Statistics and Econometrics: Methods and Applications*, by Ashenfelter, Levine and Zimmerman, 2003.

dependent variable on x and the error term from a regression of x on an instrumental variable. Then we test whether the coefficient on the error term variable is zero. If we can reject its being zero, we conclude that endogeneity is a problem.

Ⅲ. Computer Exercise[①]

Truffles are a gourmet delight. They are edible fungi that grow below the ground. Let us consider a supply and demand model for truffles:

Demand: $q_t = \alpha_1 + \alpha_2 p_t + \alpha_3 ps_t + \alpha_4 di_t + \varepsilon_t^d$

Supply: $q_t = \beta_1 + \beta_2 p_t + \beta_3 pf_t + \varepsilon_t^s$

In the demand equation,

q = the quantity of truffles traded in a particular French market at time t,

p = the market price of truffles,

ps = the market price of a substitute for real truffles,

di = per capita disposable income.

The supply equation contains the market price and quantity supplied and also includes: pf = price of a factor of production, which in this case is the hourly rental price of truffle used in the search process.

In this model, we assume that p and q are endogenous variables. The exogenous variables are ps, pf, and di.

3.1 Identification

Before thinking about estimation, let us check the identification of each equation. The rule of identifying an equation is that in a system of M equations at least $M-1$ variable must be omitted from each equation in order for it to be identified.

Is the demand equation identified? Why?

$X=1$ exogenous variable excluded,

$N=1$ endogenous variable included.

When $N=X$, the structural equation is identified.

Is the supply equation identified? Why?

$X=2$ exogenous variable excluded,

$N=1$ endogenous variable included.

When $X>N$, the structural equation is overidentified.

Now we conclude that each equation in the system is identified or over identified and

① This exercise is modified and the needed data is collected based on the example in Chapter 14.7, *Undergraduate Econometrics*, 2nd Edition, Hill, Griffiths, and Judge, 2001.

can thus be estimated by 2SLS.

3.2 The Reduced-Form Equations

The reduced-form equations express each endogenous variable, p and q, in terms of the exogenous variables ps, di, pf and the intercept variable, plus an error term.

$$q_t = \pi_{11} + \pi_{21} ps_t + \pi_{31} di_t + \pi_{41} pf_t + v_{t1}$$

$$p_t = \pi_{12} + \pi_{22} ps_t + \pi_{32} di_t + \pi_{42} pf_t + v_{t2}$$

Can we estimate the above equations by OLS? Why?

Answer: Yes, because each of the reduced-form equations does not have the endogeneity problem. As long as it satisfies all the necessary requirements, we can estimate the above equations by OLS.

Please upload the complete date file[1] named **truffle. dta** into Stata as usual. Then, in Stata, type the following commands.

```
reg q ps di pf

      Source |       SS       df       MS              Number of obs =      30
-------------+------------------------------           F(  3,    26) =   19.97
       Model |  430.382636     3  143.460879           Prob > F      =  0.0000
    Residual |  186.754175    26  7.18285287           R-squared     =  0.6974
-------------+------------------------------           Adj R-squared =  0.6625
       Total |  617.136811    29  21.2805797           Root MSE      =  2.6801

------------------------------------------------------------------------------
           q |      Coef.   Std. Err.      t    P>|t|     [95% Conf. Interval]
-------------+----------------------------------------------------------------
          ps |    .656402   .1425376     4.61   0.000     .3634118    .9493922
          di |   .2167156   .0700474     3.09   0.005     .0727312    .3607001
          pf |  -.5069824   .1212616    -4.18   0.000    -.7562393   -.2577255
       _cons |     7.8951   3.243421     2.43   0.022     1.228152    14.56205
------------------------------------------------------------------------------

predict qhat, xb
```

In the above table, we see that the estimated coefficients are statistically significant and thus we conclude that the exogenous variables affect the quantity of truffles traded. On the other hand, the R-squared$=0.697$ and the overall F-statistic is 19.97 which has the p-value of less than 5%. So we conclude that the reduced-form equation has overall significance.

In Stata, type the following commands.

```
reg p ps di pf

      Source |       SS       df       MS              Number of obs =      30
-------------+------------------------------           F(  3,    26) =   69.19
       Model |  1003.86396     3  334.621321           Prob > F      =  0.0000
    Residual |  125.744143    26  4.83631318           R-squared     =  0.8887
-------------+------------------------------           Adj R-squared =  0.8758
       Total |  1129.60811    29  38.9520036           Root MSE      =  2.1992

------------------------------------------------------------------------------
           p |      Coef.   Std. Err.      t    P>|t|     [95% Conf. Interval]
-------------+----------------------------------------------------------------
          ps |   .5693824   .1169602     4.87   0.000     .3289672    .8097976
          di |   .2534164   .0574779     4.41   0.000     .1352689    .3715638
          pf |   .4513019   .0995021     4.54   0.000     .2467725    .6558314
       _cons |  -10.83747   2.661412    -4.07   0.000    -16.30808   -5.366864
------------------------------------------------------------------------------

predict phat
option xb assumed; fitted values)
```

---

[1] Data is collected from *Undergraduate Econometrics*, 2nd Edition, Hill, Griffiths, and Judge, 2001.

In the above table, we see that the estimated coefficients are statistically significant and thus we conclude that the exogenous variables have an effect on market price p. On the other hand, the R-squared = 0.889 and the overall F-statistic is 69.19 which has the p-value of less than 0.000 1. So we conclude that the model has statistically significant explanatory power.

3.3 Indirect Least Square

$$\hat{q}_t = \hat{\pi}_{11} + \hat{\pi}_{21} ps_t + \hat{\pi}_{31} di_t + \hat{\pi}_{41} pf_t + v_{t1}$$
$$= 7.895 + 0.66 ps_t + 0.22 di_t - 0.51 pf_t$$
$$\hat{p}_t = \hat{\pi}_{12} + \hat{\pi}_{22} ps_t + \hat{\pi}_{32} di_t + \hat{\pi}_{42} pf_t$$
$$= -10.837 + 0.569 ps_t + 0.253 di_t + 0.451 pf_t$$

Substituting the above two equations into the demand equation which is exactly identified, we can solve for the estimated structural parameters:

$\hat{\alpha}_1 = -4.35$ $\hat{\alpha}_2 = -1.13$

$\hat{\alpha}_3 = 1.304$ $\hat{\alpha}_4 = 0.502\ 5$

Note that we can't use indirect least squares to estimate an over identified equation. To solve for this, we consider 2SLS approach.

3.4 Two-Stage Least Square

The reduced-form equations are used to obtain *phat* ($\hat{p}$), which will be used in place of p on the right hand side of the supply and demand equations in the second stage of two-stage least squares.

The 2SLS results are obtained by typing the following commands in Stata.

```
. ivreg  q (p=phat) ps di

Instrumental variables (2SLS) regression

      Source |       SS       df       MS              Number of obs =      30
-------------+------------------------------           F(  3,    26) =    5.90
       Model | -14.7802477     3 -4.92674922           Prob > F      =  0.0033
    Residual |  631.917058    26  24.3045022           R-squared     =       .
-------------+------------------------------           Adj R-squared =       .
       Total |  617.136811    29  21.2805797           Root MSE      =    4.93

------------------------------------------------------------------------------
           q |      Coef.   Std. Err.      t    P>|t|     [95% Conf. Interval]
-------------+----------------------------------------------------------------
           p |  -1.123377    .494255    -2.27   0.032    -2.139333   -.1074214
          ps |   1.296033   .3551932     3.65   0.001     .5659232    2.026143
          di |   .5013978   .2283556     2.20   0.037     .0320062    .9707893
       _cons |  -4.279472   5.543884    -0.77   0.447    -15.67509    7.116145
------------------------------------------------------------------------------
Instrumented:  p
Instruments:   ps di phat
------------------------------------------------------------------------------
```

Note that the coefficient of price is negative, indicating that as the market price rises, the quantity demanded of truffles declines, as predicted by the law of demand. The standard errors that are reported are obtained from 2SLS software (Stata). They and the

t-values are valid in large samples. The p-value indicates that the estimated slope of the demand curve is significantly different from zero. Increases in the price of the substitute for truffles increase the demand for truffles. Finally, the effect of income is positive, indicating that truffles are a normal good. In summary, all of these variables have statistically significant coefficients, and thus have an effect on the quantity demanded.

```
. ivreg q (p=phat) pf

Instrumental variables (2SLS) regression

      Source |       SS       df       MS              Number of obs =      30
-------------+------------------------------           F(  2,    27) =   95.26
       Model |  556.582222     2  278.291111           Prob > F      =  0.0000
    Residual |  60.5545883    27  2.24276253           R-squared     =  0.9019
-------------+------------------------------           Adj R-squared =  0.8946
       Total |  617.136811    29  21.2805797           Root MSE      =  1.4976

------------------------------------------------------------------------------
           q |      Coef.   Std. Err.      t    P>|t|     [95% Conf. Interval]
-------------+----------------------------------------------------------------
           p |   1.013945   .0747587    13.56   0.000     .8605525    1.167337
          pf |  -1.000909    .082528   -12.13   0.000    -1.170243    -.831576
       _cons |    20.0328   1.223115    16.38   0.000     17.52318    22.54243
------------------------------------------------------------------------------
Instrumented:  p
Instruments:   pf phat
```

As anticipated, increases in the price of struffles increase the quantity supplied, and increases in the rental rate for truffle-seeking pigs, which is an increase in the cost of a factor production, reduce supply. Both of these variables have statistically significant coefficient estimates.

3.5 Hausman Test

We can use Stata's hausman command to test whether the differences between the ivreg and OLS estimates are large enough to suggest that the OLS estimates are not consistent.

To use the Hausman test, one has to perform the following steps.

(1) obtain an estimator that is consistent whether or not the hypothesis is true;

(2) store the estimation results under a name-consistent using "estimates store";

(3) obtain an estimator that is efficient (and consistent) under the hypothesis that we are testing, but inconsistent otherwise;

(4) store the estimation results under a name-efficient, using "estimates store";

(5) use "hausman" to perform the test.

To conduct the test, type the following Stata codes.

```
. quietly ivreg q (p=phat) ps di
. estimates store ivreg
. quietly reg q p ps di
. estimates store ols
```

```
. hausman ivreg . , constant sigmamore

Note: the rank of the differenced variance matrix (1) does not equal the number of coefficients being tested (4); be
      sure this is what you expect, or there may be problems computing the test.  Examine the output of your
      estimators for anything unexpected and possibly consider scaling your variables so that the coefficients are on
      a similar scale.

                 ---- Coefficients ----
             |      (b)          (B)            (b-B)     sqrt(diag(V_b-V_B))
             |     ivreg         ols         Difference          S.E.
-------------+----------------------------------------------------------------
           p |   -1.123377     .0698861      -1.193263        .2591631
          ps |    1.296033     .7100395       .5859937        .1272711
          di |    .5013978     .0076445       .4937532        .1072375
       _cons |   -4.279472     1.091044      -5.370516        1.166415
------------------------------------------------------------------------------
                           b = consistent under Ho and Ha; obtained from ivreg
            B = inconsistent under Ha, efficient under Ho; obtained from regress

    Test:  Ho:  difference in coefficients not systematic

                  chi2(1) = (b-B)'[(V_b-V_B)^(-1)](b-B)
                          =       21.20
                Prob>chi2 =      0.0000
```

Since the p-value is less than 5%, indicating that we reject the null hypothesis, we conclude that there is a difference between the ivreg and OLS estimates, and the OLS estimates are not consistent.

Ⅳ. Additional Computer Exercise

Consider the following two-equation simultaneous model for the agricultural labor market in the United States:

$$\ln(L_i)=\beta_0+\beta_1\ln(W_i)+\beta_2\ln(Land_i)+\beta_3\ln(RE_i)+\beta_4\ln(Othexp_i)+\beta_5\ln(Sch_i)+\varepsilon_i \quad (*)$$

$$\ln(W_i)=\alpha_0+\alpha_1\ln(L_i)+\alpha_2\ln(Sch_i)+\alpha_3\ln(Othwag_i)+\mu_i \quad (**)$$

where L=labor (total person days of farm labor by state),

W=wage (annual average composite farm wage per hour),

RE=research and extension service expenditures (a proxy for innovations),

$Land$=value of stock of farmland,

$Othexp$=nonlabor operating expenses,

Sch=median years of formal schooling of rural males,

$Othwag$=alternative wage (weighted average) for craftsmen, foremen, etc.

a) Which variables are exogenous? Which variables are endogenous?

Labor and the wage are endogenous. The remainders of the variables are exogenous.

b) Solve analytically (i. e. do the algebra) for the two reduced-form equations.

The reduced-form equation for $\ln(L)$ is:

$$\ln(L_i)=\frac{1}{1-a_1}b_0+\frac{a_0b_1}{1-a_1}+\left(\frac{a_2b_1+b_5}{1-a_1}\right)\ln(Sch_i)+\frac{a_3b_1}{1-a_1}\ln(Othwag_i)$$

$$+\frac{b_2}{1-a_1}\ln(Land_i)+\frac{b_3}{1-a_1}\ln(RE_i)+\frac{b_4}{1-a_1}\ln(Othexp_i)+\frac{b_1e_2+e_1}{1-a_1}$$

The reduced-form equation for ln(W) is:

$$\ln(W_i)=\frac{1}{1-b_1}a_0+\frac{a_1b_0}{1-b_1}+\left(\frac{a_1b_5+a_2}{1-b_1}\right)\ln(Sch_i)+\frac{a_3}{1-b_1}\ln(Othwag_i)$$
$$+\frac{a_1b_2}{1-b_1}\ln(Land_i)+\frac{a_1b_3}{1-b_1}\ln(RE_i)+\frac{a_3}{1-b_1}\ln(Othexp_i)+\frac{a_1e_1+e_2}{1-b_1}$$

c) Using the order condition, show that equation (*) is exactly identified while equation (**) is over identified.

Equation (*) is exactly identified because there is only 1 exogenous variable in equation (**) that is not also contained in equation (*). Equation (**) is overidentified because there are 3 exogenous variables contained in equation (*) that are not contained in equation (**).

d) Use the data set: **labor. dta.** [1]Estimate (*) and (**) using OLS. Also estimate (*) and (**) using two-stage least squares (2SLS). Compare results. Do you think OLS is an inappropriate method of estimation for this problem?

The OLS estimates of these equations are:

. regress lnlabor lnwage lnland lnre lnothexp lnsch

Source	SS	df	MS		
Model	11.0167377	5	2.20334753	Number of obs =	39
Residual	1.61159521	33	.048836218	F(5, 33) =	45.12
Total	12.6283329	38	.332324549	Prob > F =	0.0000
				R-squared =	0.8724
				Adj R-squared =	0.8530
				Root MSE =	.22099

lnlabor	Coef.	Std. Err.	t	P>|t|	[95% Conf.	Interval]
lnwage	-1.105774	.2893065	-3.82	0.001	-1.694373	-.517176
lnland	.3118018	.0837263	3.72	0.001	.1414594	.4821441
lnre	.4446036	.1140206	3.90	0.000	.2126269	.6765803
lnothexp	.2645385	.1127825	2.35	0.025	.0350808	.4939961
lnsch	-.2623222	.6082036	-0.43	0.669	-1.499722	.9750773
_cons	.8757252	1.943497	0.45	0.655	-3.078349	4.8298

. regress lnwage lnlabor lnsch lnothwag

Source	SS	df	MS		
Model	1.871368	3	.623789334	Number of obs =	39
Residual	.465284236	35	.013293835	F(3, 35) =	46.92
Total	2.33665224	38	.061490848	Prob > F =	0.0000
				R-squared =	0.8009
				Adj R-squared =	0.7838
				Root MSE =	.1153

lnwage	Coef.	Std. Err.	t	P>|t|	[95% Conf.	Interval]
lnlabor	-.0109471	.0340323	-0.32	0.750	-.0800364	.0581422
lnsch	1.164415	.2384458	4.88	0.000	.6803442	1.648486
lnothwage	.4682868	.1323288	3.54	0.001	.1996451	.7369286
_cons	-2.972985	.6356697	-4.68	0.000	-4.263463	-1.682507

[1] The dataset is collected from Chapter 15, *Statistics and Econometrics: Methods and Applications*, by Ashenfelter, Levine and Zimmerman, 2003.

Two-stage least squares estimates are:

. regress lnlabor lnwage lnland lnre lnothexp lnsch (lnland lnre lnothexp lnsch lnothwag)

```
Instrumental variables (2SLS) regression

      Source |       SS       df       MS              Number of obs =      39
-------------+------------------------------           F(  5,    33) =   41.63
       Model |  10.9478902     5  2.18957803           Prob > F      =  0.0000
    Residual |  1.68044271    33  .050922506           R-squared     =  0.8669
-------------+------------------------------           Adj R-squared =  0.8468
       Total |  12.6283329    38  .332324549           Root MSE      =  .22566

------------------------------------------------------------------------------
     lnlabor |      Coef.   Std. Err.      t    P>|t|     [95% Conf. Interval]
-------------+----------------------------------------------------------------
      lnwage |  -1.449278   .6012275    -2.41   0.022    -2.672485   -.2260714
      lnland |   .3286769   .0892823     3.68   0.001     .1470308    .5103231
        lnre |   .4687022   .1220887     3.84   0.001     .2203109    .7170935
    lnothexp |   .2497877    .117341     2.13   0.041     .0110556    .4885198
       lnsch |   .3420969   1.111155     0.31   0.760    -1.918564    2.602758
       _cons |  -.8591309   3.306457    -0.26   0.797    -7.586169    5.867907
------------------------------------------------------------------------------
```

. regress lnwage lnlabor lnsch lnothwag (lnsch lnothwag lnland lnre lnothexp)

```
Instrumental variables (2SLS) regression

      Source |       SS       df       MS              Number of obs =      39
-------------+------------------------------           F(  3,    35) =   44.97
       Model |  1.84881748     3  .616272493           Prob > F      =  0.0000
    Residual |  .487834759    35  .013938136           R-squared     =  0.7912
-------------+------------------------------           Adj R-squared =  0.7733
       Total |  2.33665224    38  .061490848           Root MSE      =  .11806

------------------------------------------------------------------------------
      lnwage |      Coef.   Std. Err.      t    P>|t|     [95% Conf. Interval]
-------------+----------------------------------------------------------------
     lnlabor |   .0333775   .0384072     0.87   0.391    -.0445932    .1113482
       lnsch |   1.234335    .245481     5.03   0.000     .7359817    1.732687
  lnothwage |   .4643323   .1355053     3.43   0.002      .189242    .7394226
       _cons |  -3.576787   .6870601    -5.21   0.000    -4.971593   -2.181981
------------------------------------------------------------------------------
```

OLS and 2SLS estimates are not that much different, particularly when you take into consideration the increase in the size of the standard errors associated with the 2SLS estimates. Although technically OLS is an inappropriate technique to use for this problem because of the endogeneity problem, in practice correcting the problem by estimating the model using 2SLS does not change the results much.

第 14 章

时间序列模型中的计量问题

Ⅰ. 利用 OLS 处理时间序列数据所考虑的问题

1.1 Gauss-Markov 假设

OLS 方法依然可以运用于时间序列回归模型。在本章中，我们先研究 OLS 的性质。不同于横截面数据，时间序列数据有时间顺序。鉴于时间序列模型不是依赖于个体的随机抽样，我们需要改变一些假设。在保证无偏性的假设中，ⅰ）我们仍假定所建立的模型关于参数为线性的：$y_t=\beta_0+\beta_1 x_{t1}+\cdots+\beta_k x_{tk}+u_t$。ⅱ）我们仍需要一个零条件均值的假设：$E(u_t \mid x)=0$，$t=1, 2, \cdots, n$。注意，这意味着任何时期里的误差和所有时间段里的解释变量是不相关的。这个零条件均值假设意味着解释变量 x 是完全外生的。另一种替代假设和处理横截面数据时所采取的假设更相近，即 $E(u_t \mid x_t)=0$。这一假设将意味着 x 是同期外生的。同期外生性只在大样本的情况下才有效。ⅲ）我们仍然需要假设没有一个 x 是固定常数，而且彼此之间没有完全的线性相关性。注意：我们放弃了随机抽样的假设。这一假设的关键作用在于，每一个 u_i 都是相互独立的。严格外生性假设已经将此随机抽样假设考虑进去了。基于这三个假设，当我们使用时间序列数据时，OLS 估计是无偏的。ⅳ）正如处理横截面数据一样，我们需要加入同方差性的假设，以便能够推算方差。我们假设 $\text{Var}(u_t \mid x)=\text{Var}(u_t)=\sigma^2$。因此，误差方差和所有的 x 是相互独立的，并且不会随着时间的推移而变动。ⅴ）我们还需要假设没有序列相关：$\text{Corr}(u_t, u_s \mid x)=0$，$t\neq s$。根据上述 5 个假设，在时间序列的情况下所得的 OLS 方差和在横截面数据情况下所得的是一样的。此外，σ^2 的估计也是相同的。OLS 仍然是最优线性无偏估计量（BLUE）。如果加入误差服从正态分布的假设，我们过去的统计检验方法也是相同的。

1.2 时间趋势和季节性

除了确保我们建立的时间序列模型满足上述基本要求之外，在回归估计之前，我们还应该考虑其他两个问题：趋势和季节性因素的影响。时间序列的经济数据往往有随着时间的推移而增长的趋势。如果两个变量都有时间趋势性，我们不能认为它们之间一定有因果关系，这是因为有些不可观测的具有时间趋势性的因素可能与解释变量相关。如果我们忽视了这种可能性，会发现因变量与一个或多个解释变量之间实际上存在着虚假的关系。为了消除这个问题，我们可以添加一个时间趋势变量。

在回归模型里增加线性时间趋势项和在回归里使用“去趋势化的”序列的效果是一样的。例如，我们回归模型：$y_t=\beta_0+\beta_1 x_{1t}+\beta_2 x_{2t}+t+\mu$，从而可以得到 $\hat{\beta}_1$ 和 $\hat{\beta}_2$。我们也可以通过以下的方法得到相同的估计。ⅰ）对于每一个 y_t，x_{1t}和 x_{2t}对常数项及时间趋势 t 进行回归，并存贮残差，也就是，$\tilde{y}_t$，$\tilde{x}_{1t}$和 $\tilde{x}_{2t}$。例如，$\tilde{y}_t=y_t-\hat{\alpha}_0-\hat{\alpha}_1 t$，这里，$\tilde{y}_t$ 被视为被线性去趋势化的变量。ⅱ）用 $\tilde{y}_t$对 $\tilde{x}_{1t}$和 $\tilde{x}_{2t}$进行回归，从而得到 $\hat{\beta}_1$和 $\hat{\beta}_2$。

采用去趋势化的变量的优点（相对于加入线性趋势项）体现在拟合优度的计算上。对已去趋势化的变量进行回归所得的 R^2 能更好地反映 x_t是如何影响 y_t的。

另一个涉及时间序列数据的问题是季节性因素的影响。很多时候，时间序列数据具有周期性，也就是，受到季节性因素的影响。例如：零售业的销货额的季度数据往往在第四季度趋于增加。季节性问题是通过增加一系列的季节虚拟变量来解决的。正如我们处理时间趋势问题，受到季节性因素影响的变量可以经过相关调整之后再进行回归。

例如，我们有一个月度数据模型：$y_t=\beta_0+\beta_1 x_{1t}+\beta_2 x_{2t}+\mu$，其中 x_1 有季节性因素的问题。我们可以用 x_{1t}对常数项和一系列虚拟变量 jan_t，feb_t，mar_t，…，nov_t进行回归，这里 jan_t，feb_t，mar_t，…，nov_t 分别是对应一年中前十一个月的虚拟变量。回归后，我们保存残差，也就是 $\tilde{x}_{1t}$，这是从 $\tilde{x}_{1t}=x_{1t}-\hat{\alpha}_0-\hat{\alpha}_1 jan_t-\hat{\alpha}_2 feb_t-\hat{\alpha}_3 mar_t-\cdots-\hat{\alpha}_{11} nov_t$ 得到的。这里，$\tilde{x}_{1t}$视为被线性去季节性的变量。

Ⅱ. 常用的时间序列模型

迄今为止我们讨论的线性回归模型都是围绕寻找因变量和一系列自变量之间的因果关系。时间序列模型往往着眼于分析因变量的当前变化和它自身过去值的联系，以及误差项之间存在的潜在相关关系。以下的时间序列模型在时间序列分析中很有用，并且这些类型对于短期预测非常有效。

2.1 有限分布滞后模型（FDL 模型）

相对于仅涉及当期变量的静态模型 $y_t=\beta_0+\beta_1 z_t+u_t$而言，有限分布滞后模型允许一个或多个变量对 y 有滞后影响：$y_t=a_0+d_0 z_t+d_1 z_{t-1}+d_2 z_{t-2}+\cdots+d_q z_{t-q}+u_t$。一般来说，$q$ 阶有限分布滞后模型包括变量 z 的 q 个滞后变量。如何解释 FDL 模型里的系数呢？我们来考虑如下的二阶 FDL 模型：$y_t=a_0+d_0 z_t+d_1 z_{t-1}+d_2 z_{t-2}+u_t$。我们称：

d_0=即期倾向，表示本期 z 短暂变化一单位对 y 平均值的影响程度。

$d_1=y_{t+1}-y_{t-1}$，表示本期 z 短暂变动一个时间段后 y 平均值变化的大小。

$d_2=y_{t+2}-y_{t-1}$，表示本期 z 短暂变动两个时间段后 y 平均值变化的大小。

本期 z 短暂变动三个时间段后，y 重新回归到它的初始值：$y_{t+3}=y_t$。

我们对 d_i 画图，可以获取滞后分布图，它总结了 z 的临时变化对于 y 的动态影响。如果在我们所举的二阶 FDL 模型的例子中，z 的变化是永久的，那么我们称 $d_0+d_1+\cdots+d_q$ 为长期倾向（LRP）——它反映了 z 的永久性变化之后 y 的长期变化量。

2.2 移动平均模型（MA 模型）

这种类型的模型假定过去时期的变化会影响当期的结果。在这个模型：

$$y_t=\beta_0+\varepsilon_t+\delta_1\varepsilon_{t-1}+\delta_2\varepsilon_{t-2}+\cdots+\delta_m\varepsilon_{t-m}$$

ε_t＝发生在时间 t 影响 y_t 的随机冲击项。

如果没有随机冲击的存在，那么其结果是 β_0——稳定状态。过去 m 期产生的冲击会影响目前的结果。但冲击在不同时期的影响被假定为有差别的。举例来说，在很久以前发生的冲击其影响可能比目前的冲击所产生的影响要小。上面的模型表明了一个 m 阶移动平均过程：MA(m)。如果 $m=1$，我们便得到一阶移动平均，MA(1)：$y_t=\beta_0+\varepsilon_t+\delta_1\varepsilon_{t-1}$。

2.3 自回归模型（AR 模型）

在自回归（AR）模型，今天的结果是过去结果的函数并写为：

$$y_t=\alpha_0+\phi_1 y_{t-1}+\phi_2 y_{t-2}+\cdots+\phi_m y_{t-m}+\varepsilon_t$$

一阶自回归过程 AR(1) 是：

$$y_t=\alpha_0+\phi_1 y_{t-1}+\varepsilon_t$$

这种模型要比方程式表面上看起来有更长的记忆量。假设 $\alpha_0=0$，而且有几个时间段内没有冲击，或 ε_0，ε_1，ε_2，$\cdots=0$。在所有时期内，经过第一时期后，$y^s=\phi_1 y_{t-1}=0$，这里，y^s＝稳定状态的结果。如果在时期 t 随机冲击发生，之后没有随机冲击发生，即 $\varepsilon_t\neq 0$，ε_{t+1}，ε_{t+2}，ε_{t+3}，$\cdots=0$。那么我们有：

$$y_{t-1}=\phi_1 y_{t-2}+\varepsilon_{t-1}=0$$
$$y_t=\phi_1 y_{t-1}+\varepsilon_t=\varepsilon_t$$
$$y_{t+1}=\phi_1 y_t=\phi_1\varepsilon_t$$
$$y_{t+2}=\phi_1 y_{t+1}=\phi_1^2 y_t=\phi_1^2\varepsilon_t$$
$$y_{t+3}=\phi_1 y_{t+2}=\phi_1^3 y_t=\phi_1^3\varepsilon_t$$
$$\vdots$$

在某个时期产生的冲击会对以后的一些时期产生较持久的影响。当 $\phi_1<1$ 时，经过后来的一些时期，影响结果将逐渐收敛到稳定状态。收敛到稳定状态的速度取决于 ϕ_1 的大小。下面的图表[①]显示了在 ϕ_1 小于 1 的情况下受到冲击影响的变量是如何收敛到稳定状态

---

① 该图选自 Chapter 17.2.2，*Statistics and Econometrics：Methods and Applications*，by Ashenfelter，Levine and Zimmerman，2003.

的。ϕ_1 的数值越接近 1，收敛速度越慢。

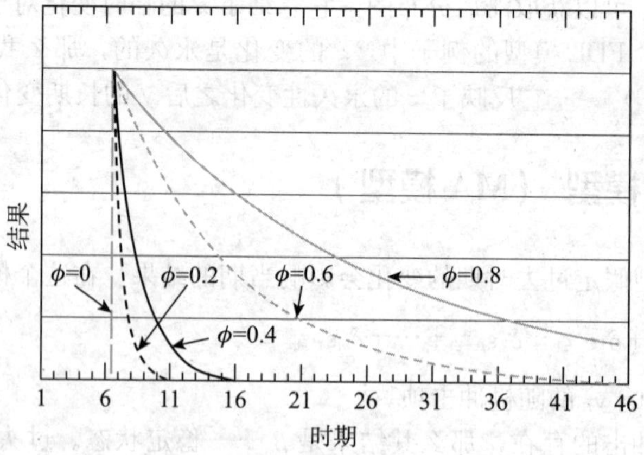

如果 $\phi_1=1$，我们得到的结果是一个随机游走，或者说 AR(1) 模型有一个单位根。单位根对时间序列过程的演变会产生重大影响：

$$y_{t-1}=\phi_1 y_{t-2}+\varepsilon_{t-1}=0$$
$$y_t=\phi_1 y_{t-1}+\varepsilon_t=\varepsilon_t$$
$$y_{t+1}=\phi_1 y_t=\varepsilon_t$$
$$y_{t+2}=\phi_1 y_{t+1}=\phi_1^2\, y_t=\varepsilon_t$$
$$y_{t+3}=\phi_1 y_{t+2}=\phi_1^3\, y_t=\varepsilon_t$$
$$\vdots$$

当 $\phi_1>1$ 时，y 将没有约束地增长下去。

2.4 自回归移动平均模型（ARMA 模型）

自回归和移动平均过程不是相互排斥的。时间序列模型可能会同时具有这两种属性，故而被称为自回归移动平均（或 ARMA）模型。ARMA 模型写为：

$$y_t=\alpha_0+\phi_1 y_{t-1}+\phi_2 y_{t-2}+\cdots+\phi_m y_{t-m}+\varepsilon_t+\delta_1\varepsilon_{t-1}+\delta_2\varepsilon_{t-2}+\cdots+\delta_m\varepsilon_{t-m}$$

ARMA 模型的一般版本是 ARMA(m，k)。ARMA(1，1) 写为：

$$y_t=\alpha_0+\phi_1 y_{t-1}+\varepsilon_t+\delta_1\varepsilon_{t-1}$$

Ⅲ. 平稳性问题的分析

3.1 平稳性的定义

时间序列和横截面数据分析的主要差异是每个时间序列观察值是某个随机变量的特定

实现，并且这一实现可能随着时间而改变，而横截面观察值代表一个服从特定分布的随机值。分析时间序列数据时一个重要的考虑因素是，作为随机变量的时间序列观察值是否服从相同的分布。如果是这样，先前所学的横截面数据分析方法也同样适用于时间序列分析。如果不是，我们需要采用其他一些分析方法。

如果时间序列观察值服从相同的分布，该时间序列是平稳的。用于描述该特征的联合概率密度函数 $f(y_1, y_2, y_3, \cdots, y_T)$ 不随时间位移而变化：$f(y_t, y_{t+1}, y_{t+2}, \cdots, y_{t+k}) = f(y_{t+m}, \cdots, y_{t+m+k})$，对所有的 m 和 k。如果以下条件成立，这样的过程称为弱平稳。ⅰ）y_t的均值不随时间而变化，即 $E(y_t)=\mu$；ⅱ）y_t的方差不随时间而变化，即 $\mathrm{Var}(y_t)=E[(y_t-\mu)^2]=\sigma^2$；ⅲ）$y_t$和 y_{t+k}的协方差是 k 的方程，而不是 t 的方程，即 $\mathrm{Cov}(y_t, y_{t+k})=E[(y_t-\mu)(y_{t+k}-\mu)]={}_k$。

一个平稳的时间序列满足上述弱平稳性所需要的条件。如果一个时间序列过程中有单位根的存在（显示为随机游走形式），它就不是平稳的。尽管时间序列过程本身并不平稳，但有时它的一阶差分是平稳的。

平稳性的条件可能难以把握，但是通过学习以下一些模型会帮助我们理解这一概念。我们从 AR(1) 过程开始：$y_t=\alpha+\rho y_{t-1}+v_t$。如果$|\rho|<1$，那么 AR(1) 过程是平稳的。如果 $\alpha=0$ 和 $\rho=1$，AR(1) 过程变为非平稳的随机游走形式。随机游走的形式是 $y_t=\alpha+y_{t-1}+v_t$，没有呈现明显的趋势，并且缓慢地增长或下跌。如果 $\alpha\neq0$ 和 $\rho=1$，AR(1) 成为 $y_t=y_{t-1}+v_t$，这也是非平稳的，称为带漂移项的随机游走。

许多宏观经济变量和金融时间序列是不平稳的。假设有两个随机游走变量。当我们画图时，可以看到它们之间存在反比关系。然而实际上，它们是独立产生的，并且彼此没有任何关系。如果我们用序列 1 对序列 2 回归，会面临这样一种危险，即使用彼此无关联的非平稳数据却能取得具有显著性的回归结果。这种回归称为伪回归。

3.2　检查平稳性

ⅰ）相关图。

变量 y_t的自相关函数 ρ_s 是 $\rho_s=\dfrac{\mathrm{Cov}(y_t, y_{t+s})}{\mathrm{Var}(y_t)}=\dfrac{\gamma_s}{\gamma_0}$。如果我们画样本相关值和 s 之间的图表，获得的就是所谓的相关图。对于平稳序列，自相关的数值会逐渐减弱，这表明过去的数值发生的时间越久和当前值之间的相关性越小。对于非平稳序列，自相关不会很迅速地消失。

ⅱ）平稳性的单位根检验。

时间序列的平稳性可以通过单位根检验。时间序列变量 y_t 的 AR(1) 模型是 $y_t=\rho y_{t-1}+v_t$。假设 v_t 是随机干扰项，其均值为零且方差恒定。我们回忆一下，如果$|\rho|<1$，那么 AR(1) 过程是平稳的。如果 $\rho=1$，那么 y_t是不平稳的随机游走，称为有一个单位根。

用于检验非平稳性的零假设为 $\rho=1$，而备择假设为 $\rho\neq1$，或仅仅为 $\rho<1$。检验单位根的方法称为迪基-富勒（DF）检验。检验可以通过从原 AR(1) 模型的方程式两边减去 y_{t-1}得到一个简便形式：

$$
\begin{aligned}
y_t-y_{t-1}&=\rho y_{t-1}-y_{t-1}+v_t\\
\Delta y_t&=(\rho-1)y_{t-1}+v_t\\
&=\gamma y_{t-1}+v_t
\end{aligned}
$$

其中，$\Delta y_t = y_t - y_{t-1}$ 且 $\gamma = \rho - 1$。因此，

$$H_0: \rho = 1 \quad \leftrightarrow \quad H_0: \gamma = 0$$

$$H_1: \rho < 1 \quad \leftrightarrow \quad H_1: \gamma < 0$$

变量 Δy_t 称为 y_t 的一阶差分。如果 y_t 服从随机游走，那么 $\gamma=0$ 且 $\Delta y_t = y_t - y_{t-1} = v_t$。

时间序列的一个有趣的特点是，如果我们已经假设的随机误差 v_t 是完全随机的，那么时间序列是平稳的。时间序列中，例如序列 y_t，可以通过一阶差分方法变为平稳序列。这样的序列被认为具有一阶单整，并命名为 I(1)。平稳变量具有零阶单整，并命名为 I(0)。一般来说，如果一个序列进行 d 次差分后成为平稳序列，那么它具有 d 阶单整，并命名为 I(d)。

ⅲ）增广的迪基-富勒检验。

为了控制方程组中某个方程式的误差项存在自相关的可能性，我们加入另外一些项。修改后的模型是：

$$\Delta y_t = \alpha_0 + \gamma y_{t-1} + \sum_{i=1}^{m} a_i \Delta y_{t-i} + v_t$$

其中 $\Delta y_{t-1} = (y_{t-1} - y_{t-2})$，$\Delta y_{t-2} = (y_{t-2} - y_{t-3})$，…。

在这个模型中，我们检验的零假设为 $\gamma=0$。这种检验方法称为增广的迪基-富勒检验。

Ⅳ. 协整现象分析

作为一般规则，为了避免伪回归问题，非平稳时间序列变量不应在回归模型中使用。但有一个例外。如果 y_t 和 x_t 是非平稳的且具有一阶单整，那么我们期望它们的差或者它们的任何线性组合，例如，$e_t = y_t - \beta_1 - \beta_2 x_t$ 也将具有一阶单整。但是，在某些重要情况下，e_t 是平稳的，具有零阶单整。在这种情况下，y_t 和 x_t 称为协整。

协整意味着，y_t 和 x_t 有着类似的随机趋势，实际上，因为它们的差异是平稳的，它们从来没有偏离对方太远。协整变量 y_t 和 x_t 所展现的长期均衡关系定义为：$y_t = \beta_1 + \beta_2 x_t$，而且 e_t 是均衡误差，它代表了对长期均衡关系的短期偏离。

我们可以通过检验 $e_t = y_t - \beta_1 - \beta_2 x_t$ 是否平稳来检验 y_t 和 x_t 是否协整。因为我们不能观察到 e_t，却可以通过使用迪基-富勒检验方法来检验最小二乘残差 $\hat{e}_t = y_t - \hat{\beta}_1 - \hat{\beta}_2 x_t$ 是否平稳。如果迪基-富勒检验拒绝了有单位根的零假设，那么我们可以说 y 和 x 是协整的。

假设我们对估计两个变量之间的关系有兴趣。两者的水平值都是非平稳的。两者都是差分平稳的。回归模型 $y_t = \beta_0 + \beta_1 x_t + \varepsilon_t$ 会遇到伪回归问题。因为 y_t 和 x_t 遵循随机游动形式，它们表现出一定的时间趋势。如果它们都倾向于同一（相反的）方向，回归估计会发现这两个变量是正（负）相关，尽管这样的关系并不存在。什么时候我们能预见一个非平稳随机变量对另一个非平稳随机变量的回归会导致伪回归问题？答案取决于协整的概念。如果 y_t 和 x_t 协整，那么 y_t 和 x_t 都是一阶单整而且 $\varepsilon_t = y_t - \beta_1 x_t$ 是 I(0)。β_1 是协整因子。这样的回归不会导致伪回归问题，但会显示出它们之间的真实关系。

如何检验两个变量是否协整？从理论上讲，我们可以进行迪基-富勒检验或者采用增广的迪基-富勒检验来检验残差项 $\varepsilon_t = y_t - \beta_1 x_t$ 是否平稳。但在实践中，因为 β_1 是未知的，我们必须首先估计回归模型 $y_t = \beta_0 + \beta_1 x_t + \varepsilon_t$，然后，计算估计残差 $\hat{e}_t = y_t - \hat{\beta}_0 - \hat{\beta}_1 x_t$，从而用它来检验非平稳性问题。

总而言之，我们有 4 种涉及协整问题的情况。

情况 1：如果两个变量是平稳的，本书中先前提到的隐含的假设条件依然存在。在这种情况下，最小二乘法或广义最小二乘法二者哪种更合适，哪种就可以用来估计 y 和 x 之间的关系。

情况 2：如果两个变量非平稳，而且也不协整，一个潜在的解决用非平稳变量进行回归而导致的伪回归问题的方案是，如果这两个变量都是 I(1)，我们可以估计一阶差分模型。例如，我们要估计模型 $y_t=\beta_0+\beta_1 x_t+\varepsilon_t$，但是 x_t 和 y_t 非平稳。我们可以考虑滞后一个时期的回归模型：$y_{t-1}=\beta_0+\beta_1 x_{t-1}+\varepsilon_{t-1}$。将此方程和相应的同期方程的左右两边相减，我们得到：

$$y_t-y_{t-1}=\beta_1(x_t-x_{t-1})+(\varepsilon_t-\varepsilon_{t-1})\rightarrow \Delta y_t=\beta_1\Delta x_t+\Delta\varepsilon_t。$$

估计这样的方程将给出变量变化量之间的关系。

情况 3：协整变量 y_t 和 x_t 的长期均衡关系定义为 $y_t=\beta_1+\beta_2 x_t$，而且 e_t 是均衡误差项，代表了对长期均衡关系的短期偏离。

情况 4：还有一种有趣的关系，可以由所谓的误差修正模型来衡量。当 y 和 x 非平稳但协整时，该模型可以采用。例如：对于 I(1) 变量，误差修正模型将变量的变化值，即 Δy_t，与前一时期长期均衡的偏离联系起来。它可以写成：$\Delta y_t=\alpha_1+\alpha_2(y_{t-1}-\beta_1-\beta_2 x_{t-1})+v_t$。

V．上机操作练习

在这个练习中，我们延伸了关于利用时间序列数据进行动态建模的分析。利用时间序列数据进行的最小二乘估计的基本性质取决于时间序列变量服从平稳随机过程的假设。如果时间序列的平均值和方差随着时间变化是不变的，并且序列中两个值的协方差只与两者之间的时间长短有关，而与观察变量的实际时间无关，那么随机过程就是平稳的。

我们使用 Excel 格式的数据文件 **timeseries. xls**。[①] 其中有 6 个序列 $s1$、$s2$、$rw1$、$rw2$、$rwd1$、$rwd2$ 的 1 001 个观测值。

（1）采用 EViews 画图。

a）$s1$ 的图像（平稳过程）。

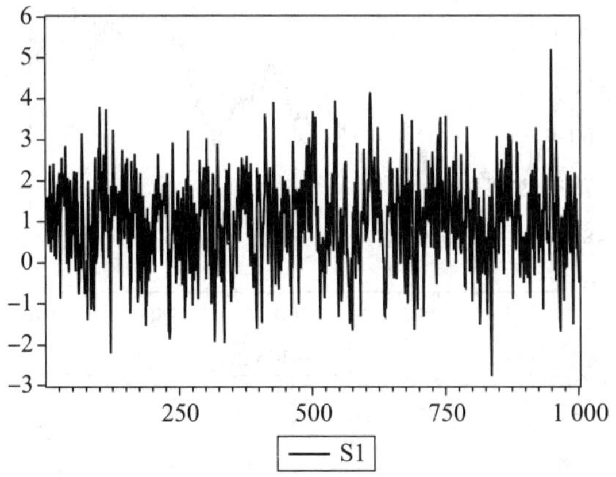

① 资料来源：http://shazam. econ. ubc. ca/student/hill/FIG16－1. txt。

b）$s2$ 的图像（平稳过程）。

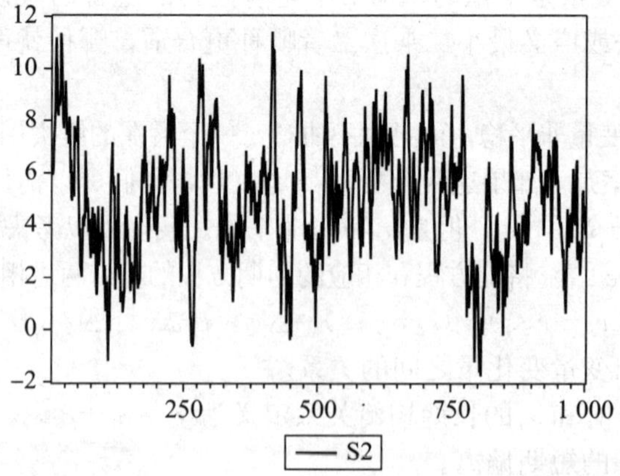

c）$rw1$ 的图像（随机游走）。

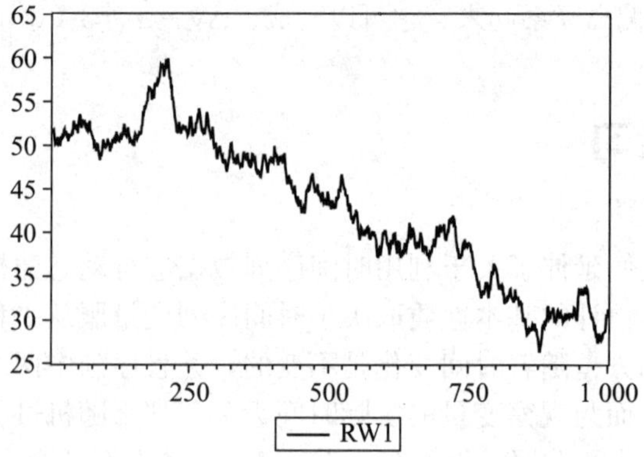

d）$rw2$ 的图像（随机游走）。

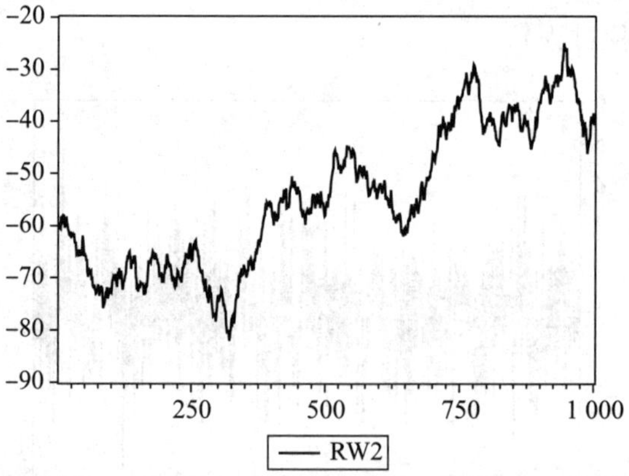

e）$rwd1$ 的图像（带漂移项的随机游走）。

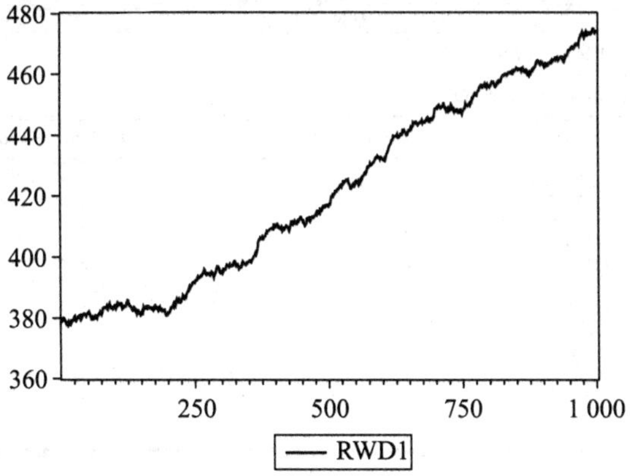

f）$rwd2$ 的图像（带漂移项的随机游走）。

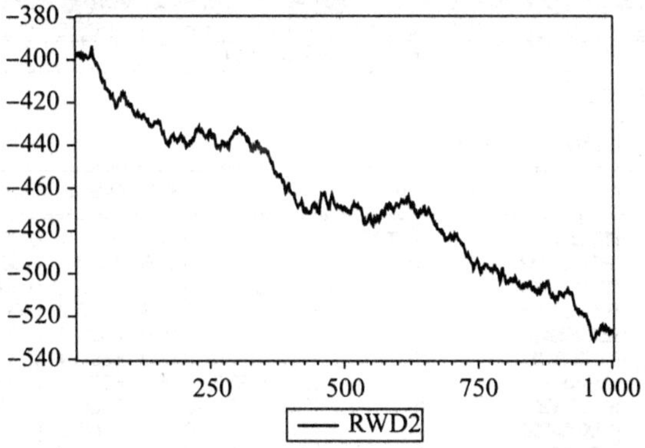

图（a）～图（b）中有两个平稳序列。它们在一个固定的水平上随机变化并且有不变的方差。在图（c）～图（d）中，两个序列不平稳。这样的序列叫做随机游走，因为它们慢慢向上或向下游走但是并没有规律。图（e）～图（f）中的两个序列更加不平稳，但是显示出了明显的上升或下降的趋势。这样的序列叫做带漂移项的随机游走。

（2）我们可以用自相关函数来检验平稳性。如果相对于 s 画出样本相关函数我们可以得到一个相关图。经济软件可以计算样本相关函数。按以下步骤在 EViews 中计算出自相关函数（ACF）。

第一步：在 workfile 窗口中双击序列图标，在窗口中打开 $s2$。

第二步：要查看自相关，选择“View/Correlogram”，在 $s2$ 序列的菜单栏会有一个“Correlogram Specification”对话框显示出来。在“Correlogram of:”窗口中选择“Level”，并在“Lag Specification：lags to include:”窗口中输入“10”，然后点击“OK”来查看 EViews 的结果。

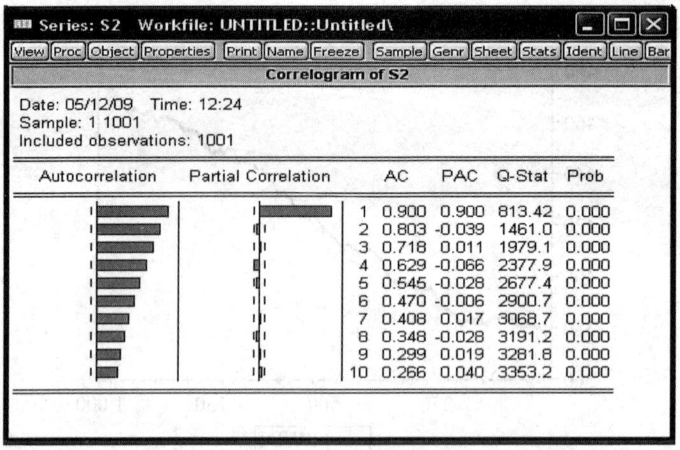

Series: S2 Workfile: UNTITLED::Untitled\

Correlogram of S2

Date: 05/12/09 Time: 12:24
Sample: 1 1001
Included observations: 1001

	AC	PAC	Q-Stat	Prob
1	0.900	0.900	813.42	0.000
2	0.803	-0.039	1461.0	0.000
3	0.718	0.011	1979.1	0.000
4	0.629	-0.066	2377.9	0.000
5	0.545	-0.028	2677.4	0.000
6	0.470	-0.006	2900.7	0.000
7	0.408	0.017	3068.7	0.000
8	0.348	-0.028	3191.2	0.000
9	0.299	0.019	3281.8	0.000
10	0.266	0.040	3353.2	0.000

我们可以按上述步骤计算出 $rw1$ 的自相关函数。

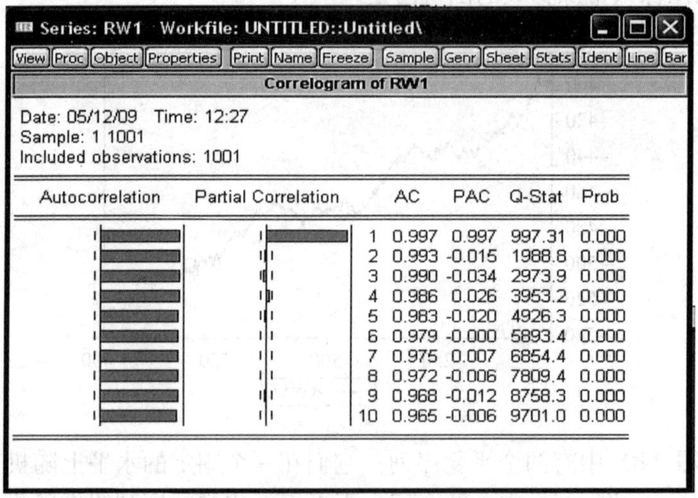

Series: RW1 Workfile: UNTITLED::Untitled\

Correlogram of RW1

Date: 05/12/09 Time: 12:27
Sample: 1 1001
Included observations: 1001

	AC	PAC	Q-Stat	Prob
1	0.997	0.997	997.31	0.000
2	0.993	-0.015	1988.8	0.000
3	0.990	-0.034	2973.9	0.000
4	0.986	0.026	3953.2	0.000
5	0.983	-0.020	4926.3	0.000
6	0.979	-0.000	5893.4	0.000
7	0.975	0.007	6854.4	0.000
8	0.972	-0.006	7809.4	0.000
9	0.968	-0.012	8758.3	0.000
10	0.965	-0.006	9701.0	0.000

在以上图表中，我们展示了平稳序列 $s2$ 和非平稳序列 $rw1$ 的前 10 个相关系数。

平稳序列 $s2$ 和非平稳序列 $rw1$ 的相关图有很大差别。平稳序列的自相关逐渐消失，显示出越早的数据与当前的数据越没有关联。非平稳序列的自相关完全没有很快消失。$rw1_t$ 和 $rw1_{t-10}$ 的相关系数是 0.965。因此，对于这些函数的视觉检验是检查非平稳性的第一指标。

（3）平稳性的单位根检验。

时间序列的平稳性可以直接用单位根检验来检验。按以下步骤来做迪基-富勒检验，检验 $rw1$ 序列是非平稳的假设。

第一步：在“workfile”窗口中双击序列图标，在窗口中打开 $rw1$。注意，EViews 可能会显示 $rw1$ 的相关图，因为这是上一个指令。我们可以选择“View/Spreadsheet”来查看序列数据或者直接进入下一步来检验平稳性。

第二步：在 $rw1$ 序列窗口的菜单栏中选择“View/Unit Root Test”来做 DF 检验。

第三步：要做单位根检验，我们需要在“Unit Root Test”对话框中给出一定指示。首先，选择检验的种类——Augmented Dickey-Fuller（ADF）检验或者 Phillips-Perron（PP）检验（在这个练习中选择 ADF）。然后，选择检验哪种单位根，“Level”，“1st difference”，或者“2nd difference”(在这个练习中选择“Level”)。之后，指定是否要包括截距、趋势和截距或者都不包括（在这个练习中尝试每一个选项)。接着，确定要在检验的回归中包括的滞后的一阶差分项的数量（在这个练习中为 0)。当完成这些选项后，点击“OK”来获取回归结果。

等式 1:（没有截距和趋势）

$$\Delta \hat{rw}1_t = -\underset{(-1.400\,9)}{0.000\,5} rw1_{t-1} + \varepsilon_t$$

等式 2:（有截距）

$$\Delta \hat{rw}1_t = \underset{(0.456)}{0.038} - \underset{(-0.7142)}{0.001\,36} rw1_{t-1} + \varepsilon_t$$

等式 3:（有截距和趋势）

$$\Delta \hat{rw}1_t = \underset{(3.097)}{1.016} - \underset{(-3.081)}{0.000\,5} t - \underset{(-3.145)}{0.018} rw1_{t-1} + \varepsilon_t$$

第四步：在上述每种情况中，在 5%的显著性水平上检验不能拒绝 $rw1$ 序列有单位根的零假设，因为 ADF 检验统计量没有小于 MacKinnon 临界值。并且，对应的 p 值是 0.150 2，0.844 和 0.096 4，显示出我们不能拒绝 $rw1$ 序列有单位根的零假设。

(4) 如何使非平稳变量变成平稳变量。

我们创建 $rw1$ 的一阶差分，用 $rw1\_first_t$ 来命名并画出一阶差分图，它看起来像平稳序列的图像。

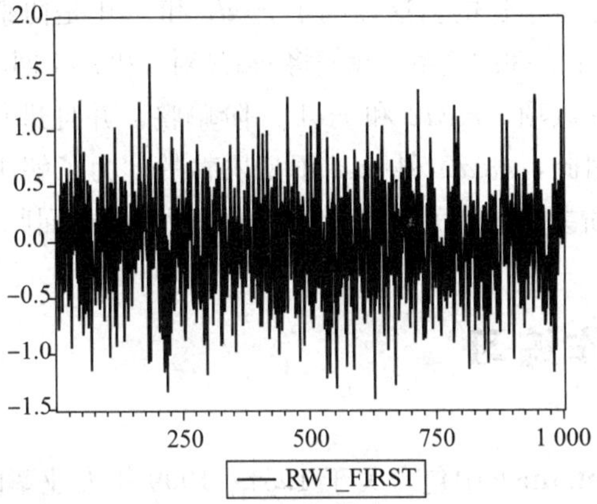

相关图显示出很小的关联，所以序列是平稳的。

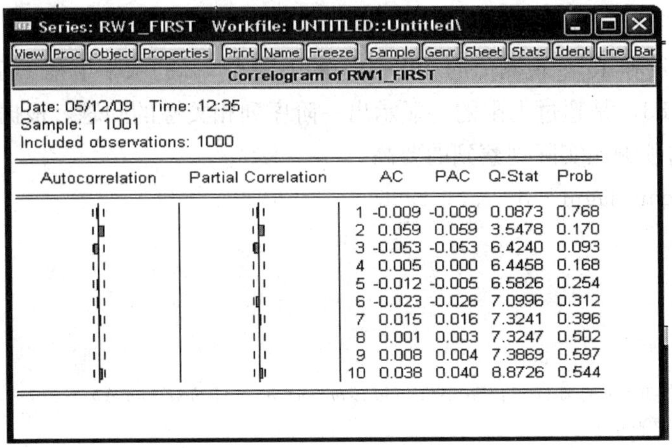
Series: RW1_FIRST　Workfile: UNTITLED::Untitled\

View Proc Object Properties Print Name Freeze Sample Genr Sheet Stats Ident Line Bar

Correlogram of RW1_FIRST

Date: 05/12/09　Time: 12:35
Sample: 1 1001
Included observations: 1000

Autocorrelation	Partial Correlation		AC	PAC	Q-Stat	Prob
		1	-0.009	-0.009	0.0873	0.768
		2	0.059	0.059	3.5478	0.170
		3	-0.053	-0.053	6.4240	0.093
		4	0.005	0.000	6.4458	0.168
		5	-0.012	-0.005	6.5826	0.254
		6	-0.023	-0.026	7.0996	0.312
		7	0.015	0.016	7.3241	0.396
		8	0.001	0.003	7.3247	0.502
		9	0.008	0.004	7.3869	0.597
		10	0.038	0.040	8.8726	0.544

将 Dickey-Fuller 检验用于序列 $rw1\_first$，显示它是平稳的。

根据 $rw1$ 和 $rw1\_first$（$\Delta rw1$）的单位根检验，我们可以得出结论：序列 $rw1$ 是 I(1)。根据单位根的零假设没有被拒绝，我们可以得出 $rw1$ 是 I(2) 或者二阶以上单整。

（5）协整。

我们来考虑 $rw1$ 和 $rwd2$ 之间的关系。我们已经注意到它们是不平稳的并且都是一阶单整。要检验它们是否协整，我们将 $rwd2$ 对 c 和 $rw1$ 回归并得到残差，将其命名为 *residual*。

第一步：在 EViews 中，在主菜单栏，从“workfile”菜单中选择“Quic/Estimate Equation”。

第二步：在“Equation Estimation（specification）:”窗口中输入因变量 $rwd2$（y）和 c（常数项），然后输入自变量 $rw1$（x）。必须要先输入因变量(y)。

第三步：选择估计方法“{LS－Least Squares（NLS and ARMA)}”。这是大部分时间的默认设置。

第四步：“workfile”的样本范围是自动输入的，但如果需要另一个样本范围我们可以进行更改。点击“OK”来查看 EViews 的回归结果。

第五步：在主菜单栏中选择“Quic/Generate Series”并在“Generate Series by Equation:”窗口中输入“residual＝resid”。

第六步：按照之前做迪基-富勒检验的步骤来检验残差变量是否平稳。

在这个练习中，残差是平稳的。这证明了 $rwd2$ 和 $rw1$ 是协整的。

为了探究 $rwd2$ 和 $rw1$ 之间的关系，我们将 $rwd2$ 对 c 和 $rw1$ 回归来检验它们的长期关系。

另一个例子：没有常数项，$rwd2$ 和 $rw1$ 一阶单整，并且进行在 DF 检验之后，它们的残差都是不平稳的。因此，$rwd2$ 和 $rw1$ 不是协整的。为了解决这些问题，我们先分别求出 $rwd2$ 和 $rw1$ 的一阶差分。然后我们将 $\Delta rwd2$ 对 $\Delta rw1$ 回归。

Ⅵ. 附加上机操作练习

数据集 **unemployment. dta**[①] 中包含关于 1951—1999 年失业率的信息。

a）估计 AR(1) 模型。检验一阶序列相关性。将最近三年排除在外。用模型的参数估计值为那三年做一个“样本内的”预测。模型预测的效果如何?

有一个自变量和 45 个观测值的 DW 检验的上限在 5%的水平上是 1.566。这个模型的 DW 统计量是 1.83，是超过上限的，显示出一阶序列相关性的问题。根据这个模型做出的 1997—1999 年的预测比实际观察到的要高。

```
. regress unemp lagun1 if year≤1996
```

① 该数据集取自如下书的第 17 章：*Statistics and Econometrics: Methods and Applications*, by Ashenfelter, Levine and Zimmerman, 2003。

```
      Source |       SS       df       MS              Number of obs =      45
-------------+------------------------------           F(  1,    43) =   63.29
       Model |  63.2154238     1  63.2154238           Prob > F      =  0.0000
    Residual |  42.9476863    43  .998783403           R-squared     =  0.5955
-------------+------------------------------           Adj R-squared =  0.5860
       Total |   106.16311    44  2.41279796           Root MSE      =  .99939

------------------------------------------------------------------------------
       unemp |      Coef.   Std. Err.      t    P>|t|     [95% Conf. Interval]
-------------+----------------------------------------------------------------
      lagun1 |   .7502622   .0943055     7.96   0.000     .5600769    .9404474
       _cons |   1.492371   .5658874     2.64   0.012     .3511505    2.633592
------------------------------------------------------------------------------
```

. dwstat

Durbin-Watson d-statistic（2，45）＝1.831658

根据这个模型做出的 1997—1999 年的预测比实际观察到的要高。

year	unemp	unemphat
1997	4.9	5.543787
1998	4.5	5.168656
1999	4.2	4.868551

b）重复 a）部分，但这次使用 AR(2）模型。哪个模型更好？

在 AR(2）模型中，失业率的二阶滞后不统计显著。另外，对于随后的失业率的预测很相似，但是比我们用 AR(1）模型预测的要差一些。因此，可能 AR(1）模型更合适一些。

. regress unemp lagun1 lagun2 if year ≤1996

```
      Source |       SS       df       MS              Number of obs =      44
-------------+------------------------------           F(  2,    41) =   28.14
       Model |  56.6636686     2  28.3318343           Prob > F      =  0.0000
    Residual |  41.2763304    41  1.00673977           R-squared     =  0.5786
-------------+------------------------------           Adj R-squared =  0.5580
       Total |  97.9399991    43   2.2776744           Root MSE      =  1.0034

------------------------------------------------------------------------------
       unemp |      Coef.   Std. Err.      t    P>|t|     [95% Conf. Interval]
-------------+----------------------------------------------------------------
      lagun1 |   .8224242   .1532625     5.37   0.000     .5129044    1.131944
      lagun2 |  -.1201272    .148901    -0.81   0.424    -.4208388    .1805844
       _cons |   1.788476   .6138583     2.91   0.006     .5487635    3.028188
------------------------------------------------------------------------------
```

. list year unemp unemphat if year ≥1997

	year	unemp	unemphat
47.	1997	4.9	5.556854
48.	1998	4.5	5.169667
49.	1999	4.2	4.900761

Chapter 14

Time Series Econometrics

Ⅰ. Issues in Using OLS with Time Series Data

1.1 Gauss-Markov Assumptions

In this chapter, we will start to study the properties of OLS for estimating linear time series regression models using time series data. Unlike cross-section data, time series data has a temporal ordering. Given that a time series model no longer has a random sample of individuals, we will need to alter some of our assumptions to take this fact into account. Among the assumptions for unbiasedness, ⅰ) we still assume the model that is linear in parameters: $y_t=\beta_0+\beta_1 x_{t1}+\cdots+\beta_k x_{tk}+u_t$. ⅱ) We still need to make the zero conditional mean assumption: $E(u_t \mid x)=0$, $t=1, 2, \cdots, n$. Note that this implies the error term in any given period is uncorrelated with the explanatory variables in all time periods. This zero conditional mean assumption implies the x's are strictly exogenous. An alternative assumption, more parallel to the cross-sectional case, is $E(u_t \mid x_t)=0$. This assumption would imply the x's are contemporaneously exogenous. Contemporaneous exogeneity will only be sufficient in large samples. ⅲ) We still need to assume that no x is constant, and that there is no perfect collinearity. Note that we have skipped the assumption of a random sample. The key impact of the random sample assumption is that each u_i is independent. Our strict exogeneity assumption takes care of it in this case. Based on these three assumptions, when we use time series data, the OLS estimators are unbiased. ⅳ) Like in the cross-section case, we need to add an assumption of homoskedasticity in order to be able to derive variances. Now we assume $\mathrm{Var}(u_t \mid x)=\mathrm{Var}(u_t)=\sigma^2$. Thus, the error variance is independent of all the x's, and it is constant over time. ⅴ) We also need the assumption of no serial correlation: $\mathrm{Corr}(u_t, u_s \mid x)=0$ for $t\neq s$. Under these five assumptions, the OLS variances in the time-series case are the same as in the cross-section case. Also, the estimator of σ^2 is the same. OLS remains BLUE. With the additional assumption of normal errors, inference is the same.

1.2 Trending and Seasonality

In addition to making sure the time series model we set up satisfies the above basic requirements, prior to estimation, we should also take care of the other two issues: trending and seasonality. Economic time series often have a trend of growing over time. If two series are trending together, we can't assume that the relation is causal because the unobserved trending factors might be correlated with the explanatory variables. If we ignore this possibility, we may find a spurious relationship between the dependent variable and one or more explanatory variables. To eliminate this problem, we can add a time trend.

Adding a linear trend term to a regression is the same as using "detrended" series in a regression. For example, we regress the model: $y_t=\beta_0+\beta_1 x_{1t}+\beta_2 x_{2t}+t+\mu$ to get $\hat{\beta}_1$ and $\hat{\beta}_2$. We can get the same estimates as follows. i) We regress each of y_t, x_{1t}, and x_{2t} on a constant and the time trend t and save the residuals, say, $\tilde{y}_t$, $\tilde{x}_{1t}$, and $\tilde{x}_{2t}$. For example, $\tilde{y}_t=y_t-\hat{\alpha}_0-\hat{\alpha}_1 t$, where $\tilde{y}_t$ is thought of being linearly detrended. ii) We run the regression of $\tilde{y}_t$ on $\tilde{x}_{1t}$ and $\tilde{x}_{2t}$ to get exactly $\hat{\beta}_1$ and $\hat{\beta}_2$.

An advantage to actually detrending the data (vs. adding a trend) involves the calculation of goodness of fit. The R^2 from a regression on detrended data better reflects how well the x_t's explain y_t.

Another issue related to time series data is seasonality. Very often, time-series data exhibits some periodicity, referred to as seasonality. For example, quarterly data on retail sales will tend to jump up in the 4th quarter. Seasonality can be dealt with by adding a set of seasonal dummies. As with trends, the series can be seasonally adjusted before we run the regression.

For example, we have a model for monthly data: $y_t=\beta_0+\beta_1 x_{1t}+\beta_2 x_{2t}+\mu$, where x_1 exhibits the issue of seasonality. We can deseasonalize it by regressing x_{1t} on a constant and jan_t, feb_t, mar_t, $\cdots$, and nov_t, where jan_t, feb_t, mar_t, $\cdots$, and nov_t are dummy variables corresponding to the appropriate month. After regression, we save the residual, say, $\tilde{x}_{1t}$, which is obtained from $\tilde{x}_{1t}=x_{1t}-\hat{\alpha}_0-\hat{\alpha}_1 jan_t-\hat{\alpha}_2 feb_t-\hat{\alpha}_3 mar_t-\cdots-\hat{\alpha}_{11} nov_t$. Here, $\tilde{x}_{1t}$ is thought of being linearly deseasonalized.

Ⅱ. Commonly Used Time Series Models

The linear regression model presented so far has centered on finding a causal relationship between a dependent variable and a series of independent variables. Time series models often aim at relating movements in the dependent variable to its own past values and a set of potential correlated error terms. The following types of time series models are useful in empirical time series analysis and show that such models are quite effective in making short-run forecasts.

2.1 Finite Distributed Lag Models (FDL Models)

Relative to a static model that relates contemporaneous variables: $y_t=\beta_0+\beta_1 z_t+u_t$, a finite distributed lag (FDL) model allows one or more variables to affect y with a lag: $y_t=a_0+d_0 z_t+d_1 z_{t-1}+d_2 z_{t-2}+\cdots+d_q z_{t-q}+u_t$. Generally, a finite distributed lag model of order q will include q lags of z. How do we interpret the coefficients in the FDL model? Consider the FDL Model of order two as follows: $y_t=a_0+d_0 z_t+d_1 z_{t-1}+d_2 z_{t-2}+u_t$. We can call:

$d_0=$the impact propensity—it reflects the immediate change in y.

$d_1=y_{t+1}-y_{t-1}$ is the change in y one period after the temporary shock.

$d_2=y_{t+2}-y_{t-1}$ is the change in y two periods after the temporary shock.

At time $t+3$, y has reverted back to its initial level: $y_{t+3}=y_t$.

When we graph d_i, we obtain the lag distribution, which summarizes the dynamic effect that a temporary increase in z has on y. If there is a permanent increase in z, in the example of the FDL model of order 2, we can call $d_0+d_1+\cdots+d_q$ the long-run propensity (LRP) —it reflects the long-run change in y after a permanent change in z.

2.2 Moving Average Models (MA Models)

This type of model assumes that shocks from past periods affect the outcome in the current period. In this model:

$$y_t=\beta_0+\varepsilon_t+\delta_1\varepsilon_{t-1}+\delta_2\varepsilon_{t-2}+\cdots+\delta_m\varepsilon_{t-m}$$

where $\varepsilon_t=$a random shock occurring at time t to y_t.

If there are no shocks, then the outcome is β_0—the steady state. Shocks going back m periods affect present outcome. But the influences of shocks in different periods are assumed to have differential impacts. For instance, a shock occurring farther in the past may have less influence than a current shock. The above model shows a moving average process of order m: MA(m). If $m=1$ we have a first-order moving average, MA(1): $y_t=\beta_0+\varepsilon_t+\delta_1\varepsilon_{t-1}$.

2.3 Autoregressive Models (AR models)

In an autoregressive (AR) model, today's outcome is a function of past outcomes and is written formally as:

$$y_t = \alpha_0 + \phi_1 y_{t-1} + \phi_2 y_{t-2} + \cdots + \phi_m y_{t-m} + \varepsilon_t$$

A first-order autoregressive process AR(1) is:

$$y_t = \alpha_0 + \phi_1 y_{t-1} + \varepsilon_t$$

This model has a longer memory than one would infer from the statement. Suppose that $\alpha_0 = 0$ and that for several periods there is no shock to the series, or ε_0, ε_1, ε_2, $\cdots = 0$. For all periods after the first, $y^s = \phi_1 y_{t-1} = 0$, where y^s = the steady-state outcome. If a shock occurs in period t but no shocks occur after that, $\varepsilon_t \neq 0$, ε_{t+1}, ε_{t+2}, ε_{t+3}, $\cdots = 0$. Then we have:

$$y_{t-1} = \phi_1 y_{t-2} + \varepsilon_{t-1} = 0$$
$$y_t = \phi_1 y_{t-1} + \varepsilon_t = \varepsilon_t$$
$$y_{t+1} = \phi_1 y_t = \phi_1 \varepsilon_t$$
$$y_{t+2} = \phi_1 y_{t+1} = \phi_1^2 y_t = \phi_1^2 \varepsilon_t$$
$$y_{t+3} = \phi_1 y_{t+2} = \phi_1^3 y_t = \phi_1^3 \varepsilon_t$$
$$\vdots$$

The shock in one period will have a lasting impact for several subsequent periods. For $\phi_1 < 1$, outcomes in subsequent periods will converge back to the steady state. The rate of convergence depends upon the value of ϕ_1. The following graph① shows how a shock to the series would result in a steady state convergence if ϕ_1 is less than 1. The closer ϕ_1 is to unity, the slower the rate of convergence.

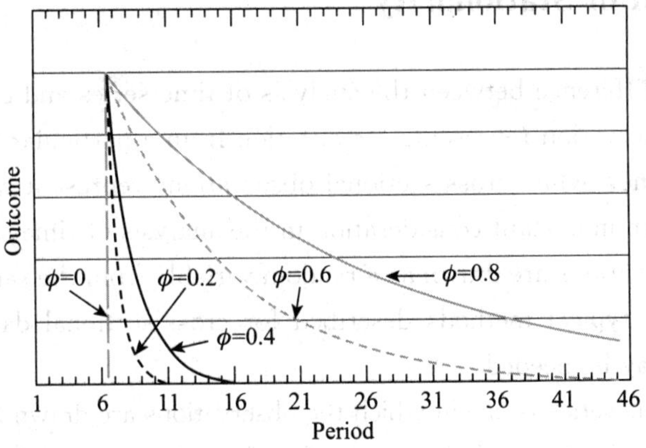

If $\phi_1 = 1$, the result is a random walk, or the AR(1) model is said to have a unit root. A unit root has significant implications for the evolution of a time series process:

$$y_{t-1} = \phi_1 y_{t-2} + \varepsilon_{t-1} = 0$$

---

① This graph is selected from Chapter 17.2.2, *Statistics and Econometrics: Methods and Applications*, by Ashenfelter, Levine and Zimmerman, 2003.

$$y_t = \phi_1 y_{t-1} + \varepsilon_t = \varepsilon_t$$
$$y_{t+1} = \phi_1 y_t = \varepsilon_t$$
$$y_{t+2} = \phi_1 y_{t+1} = \phi_1^2 y_t = \varepsilon_t$$
$$y_{t+3} = \phi_1 y_{t+2} = \phi_1^3 y_t = \varepsilon_t$$
$$\vdots$$

When $\phi_1 > 1$, y will grow without bound.

2.4 Autoregressive-Moving Average Models (ARMA Models)

Autoregressive and moving average processes are not mutually exclusive. A time series may exhibit both properties, called autoregressive moving average (or ARMA) model. An ARMA model is specified as:

$$y_t = \alpha_0 + \phi_1 y_{t-1} + \phi_2 y_{t-2} + \cdots + \phi_m y_{t-m} + \varepsilon_t + \delta_1 \varepsilon_{t-1} + \delta_2 \varepsilon_{t-2} + \cdots + \delta_m \varepsilon_{t-m}$$

The general version of the model is an ARMA(m, k). An ARMA(1, 1) would be

$$y_t = \alpha_0 + \phi_1 y_{t-1} + \varepsilon_t + \delta_1 \varepsilon_{t-1}$$

Ⅲ. Stationarity

3.1 Definition of Stationarity

The principal difference between the analysis of time series and cross-sectional data is each time series observation represents a realization from a particular random variable that may change over time, while cross-sectional observations represent random draws from a fixed distribution. An important consideration in the analysis of time series data is whether all time series observations are drawn as a random variable from the same underlying distribution. If they are, typical methods described for cross-sectional data apply. If they are not, alternatives may be needed.

A stationary time series is one in which the observations are drawn from the same underlying distribution. The joint probability density function $f(y_1, y_2, y_3, \cdots, y_T)$ characterizing the process is invariant to any displacement in time $f(y_t, y_{t+1}, y_{t+2}, \cdots, y_{t+k}) = f(y_{t+m}, \cdots, y_{t+m+k})$ for all m and k. A process is weakly stationary if ⅰ) the mean of y_t is a constant over time, i. e. $E(y_t) = \mu$; ⅱ) the variance of y_t is constant over time, i. e. $\mathrm{Var}(y_t) = E[(y_t - \mu)^2] = \sigma^2$; ⅲ) the covariance of y_t and y_{t+k} is only a function of k, not t, i. e. $\mathrm{Cov}(y_t, y_{t+k}) = E[(y_t - \mu)(y_{t+k} - \mu)] = \pi_k$.

A stationary process satisfies the conditions required for weak stationarity. If a time series process has a unit root (exhibits a random walk), it is not stationary. Even if a time series process itself is not stationary, sometimes its first difference is if it follows a different stationary process.

The conditions for stationarity may be difficult to grasp, but looking at some models may help. Let us start from AR(1) process: $y_t=\alpha+\rho y_{t-1}+v_t$. The AR(1) process is stationary if $|\rho|<1$. If $\alpha=0$ and $\rho=1$, the AR(1) process reduces to a nonstationary random walk series. A Random Walk, written as $y_t=\alpha+y_{t-1}+v_t$, shows no definite trend, and slowly turns one way or the other. If $\alpha\neq 0$ and $\rho=1$ the series produced $y_t=y_{t-1}+v_t$ is also nonstationary and is called a random walk with a drift.

Many macroeconomic and financial time series are nonstationary. Suppose there are two random walk series. When we plot them, we see an inverse relationship between them. However, they were generated independently and have no relation to one another. If we regress series one on series two, there is a danger of obtaining apparently significant regression results from unrelated data when using nonstationary series in regression analysis. Such regressions are said to be spurious.

3.2 Checking Stationarity

i) Correlogram.

The autocorrelation function, ρ_s, of the series y_t is $\rho_s=\frac{\text{Cov}(y_t, y_{t+s})}{\text{Var}(y_t)}=\frac{\gamma_s}{\gamma_0}$. If we plot the sample correlations against s, we obtain what is called a correlogram. For the stationary series the autocorrelations gradually die out, indicating the values farther in the past are less correlated with the current value. For the nonstationary series, the autocorrelations do not die out rapidly at all.

ii) Unit Root Tests for Stationarity.

The stationarity of a time series can be tested directly with a unit root test. The AR(1) model for the time series variable y_t is $y_t=\rho y_{t-1}+v_t$. Assume that v_t is a random disturbance with zero mean and constant variance. Recall that if $|\rho|<1$, then the AR(1) process is stationary. If $\rho=1$, then y_t is the nonstationary random walk, and is said to have a unit root.

We can test for nonstationarity by testing the null hypothesis that $\rho=1$ against the alternative that $\rho\neq 1$, or simply $\rho<1$. The test for unit root is called the Dickey-Fuller (DF) test. The test is put into a convenient form by subtracting y_{t-1} from both sides of the original AR(1) equation to obtain:

$$\begin{aligned} y_t-y_{t-1}&=\rho y_{t-1}-y_{t-1}+v_t \\ \Delta y_t&=(\rho-1)y_{t-1}+v_t \\ &=\gamma y_{t-1}+v_t \end{aligned}$$

where $\Delta y_t = y_t - y_{t-1}$, and $\gamma = \rho - 1$. Then:

$H_0: \rho = 1 \leftrightarrow H_0: \gamma = 0$

$H_1: \rho < 1 \leftrightarrow H_1: \gamma < 0$

The variable Δy_t is called the first difference of the series y_t.

If y_t follows a random walk, then $\gamma = 0$ and $\Delta y_t = y_t - y_{t-1} = v_t$.

An interesting feature of the series is that it is stationary if, as we have assumed, the random error v_t is purely random. Series like y_t, which can be made stationary by taking its first difference, are said to be integrated of order 1, and denoted I(1). Stationary series are said to be integrated of order zero, I(0). In general, if a series must be differenced d times to be made stationary it is integrated of order d, or I(d).

ⅲ) Augmented Dickey-Fuller Test.

To control for the possibility that the error terms in one of the equations are autocorrelated, additional terms are included. The modified model is:

$$\Delta y_t = \alpha_0 + \gamma y_{t-1} + \sum_{i=1}^{m} a_i \Delta y_{t-i} + v_t$$

where $\Delta y_{t-1} = (y_{t-1} - y_{t-2})$, $\Delta y_{t-2} = (y_{t-2} - y_{t-3})$, ….

Testing the null hypothesis that $\gamma = 0$ in the context of this model is called the augmented Dickey-Fuller test.

Ⅳ. Cointegration

As a general rule, nonstationary time series variables should not be used in regression models, in order to avoid the problem of spurious regression. There is an exception to this rule. If y_t and x_t are nonstationary I(1) variables, then we would expect that their difference, or any linear combination of them, such as, $e_t = y_t - \beta_1 - \beta_2 x_t$ to be I(1) as well. However there are important cases when e_t is a stationary I(0) process. In this case y_t and x_t are said to be cointegrated.

Cointegration implies that y_t and x_t share similar stochastic trends, and in fact since their difference e_t is stationary, they never diverge too far from each other. The cointegrated variables y_t and x_t exhibit a long term equilibrium relationship defined by $y_t = \beta_1 + \beta_2 x_t$, and e_t is the equilibrium error, which represents short term deviations from the long-term relationship.

We can test whether y_t and x_t are cointegrated by testing whether the errors $e_t = y_t - \beta_1 - \beta_2 x_t$ are stationary. Since we cannot observe e_t, we instead test the stationarity of the least squares residuals, $\hat{e}_t = y_t - \hat{\beta}_1 - \hat{\beta}_2 x_t$, using a Dickey-Fuller test. If the DF test rejects the null hypothesis of a unit root, we can say y and x are cointegrated.

Suppose we are interested in estimating the relationship between two variables. Both are nonstationary in levels. Both are difference stationary. A regression of the form $y_t=\beta_0+\beta_1 x_t+\varepsilon_t$ is subject to the problem of spurious regression, and because both y_t and x_t follow a random walk, they have a tendency to appear to trend over time. If they both tend to move in the same (opposite) direction, regression estimates will find the two variables to be positively (negatively) related, even though no such relationship exists. When can we expect a regression of one nonstationary random variable on another to result in a non-spurious relationship? The answer has to do with the concept of cointegration. If y_t and x_t are cointegrated, i. e. y_t and x_t are both I (1) and $\varepsilon_t=y_t-\beta_1 x_t$ is I(0), β_1 is the cointegrating factor. A regression of one on the other does not yield a spurious regression, but indicates an estimate of the true relationship between them.

How can we test whether two variables are cointegrated? In theory, we can conduct a Dickey-Fuller or augmented Dickey-Fuller test for stationarity on the residual, $\varepsilon_t=y_t-\beta_1 x_t$. In practice, because β_1 is unknown, we must first estimate the regression model, $y_t=\beta_0+\beta_1 x_t+\varepsilon_t$. Then we calculate the estimated residuals $\hat{e}_t=y_t-\hat{\beta}_0-\hat{\beta}_1 x_t$ before tests for nonstationarity can be conducted.

In summary, there are four cases related to cointegration.

Case 1: If two variables are stationary, the implicit assumption maintained for most of the text, least squares or generalized least squares, whichever is more appropriate, can be used to estimate a relationship between y and x.

Case 2: If two variables are nonstationary and not cointegrated, one potential solution to spurious regression with nonstationary variables is estimating regression models in first differences if these two variables are I(1). For example, suppose we want to estimate a regression model of the form $y_t=\beta_0+\beta_1 x_t+\varepsilon_t$. But both x_t and y_t are nonstationary. Consider the one-period lag of this regression model: $y_{t-1}=\beta_0+\beta_1 x_{t-1}+\varepsilon_{t-1}$. By subtracting the lagged left and right sides of this equation from the corresponding contemporaneous equation we have: $y_t-y_{t-1}=\beta_1(x_t-x_{t-1})+(\varepsilon_t-\varepsilon_{t-1})\rightarrow \Delta y_t=\beta_1\Delta x_t+\Delta\varepsilon_t$. Estimating equations like this one gives information on any relationship between the changes in the variables.

Case 3: The cointegrated variables y_t and x_t exhibit a long-term equilibrium relationship defined by $y_t=\beta_1+\beta_2 x_t$, and e_t is the equilibrium error, which represents short term deviations from the long-term relationship.

Case 4: There is another relationship that is of interest, called an error correction model, which can be estimated when y and x are nonstationary, but cointegrated. For example: For I (1) variables, the error correction model relates changes in a variable, say Δy_t, to departures from the long-run equilibrium in the previous period. It can be written as: $\Delta y_t=\alpha_1+\alpha_2(y_{t-1}-\beta_1-\beta_2 x_{t-1})+v_t$.

Ⅴ. Computer Exercise

In this exercise, we extend our analysis of dynamic modeling using time series data. The usual properties of the least squares estimator in a regression using time series data depend on the assumption that the time series variables involved follow a stationary stochastic process. A stochastic process (time series process) is stationary if its mean and variance are constant over time and the covariance between two values from the series depends only on the length of time between periods, not on the actual times at which the variables are observed.

Let us use the data file① named **timeseries. xls** in Excel format. There are 1 001 observations on 6 series, *s*1, *s*2, *rw*1, *rw*2, *rwd*1, *rwd*2.

(1) Plot each of these series using EViews.

a) Graph for *s*1(stationary process).

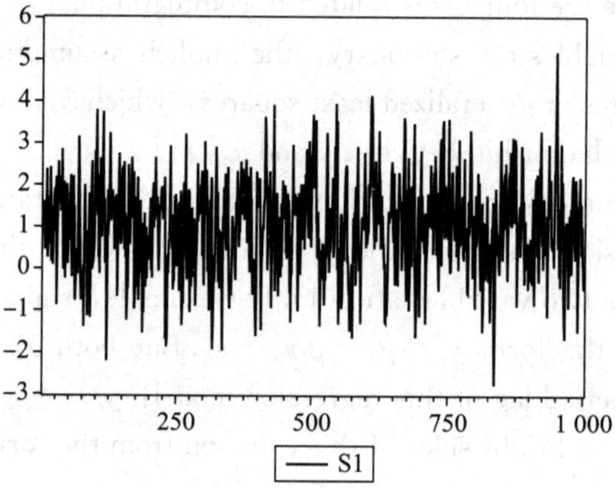

b) Graph for *s*2(stationary process).

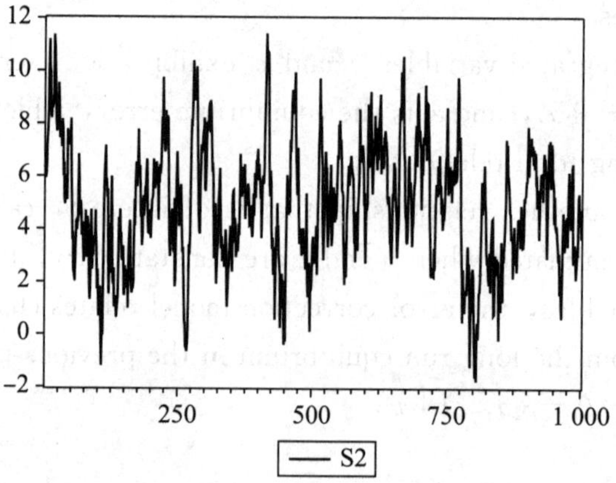

① Data is collected from http://shazam. econ. ubc. ca/student/hill/FIG16—1. txt.

c) Graph for *rw*1(random walk).

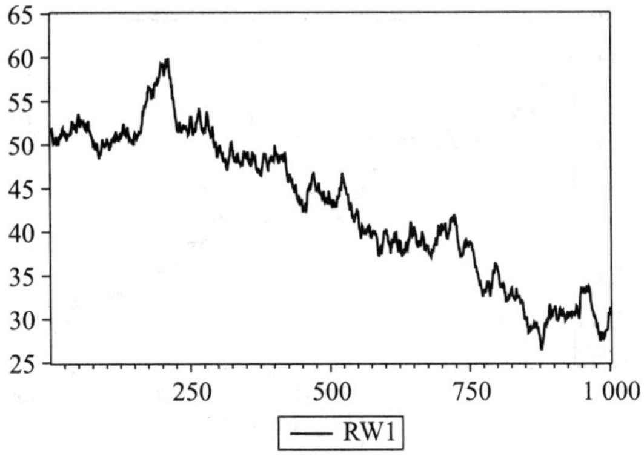

d) Graph for *rw*2(random walk).

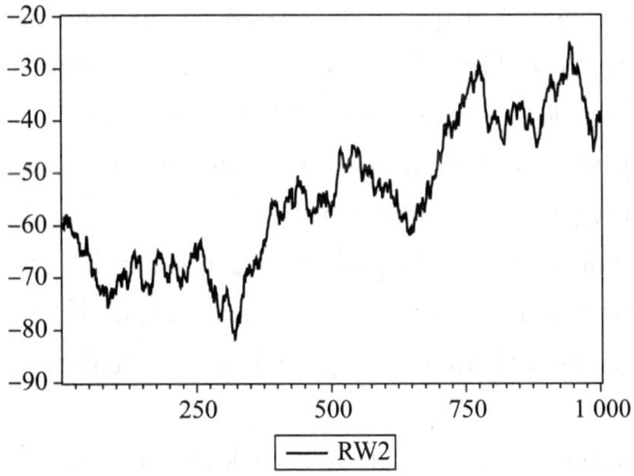

e) Graph for *rwd*1(random walk with drift).

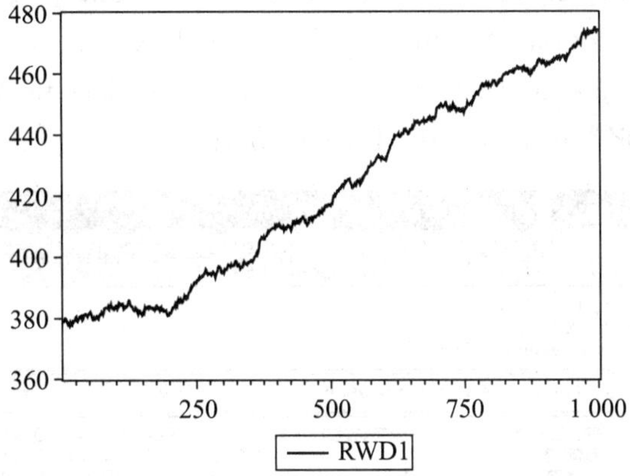

f) Graph for *rwd*2(random walk with drift).

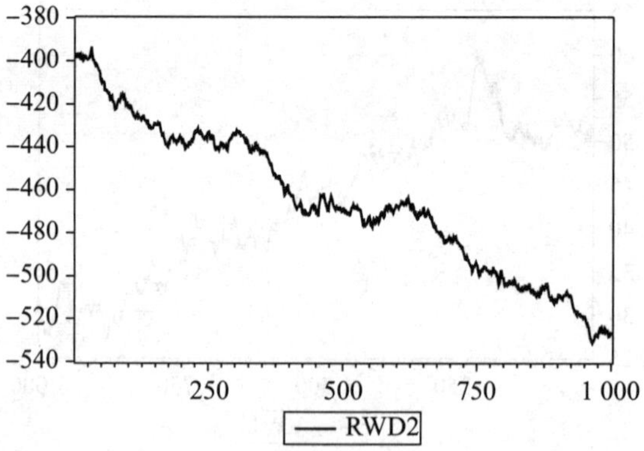

In Figures (a)~(b) there are two stationary series. They vary randomly at a constant level (mean) and with constant dispersion (variance). In Figures (c)~(d) are plots of series that are not stationary. These time series are called random walks, because they slowly wander upwards or downwards, but with no real pattern. In Figures (e)~(f) are two more nonstationary series, but these show a definite trend either upwards or downwards. These are called random walks with a drift.

(2) We can check stationarity using the autocorrelation function. If we plot the sample correlations against *s* we obtain what is called a correlogram. Economic software will compute the sample correlations. Follow the steps below to calculate the autocorrelation function (ACF) in EViews.

Step 1: Open *s*2 in one window by double clicking the series icon in the workfile window.

Step 2: To view the autocorrelation, select "View/Correlogram", on the *s*2 series menu bar and a "Correlogram Specification" dialog box appears. Select "Level" in the "Correlogram of:" window and enter "10" in the "Lag Specification: lags to include:" window, and click "OK" to reveal the EViews output.

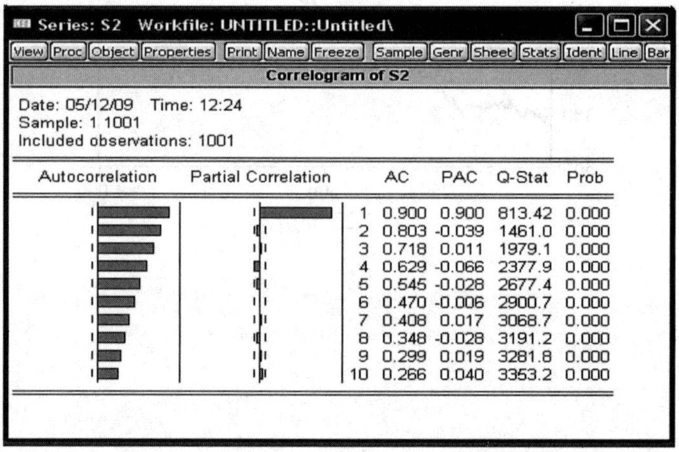

We can follow the above steps and calculate autocorrelation function for $rw1$.

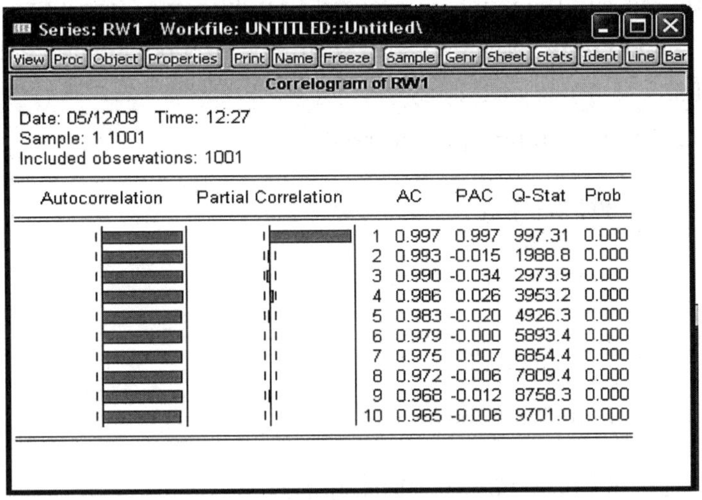

In the above tables, we show the first 10 correlations (AC) for the stationary series $s2$ and nonstationary series $rw1$.

There is a dramatic difference between the correlograms for the stationary series $s2$ and nonstationary series $rw1$. For the stationary series the autocorrelations gradually die out, indicating the values further in the past are less correlated with the current value. For the nonstationary series, the autocorrelations do not die out rapidly at all. The correlation between $rw1_t$ and $rw1_{t-10}$ is 0.965. Thus, visual inspection of these functions can be a first indicator of nonstationarity.

(3) Unit Root Tests for Stationarity.

The stationarity of a time series can be tested directly with a unit root test. Follow these steps to conduct the Dickey-Fuller test of the hypothesis that the $rw1$ series is nonstationary.

Step 1: Open $rw1$ in one window by double clicking the series icon in the workfile window. Note that EViews will probably display the correlogram view for $rw1$ since that was the last view selected. We can select "View/Spreadsheet" to view the series data or just proceed with the next step to test for stationarity.

Step 2: To conduct the DF test, select "View/Unit Root Test" on the $rw1$ series window menu bar.

Step 3: Several things have to be specified in the "Unit Root Test" dialog box to carry out a unit root test. First, choose the type of the test—either the Augmented Dickey-Fuller (ADF) test or the Phillips-Perron (PP) test (select ADF for this exercise). Second, specify whether to test for a unit root in the "Level", "1st difference", or "2nd difference" of the series (select "Level" for this exercise). Third, specify whether to include an intercept, a trend and intercept, or none in the test regression (try each of them in this exercise). Fourth, specify the number of lagged first difference terms to add in the test regression (0 for the DF test). When finished with the selections, click "OK" to reveal the regression results.

Equations 1: (without intercept and trend)

$$\Delta \hat{rw1}_t = \underset{(-1.4009)}{-0.0005} rw1_{t-1} + \varepsilon_t$$

Equation 2: (with intercept)

$$\Delta \hat{rw1}_t = \underset{(0.456)}{0.038} - \underset{(-0.7142)}{0.00136} rw1_{t-1} + \varepsilon_t$$

Equation 3: (with intercept and trend)

$$\Delta \hat{rw1}_t = \underset{(3.097)}{1.016} - \underset{(-3.081)}{0.0005} t - \underset{(-3.145)}{0.018} rw1_{t-1} + \varepsilon_t$$

Step 4: In each of the above cases, the test fails to reject the null hypothesis of a unit root in the *rw*1 series at 5% of the reported significance levels, since the ADF test statistic is not less than the MacKinnon critical values. In addition, the *p*-values are 0.150 2, 0.844 and 0.096 4 respectively for each case, indicating that we don't reject the null hypothesis that *rw*1 has a unit root.

(4) How to make nonstationary variable stationary.

Let us generate the first difference of *rw*1, denoted by $rw1\_first_t$, and plot the first difference, which looks like the plots of stationary process.

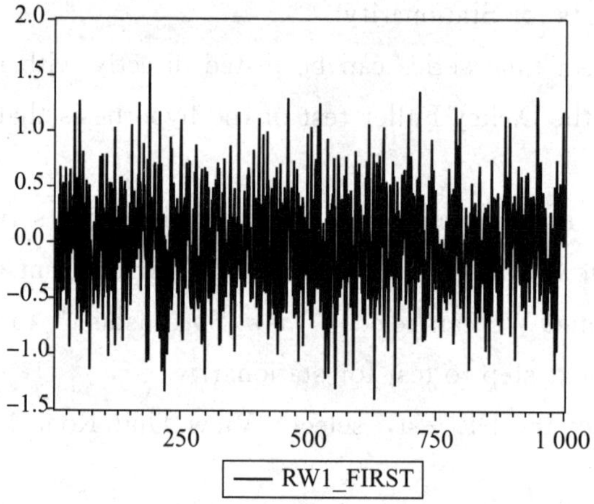

The correlogram shows small correlations at all lags, suggesting stationarity.

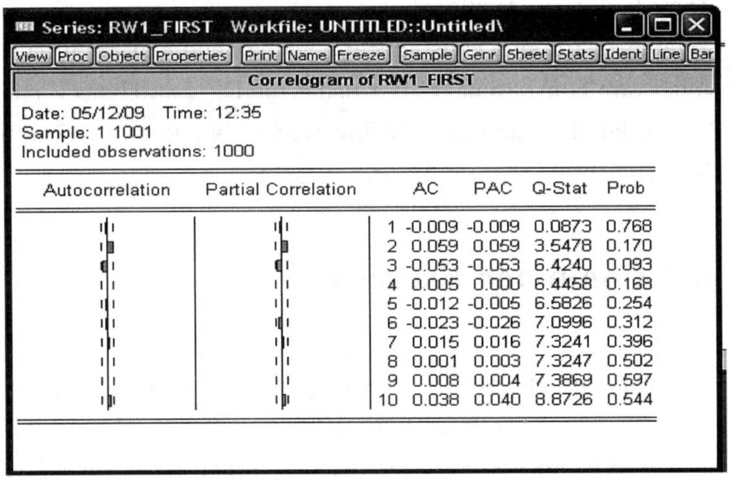

Correlogram of RW1_FIRST

Date: 05/12/09 Time: 12:35
Sample: 1 1001
Included observations: 1000

Autocorrelation	Partial Correlation		AC	PAC	Q-Stat	Prob
		1	-0.009	-0.009	0.0873	0.768
		2	0.059	0.059	3.5478	0.170
		3	-0.053	-0.053	6.4240	0.093
		4	0.005	0.000	6.4458	0.168
		5	-0.012	-0.005	6.5826	0.254
		6	-0.023	-0.026	7.0996	0.312
		7	0.015	0.016	7.3241	0.396
		8	0.001	0.003	7.3247	0.502
		9	0.008	0.004	7.3869	0.597
		10	0.038	0.040	8.8726	0.544

The result of the Dickey-Fuller test for a random walk (since no trend) applied to the series *rw*1 _ *first*, shows that it is stationary.

Collecting the results from the unit root tests on *rw*1 and *rw*1 _ *first* ($\Delta rw1$), we can say that the series *rw*1 is I(1). Had the null hypothesis of a unit root not been rejected, we would have concluded that *rw*1 is I(2) or integrated of an order higher than two.

(5) Cointegration.

Let us consider the relationship between *rw*1 and *rwd*2. We have noticed that they are nonstationary and both integrated of order one. To check whether they are cointegrated, we regress *rwd*2 on *c* and *rw*1 and get the residuals, denoted by *residual*.

In EViews, follow Step 1. On the major menu bar, select "Quic/Estimate Equation" from the workfile menu.

Step 2: Enter the dependent variable *rwd*2 (*y*) and *c* (constant term) and then the independent variable *rw*1 (*x*) in the "Equation Estimation (specification):" window. It is important to enter the dependent variable first (*y* in this case).

Step 3: Select the estimation method "{LS—Least Squares (NLS and ARMA)}". This is the default that will be used most of the time.

Step 4: The workfile sample range is automatically entered but it can be changed if another sample range is desired. Click "OK" to view the EViews Least Squares regression output table.

Step 5: Go to the major menu bar, select "Quic/Generate Series" and then enter "residual=resid" in the "Generate Series by Equation:" window.

Step 6: Follow the previous steps to conduct a Dickey-Fuller test to check whether the residual variable is stationary or not.

In this exercise, the residual is stationary. This indicates that *rwd*2 and *rw*1 are cointegrated.

To explore the relationship between *rwd*2 and *rw*1, we just regress *rwd*2 on *c* and *rw*1 to examine their long-term relationship.

One more example, without a constant term, *rwd*2 and *rw*1 are integrated with order 1, and their residuals are nonstationary after using the DF test. Hence, *rwd*2 and *rw*1 are not cointegrated. To solve the existing problem, we firstly take the first difference of *rwd*2 and *rw*1 respectively. Then we regress Δ*rwd*2 on Δ*rw*1.

Ⅵ. Additional Computer Exercise

The dataset (**unemployment. dta**[①]) contains information on the unemployment rate (monthly and seasonally adjusted) from 1951 to 1999 with a year variable.

a) Estimate an AR(1) model. Test for the first order serial correlation. Conduct the estimation excluding the three most recent years. Using the model's parameter estimates, perform an "in-sample" prediction for those three periods. How well does the model do?

The upper bound for a Durbin-Watson test with 1 explanatory variable and 45 observations at the 5% level is 1. 566. The Durbin-Watson statistic for this model 1. 83, which is well above this cut-off, providing little evidence of first order serial correlation. Based on this model the predictions that we get for 1997 through 1999 are considerably higher than what we actually observed.

. regress unemp lagunl if year ⩽1996

```
      Source |       SS       df       MS              Number of obs =      45
-------------+------------------------------           F(  1,    43) =   63.29
       Model |  63.2154238     1  63.2154238           Prob > F      =  0.0000
    Residual |  42.9476863    43  .998783403           R-squared     =  0.5955
-------------+------------------------------           Adj R-squared =  0.5860
       Total |   106.16311    44  2.41279796           Root MSE      =  .99939

------------------------------------------------------------------------------
       unemp |      Coef.   Std. Err.      t    P>|t|     [95% Conf. Interval]
-------------+----------------------------------------------------------------
      lagunl |   .7502622   .0943055     7.96   0.000     .5600769    .9404474
       _cons |   1.492371   .5658874     2.64   0.012     .3511505    2.633592
------------------------------------------------------------------------------
```

. dwstat

Durbin-Watson d-statistic (2, 45) =1. 831658

Based on this model the predictions that we get for 1997 through 1999 are considerably higher than what we actually observed.

year	unemp	unemphat
1997	4. 9	5. 543787
1998	4. 5	5. 168656
1999	4. 2	4. 868551

b) Repeat part (a) using an AR(2) model. Which model do you prefer?

In the AR(2) model, the 2nd lag of the unemployment rate is not statistically signifi-

① The dataset is collected from Chapter 17, *Statistics and Econometrics: Methods and Applications*, by Ashenfelter, Levine and Zimmerman, 2003.

cant. In addition, the predictions for subsequent unemployment are similar, but slightly worse than what we obtained in the AR(1) model. As a result, one would probably prefer the AR(1).

. regress unemp lagunl lagun2 if year ≤1996

```
      Source |       SS       df       MS              Number of obs =      44
-------------+------------------------------           F(  2,    41) =   28.14
       Model |  56.6636686     2  28.3318343           Prob > F      =  0.0000
    Residual |  41.2763304    41  1.00673977           R-squared     =  0.5786
-------------+------------------------------           Adj R-squared =  0.5580
       Total |  97.9399991    43   2.2776744           Root MSE      =  1.0034

------------------------------------------------------------------------------
       unemp |      Coef.   Std. Err.      t    P>|t|     [95% Conf. Interval]
-------------+----------------------------------------------------------------
      lagun1 |   .8224242   .1532625     5.37   0.000     .5129044    1.131944
      lagun2 |  -.1201272    .148901    -0.81   0.424    -.4208388    .1805844
       _cons |   1.788476   .6138583     2.91   0.006     .5487635    3.028188
------------------------------------------------------------------------------
```

. list year unemp unemphat if year ≥1997

	year	unemp	unemphat
47.	1997	4. 9	5. 556854
48.	1998	4. 5	5. 169667
49.	1999	4. 2	4. 900761

第 15 章

向量自回归模型（VAR 模型）

Ⅰ. 如何建立一个 VAR 模型

大规模的联立方程模型有时候会包含上百个方程式，它们可以用于预测经济运行中的一些重要经济变量的变化情况。然而，这样的模型往往会受到一些攻击。例如，这些模型的参数可能会依赖于经济政策的状况并会随这些政策的改变而有所变化。因此，支持这些方程组建立的理论依据往往会受到质疑。这种担忧也导致我们去寻求另一种办法来预测宏观经济运行：向量自回归模型（VAR 模型），它可以使构建这些联立方程模型所需要的各种假设数量最小化。

一个 VAR 模型通常采用以下形式：

$$
\begin{aligned}
y_{1t} = {} & \alpha_{01} + \sum_{j=1}^{m}\beta_{11j}y_{1(t-j)} + \sum_{j=1}^{m}\beta_{12j}y_{2(t-j)} + \cdots + \sum_{j=1}^{m}\beta_{1rj}y_{n(t-j)} + \cdots + \sum_{j=1}^{l}\gamma_{11j}z_{1(t-j)} + \\
& \cdots \\
& + \sum_{j=1}^{l}\gamma_{1rj}z_{r(t-j)} + \varepsilon_{1t} \\
\cdots & \\
y_{nt} = {} & \alpha_{0n} + \sum_{j=1}^{m}\beta_{n1j}y_{1(t-j)} + \sum_{j=1}^{m}\beta_{n2j}y_{2(t-j)} + \cdots + \sum_{j=1}^{m}\beta_{nrj}y_{n(t-j)} + \cdots + \sum_{j=1}^{l}\gamma_{n1j}z_{1(t-j)} + \cdots \\
& + \sum_{j=1}^{l}\gamma_{nrj}z_{r(t-j)} + \varepsilon_{nt}
\end{aligned}
$$

在这个模型，我们可以允许每个变量任意带有一系列滞后项。虽然我们可以包括许多滞后项，但是当越来越多的变量加入模型内，自由度会因此而降低。

通常情况下，从 VAR 模型里，我们比较希望能获知以下两个结果：

· 脉冲响应函数：它可通过图表形式来描述当结构冲击值发生一个标准差变化时，模型里每个变量随之产生的变化量。通常这种变化是（并不总是）通过标准误区间来表示的。

· 方差分解：通过图形或表格显示在不同时间段，由于冲击值的变化而导致的每个变量的方差的百分比变化。

Ⅱ．如何估计 VAR 模型

假如我们想研究货币政策对国内生产总值的影响。是否加息会减少国内生产总值呢？我们采用 r_t 作为衡量利息率（货币政策）的变量，用 y_t 来衡量实际国内生产总值（GDP）的对数。

方法 1：单方程估计（例如 Romer & Romer[①]）：

$$y_t = \alpha_0 + \alpha(L) y_{t-1} + \beta(L) r_t + u_t$$

我们可以检验对于所有的 i，$\beta_i = 0$ 这一假设。但这个方法所带来的问题是，我们要假设没有 $y \rightarrow r$ 的反作用。但合理的推测往往是 $\uparrow r \rightarrow \downarrow y \rightarrow \downarrow r$。换句话说，真正的模式可能应该是：

$$y_t = \kappa_y + \alpha_y(L) y_{t-1} + \beta_y(L) r_t + u_{yt}$$
$$r_t = \kappa_r + \alpha_r(L) y_t + \beta_r(L) r_{t-1} + u_{rt}$$

方法 2：向量自回归模型（VAR 模型）。

我们简化上述方程组并把它们改写为：

$$y_t = \kappa_y + \alpha_{y1} y_{t-1} + \beta_{y0} r_t + \beta_{y1} r_{t-1} + u_{yt}$$
$$r_t = \kappa_r + \alpha_{r0} y_t + \alpha_{r1} y_{t-1} + \beta_{r1} r_{t-1} + u_{rt}$$

其中 $\mathrm{Var}(u_{yt}) = \sigma_y^2$，$\mathrm{Var}(u_{rt}) = \sigma_r^2$ 和 $\mathrm{Cov}(u_{yt}, u_{yt}) = 0$。

上述模型无法用 OLS 估计，因为在第一个方程式里，r_t 和 u_{yt} 相关，而且在第二个方程式里 y_t 和 u_{rt} 相关（由于 $u_{yt} \rightarrow y_t \rightarrow r_t$）。如果要估计这种模型，我们需要添加一些关于 r_t 和 y_t 是否同期相关的限制条件。最常用的方法是递归排序。例如，我们假设 $y_t \rightarrow r_t$，但是 $r_t \not\rightarrow y_t$，于是 $\beta_{y0} = 0$：

$$y_t = \kappa_y + \alpha_{y1} y_{t-1} + \beta_{y1} r_{t-1} + u_{yt}$$
$$r_t = \kappa_r + \alpha_{r0} y_t + \alpha_{r1} y_{t-1} + \beta_{r1} r_{t-1} + u_{rt}$$

当我们学习联立方程组模型时，我们知道，一般情况下，用 OLS 估计联立方程模型里的每个方程式并不是有效的。但有一个例外：如果每个方程式的等式右边的变量都是相同的，那么 OLS 估计是 BLUE。因此，如果我们能处理 $\alpha_{r0} y_t$ 这一项，那么估计会比较简单。我们可以通过替代实现这一目的：

$$y_t = \kappa_y + \alpha_{y1} y_{t-1} + \beta_{y1} r_{t-1} + u_{yt}$$
$$r_t = (\kappa_r + \alpha_{r0}\kappa_y) + (\alpha_{r1} + \alpha_{r0}\alpha_{y1}) y_{t-1} + (\beta_{r1} + \alpha_{r0}\beta_{y1}) r_{t-1} + (u_{rt} + \alpha_{r0} u_{yt})$$

或者：

---

① Romer, Christina D. and David H. Romer (1994), "Monetary Policy Matters", *Journal of Monetary Economics*, 34 (August): 75－88.

$$y_t = k_y + \alpha_{y1} y_{t-1} + b_{y1} r_{t-1} + v_{yt}$$
$$r_t = k_r + a_{r1} y_{t-1} + b_{r1} r_{t-1} + v_{rt}$$

该方程组可以用 OLS 对每个方程式逐一估计。我们可以使用估计值来恢复模型里的结构参数：

$$\kappa_y = k_y$$
$$\alpha_{y1} = \alpha_{y1}$$
$$\beta_{y1} = b_{y1}$$
$$k_r = \kappa_r + \alpha_{r0} \kappa_y$$
$$a_{r1} = \alpha_{r1} + \alpha_{r0} \alpha_{y1}$$
$$b_{r1} = \beta_{r1} + \alpha_{r0} \beta_{y1}$$

如果我们知道 α_{r0}（y 对 x 的同期影响），就可以求解 κ_r，a_{r1} 和 b_{r1}。可以根据残差的方差—协方差矩阵来求解：

$$v_{yt} = u_{yt}$$
$$v_{rt} = u_{rt} + \alpha_{r0} u_{yt}$$
$$\mathrm{Var}(v_{yt}) = \sigma_y^2$$
$$\mathrm{Var}(v_{rt}) = \sigma_r^2 + \alpha_{r0}^2 \sigma_y^2$$
$$\mathrm{Cov}(v_{yt}, v_{rt}) = \alpha_{r0} \sigma_y^2$$

这样我们有 3 个方程和 3 个未知数；求解这 3 个方程便可以得到 α_{r0}，然后可用该估计来求解 κ_r，a_{r1} 和 b_{r1}。

Ⅲ. 上机操作练习①

这个练习告诉我们如何得出 VAR 分析的结果。下面这些步骤是人为简单化的，使用的是 EViews 的点击菜单方法。

启动 EViews。

选择菜单选项“File/Open/Workfile”。

选择并上传 **var. wf1** 到 EViews。

这个数据文件中包含了 1965 年 1 月到 1995 年 12 月每月观测值的时间序列数据：

ftaprice＝富时全股价格指数

ftadiv＝富时全股红利指数

*r*20＝20 年政府债券的收益率

rs＝ 90 天国库券的收益率

lprice＝log(*ftaprice*)

ldiv＝log(*ftadiv*)

---

① 该练习基于 http：//people. few. eur. nl/smant/econometrics 的任务和论点进行了修改。

$dlprice = lprice - lprice(-1)$

$dldiv = ldiv - ldiv(-1)$

$dr20 = r20 - r20(-1)$

$drs = rs - rs(-1)$

（1）描述性统计分析。

选择 *lprice* 序列。选择“View/Graph/Line”。

观察到 *lprice* 是逐渐上移的时间序列，但是对数值是沿着直线移动的并且没有急剧扩展，*ftaprice* 也有同样的观测结果。

通过选择“View/Graph/Line”来对 *ldiv*，*r*20 和 *rs* 做相同检查。

（2）单位根检验。

前面已经讨论过在时间序列例子中如何做单位根检验。我们对 VAR 模型做这个检验，通常使用水平变量或者一阶差分变量。

检验 *ldive*，*lprice*，*r*20 和 *rs* 是否平稳。

检验 *dldiv*，*dlprice*，*dr*20 和 *drs* 是否为平稳变量。

（3）估计 VAR 模型。

首先选择我们要分析的序列。在这里我们选择 *dldiv*，*dlprice*，*dr*20 和 *drs*。

按住“CTRL”键并左击这些变量。

在“Workfile”窗口中选择“Objects/New Object/Group”。（注意，如果需要存储结果，可以另取名。）

在“Group”窗口中选择“Procs/Make Vector Autoregression”。

选择“Unrestricted VAR”，样本范围设置为“1965：01 1995：12”。

（4）滞后长度的选择标准。

在“VAR”窗口中选择“View/Lag Structure/Lag length criteria”，最大滞后长度为 12。

（注意：你会发现模型选择标准：对数似然，AIC，SIC，HQ。VAR 的估计时间段只取决于你想考虑的最大滞后数量，因为对所有模型都选择相同的估计时间段。只要决定了最优滞后数量，估计时间段会根据选择的滞后数量而改变。）

滞后长度标准建议选择带有一个或两个滞后的模型。

在“VAR”窗口中选择“Estimate”，然后选择“Lag”间隔为“11”。

然后重复以上步骤，并选择“Lag”间隔为“12”。

检验残差相关性。根据传统的方法，在 VAR 模型中使用平稳变量时 VAR 方程的残差没有相关性。（如果你使用存在长期、水平形式的 VAR 模型，并且不担心 I(1) 变量，残差相关性的检验就不是那么重要。）

在“VAR”窗口中选择“View/Residual Tests/Portmanteau Autocorrelation Test/Lags 12”。

综合以上各种标准，我们选择有两个滞后的 VAR 模型。在 VAR 窗口中选择“Stats”来查看最终的 VAR 估计结果。注意 VAR 模型已经有两个滞后。

（5）残差的相关矩阵。

在“VAR”窗口中选择“View/Residual Tests/Correlograms”。选择“Tabulated by variable”和“Lags 0”。

（注意：关联矩阵可以用来判断递归 VAR 模型里的顺序（Cholesky 分解）是否可能影响结果。对脉冲响应和方差分解操作来说，VAR 方程的残差必须正交化。）

（6）脉冲响应函数（IRF）。

脉冲响应函数追踪内生变量对其他变量的冲击影响。

在“VAR”窗口中选择“Impulse”（或者“View/Impulse Response…”）。在“Impulse Definition”下，选择“Cholesky-dof adjusted”和“Cholesky Ordering dldiv dlprice dr20 drs”。在“Display”下，选择“Multiple Graphs”，“Response standard errors-Monte Carlo”和“periods 10”（你可以选择更多时间段，但是在这个例子中并不考虑）。

注意：我们可以更改变量的顺序，这会改变 VAR 冲击的识别格式并且影响脉冲响应和方差分解。EViews 允许我们选择表格或图像作为计算的方式。后者通常对 IRF 更有效，表格通常对 FEDV 更好。

（7）预测误差项的方差分解（FEDV）。

方差分解可以将内生变量的变化分解为 VAR 的成分冲击。因此，方差分解提供了关于每个影响 VAR 中变量的随机新息的相对重要性。

在“VAR”窗口中选择“View/Variance Decomposition…”。选择“Multiple Graphs”，“Standard errors-None”，“Periods 10”。

我们也可以将结果以表格形式展示出来。

（8）预测。

用 VAR 模型来预测或模拟，我们必须将估计等式转化成一个可以在 EViews 模型操作中使用的模型（一系列方程）。EViews 使我们非常容易地创建这个模型。

在“Workfile”窗口中选择“Procs/Structure/Resize Current Page”。将截止日期设为“2000:12”。

在“VAR”窗口中选择“Procs/Make Model/Solve”。将样本设为“1996:01 2000:12”。

我们可以看到预测的结果显示在“Workfile”窗口中，因为这里有新创建的命名为 **name _ 0** 的变量。这些变量包含了 VAR 变量的模拟或预测值。

我们可以通过在“Model”窗口中选择“Procs/Make Graph”，然后选择“Endogenous variables”，“series grouping Each series in its own graph”来创建图像。在命令窗口中将样本时间段设为“1995:01 1996:12”。我们也可以选择“variables _ 0”并且打开一个新的“EViews Object/Group”窗口。

Chapter 15

Vector Autoregression (VAR)

Ⅰ. How to Develop a VAR Model

Large-scale simultaneous equation models, sometimes containing several hundred equations, can be developed to help forecast key variables in the economy. However, these models are open to a variety of attacks. For instance, the parameters in these models might themselves be dependent on the state of economic policy and would change when the policy changes. Thus, the theory underlying the specification of the equations could be challenged. This concern leads to an alternative approach for forecasting the macroeconomy: the vector autoregression model (VAR), which is able to make minimal assumptions about the structure underlying the model.

A VAR model generally takes the following form:

$$y_{1t} = \alpha_{01} + \sum_{j=1}^{m} \beta_{11j} y_{1(t-j)} + \sum_{j=1}^{m} \beta_{12j} y_{2(t-j)} + \cdots + \sum_{j=1}^{m} \beta_{1rj} y_{n(t-j)} + \cdots + \sum_{j=1}^{l} \gamma_{11j} z_{1(t-j)} + \cdots + \sum_{j=1}^{l} \gamma_{1rj} z_{r(t-j)} + \varepsilon_{1t}$$

$$\cdots$$

$$y_{nt} = \alpha_{0n} + \sum_{j=1}^{m} \beta_{n1j} y_{1(t-j)} + \sum_{j=1}^{m} \beta_{n2j} y_{2(t-j)} + \cdots + \sum_{j=1}^{m} \beta_{nrj} y_{n(t-j)} + \cdots + \sum_{j=1}^{l} \gamma_{n1j} z_{1(t-j)} + \cdots + \sum_{j=1}^{l} \gamma_{nrj} z_{r(t-j)} + \varepsilon_{nt}$$

In the model, we can allow for an arbitrary set of lags for each variable. Although we can include as many lags as desired, the degrees of freedom fall as additional variables are included.

Usually, we are interested in obtaining two main pieces of output from VARs:

- Impulse response functions: graphs of estimated dynamic response of each variable to a one standard deviation change in each structural shock. Usually (not always) shown with standard error bands.

• Variance decompositions: graphs or tables showing percentage of the variance of each variable due to variance in each shock, at different horizons.

Ⅱ. How to Estimate a VAR Model

Suppose we're interested in the effect of monetary policy on GDP. Does an increase in interest rates reduce output? Use r_t for interest rate (monetary policy) variable, log real GDP (y_t) for output.

Method 1: single-equation estimation (e. g. Romer & Romer①):

$$y_t = \alpha_0 + \alpha(L) y_{t-1} + \beta(L) r_t + u_t$$

We can test the hypothesis $\beta_i = 0$, for all i. The problem with this method is that we're assuming there's no feedback from $y \rightarrow r$. But it's reasonable to assume that $\uparrow r \rightarrow \downarrow y \rightarrow \downarrow r$. In other words, the true model may be:

$$y_t = \kappa_y + \alpha_y(L) y_{t-1} + \beta_y(L) r_t + u_{yt}$$
$$r_t = \kappa_r + \alpha_r(L) y_t + \beta_r(L) r_{t-1} + u_{rt}$$

Method 2: vector autoregressions (VARs).

Let us simplify the above equations and rewrite them a bit:

$$y_t = \kappa_y + \alpha_{y1} y_{t-1} + \beta_{y0} r_t + \beta_{y1} r_{t-1} + u_{yt}$$
$$r_t = \kappa_r + \alpha_{r0} y_t + \alpha_{r1} y_{t-1} + \beta_{r1} r_{t-1} + u_{rt}$$

where $\mathrm{Var}(u_{yt}) = \sigma_y^2$, $\mathrm{Var}(u_{rt}) = \sigma_r^2$, and $\mathrm{Cov}(u_{yt}, u_{yt}) = 0$.

The model above cannot be estimated by OLS because in the first equation, r_t is correlated with u_{yt}, and in the second equation y_t is correlated with u_{rt} (since e. g. $u_{yt} \rightarrow y_t \rightarrow r_t$). To estimate this, we need to impose some restrictions on how r_t and y_t interact contemporaneously. The most common approach is recursive ordering. Assume $y_t \rightarrow r_t$, but not $r_t \rightarrow y_t$. So $\beta_{y0} = 0$:

$$y_t = \kappa_y + \alpha_{y1} y_{t-1} + \beta_{y1} r_{t-1} + u_{yt}$$
$$r_t = \kappa_r + \alpha_{r0} y_t + \alpha_{r1} y_{t-1} + \beta_{r1} r_{t-1} + u_{rt}$$

When we study simultaneous equations models, we have learned that, in general, equation-by-equation OLS is at best inefficient in simultaneous equations models. But there's one exception: when the right-hand-side variables in each equation are identical,

① Romer, Christina D. and David H. Romer (1994), "Monetary Policy Matters", *Journal of Monetary Economics*, 34 (August): 75—88.

equation-by-equation OLS estimators are BLUE. So estimation is simpler if we get rid of the $\alpha_{r0} y_t$ term. Do this by substitution:

$$y_t = \kappa_y + \alpha_{y1} y_{t-1} + \beta_{y1} r_{t-1} + u_{yt}$$
$$r_t = (\kappa_r + \alpha_{r0}\kappa_y) + (\alpha_{r1} + \alpha_{r0}\alpha_{y1}) y_{t-1} + (\beta_{r1} + \alpha_{r0}\beta_{y1}) r_{t-1} + (u_{rt} + \alpha_{r0} u_{yt})$$

or

$$y_t = k_y + a_{y1} y_{t-1} + b_{y1} r_{t-1} + v_{yt}$$
$$r_t = k_r + a_{r1} y_{t-1} + b_{r1} r_{t-1} + v_{rt}$$

This system can now be estimated by equation-by-equation OLS. We can use estimates to uncover the structural parameters above:

$$\kappa_y = k_y$$
$$\alpha_{y1} = a_{y1}$$
$$\beta_{y1} = b_{y1}$$
$$k_r = \kappa_r + \alpha_{r0}\kappa_y$$
$$a_{r1} = \alpha_{r1} + \alpha_{r0}\alpha_{y1}$$
$$b_{r1} = \beta_{r1} + \alpha_{r0}\beta_{y1}$$

If we knew α_{r0} (contemporaneous effect of y on r), we could solve for κ_r, a_{r1}, and b_{r1}. We can get this from the variance-covariance matrix of residuals:

$$v_{yt} = u_{yt}$$
$$v_{rt} = u_{rt} + \alpha_{r0} u_{yt}$$
$$\mathrm{Var}(v_{yt}) = \sigma_y^2$$
$$\mathrm{Var}(v_{rt}) = \sigma_r^2 + \alpha_{r0}^2 \sigma_y^2$$
$$\mathrm{Cov}(v_{yt}, v_{rt}) = \alpha_{r0}\sigma_y^2$$

These are 3 equations and 3 unknowns; solve them to find α_{r0}, then use that estimate to solve for κ_r, a_{r1}, and b_{r1}.

Ⅲ. Computer Exercise①

This exercise shows us how to create the results for the VAR analysis. The following steps are deliberately kept easy, using the EViews point-and-click approach.

Start EViews.

Select Menu options "File/Open/Workfile".

---

① This exercise is modified, based on the assignments and thesis from http://people.few.eur.nl/smant/econometrics.

Select and upload the existing workfile① **var. wf1** onto EViews.

The workfile contains the time series data with monthly observations from January 1965 to December 1995:

ftaprice=the FT-All Share price index

ftadiv=the FT-All Share dividend index

*r*20=the yield on 20-year government bonds

rs=the rate on 90-day treasury bills

lprice=log(*ftaprice*)

ldiv=log(*ftadiv*)

dlprice=*lprice*−*lprice*(−1)

dldiv=*ldiv*−*ldiv*(−1)

*dr*20=*r*20−*r*20(−1)

drs=*rs*−*rs*(−1)

(1) Descriptive Statistics.

Select series *lprice*. Select "View/Graph/Line".

Observe that *lprice* is a gradually upward moving time series, but the log values appear to move along a straight line and not explode, as did the series *ftaprice*.

Do the same check-up for *ldiv*, *r*20, and *rs* by selecting "View/Graph/Line".

(2) Unit Root Tests.

We have already discussed how to perform unit root tests in the time series example. We normally perform these tests to decide on a VAR model in levels or first-differences of the variables.

Check whether *ldive*, *lprice*, *r*20, and *rs* are stationary.

Check whether *dldiv*, *dlprice*, *dr*20, and *drs* are stationary variables.

(3) Estimate the VAR Model.

First select the series we wish to analyze. Here we look at the series *dldiv*, *dlprice*, *dr*20, and *drs*.

Hold "CTRL" and left-click on the variables.

Select "Workfile" window "Objects/New Object/Group". (Note that you can provide a name for the group if you need to save your results.)

Select "Group" window "Procs/Make Vector Autoregression".

Select "Unrestricted VAR", sample "1965: 01 1995: 12".

(4) Lag length selection criteria.

Select "VAR" window "View/Lag Structure/Lag length criteria", max lags "12".

(Note: you will find the model selection criteria log-likelihood, AIC, SIC, HQ. The estimation period of the VARs in this option just depends on the maximum number of lags you want to consider because we choose the same estimation period for all the models con-

① Data is collected from http: //people. few. eur. nl/smant/econometrics/exerc/fta. wf1.

sidered. Once you have decided the optimal number of lags, the estimation period changes according to the selected lag number.)

The lag length criteria suggest a model with either 1 or 2 lags.

Select "VAR" window "Estimate". Select "Lag" intervals "11".

Repeat for VAR model with "Lag" intervals "12".

Check for residual correlation. According to the traditional approach, using stationary variables in the VAR model, residuals of the VAR equations do not exhibit residual correlation. (If you use the VAR in its long run, levels form, and do not worry about I(1) variables, the test on residual correlation is considered less important.)

Select "VAR" window "View/Residual Tests/Portmanteau Autocorrelation Test/Lags 12".

Combining the above criterions, we select a VAR model with 2 lags. View the final VAR estimation results by selecting VAR window "Stats". Please note that the VAR model is already in its 2 lag form.

(5) Residual correlation matrix.

Select "VAR" window "View/Residual Tests/Correlograms". Select "Tabulated by variable" and "Lags 0".

(Note: the correlation matrix is useful to determine whether the ordering in the recursive VAR method (Cholesky decomposition) is likely to influence results. For the impulse response and variance decomposition operations, the residuals of the VAR equations must be orthogonalized.)

(6) Impulse response functions (IRF).

Impulse response functions trace the effects of a shock to one endogenous variable on the other variables in the VAR.

Select "VAR" window "Impulse" (or "View/Impulse Response ... "). Under "Impulse Definition", select "Cholesky-dof adjusted" and "Cholesky Ordering dldiv dlprice dr20 drs". Under "Display" select "Multiple Graphs", "Response standard errors-Monte Carlo", and "periods 10" (you can select more periods, but the results are not interesting in this case).

Note that we can modify the order of the variables, which changes the identification scheme of the VAR shocks and affects the impulse responses and variance decompositions. EViews allows us to choose the format of the calculations as tabular or graph. The latter is usually better for IRF while tabular is often preferred for FEDV, as discussed below.

(7) Forecast error decomposition of variances (FEDV).

Variance decomposition is able to separate the variation in an endogenous variable into the component shocks to the VAR. Thus, the variance decomposition provides information about the relative importance of each random innovation in affecting the variables in the VAR.

Select "VAR" window "View/Variance Decomposition ...", Select "Multiple Graphs", "Standard errors-None", "Periods 10".

If we want, we can produce the output as tables rather than graphs.

(8) Forecasts.

To work with the estimated VAR model in forecasts and simulations, we have to transform the estimated equations into a model (a set of equations) to be used in EViews model operations. EViews allows us to make this model very easily.

Select "Workfile" window "Procs/Structure/Resize Current Page". Set end date to "2000:12".

Select "VAR" window "Procs/Make Model/Solve". Set solution sample to "1996:01 2000:12".

We can see the results of the forecast appearing in the "Workfile" window because there are new variables being generated called **name _ 0**. These variables contain the simulated, or forecasted in this case, values of the VAR variables.

We can produce the graphs by selecting "Model" window "Procs/Make Graph" and selecting "Endogenous variables", "series grouping Each series in its own graph", for the Baseline scenario (the variables referred to as _ 0). Set the sample period to "1995:01 1996:12" in the command window. We can also select the "variables _ 0" and make a new "EViews Object/Group" window.

Appendix（附录）

Table 1：Standard Normal（Z）Table Area between 0 and z

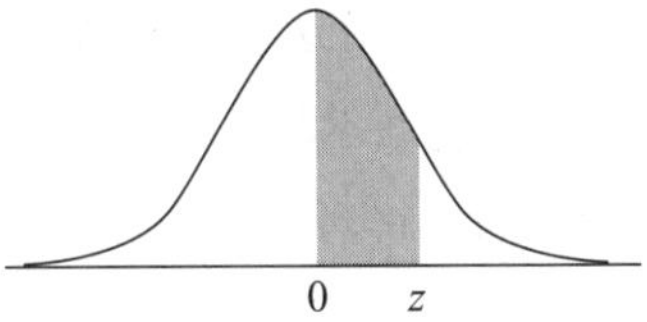

	0	0.01	0.02	0.03	0.04	0.05	0.06	0.07	0.08	0.09
0	0	0.004	0.008	0.012	0.016	0.0199	0.0239	0.0279	0.0319	0.0359
0.1	0.0398	0.0438	0.0478	0.0517	0.0557	0.0596	0.0636	0.0675	0.0714	0.0753
0.2	0.0793	0.0832	0.0871	0.091	0.0948	0.0987	0.1026	0.1064	0.1103	0.1141
0.3	0.1179	0.1217	0.1255	0.1293	0.1331	0.1368	0.1406	0.1443	0.148	0.1517
0.4	0.1554	0.1591	0.1628	0.1664	0.17	0.1736	0.1772	0.1808	0.1844	0.1879
0.5	0.1915	0.195	0.1985	0.2019	0.2054	0.2088	0.2123	0.2157	0.219	0.2224
0.6	0.2257	0.2291	0.2324	0.2357	0.2389	0.2422	0.2454	0.2486	0.2517	0.2549
0.7	0.258	0.2611	0.2642	0.2673	0.2704	0.2734	0.2764	0.2794	0.2823	0.2852
0.8	0.2881	0.291	0.2939	0.2967	0.2995	0.3023	0.3051	0.3078	0.3106	0.3133
0.9	0.3159	0.3186	0.3212	0.3238	0.3264	0.3289	0.3315	0.334	0.3365	0.3389
1.0	0.3413	0.3438	0.3461	0.3485	0.3508	0.3531	0.3554	0.3577	0.3599	0.3621
1.1	0.3643	0.3665	0.3686	0.3708	0.3729	0.3749	0.377	0.379	0.381	0.383
1.2	0.3849	0.3869	0.3888	0.3907	0.3925	0.3944	0.3962	0.398	0.3997	0.4015
1.3	0.4032	0.4049	0.4066	0.4082	0.4099	0.4115	0.4131	0.4147	0.4162	0.4177

1.4	0.4192	0.4207	0.4222	0.4236	0.4251	0.4265	0.4279	0.4292	0.4306	0.4319
1.5	0.4332	0.4345	0.4357	0.437	0.4382	0.4394	0.4406	0.4418	0.4429	0.4441
1.6	0.4452	0.4463	0.4474	0.4484	0.4495	0.4505	0.4515	0.4525	0.4535	0.4545
1.7	0.4554	0.4564	0.4573	0.4582	0.4591	0.4599	0.4608	0.4616	0.4625	0.4633
1.8	0.4641	0.4649	0.4656	0.4664	0.4671	0.4678	0.4686	0.4693	0.4699	0.4706
1.9	0.4713	0.4719	0.4726	0.4732	0.4738	0.4744	0.475	0.4756	0.4761	0.4767
2.0	0.4772	0.4778	0.4783	0.4788	0.4793	0.4798	0.4803	0.4808	0.4812	0.4817
2.1	0.4821	0.4826	0.483	0.4834	0.4838	0.4842	0.4846	0.485	0.4854	0.4857
2.2	0.4861	0.4864	0.4868	0.4871	0.4875	0.4878	0.4881	0.4884	0.4887	0.489
2.3	0.4893	0.4896	0.4898	0.4901	0.4904	0.4906	0.4909	0.4911	0.4913	0.4916
2.4	0.4918	0.492	0.4922	0.4925	0.4927	0.4929	0.4931	0.4932	0.4934	0.4936
2.5	0.4938	0.494	0.4941	0.4943	0.4945	0.4946	0.4948	0.4949	0.4951	0.4952
2.6	0.4953	0.4955	0.4956	0.4957	0.4959	0.496	0.4961	0.4962	0.4963	0.4964
2.7	0.4965	0.4966	0.4967	0.4968	0.4969	0.497	0.4971	0.4972	0.4973	0.4974
2.8	0.4974	0.4975	0.4976	0.4977	0.4977	0.4978	0.4979	0.4979	0.498	0.4981
2.9	0.4981	0.4982	0.4982	0.4983	0.4984	0.4984	0.4985	0.4985	0.4986	0.4986
3.0	0.4987	0.4987	0.4987	0.4988	0.4988	0.4989	0.4989	0.4989	0.499	0.499

Table 2: *t* table with right tail probabilities

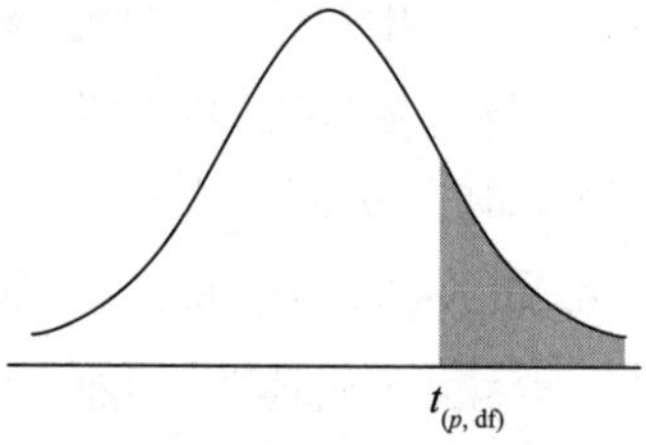

df \ p	0.4	0.25	0.1	0.05	0.025	0.01	0.005	0.0005
1	0.32492	1	3.077684	6.313752	12.7062	31.82052	63.65674	636.6192
2	0.288675	0.816497	1.885618	2.919986	4.30265	6.96456	9.92484	31.5991
3	0.276671	0.764892	1.637744	2.353363	3.18245	4.5407	5.84091	12.924
4	0.270722	0.740697	1.533206	2.131847	2.77645	3.74695	4.60409	8.6103
5	0.267181	0.726687	1.475884	2.015048	2.57058	3.36493	4.03214	6.8688

6	0.264835	0.717558	1.439756	1.94318	2.44691	3.14267	3.70743	5.9588
7	0.263167	0.711142	1.414924	1.894579	2.36462	2.99795	3.49948	5.4079
8	0.261921	0.706387	1.396815	1.859548	2.306	2.89646	3.35539	5.0413
9	0.260955	0.702722	1.383029	1.833113	2.26216	2.82144	3.24984	4.7809
10	0.260185	0.699812	1.372184	1.812461	2.22814	2.76377	3.16927	4.5869
11	0.259556	0.697445	1.36343	1.795885	2.20099	2.71808	3.10581	4.437
12	0.259033	0.695483	1.356217	1.782288	2.17881	2.681	3.05454	4.3178
13	0.258591	0.693829	1.350171	1.770933	2.16037	2.65031	3.01228	4.2208
14	0.258213	0.692417	1.34503	1.76131	2.14479	2.62449	2.97684	4.1405
15	0.257885	0.691197	1.340606	1.75305	2.13145	2.60248	2.94671	4.0728
16	0.257599	0.690132	1.336757	1.745884	2.11991	2.58349	2.92078	4.015
17	0.257347	0.689195	1.333379	1.739607	2.10982	2.56693	2.89823	3.9651
18	0.257123	0.688364	1.330391	1.734064	2.10092	2.55238	2.87844	3.9216
19	0.256923	0.687621	1.327728	1.729133	2.09302	2.53948	2.86093	3.8834
20	0.256743	0.686954	1.325341	1.724718	2.08596	2.52798	2.84534	3.8495
21	0.25658	0.686352	1.323188	1.720743	2.07961	2.51765	2.83136	3.8193
22	0.256432	0.685805	1.321237	1.717144	2.07387	2.50832	2.81876	3.7921
23	0.256297	0.685306	1.31946	1.713872	2.06866	2.49987	2.80734	3.7676
24	0.256173	0.68485	1.317836	1.710882	2.0639	2.49216	2.79694	3.7454
25	0.25606	0.68443	1.316345	1.708141	2.05954	2.48511	2.78744	3.7251
26	0.255955	0.684043	1.314972	1.705618	2.05553	2.47863	2.77871	3.7066
27	0.255858	0.683685	1.313703	1.703288	2.05183	2.47266	2.77068	3.6896
28	0.255768	0.683353	1.312527	1.701131	2.04841	2.46714	2.76326	3.6739
29	0.255684	0.683044	1.311434	1.699127	2.04523	2.46202	2.75639	3.6594
30	0.255605	0.682756	1.310415	1.697261	2.04227	2.45726	2.75	3.646
inf	0.253347	0.67449	1.281552	1.644854	1.95996	2.32635	2.57583	3.2905

Table 3: Right tail area for the Chi-square Distribution

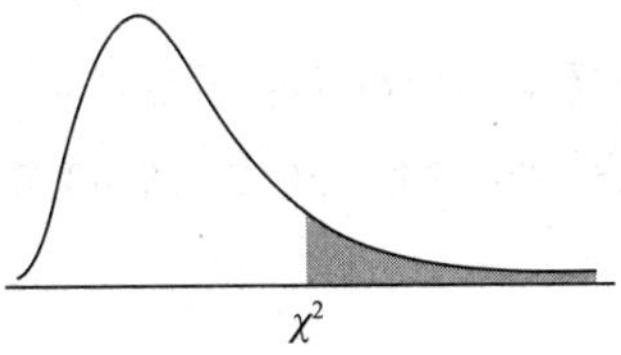

df \ area	0.99	0.975	0.95	0.9	0.1	0.05	0.025	0.01	0.005
1	0.00016	0.00098	0.00393	0.01579	2.70554	3.84146	5.02389	6.6349	7.87944
2	0.0201	0.05064	0.10259	0.21072	4.60517	5.99146	7.37776	9.21034	10.59663
3	0.11483	0.2158	0.35185	0.58437	6.25139	7.81473	9.3484	11.34487	12.83816
4	0.29711	0.48442	0.71072	1.06362	7.77944	9.48773	11.14329	13.2767	14.86026
5	0.5543	0.83121	1.14548	1.61031	9.23636	11.0705	12.8325	15.08627	16.7496
6	0.87209	1.23734	1.63538	2.20413	10.64464	12.59159	14.44938	16.81189	18.54758
7	1.23904	1.68987	2.16735	2.83311	12.01704	14.06714	16.01276	18.47531	20.27774
8	1.6465	2.17973	2.73264	3.48954	13.36157	15.50731	17.53455	20.09024	21.95495
9	2.0879	2.70039	3.32511	4.16816	14.68366	16.91898	19.02277	21.66599	23.58935
10	2.55821	3.24697	3.9403	4.86518	15.98718	18.30704	20.48318	23.20925	25.18818
11	3.05348	3.81575	4.57481	5.57778	17.27501	19.67514	21.92005	24.72497	26.75685
12	3.57057	4.40379	5.22603	6.3038	18.54935	21.02607	23.33666	26.21697	28.29952
13	4.10692	5.00875	5.89186	7.0415	19.81193	22.36203	24.7356	27.68825	29.81947
14	4.66043	5.62873	6.57063	7.78953	21.06414	23.68479	26.11895	29.14124	31.31935
15	5.22935	6.26214	7.26094	8.54676	22.30713	24.99579	27.48839	30.57791	32.80132
16	5.81221	6.90766	7.96165	9.31224	23.54183	26.29623	28.84535	31.99993	34.26719
17	6.40776	7.56419	8.67176	10.08519	24.76904	27.58711	30.19101	33.40866	35.71847
18	7.01491	8.23075	9.39046	10.86494	25.98942	28.8693	31.52638	34.80531	37.15645
19	7.63273	8.90652	10.11701	11.65091	27.20357	30.14353	32.85233	36.19087	38.58226
20	8.2604	9.59078	10.85081	12.44261	28.41198	31.41043	34.16961	37.56623	39.99685
21	8.8972	10.2829	11.59131	13.2396	29.61509	32.67057	35.47888	38.93217	41.40106
22	9.54249	10.98232	12.33801	14.04149	30.81328	33.92444	36.78071	40.28936	42.79565
23	10.19572	11.68855	13.09051	14.84796	32.0069	35.17246	38.07563	41.6384	44.18128
24	10.85636	12.40115	13.84843	15.65868	33.19624	36.41503	39.36408	42.97982	45.55851
25	11.52398	13.11972	14.61141	16.47341	34.38159	37.65248	40.64647	44.3141	46.92789
26	12.19815	13.8439	15.37916	17.29188	35.56317	38.88514	41.92317	45.64168	48.28988
27	12.8785	14.57338	16.1514	18.1139	36.74122	40.11327	43.19451	46.96294	49.64492
28	13.56471	15.30786	16.92788	18.93924	37.91592	41.33714	44.46079	48.27824	50.99338
29	14.25645	16.04707	17.70837	19.76774	39.08747	42.55697	45.72229	49.58788	52.33562
30	14.95346	16.79077	18.49266	20.59923	40.25602	43.77297	46.97924	50.89218	53.67196

Table 4a: *F* Table for alpha=0.10

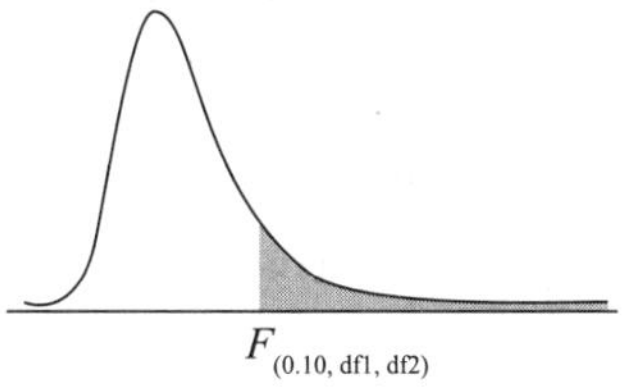

df2/df1	1	2	3	4	5	6	7	8	9	10	30	60	120	inf
1	39.9	49.5	53.6	55.8	57.2	58.2	58.9	59.4	59.9	60.2	62.3	62.8	63.1	63.3
2	8.53	9	9.16	9.24	9.29	9.33	9.35	9.37	9.38	9.39	9.46	9.47	9.48	9.49
3	5.54	5.46	5.39	5.34	5.31	5.28	5.27	5.25	5.24	5.23	5.17	5.15	5.14	5.13
4	4.54	4.32	4.19	4.11	4.05	4.01	3.98	3.95	3.94	3.92	3.82	3.79	3.78	3.76
5	4.06	3.78	3.62	3.52	3.45	3.4	3.37	3.34	3.32	3.3	3.17	3.14	3.12	3.11
6	3.78	3.46	3.29	3.18	3.11	3.05	3.01	2.98	2.96	2.94	2.8	2.76	2.74	2.72
7	3.59	3.26	3.07	2.96	2.88	2.83	2.78	2.75	2.72	2.7	2.56	2.51	2.49	2.47
8	3.46	3.11	2.92	2.81	2.73	2.67	2.62	2.59	2.56	2.54	2.38	2.34	2.32	2.29
9	3.36	3.01	2.81	2.69	2.61	2.55	2.51	2.47	2.44	2.42	2.25	2.21	2.18	2.16
10	3.29	2.92	2.73	2.61	2.52	2.46	2.41	2.38	2.35	2.32	2.16	2.11	2.08	2.06
11	3.23	2.86	2.66	2.54	2.45	2.39	2.34	2.3	2.27	2.25	2.08	2.03	2	1.97
12	3.18	2.81	2.61	2.48	2.39	2.33	2.28	2.24	2.21	2.19	2.01	1.96	1.93	1.9
13	3.14	2.76	2.56	2.43	2.35	2.28	2.23	2.2	2.16	2.14	1.96	1.9	1.88	1.85
14	3.1	2.73	2.52	2.39	2.31	2.24	2.19	2.15	2.12	2.1	1.91	1.86	1.83	1.8
15	3.07	2.7	2.49	2.36	2.27	2.21	2.16	2.12	2.09	2.06	1.87	1.82	1.79	1.76
16	3.05	2.67	2.46	2.33	2.24	2.18	2.13	2.09	2.06	2.03	1.84	1.78	1.75	1.72
17	3.03	2.64	2.44	2.31	2.22	2.15	2.1	2.06	2.03	2	1.81	1.75	1.72	1.69
18	3.01	2.62	2.42	2.29	2.2	2.13	2.08	2.04	2	1.98	1.78	1.72	1.69	1.66
19	2.99	2.61	2.4	2.27	2.18	2.11	2.06	2.02	1.98	1.96	1.76	1.7	1.67	1.63
20	2.97	2.59	2.38	2.25	2.16	2.09	2.04	2	1.96	1.94	1.74	1.68	1.64	1.61
21	2.96	2.57	2.36	2.23	2.14	2.08	2.02	1.98	1.95	1.92	1.72	1.66	1.62	1.59
22	2.95	2.56	2.35	2.22	2.13	2.06	2.01	1.97	1.93	1.9	1.7	1.64	1.6	1.57
23	2.94	2.55	2.34	2.21	2.11	2.05	1.99	1.95	1.92	1.89	1.69	1.62	1.59	1.55
24	2.93	2.54	2.33	2.19	2.1	2.04	1.98	1.94	1.91	1.88	1.67	1.61	1.57	1.53

25	2.92	2.53	2.32	2.18	2.09	2.02	1.97	1.93	1.89	1.87	1.66	1.59	1.56	1.52
26	2.91	2.52	2.31	2.17	2.08	2.01	1.96	1.92	1.88	1.86	1.65	1.58	1.54	1.5
27	2.9	2.51	2.3	2.17	2.07	2	1.95	1.91	1.87	1.85	1.64	1.57	1.53	1.49
28	2.89	2.5	2.29	2.16	2.06	2	1.94	1.9	1.87	1.84	1.63	1.56	1.52	1.48
29	2.89	2.5	2.28	2.15	2.06	1.99	1.93	1.89	1.86	1.83	1.62	1.55	1.51	1.47
30	2.88	2.49	2.28	2.14	2.05	1.98	1.93	1.88	1.85	1.82	1.61	1.54	1.5	1.46
40	2.84	2.44	2.23	2.09	2	1.93	1.87	1.83	1.79	1.76	1.54	1.47	1.42	1.38
60	2.79	2.39	2.18	2.04	1.95	1.87	1.82	1.77	1.74	1.71	1.48	1.4	1.35	1.29
120	2.75	2.35	2.13	1.99	1.9	1.82	1.77	1.72	1.68	1.65	1.41	1.32	1.26	1.19
inf	2.71	2.3	2.08	1.94	1.85	1.77	1.72	1.67	1.63	1.6	1.34	1.24	1.17	1

Table 4b: *F* Table for alpha=0.05

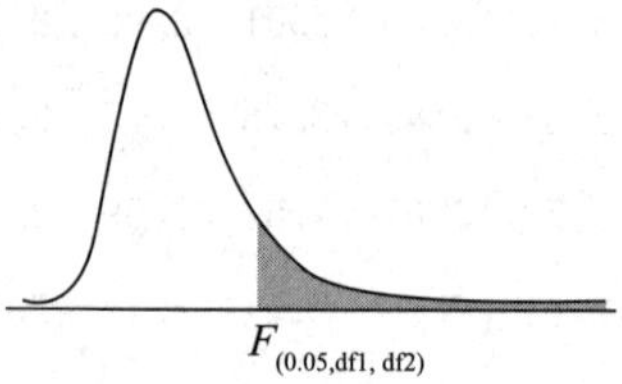

df2/df1	1	2	3	4	5	6	7	8	9	10	30	60	120	inf
1	161	200	216	225	230	234	237	239	241	242	250	252	253	254
2	18.5	19	19.2	19.2	19.3	19.3	19.4	19.4	19.4	19.4	19.5	19.5	19.5	19.5
3	10.1	9.55	9.28	9.12	9.01	8.94	8.89	8.85	8.81	8.79	8.62	8.57	8.55	8.53
4	7.71	6.94	6.59	6.39	6.26	6.16	6.09	6.04	6	5.96	5.75	5.69	5.66	5.63
5	6.61	5.79	5.41	5.19	5.05	4.95	4.88	4.82	4.77	4.74	4.5	4.43	4.4	4.37
6	5.99	5.14	4.76	4.53	4.39	4.28	4.21	4.15	4.1	4.06	3.81	3.74	3.7	3.67
7	5.59	4.74	4.35	4.12	3.97	3.87	3.79	3.73	3.68	3.64	3.38	3.3	3.27	3.23
8	5.32	4.46	4.07	3.84	3.69	3.58	3.5	3.44	3.39	3.35	3.08	3.01	2.97	2.93
9	5.12	4.26	3.86	3.63	3.48	3.37	3.29	3.23	3.18	3.14	2.86	2.79	2.75	2.71
10	4.96	4.1	3.71	3.48	3.33	3.22	3.14	3.07	3.02	2.98	2.7	2.62	2.58	2.54
11	4.84	3.98	3.59	3.36	3.2	3.09	3.01	2.95	2.9	2.85	2.57	2.49	2.45	2.4
12	4.75	3.89	3.49	3.26	3.11	3	2.91	2.85	2.8	2.75	2.47	2.38	2.34	2.3
13	4.67	3.81	3.41	3.18	3.03	2.92	2.83	2.77	2.71	2.67	2.38	2.3	2.25	2.21

14	4.6	3.74	3.34	3.11	2.96	2.85	2.76	2.7	2.65	2.6	2.31	2.22	2.18	2.13
15	4.54	3.68	3.29	3.06	2.9	2.79	2.71	2.64	2.59	2.54	2.25	2.16	2.11	2.07
16	4.49	3.63	3.24	3.01	2.85	2.74	2.66	2.59	2.54	2.49	2.19	2.11	2.06	2.01
17	4.45	3.59	3.2	2.96	2.81	2.7	2.61	2.55	2.49	2.45	2.15	2.06	2.01	1.96
18	4.41	3.55	3.16	2.93	2.77	2.66	2.58	2.51	2.46	2.41	2.11	2.02	1.97	1.92
19	4.38	3.52	3.13	2.9	2.74	2.63	2.54	2.48	2.42	2.38	2.07	1.98	1.93	1.88
20	4.35	3.49	3.1	2.87	2.71	2.6	2.51	2.45	2.39	2.35	2.04	1.95	1.9	1.84
21	4.32	3.47	3.07	2.84	2.68	2.57	2.49	2.42	2.37	2.32	2.01	1.92	1.87	1.81
22	4.3	3.44	3.05	2.82	2.66	2.55	2.46	2.4	2.34	2.3	1.98	1.89	1.84	1.78
23	4.28	3.42	3.03	2.8	2.64	2.53	2.44	2.37	2.32	2.27	1.96	1.86	1.81	1.76
24	4.26	3.4	3.01	2.78	2.62	2.51	2.42	2.36	2.3	2.25	1.94	1.84	1.79	1.73
25	4.24	3.39	2.99	2.76	2.6	2.49	2.4	2.34	2.28	2.24	1.92	1.82	1.77	1.71
26	4.23	3.37	2.98	2.74	2.59	2.47	2.39	2.32	2.27	2.22	1.9	1.8	1.75	1.69
27	4.21	3.35	2.96	2.73	2.57	2.46	2.37	2.31	2.25	2.2	1.88	1.79	1.73	1.67
28	4.2	3.34	2.95	2.71	2.56	2.45	2.36	2.29	2.24	2.19	1.87	1.77	1.71	1.65
29	4.18	3.33	2.93	2.7	2.55	2.43	2.35	2.28	2.22	2.18	1.85	1.75	1.7	1.64
30	4.17	3.32	2.92	2.69	2.53	2.42	2.33	2.27	2.21	2.16	1.84	1.74	1.68	1.62
40	4.08	3.23	2.84	2.61	2.45	2.34	2.25	2.18	2.12	2.08	1.74	1.64	1.58	1.51
60	4	3.15	2.76	2.53	2.37	2.25	2.17	2.1	2.04	1.99	1.65	1.53	1.47	1.39
120	3.92	3.07	2.68	2.45	2.29	2.18	2.09	2.02	1.96	1.91	1.55	1.43	1.35	1.25
inf	3.84	3	2.6	2.37	2.21	2.1	2.01	1.94	1.88	1.83	1.46	1.32	1.22	1

Table 4c: *F* Table for alpha=0.01

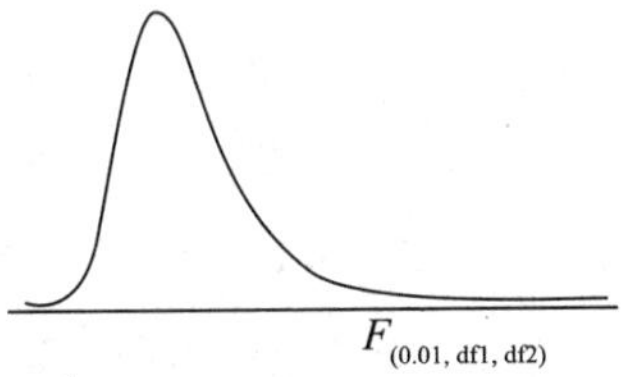

df2/df1	1	2	3	4	5	6	7	8	9	10	30	60	120	inf
1	4052	5000	5403	5625	5764	5859	5928	5981	6022	6056	6261	6313	6339	6366
2	98.5	99	99.2	99.2	99.3	99.3	99.4	99.4	99.4	99.4	99.5	99.5	99.5	99.5

3	34.1	30.8	29.5	28.7	28.2	27.9	27.7	27.5	27.3	27.2	26.5	26.3	26.2	26.1
4	21.2	18	16.7	16	15.5	15.2	15	14.8	14.7	14.5	13.8	13.7	13.6	13.5
5	16.3	13.3	12.1	11.4	11	10.7	10.5	10.3	10.2	10.1	9.38	9.2	9.11	9.02
6	13.7	10.9	9.78	9.15	8.75	8.47	8.26	8.1	7.98	7.87	7.23	7.06	6.97	6.88
7	12.2	9.55	8.45	7.85	7.46	7.19	6.99	6.84	6.72	6.62	5.99	5.82	5.74	5.65
8	11.3	8.65	7.59	7.01	6.63	6.37	6.18	6.03	5.91	5.81	5.2	5.03	4.95	4.86
9	10.6	8.02	6.99	6.42	6.06	5.8	5.61	5.47	5.35	5.26	4.65	4.48	4.4	4.31
10	10	7.56	6.55	5.99	5.64	5.39	5.2	5.06	4.94	4.85	4.25	4.08	4	3.91
11	9.65	7.21	6.22	5.67	5.32	5.07	4.89	4.74	4.63	4.54	3.94	3.78	3.69	3.6
12	9.33	6.93	5.95	5.41	5.06	4.82	4.64	4.5	4.39	4.3	3.7	3.54	3.45	3.36
13	9.07	6.7	5.74	5.21	4.86	4.62	4.44	4.3	4.19	4.1	3.51	3.34	3.26	3.17
14	8.86	6.52	5.56	5.04	4.7	4.46	4.28	4.14	4.03	3.94	3.35	3.18	3.09	3
15	8.68	6.36	5.42	4.89	4.56	4.32	4.14	4	3.9	3.81	3.21	3.05	2.96	2.87
16	8.53	6.23	5.29	4.77	4.44	4.2	4.03	3.89	3.78	3.69	3.1	2.93	2.85	2.75
17	8.4	6.11	5.19	4.67	4.34	4.1	3.93	3.79	3.68	3.59	3	2.84	2.75	2.65
18	8.29	6.01	5.09	4.58	4.25	4.02	3.84	3.71	3.6	3.51	2.92	2.75	2.66	2.57
19	8.19	5.93	5.01	4.5	4.17	3.94	3.77	3.63	3.52	3.43	2.84	2.67	2.58	2.49
20	8.1	5.85	4.94	4.43	4.1	3.87	3.7	3.56	3.46	3.37	2.78	2.61	2.52	2.42
21	8.02	5.78	4.87	4.37	4.04	3.81	3.64	3.51	3.4	3.31	2.72	2.55	2.46	2.36
22	7.95	5.72	4.82	4.31	3.99	3.76	3.59	3.45	3.35	3.26	2.67	2.5	2.4	2.31
23	7.88	5.66	4.77	4.26	3.94	3.71	3.54	3.41	3.3	3.21	2.62	2.45	2.35	2.26
24	7.82	5.61	4.72	4.22	3.9	3.67	3.5	3.36	3.26	3.17	2.58	2.4	2.31	2.21
25	7.77	5.57	4.68	4.18	3.86	3.63	3.46	3.32	3.22	3.13	2.54	2.36	2.27	2.17
26	7.72	5.53	4.64	4.14	3.82	3.59	3.42	3.29	3.18	3.09	2.5	2.33	2.23	2.13
27	7.68	5.49	4.6	4.11	3.79	3.56	3.39	3.26	3.15	3.06	2.47	2.29	2.2	2.1
28	7.64	5.45	4.57	4.07	3.75	3.53	3.36	3.23	3.12	3.03	2.44	2.26	2.17	2.06
29	7.6	5.42	4.54	4.05	3.73	3.5	3.33	3.2	3.09	3.01	2.41	2.23	2.14	2.03
30	7.56	5.39	4.51	4.02	3.7	3.47	3.3	3.17	3.07	2.98	2.39	2.21	2.11	2.01
40	7.31	5.18	4.31	3.83	3.51	3.29	3.12	2.99	2.89	2.8	2.2	2.02	1.92	1.81
60	7.08	4.98	4.13	3.65	3.34	3.12	2.95	2.82	2.72	2.63	2.03	1.84	1.73	1.6
120	6.85	4.79	3.95	3.48	3.17	2.96	2.79	2.66	2.56	2.47	1.86	1.66	1.53	1.38
inf	6.64	4.61	3.78	3.32	3.02	2.8	2.64	2.51	2.41	2.32	1.7	1.47	1.33	1

Table 5a: Critical Values for the Durbin-Watson Statistic
(Level of Significance $\alpha=0.05$)

n	$k=1$		$k=2$		$k=3$		$k=4$		$k=5$	
	dL	dU	dL	dU	dL	dU	dL	dU	dL	dU
6	0.61	1.4								
7	0.7	1.36	0.47	1.9						
8	0.76	1.33	0.56	1.78	0.37	2.29				
9	0.82	1.32	0.63	1.7	0.46	2.13	0.3	2.59		
10	0.88	1.32	0.7	1.64	0.53	2.02	0.38	2.41	0.24	2.82
11	0.93	1.32	0.66	1.6	0.6	1.93	0.44	2.28	0.32	2.65
12	0.97	1.33	0.81	1.58	0.66	1.86	0.51	2.18	0.38	2.51
13	1.01	1.34	0.86	1.56	0.72	1.82	0.57	2.09	0.45	2.39
14	1.05	1.35	0.91	1.55	0.77	1.78	0.63	2.03	0.51	2.3
15	1.08	1.36	0.95	1.54	0.82	1.75	0.69	1.97	0.56	2.21
16	1.1	1.37	0.98	1.54	0.86	1.73	0.74	1.93	0.62	2.15
17	1.13	1.38	1.02	1.54	0.9	1.71	0.78	1.9	0.67	2.1
18	1.16	1.39	1.05	1.53	0.93	1.69	0.92	1.87	0.71	2.06
19	1.18	1.4	1.08	1.53	0.97	1.68	0.86	1.85	0.75	2.02
20	1.2	1.41	1.1	1.54	1	1.68	0.9	1.83	0.79	1.99
21	1.22	1.42	1.13	1.54	1.03	1.67	0.93	1.81	0.83	1.96
22	1.24	1.43	1.15	1.54	1.05	1.66	0.96	1.8	0.96	1.94
23	1.26	1.44	1.17	1.54	1.08	1.66	0.99	1.79	0.9	1.92
24	1.27	1.45	1.19	1.55	1.1	1.66	1.01	1.78	0.93	1.9
25	1.29	1.45	1.21	1.55	1.12	1.66	1.04	1.77	0.95	1.89
26	1.3	1.46	1.22	1.55	1.14	1.65	1.06	1.76	0.98	1.88
27	1.32	1.47	1.24	1.56	1.16	1.65	1.08	1.76	1.01	1.86
28	1.33	1.48	1.26	1.56	1.18	1.65	1.1	1.75	1.03	1.85
29	1.34	1.48	1.27	1.56	1.2	1.65	1.12	1.74	1.05	1.84
30	1.35	1.49	1.28	1.57	1.21	1.65	1.14	1.74	1.07	1.83
31	1.36	1.5	1.3	1.57	1.23	1.65	1.16	1.74	1.09	1.83
32	1.37	1.5	1.31	1.57	1.24	1.65	1.18	1.73	1.11	1.82

33	1.38	1.51	1.32	1.58	1.26	1.65	1.19	1.73	1.13	1.81
34	1.39	1.51	1.33	1.58	1.27	1.65	1.21	1.73	1.15	1.81
35	1.4	1.52	1.34	1.58	1.28	1.65	1.22	1.73	1.16	1.8
36	1.41	1.52	1.35	1.59	1.29	1.65	1.24	1.73	1.18	1.8
37	1.42	1.53	1.36	1.59	1.31	1.66	1.25	1.72	1.19	1.8
38	1.43	1.54	1.37	1.59	1.32	1.66	1.26	1.72	1.21	1.79
39	1.43	1.54	1.38	1.6	1.33	1.66	1.27	1.72	1.22	1.79
40	1.44	1.54	1.39	1.6	1.34	1.66	1.29	1.72	1.23	1.79
45	1.48	1.57	1.43	1.62	1.38	1.67	1.34	1.72	1.29	1.78
50	1.5	1.59	1.46	1.63	1.42	1.67	1.38	1.72	1.34	1.77
55	1.53	1.6	1.49	1.64	1.45	1.68	1.41	1.72	1.38	1.77
60	1.55	1.62	1.51	1.65	1.48	1.69	1.44	1.73	1.41	1.77
65	1.57	1.63	1.54	1.66	1.5	1.7	1.47	1.73	1.44	1.77
70	1.58	1.64	1.55	1.67	1.52	1.7	1.49	1.74	1.46	1.77
75	1.6	1.65	1.57	1.68	1.54	1.71	1.51	1.74	1.49	1.77
80	1.61	1.66	1.59	1.69	1.56	1.72	1.53	1.74	1.51	1.77
85	1.62	1.67	1.6	1.7	1.57	1.72	1.55	1.75	1.52	1.77
90	1.63	1.68	1.61	1.7	1.59	1.73	1.57	1.75	1.54	1.78
95	1.64	1.69	1.62	1.71	1.6	1.73	1.58	1.75	1.56	1.78
100	1.65	1.69	1.63	1.72	1.61	1.74	1.59	1.76	1.57	1.78
150	1.72	1.75	1.71	1.76	1.69	1.77	1.68	1.79	1.66	1.8
200	1.76	1.78	1.75	1.79	1.74	1.8	1.73	1.81	1.72	1.82

Where n=number of observations and k=number of independent variables

Continued....

Table 5b: Critical Values for the Durbin-Watson Statistic (Level of Significance $\alpha=0.05$)

n	k=6		k=7		k=8		k=9		k=10	
	dL	dU	dL	dU	dL	dU	dL	dU	dL	dU
11	0.2	3.01								
12	0.27	2.83	0.17	3.15						
13	0.33	2.7	0.23	2.99	0.15	3.27				

14	0.39	2.57	0.29	2.85	0.2	3.11	0.13	3.36		
15	0.45	2.47	0.34	2.73	0.25	2.98	0.18	3.22	0.11	3.44
16	0.5	2.39	0.4	2.62	0.3	2.86	0.22	3.09	0.16	3.3
17	0.55	2.32	0.45	2.54	0.36	2.76	0.27	2.98	0.2	3.18
18	0.6	2.26	0.5	2.47	0.41	2.67	0.32	2.87	0.24	3.07
19	0.65	2.21	0.55	2.4	0.46	2.59	0.37	2.78	0.29	2.97
20	0.69	2.16	0.6	2.34	0.5	2.52	0.42	2.7	0.34	2.89
21	0.73	2.12	0.64	2.3	0.55	2.46	0.46	2.63	0.38	2.81
22	0.77	2.09	0.68	2.25	0.59	2.41	0.51	2.57	0.42	2.73
23	0.8	2.06	0.72	2.21	0.63	2.36	0.55	2.51	0.47	2.67
24	0.84	2.04	0.75	2.17	0.67	2.32	0.58	2.46	0.51	2.61
25	0.87	2.01	0.78	2.14	0.7	2.28	0.62	2.42	0.54	2.56
26	0.9	1.99	0.82	2.12	0.74	2.24	0.66	2.38	0.58	2.51
27	0.93	1.97	0.85	2.09	0.77	2.22	0.69	2.34	0.62	2.47
28	0.95	1.96	0.87	2.07	0.8	2.19	0.72	2.31	0.65	2.43
29	0.98	1.94	0.9	2.05	0.83	2.16	0.75	2.28	0.68	2.4
30	1	1.93	0.93	2.03	0.85	2.14	0.78	2.25	0.71	2.36
31	1.02	1.92	0.95	2.02	0.88	2.12	0.81	2.23	74	2.33
32	1.04	1.91	0.97	2	0.9	2.1	0.84	2.2	0.77	2.31
33	1.06	1.9	0.99	1.99	0.93	2.09	0.86	2.18	0.8	2.28
34	1.08	1.89	1.02	1.98	0.95	2.07	0.89	2.16	0.82	2.26
35	1.1	1.88	1.03	1.97	0.97	2.05	0.91	2.14	0.85	2.24
36	1.11	1.88	1.05	1.96	0.99	2.04	0.93	2.13	0.87	2.22
37	1.13	1.87	1.07	1.95	1.01	2.03	0.95	2.11	0.89	2.2
38	1.5	1.86	1.09	1.94	1.03	2.02	0.97	2.1	0.91	2.18
39	1.16	1.86	1.1	1.93	1.05	2.01	0.99	2.09	0.93	2.16
40	1.18	1.85	1.12	1.92	1.06	2	1.01	2.07	0.95	2.15
45	1.24	1.84	1.19	1.9	1.14	1.96	1.09	2.02	1.04	2.09
50	1.29	1.82	1.25	1.88	1.2	1.93	1.16	1.99	1.11	2.04
55	1.33	1.81	1.29	1.86	1.25	1.91	1.21	1.96	1.17	2.01
60	1.37	1.81	1.34	1.85	1.3	1.89	1.26	1.94	1.22	1.98
65	1.4	1.81	1.37	1.84	1.34	1.88	1.3	1.92	1.27	1.96
70	1.43	1.8	1.4	1.84	1.37	1.87	1.34	1.91	1.31	1.95

75	1.46	1.8	1.43	1.83	1.4	1.87	1.37	1.9	1.34	1.94
80	1.48	1.8	1.45	1.83	1.43	1.86	1.4	1.89	1.37	1.93
85	1.5	1.8	1.47	1.83	1.49	1.86	1.42	1.89	1.4	1.92
90	1.52	1.8	1.49	1.83	1.47	1.85	1.45	1.88	1.42	1.91
95	1.54	1.8	1.51	1.83	1.49	1.85	1.46	1.88	1.44	1.9
100	1.55	1.8	1.53	1.83	1.5	1.85	1.48	1.87	1.46	1.9
150	1.65	1.82	1.64	1.83	1.62	1.85	1.6	1.86	1.59	1.88
200	1.71	1.83	1.7	1.84	1.69	1.85	1.68	1.86	1.67	1.87

Where n=number of observations and k=number of independent variables

References（参考文献）

References in Chinese（中文参考文献）

1. A. H. 施图德蒙德．应用计量经济学．北京：机械工业出版社，2006。
2. 程振源．计量经济学：理论和试验．上海：上海财经大学出版社，2009。
3. 达摩达尔·N·古扎拉蒂．计量经济学基础（第四版）．北京：中国人民大学出版社，1996。
4. 樊丽淑．计量经济学．杭州：浙江大学出版社，2007。
5. 高铁梅．计量经济分析方法与建模：EViews 应用及实例（第二版）．北京：清华大学出版社，2009。
6. 黄少敏．计量经济学入门．北京：北京大学出版社，2004。
7. 黄浩，白鸿钧．计量经济学．厦门：厦门大学出版社，2008。
8. 李宝仁．计量经济学．北京：机械工业出版社，2008。
9. 李子奈．计量经济学（方法和应用）．北京：清华大学出版社，1992。
10. 李子奈，潘文卿．计量经济学．北京：高等教育出版社，2005。
11. 李忠民，张世英，袁学民．经济计量学教程（第二版）．天津：天津大学出版社，2009。
12. 罗素·戴维森，詹姆斯·G·麦金农．计量经济理论和方法．上海：上海财经大学出版社，2006。
13. 刘振亚．计量经济学教程．北京：中国人民大学出版社，1999。
14. 迈克尔·P·莫瑞．现代计量经济学（上下册）．北京：机械工业出版社，2009。
15. 林清泉．计量经济学（第二版）．北京：中国人民大学出版社，2009。
16. 曼纽尔·阿雷拉诺．面板数据计量经济学．上海：上海财经大学出版社，2008。
17. 聂巧平．计量经济学同步辅导．北京：中国时代经济出版社，2006。
18. 庞皓．计量经济学．北京：科学出版社，2007。
19. 斯托克，沃森．计量经济学导论．上海：上海财经大学出版社，2004。
20. 孙敬水．计量经济学．北京：清华大学出版社，2004。

21. 孙敬水．计量经济学教程．北京：清华大学出版社，2005。
22. 孙敬水．中级计量经济学教程．上海：上海财经大学出版社，2009。
23. 威廉·H·格林．计量经济分析（第五版）．北京：中国人民大学出版社，2007。
24. 沃尔特·恩德斯．应用计量经济学：时间序列分析．北京：高等教育出版社，2006。
25. 伍德里奇．计量经济学导论：现代观点．北京：清华大学出版社，2007。
26. 谢识予．计量经济学教程．上海：复旦大学出版社，2005。
27. 于俊年．计量经济学软件 Eviews 的使用．北京：对外经济贸易大学出版社，2006。
28. 张晓峒．计量经济学基础．天津：南开大学出版社，1994。
29. 张晓峒．计量经济学软件 Eviews 使用指南．天津：南开大学出版社，2004。
30. 朱平芳．现代计量经济学．上海：上海财经大学出版社，2004。

References in English（英文参考文献）

1. Ashenfelter, Orley, Phillip Levine, and David Zimmerman, *Statistics and Econometrics: Methods and Applications*, John Wiley & Sons, New York, 2003.
2. Asteriou, Dimitrios, *Applied Econometrics*, Macmillan, New York, 2006.
3. Asteriou, Dimitrios and Stephen Hall, *Applied Econometrics*, Revised Edition, Macmillan, New York, 2007.
4. Barreto, Humberto and Frank Howland, *Introductory Econometrics: Using Monte Carlo Simulation with Microsoft Excel*, Cambridge University Press, New York, 2006.
5. Casella, George and Roger Berger, *Statistical Inference*, Second Edition, Thomson Learning, Pacific Grove, 2002.
6. Chow, Gregory, *Econometric Methods*, McGraw-Hill, New York, 1983.
7. Davidson, Russell and James MacKinnon, *Econometric Theory and Methods*, Oxford University Press, New York, 2004.
8. Davidson, Russell and James MacKinnon, *Estimation and Inference in Econometrics*, Oxford University Press, New York, 1993.
9. Enders, Walter, *Applied Econometric Time Series*, Second Edition, John Wiley & Sons, New York, 2004.
10. Goldberger, A. S., *Econometric Theory*, Harvard University Press, Cambridge, 1991.
11. Greene, William, *Econometric Analysis*, Fourth Edition, Prentice Hall, 2000.
12. Griffiths, William, Carter Hill, and Guay Lim, *Using EViews for Principles of Econometrics*, Third Edition, John Wiley & Sons, New York, 2008.
13. Gujarati, Damodar N., *Essential of Econometrics*, Third Edition, McGraw-Hill, New York, 2006.
14. Gujarati, Damodar N., *Basic Econometrics*, Fourth Edition, McGraw-Hill, New York, 2003.

15. Halcoussis, Dennis, *Understanding Econometrics*, South-Western, Mason, 2005.
16. Hamilton, James, *Time Series Analysis*, Princeton University Press, Princeton, 1994.
17. Hamilton, Lawrence, *Statistics with Stata: Updated for Version 9*, Brooks/Cole, Belmont, 2006.
18. Hayashi, Fumio, *Econometrics*, Princeton University Press, Princeton, 2000.
19. Hill, Carter, William Griffiths, and George Judge, *Undergraduate Econometrics*, Second Edition, John Wiley & Sons, New York, 2001.
20. Hill, Carter, William Griffiths, and George Judge, *Principles of Econometrics*, Third Edition, John Wiley & Sons, New York, 2008.
21. Maddala, G. S., *Introduction to Econometrics*, Third Edition, John Wiley & Sons, New York, 2002.
22. Maddala, G. S. and In-Moo Kim, *Unit Roots, Cointegration and Structural Change*, Second Edition, Cambridge University Press, New York, 2003.
23. Murray, Michael, *Econometrics: A Modern Introduction*, Addison Wesley, Boston, 2006.
24. Ramananthan, Ramu, *Introductory Econometrics with Applications*, Fifth Edition, South-Western, Mason, 2002.
25. Salvatore, Dominich and Derrick Reagle, *Statistics and Econometrics*, Second Edition, McGraw-Hill, New York, 2002.
26. Schmidt, Stephen, *Econometrics*, McGraw-Hill, New York, 2005.
27. Stewart, Kenneth, *Introduction to Applied Econometrics*, Brooks/Cole, Belmont, 2005.
28. Verbeek, Marno, *A Guide to Modern Econometrics*, John Wiley & Sons, New York, 2004.
29. Wooldridge, Jeffrey, *Introductory Econometrics: a Modern Approach*, Third Edition, South-Western, Mason, 2006.
30. Wooldridge, Jeffrey, *Econometric Analysis of Cross Section and Panel Data*, MIT Press, Cambridge, 2002.

图书在版编目（CIP）数据

Stata/EViews计量经济分析/胡志宁编著. —2版. —北京：中国人民大学出版社，2016.1
新编21世纪经济学系列教材
ISBN 978-7-300-22264-6

Ⅰ.①S… Ⅱ.①胡… Ⅲ.①计量经济学-应用软件-高等学校-教材 Ⅳ.①F224.0-39

中国版本图书馆CIP数据核字（2015）第310489号

新编21世纪经济学系列教材
Stata/EViews计量经济分析（第二版）
胡志宁　编著
Stata/EViews Jiliang Jingji Fenxi

出版发行	中国人民大学出版社		
社　　址	北京中关村大街31号	邮政编码	100080
电　　话	010－62511242（总编室）		010－62511770（质管部）
	010－82501766（邮购部）		010－62514148（门市部）
	010－62515195（发行公司）		010－62515275（盗版举报）
网　　址	http://www.crup.com.cn		
	http://www.ttrnet.com（人大教研网）		
经　　销	新华书店		
印　　刷	北京密兴印刷有限公司	版　　次	2010年7月第1版
规　　格	185 mm×260 mm　16开本		2016年1月第2版
印　　张	20.25	印　　次	2020年3月第3次印刷
字　　数	476 000	定　　价	35.00元